KT-493-055

REVISE AQA A LEVEL
Sociology
REVISION
GUIDE AND WORKBOOK

Series Consultant: Harry Smith

Authors: Steven Chapman and Harrison White

Our study resources are the smart choice for those studying AQA A Level Sociology, This book will help you to:

- **Organise** your study with the one-topic-per-page format
- **Speed up** your revision with summary notes in short, memorable chunks
- **Track** your revision progress with at-a-glance check boxes
- **Check** your understanding and exam skills with worked examples
- **Develop** your exam technique with exam-style practice questions and full answers.

For the full range of Pearson revision titles across KS2, KS3, GCSE, Functional Skills, AS/A Level and BTEC visit: www.pearsonschools.co.uk/revise

Contents

• •

A small bit of small print
AQA publishes Sample Assessment Material and the Specification on its website. This is the official content and this book should be used in conjunction with it. The questions in Now try this have been written to help you practise every topic in the book. Remember: the real exam questions may not look like this.

Culture

In order to understand how societies like the UK work, you need to know and be able to illustrate the core themes of **culture**, **socialisation** and **identity**. **Culture** refers to the shared beliefs and behaviour of those who make up a society. For information on socialisation and identity, see pages 2–4.

Values
Values are widely held beliefs that particular ways of behaving deserve special status and are worth aspiring to.
For example, UK culture values marriage, family life, privacy, educational achievement, tolerance, individual liberty and the rule of law.

Norms
Norms are the social rules that govern everyday behaviour.
For example, British cultural norms mean that British people consider it unacceptable and abnormal to eat dogs, horses, frogs, snails and insects. However, other cultures view eating these creatures as quite normal.
Norms also govern behaviour in particular social situations.
For example, there are norms that shape our toilet habits, and our behaviour in libraries and classrooms, at parties and so on.
Even our homes are organised according to cultural norms.
In the UK, for example, bedrooms tend to be situated upstairs, whereas kitchens and reception rooms tend to be downstairs.

Culture
Culture is the way of life of a society. It includes the dominant values, norms, beliefs, customs, laws, traditions and language of a society. It is culture that links the individual to society.

Language
This is the means by which culture is transmitted to the next generation.

Customs and traditions
These are values and norms that have been passed down through the generations.
For example, UK culture celebrates Bonfire Night on 5 November and Christmas Day on 25 December, whereas Muslim culture fasts during the month of Ramadan and celebrates at the end of the month with the festival of Eid.

Beliefs
Beliefs are convictions and assumptions, often originating in religious and historical experiences, that something is true, that underpin cultural identity.
For example, the UK is a multicultural society. Most people in the UK are white Anglo-Saxons who subscribe to Christian beliefs. However, there are also significant Muslim, Hindu, Sikh, Chinese and Jewish subcultures and communities that exist alongside the Christian majority.
Some British beliefs are historical in origin.
For example, many people strongly believe in the need for the monarchy.

Now try this

1. Illustrate the difference between values and norms using the concept of privacy.
2. Briefly explain why the UK is regarded as a multicultural society.

Socialisation

Socialisation is the process through which children learn to be effective members of society. It is the means by which the older generation (parents, teachers) pass on the core values, beliefs, norms and traditions of a society to the next generation. Socialisation and culture help to shape the **identity** of the individuals who make up society (see page 4).

Social beings

Humans are essentially social beings because when we are born we are helpless. We are entirely dependent on others to meet our most basic physiological needs for food, drink, warmth and shelter. Socialisation enables us to develop the **social skills** needed to successfully fit into society. It also prevents us being defined as 'deviant' for failing to conform to social norms.

Feral children

The importance of socialisation to human development can be seen when we examine the experience of **feral children**. These children have experienced little or no social contact during their early years with other humans.

Genie, a young American girl, was locked away (by her father) in a room until she was 13. This act deprived her of all contact with other humans. When she was rescued in the 1970s, she was severely malnourished and completely lacked language and other social skills.

Genie was socially isolated from a young age until she was 13.

Feral children and animals

Some feral children have spent their early years with animals. When Oxana Malaya was three years old, her alcoholic parents left her outside one night, so she crawled into a hovel where they kept dogs.

It is possible that, in some cases, an animal may have 'raised' the child as its own. However, there is no real evidence of this. In Oxana's case, it is more likely that she copied the dogs' behaviour in order to survive.

Nature versus nurture

Some people believe human behaviour, culture and identity are the result of **nature** – inherited biological or genetic patterns of behaviour or instincts.

For example, it is claimed that humans have instincts for survival and that women have a maternal instinct.

However, sociologists reject this idea. Instead, they argue that human behaviour is learned from role models – especially our parents – and is therefore the result of **nurture**, or socialisation.

Socialisation into social skills

Feral children tend to lack human characteristics. By examining feral children, we can identify the social skills that most children acquire during socialisation – those that shape their identity as human beings.

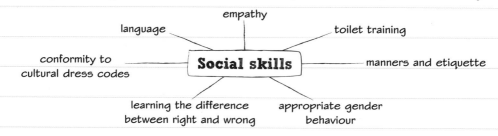

empathy

language   toilet training

conformity to cultural dress codes   **Social skills**   manners and etiquette

learning the difference between right and wrong   appropriate gender behaviour

Now try this

Sum up the nature versus nurture debate in two sentences.

Types of socialisation

Socialisation is a lifelong process whereby cultural norms and values are passed on to the next generation by the older generation via two types of socialisation: **primary** and **secondary**.

Primary socialisation

The family is the main site of primary socialisation. Ideally, parents or carers are positive **role models** who strongly encourage their children to imitate their own examples of good behaviour.

Parents often use positive and negative sanctions to reinforce primary socialisation.

- Positive sanctions are rewards.
- Negative sanctions are punishments – for example, being sent to the 'naughty step' or in extreme cases physical punishment such as smacking.

Gender role socialisation

This is an important aspect of primary socialisation. It teaches children 'appropriate' masculine and feminine behaviour.

Secondary socialisation: education

Secondary socialisation generally takes place outside the family. **Education** is the most important agency of secondary socialisation. Most children spend at least 10 years at school learning the knowledge and skills required for passing exams and acquiring qualifications through the formal curriculum.

They also learn the social skills required to get on successfully with adults in authority and fellow students. This **'hidden curriculum'** (see page 26) teaches the attitudes and behaviour that will enable children to 'progress' in society. However, there is some argument about whether such socialisation is positive or negative.

Secondary socialisation: mass media and peer groups

Mass media includes newspapers, magazines, television, advertising, films and pop music. In the past 20 years, **new media** has dramatically increased its influence on socialisation. This includes smartphones, texting, surfing the internet and using social media networks such as Facebook, Instagram, Twitter and SnapChat.

Peer groups or friendship networks are also agencies of socialisation. School is often our first experience of these. However, there are concerns that peer pressure, gang membership and bullying could result in young people breaching cultural norms and breaking the law.

Secondary socialisation: religion

In the 19th century, religion was the most important arena for teaching cultural norms and values in the UK because:

- the majority of people believed in God
- attendance at Christian churches was high on Sundays and for religious festivals such as Easter and Christmas
- many children regularly attended Sunday Schools
- most families owned a Bible.

However, Christian religious beliefs and practices declined steeply throughout the 20th century. Religious socialisation in the UK is now more likely to be practised regularly by ethnic minorities.

 Key study ## Toxic Childhood, Sue Palmer (2007)

Sociologist **Sue Palmer** argues that parents use electronic technologies such as television, computer games and the internet (secondary agents of socialisation) as alternatives to traditional parenting practices (primary agents). Instead of spending quality time with their children and reading them stories, Palmer claims parents too often use television, electronic games and junk food to keep them quiet. Children are therefore deprived of a traditional childhood and family life. She claims the effects are negative and cause social problems, and that every year children become more antisocial. They are less able to learn, enjoy life and thrive socially because of these trends.

Now try this

In what ways might media and peer group socialisation be negative and cause social problems for society?

Identity

Identity is concerned with the way we see and define ourselves in relation to others, and how others see us. Identity refers to the traits and characteristics, social relations, roles and social group memberships that define who we are.

Components of identity

Identity can be broken down into two essential components:

The self

 The self refers to a person's subjective awareness. It can also be defined as a person's sense of their individuality. This shapes how they project their personality out into the social world. For example, they may be confident or shy in the company of others.

For example, **Susie Scott** (2006) argues that shyness has come to be regarded as an 'unhealthy' state of self for individuals living in contemporary Western societies. She observes that the shy self implies a failure to achieve certain cultural values such as assertiveness. She argues that shyness has become medicalised. Medical professionals see this type of self as a form of deviant identity that should be 'treated' with counselling and drugs.

Social identity

 Social identity refers to how a person is viewed by others. It also refers to how a person manages the social expectations attached to the various social roles they play in wider society, such as occupational, family and gender roles.

In the UK, mothers and fathers generally strive to achieve the social identity of 'good parent'. A parent who fails to express love for their children, or uses 'unreasonable' force when disciplining them or is negligent in their care is likely to be labelled as a 'bad' parent. Labelling theory also observes that some social identities are imposed on individuals (see page 13). For example, if a person has been in prison for a criminal offence they might find that the imposed social identity of ex-criminal may negatively shape their interaction with others – especially employers and police officers.

Both the self and social identity are partly shaped by socialisation.

Shaping social identity

Social identity may also be shaped by:

- ethnicity
- religion
- nationality
- leisure interests.

One person may have several social identities as, for example, a doctor, a male, a husband, a father, a Muslim, a Manchester United supporter and so on.

Free will, choice and identity

Some sociological theories associated with **social action** (see page 13) and **postmodernism** (see page 14) argue that as individuals we exercise **free will**. We have a number of choices available to us that assist in the construction of our self and social identity.

For example, we may choose to use our bodies to project our identity out into the social world through our consumption of fashion, or by altering aspects of our body with cosmetic surgery, exercise, tattoos or piercings.

Social structure and identity

Some sociological theories believe that social identities are imposed on us by the **social structure** – the way societies are socially organised.

In the UK, for example, our socio-economic position – jobs and income – impose social class identities on us.

If we are male or female, society may judge us negatively if we fail to live up to social expectations about masculinity or femininity. This may explain why those who project gay, lesbian or transsexual identities are still not socially accepted by all.

Now try this

What is the difference between the self and social identity?

Social differentiation and status

All societies, including the UK, **socially differentiate** between social groups. Social differentiation often leads to **inequalities** in power and **social stratification** – a hierarchical system with different levels of wealth, status and power (see page 6).

Differentiation by nationality

Scottish, Welsh, Irish

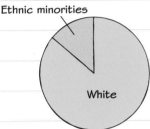

English

84% of people in the UK claim an English identity, while 16% claim a Scottish, Welsh or Irish identity.

Differentiation by social class

Social classes are groups of people who share a similar economic position because of their job, income, wealth and level of education. For example, about 7% of UK society qualify as upper class.

Age differentiation

Both young and old people experience discrimination – particularly in the workplace. For example, many employers refuse to pay teenagers the minimum wage.

Ethnic differentiation

Ethnic minorities

White

86% of the British population are white, while 14% belong to ethnic-minority groups.

Differentiation by religion

Hindu or Sikh   Other
Muslim
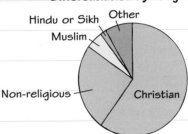
Non-religious   Christian

In the 2011 Census, approximately 60% of the UK population identified themselves as Christians, 25% claimed to have no religion, 5% identified as Muslim and 2% identified as Hindu or Sikh.

Ascribed status is an involuntary status assigned at birth and usually unchangeable.
In some societies, for example, females are ascribed very low status, as are some ethnic or religious groups.
In the UK, members of the Royal Family are born with ascribed status.

Status refers to a person's social **position** or **ranking** in a society. It refers to a high or low standing or **prestige** attached to a particular role. For example, members of the aristocracy tend to have higher status than refuse collectors in British society.

Achieved status is mainly **earned by merit**. It reflects personal skills, talent, ability, effort and hard work. It is also **chosen**.
For example, gaining qualifications and marriage may be seen as types of achieved status.

Differences in status often lead to social differentiation – inequalities in income, wealth, power, education, job opportunities, health, life expectancy and mortality.

Now try this

1 Is marriage an achieved or ascribed status?
2 Does Prince Charles occupy an achieved or ascribed status?

Stratification

Stratification refers to the hierarchical layering of a society into distinct groups. These groups each have different levels of wealth, status and power. It is generally accepted that Britain is stratified by **social class**. This type of status is generally regarded as achieved because class systems are open systems. This means people can move up or down social classes.

Social class in Britain

Social class refers to people's **socio-economic position**, which is determined by their job and the income and status attached to it. It is generally agreed that Britain can be divided into three broad social classes.

1 **Upper class (7%)**: they live off inherited wealth or rents.

2 **Middle classes (60%)**: well-paid managers and professionals, plus white collar workers.

3 **Working classes (33%)**: manual workers divided into skilled, semi-skilled and unskilled.

How social class is measured

Until the 1980s, the government measured social class using the Registrar General's **classification of occupations**, which identified five social classes. It was eventually abandoned because it left out those who lived off wealth rather than wages. It also left out the long-term unemployed and those dependent on welfare benefits.

BBC 2013 survey of class in Britain

In 1992, John Goldthorpe and Gordon Marshall developed an alternative measurement of social class known as the **National Statistics Socio-economic Classification (NS-SEC)**. It was first used in the 2001 Census because they believed changes in the economy had made the old divisions between the upper, middle and working classes obsolete. Mike Savage used a variation of the NS-SEC when he carried out a national survey of class in 2013 on behalf of the BBC.

Class	% of pop
Elite: people who earn more than £140,000 a year or who live off inherited wealth	6
Established middle class: professionals who earn £47,000 a year and own their own home	25
Technical middle class: older professionals (IT managers, engineers) who own their own homes	6
New affluent workers: younger professional or service workers on moderate incomes who own their own homes	15
Traditional working class: white-collar workers, electricians, plumbers, lorry drivers	14
Emergent service workers: young workers employed in hotels, bars, call-centres on modest incomes who rent their accommodation	19
Precariat (poorest): people on very low incomes and zero-hour contracts, often unemployed	15

The Indian–Hindu caste system

In India, Hindus are stratified along religious lines in the form of **caste**. This stratification system is **ascribed** and **closed**. The caste a person is born into determines the job they are allowed to do. Marriage between castes is not allowed. It is impossible to change caste during one's lifetime. Hindus believe that a person can only change caste by doing good throughout their life so that when they die they might be reincarnated as a member of a higher caste.

Brahmins
Priests
Academics

Kshatriyas
Warriors
Kings

Vaishyas
Business community

Kshudras
Servants, subordinate to Vaishyas, Kshatriyas and Brahmins

The Dalit
Untouchables
do all the lower-order work,
subordinate to all

Each strata is differentiated by religious purity: the Brahmin caste is regarded as the most pure; the Dalits are regarded as the most impure.

Now try this

Briefly explain the main differences between the class and caste systems of stratification.

Sociological perspectives

Sociological perspectives are different ways of explaining why societies are organised in particular ways and work the way they do. These perspectives take either a consensus or conflict approach. They can also take either a structural (structuralist) or social action (interpretivist) approach.

Consensus theories

Consensus theories suggest that some societies work well because they are based on **shared agreement** or **consensus** and cooperation. It is argued that in these societies culture is shared via socialisation. Moreover, this encourages a strong sense of belonging or **social integration** into society. Members of society are therefore happy to share the same goals, laws, morality and so on because they each benefit equally from them. The main consensus theory is **functionalism** (see page 8).

Conflict theories

Conflict theories include **Marxism** (see page 10) and **feminism** (see pages 11–12). They suggest consensus is a myth and that most modern societies are actually underpinned by some sort of **conflict**. Marxists see this conflict as caused by **social class inequalities**. Feminists see conflict as resulting from **gender inequalities**. Other sociologists such as Weber saw conflict resulting from status inequalities originating in racial, ethnic and religious differences.

In the USA, the 'Black Lives Matter' campaign suggests racial inequality is a major problem underpinning the way American society is organised.

Structural theories of society

Structuralist theories are interested in how societies are **structured** or **socially organised**.

- They take a **macro approach**. They are interested in how large-scale structures such as the economy and social institutions (the education system, political system, criminal justice system) interact with individuals and with each other.

- Structural sociologists tend to believe **society** is more important than the individual. They tend to believe people's behaviour is mainly shaped or determined by social structure. In other words, they see people as the **puppets of society**.

- Both functionalism and Marxism are structuralist theories.

Social action (interpretivist) view

The social action view rejects the idea that people are the puppets of society. Instead, it argues that people are **conscious** of what is going on around them and that they possess **free will**. They can choose to reject structural influences and embark on their own paths of action, coming together in social groups if they wish.

- Social action theory takes the **micro approach**. The **individual** is always more important than society. People are the **architects of society**.

- Social action theory prefers to focus on how people interact with one another and how they interpret one another's actions.

- Interactionism and labelling theory (see page 13) are examples of social action theories.

Structuration theory

Some sociologists, notably **Giddens**, argue that both social structure and interaction are equally important in shaping human behaviour. It is the repetition of the acts of individuals that creates and reproduces social structures and institutions.

For example, the social institution of education is created and reproduced by individuals: parents send their children to school Monday to Friday and individuals qualified as teachers turn up to teach them knowledge and skills.

Now try this

1 Explain why Marxists are critical of functionalists.
2 What, according to Giddens, creates and reproduces social structures and institutions?

Functionalism

Functionalism is a **consensus theory** (see page 7) that aims to explain why the **social structures** of modern societies like the UK are relatively well ordered. The concept of social structure refers to the ways in which societies are economically, politically and socially organised.

Society as a social system

Functionalists believe that the social structure of societies resembles social systems made up of inter-dependent social institutions. These work together and function to produce social order.

For example, a rise in divorce may affect levels of educational achievement and crime. This may consequently produce a political response in the form of new laws or social policies.

The social system

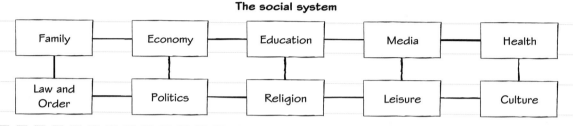

Family	Economy	Education	Media	Health
Law and Order	Politics	Religion	Leisure	Culture

The functions of the social system

When functionalists claim that something is functional, they mean it is of benefit to society. They believe that all social institutions function in three ways to bring about consensus, conformity and social order.

They function to bring about value consensus	They function to bring about social integration	They function to bring about a specialised division of labour
Members of society are socialised into broad agreement or consensus, on values, morality and norms of behaviour.	People need to be encouraged to belong to a community that has something in common. A common identity binds the individual to society so that they experience social integration or solidarity. They feel they belong to something bigger than themselves.	Members of society need to be encouraged to take their place in the economic division of labour – the organisation of jobs into hundreds of thousands of specific tasks and skills – as workers.
For example, there is broad consensus in the UK that we should tolerate one another's views whether we like them or not. Freedom of speech is therefore an important British value.	For example, it could be argued that the 2016 referendum leading to Brexit reflected a form of social integration that promoted the idea that being British was more important than being part of the EU.	For example, we are encouraged from an early age by family and school to acquire the skills needed to become productive workers as adults.

The biological analogy

Functionalists often use a biological analogy to describe how society works. They liken the social system to the human body. All the organs of the body work together to bring about good health, just as all the social institutions of society work together as a social system to bring about social order.

Evaluation

- It ignores individual choice. All behaviour is seen as shaped by the needs of the social system.
- It assumes that all members of society benefit equally. It neglects inequalities in power and wealth.
- It fails to acknowledge the dysfunctional or harmful effects of some institutions.

Now try this

1 What is meant by the 'specialised division of labour'?
2 Define what functionalists mean by 'social integration'.

New Right

The New Right refers to a collection of right-wing ideas that advocates neo-liberal economics, anti-welfarism, a belief in traditional morality and minimal government interference. In terms of its emphasis on morality and traditional family types, however, it does resemble functionalism.

Neo-liberalism

Neo-liberalism is a set of economic and political ideas which became popular with UK Conservative governments in the 1980s and the New Labour governments (1997–2010). These ideas stress the need for a free market laissez-faire economy in which free competition between manufacturers and service providers is promoted with the minimum of state regulation. Neo-liberals believe that free markets maximise both personal liberty and consumer choice. The concept of 'conservatism' that underpins New Right ideas refers to an emphasis on tradition.

Anti-welfarism and the underclass

New Right commentators argue that the state interferes too much in people's personal lives and that too many people have become over-dependent on the state, particularly the welfare state.

Murray argues that state benefits need to be cut so that members of the underclass are forced into the labour market to look for work.

Charles Murray (1990), for example, argues that government welfare policies both in the USA and UK have created an 'urban underclass' – a distinct subculture of people who are economically deprived because they have lost the inclination to look for work due to the easy availability of state benefits. This underclass is often portrayed as criminal and morally deficient. They consequently lack the cultural, moral and social skills that are required to be either good citizens or workers.

Traditional morality

New Right thinkers appeal to Conservatives because they emphasise traditional ways of thinking.

For example, New Right ideas on the family are similar to the functionalist support for heterosexual marriage and children being raised in nuclear families (see page 96). The New Right see the traditional family as under attack from liberal government social policies such as the legalisation of gay marriage, the promotion of women's rights and so on.

Rolling back the state

New Right politicians support the rolling back of state services and their replacement with private providers of, for example, education, health and adult social care. These services would compete in a free market to provide greater choice to consumers. They believe state provision of public services wastes money and is inefficient compared with the private provision offered by the free market. New Right thinkers argue that competition in the free market functions to drive down prices and raise standards – so improving the choices available to consumers.

Evaluation

👍 **Oppenheimer and Harker** (1990) argue that the concept of underclass is useful because it conveys the ways in which different aspects of poverty such as low-quality housing and a lack of paid work compound one another.

👎 Underclass theory places the blame for poverty on the poor behaviour of people who claim benefits. However, critics of the New Right point out that poverty is actually caused by wider social, economic and political factors over which people have little control. **Field** (1990) says it is unfair of the New Right to engage in victim-blaming.

👎 Critics argue there is no convincing evidence that a distinct subculture with its own unique value system actually exists in practice.

👎 The New Right emphasis on morality may be dated and fails to take account of social change and increasing family diversity.

👎 The New Right have criticised single-parent families, but evidence suggests that despite poverty single mothers do an effective job in bringing up children.

👎 There is little evidence that private provision of public services is any more efficient or effective than state provision.

Now try this

1 What is neo-liberalism?

2 Outline the relationship between state provision of welfare and the underclass according to Charles Murray.

Marxism

Marxism, a conflict theory, is essentially a critique of the economic organisation of modern capitalist societies, which Marxists see as divided into two interrelated structures: the infrastructure and the superstructure. In particular, Marxism sees capitalism as characterised by class conflict and inequality. For more on conflict and structuralist theories, see page 7.

The infrastructure

The most important part of the capitalist social system is the infrastructure or economic system, which is organised in terms of a relationship between two **social classes**: the **bourgeoisie** and the **proletariat**.

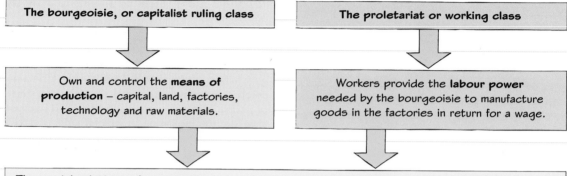

The bourgeoisie, or capitalist ruling class	The proletariat or working class
Own and control the **means of production** – capital, land, factories, technology and raw materials.	Workers provide the **labour power** needed by the bourgeoisie to manufacture goods in the factories in return for a wage.

The social relations of production
The relationship between these two groups is called '**the social relations of production**'. According to Marx, these relations are **unequal** and **exploitative** because the value of the wages paid to workers is worth less than the value of the product of their labour to the bourgeoisie. These relations also mean that these classes are in **conflict** with one another. Workers want more wages while employers want more labour for the same wage.

The superstructure

Marxists see the capitalist system as made up of two parts: the infrastructure and the superstructure. The superstructure is made up of social institutions such as the family, education, religion, legal system, mass media, politics and so on. According to Marxists, its role is to transmit ruling-class ideology, which aims to:
- hide, disguise or justify class **inequality**, or
- distract the working class from it by persuading them that the capitalist system is both meritocratic and fair.

The relationship between the infrastructure and superstructure.   **Base** shapes the superstructure

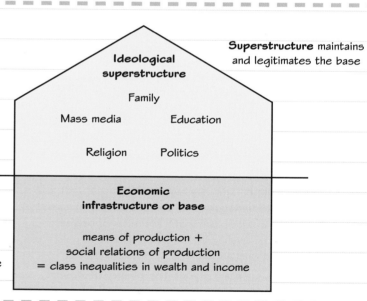

Superstructure maintains and legitimates the base

Ideological superstructure

Family

Mass media   Education

Religion   Politics

Economic infrastructure or base

means of production +
social relations of production
= class inequalities in wealth and income

Evaluation

- Marxists over-emphasise class inequalities at the expense of gender and ethnic inequalities.
- Functionalists argue that Marxists highlight conflict at the expense of consensus.
- Marxists may be guilty of underestimating working-class people's ability to see through ideology.

Now try this

What is the difference between the infrastructure and superstructure according to Marxists?

Feminism

Feminism examines society from the point of view of women. It is a structuralist theory because feminists see the social structure of most societies as patriarchal or male dominated. Within these societies, they believe that females are generally subordinate in power compared with males and are therefore regarded as second-class citizens. Feminism is also a conflict theory because it sees the conflict of interest between males and females as the most important characteristic of society.

Types of feminism

There are four broad feminist explanations for these inequalities and social differences.

1 **Radical feminism** – focuses on the problem of inequality between men and women.

2 **Marxist feminism** – focuses on the exploitation of women at home and in the workplace.

3 **Liberal feminism** – focuses on achieving equality between men and women.

4 **Difference feminism** – points out that the patriarchal experiences of women differ because of the class and ethnic differences between women.

For more on Marxist, liberal and difference feminism, see page 12.

Radical feminism

Radical feminism sees men and women as constituting social groups that have very different and conflicting interests.

Exploitation: women are exploited by and consequently subservient to men.

Separate sex/gender 'classes': men and women constitute separate and opposing 'sex classes' which are more important than economic classes or racial divisions.

Patriarchy: this is a structural feature of society as it pervades all social institutions that make up society – particularly the family and the personal or intimate relations between husband and wife.

Power: men are able to accrue more power than women in crucial social institutions such as government and the law; therefore, they are able to pass laws or introduce social policies that benefit men more than women **(Millett, 1969)**.

Radical feminism

Biology: inequality between the sexes is primarily caused by biology – specifically pregnancy and childbearing **(Firestone, 1970)**.

Violence: men's use of physical force and sexual violence, or the threat of it, is often used to oppress women in the family and in wider society.

Women are relatively **weak** and **vulnerable** and cannot compete on equal terms for **power** and **wealth** with men.

Men can **shape dominant** ideas or ideology about women's roles especially through **gender role socialisation** in the family, which further reinforce female disadvantage. This may result in females being encouraged to be less assertive and ambitious than males or to see certain roles or jobs as out of bounds **(Millett, 1969)**.

Evaluation

👍 Radical feminism highlighted important features of women's oppression, especially male use of violence.

👎 It underestimates the extent to which women have become less oppressed and liberated in modern Western societies.

👎 It implies that the patriarchal exploitation and oppression is a similar experience for all women and that all women share similar interests.

👎 Radical feminists neglect the fact that there are social and economic divisions between groups of women, which in some cases cushion the effects of patriarchy.

Now try this

Why do women experience patriarchal inequality according to Firestone?

Marxist, liberal and difference feminism

In addition to radical feminism (see page 11), there are three more feminist explanations for inequalities and social differences: Marxist, liberal and difference feminism.

Marxist feminism

Marxist feminists see women's oppression as caused by **structural factors**, specifically the **capitalist economic system**. Women are economically disadvantaged compared with men because they carry out more unpaid labour (childcare and housework). **Delphy and Leonard** (1992) claim that men exploit this. Unpaid housework maintains the health and efficiency of the present workforce free of charge; unpaid childcare ensures the future workforce is raised at relatively little cost to the capitalist class.

Marxist feminists also believe that patriarchy as an ideology benefits capitalism because it **legitimates gender inequalities**, often with reference to biological differences. It functions to divide and rule the working class by suggesting males 'deserve' greater rewards than females. **Ward** (1990) claims that global capitalism has undermined the wages of women workers in the UK because women in developing countries can be hired at much cheaper rates of pay.

Liberal feminism

Liberal feminism believes that patriarchy is in retreat as women's rights and opportunities have improved over the past century. They acknowledge that inequalities still remain, particularly in childcare, and that popular culture continues to be sexist in its portrayal of women in stereotypical ways. However, they are generally optimistic that gender inequalities will eventually disappear.

The moderate stance of liberal feminists has been instrumental in influencing political actions that have improved the opportunities of females in both the educational system and in the workplace. Liberal feminism differs from both radical and Marxist varieties of feminism because it seeks gradual reform rather than revolution.

Evaluation of Marxist feminism

- ⚐ Marxist feminism underplays the influence of non-economic factors such as culture or religion in the oppression of women.
- ⚐ Differences in the economic position of women are not emphasised.

  For example, are wealthy and working-class women exploited equally?
- ⚐ Radical feminists claim that patriarchy pre-dates capitalism and is found in a range of non-capitalist societies.
- ⚐ Liberal feminists note that Marxist feminists ignore recent social and legal changes aimed at the liberation of women in Western societies.

Evaluation of liberal feminism

- 👍 Liberal feminists have led campaigns resulting in Western governments introducing laws and social policies that improved women's position in society.
- ⚐ There is still substantial inequality between men and women (especially in the distribution of housework and childcare), and misogyny in the media, politics, some religions and popular culture.
- ⚐ There is still significant violence against women, even in modern Western societies.
- ⚐ There are still severe inequalities between men and women in the developing world.

Difference feminism

This is sometimes known as **postmodern** or **third-wave feminism**. It rejects the idea that all women share common interests or that women's experiences can be explained by a single feminist theory because there are too many divisions between women. Not all women are equally exploited or experience patriarchy in the same way: wealthy and poor; heterosexual and lesbian; young and old; black, Asian and white women. This approach therefore celebrates **difference** and suggests there may be several paths towards liberation (depending on the group to which women belong).

Now try this

Explain why difference feminism is sceptical of the idea that all women experience patriarchal inequality and exploitation in the same way.

Social action theory

Social action theory (also known as **interpretivism**) rejects the determinism of structural theories and stresses **individual free will** (see page 7). It takes a **micro-approach** – the focus is on individuals or small groups rather than the relationships between social structures.

Symbolic interactionism

G H Mead (1934) developed many of the ideas of **symbolic interactionism**. He observed that the social world (society) consists of millions of people. In order to make sense of this social world, sociologists examine how people **interact** with others in social groups – in families, in school, at work, in leisure time and so on. Mead argued that people attach meanings to **symbols** (such as facial expressions, body language, words and objects) that stand for something else. They then interact with others according to these symbols. It is this constant interaction, interpretation and reinterpretation of the meaning of symbols that is responsible for the social construction of society and social reality.

The looking-glass self

Cooley (1902) argues that a crucial component of our ability to interact successfully with others is the ability to see ourselves through the eyes of others. This '**looking-glass self**' tells us what sort of person we are – how successfully we perform our social roles, whether others regard us as reliable and so on. Mead distinguishes between two aspects of the self: the '**I**' (your opinion of yourself as a whole) and the '**me**' (what you present to the world in your various social roles – pupil, son, daughter and so on).

Blumer (1969) argues that we give meanings to action by taking the role of the other – the roles we play are based on what other people expect from us in particular situations.

Labelling theory

Labelling theory suggests that most individuals – and especially those in authority, such as teachers and police officers – engage in **labelling** when interacting with others. Labels are a form of shorthand symbolic classification. This can mean that social characteristics may be generally and unfairly applied to individuals because they are judged to be members of particular social groups. This may result in inequality as some groups are treated more favourably or negatively than others.

Society as a social construction

Interpretivists believe that **individuals** are more important than social structures (family, education system, criminal justice system and so on). Society and its social structures are the net result of people **choosing** to come together in social groups and the social meanings people apply to their interaction within these groups. Society and all its social structures are therefore **socially constructed** by the individuals who people them. Thus, people are the architects of society rather than the puppets.

Evaluation

- 💬 Social action theory fails to explain the wider social context in which small-scale interaction takes place. For example, classroom and family interactions may be influenced by structural forces such as those emanating from the economy (inequalities in income and wealth).

- 💬 Labelling often involves power but social action theory rarely explains the **origin of power** (why some groups are powerful and can therefore stereotype less powerful groups).

- 💬 Structural sociologists claim that the methods used by social action sociologists are not very scientific because they study only small-scale and unique social situations that cannot be replicated, checked and generalised from.

- 💬 The results of interactionist studies often heavily depend on the subjective interpretation of the researcher.

- 👍 Social action theory claims to produce more valid data than the quantitative methods of structuralist studies because interpretivist data 'speaks for itself' – it is often first-hand and presented in the words of those being studied.

Now try this

According to social action theory, in what way do people socially construct society?

Postmodernism

Postmodernists believe that a new type of society – **postmodern society** – dominated by media and consumption, and a mistrust of grand theories that claim to explain how societies work (particularly religious and scientific theories) has evolved out of modern industrial societies during the past 30 years.

Modern to postmodern society

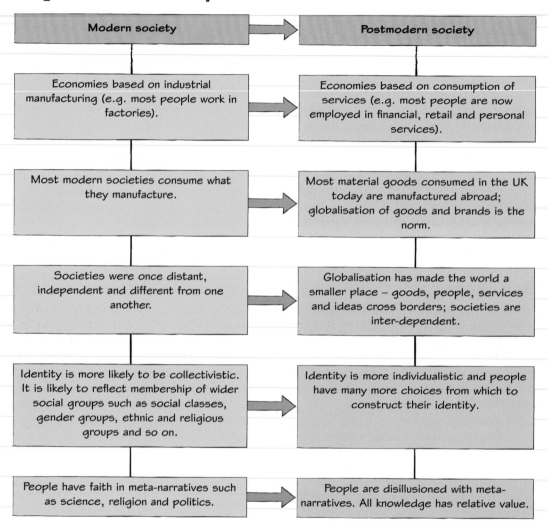

Modern society	Postmodern society
Economies based on industrial manufacturing (e.g. most people work in factories).	Economies based on consumption of services (e.g. most people are now employed in financial, retail and personal services).
Most modern societies consume what they manufacture.	Most material goods consumed in the UK today are manufactured abroad; globalisation of goods and brands is the norm.
Societies were once distant, independent and different from one another.	Globalisation has made the world a smaller place – goods, people, services and ideas cross borders; societies are inter-dependent.
Identity is more likely to be collectivistic. It is likely to reflect membership of wider social groups such as social classes, gender groups, ethnic and religious groups and so on.	Identity is more individualistic and people have many more choices from which to construct their identity.
People have faith in meta-narratives such as science, religion and politics.	People are disillusioned with meta-narratives. All knowledge has relative value.

How the cultural and economic conditions of modern society have evolved into postmodern conditions.

Evaluation

👎 Postmodernists make sweeping generalisations about social change but often fail to back these up with hard evidence.

👍 Postmodernists strongly imply that the postmodern world is one in which individuals have a variety of consumer choices at their fingertips. However, consumption and choice often depend on access to income and wealth or social class, which postmodernists claim is no longer important.

Now try this

1 Define what is meant by 'globalisation'.
2 Outline the postmodern attitude towards knowledge.

Educational policies, 1870–1978

The UK government spends approximately £90 billion per year on education. Since 1870, successive UK governments have introduced new **educational policies** and instructions that have aimed to widen participation in education and to achieve greater equality of opportunity or outcome.

Timeline of UK educational policies, 1870–1972

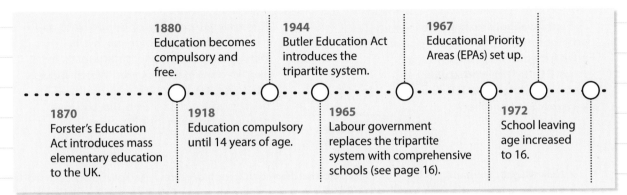

1880 Education becomes compulsory and free.

1944 Butler Education Act introduces the tripartite system.

1967 Educational Priority Areas (EPAs) set up.

1870 Forster's Education Act introduces mass elementary education to the UK.

1918 Education compulsory until 14 years of age.

1965 Labour government replaces the tripartite system with comprehensive schools (see page 16).

1972 School leaving age increased to 16.

Equal opportunities

Educational policy between 1944 and 1978 was generally based on the social democratic idea of improving **equality of opportunity**. Children from the poorest backgrounds were given the same opportunities as children from better-off social groups. This approach was based on the idea that British education should be **meritocratic** – that students should be rewarded purely on the basis of their ability. Sociologists are therefore interested in whether educational policies have been successful in tackling the inequality that exists between social classes, the genders and ethnic groups.

Education Priority Areas (EPAs)

Compensatory education policies aimed to tackle the educational inequalities caused by socio-economic disadvantages – for example, living in poverty-stricken areas. In the UK, this took the form of **Educational Priority Areas (EPAs)**. These were set up in 1967 in deprived parts of London, Birmingham, Liverpool and West Yorkshire to provide schools with extra money and resources to raise poor children's achievement and to encourage parental involvement in education.

EPAs aimed to compensate for poverty. This policy was inspired by both **cultural** and **material deprivation theories** (see pages 33–34). For example, **Douglas** (1964) believed that poorer parents were less likely than middle-class parents to take an interest in the education of their children.

EPAs were eventually abandoned because, as sociologists such as Bernstein observed, 'schools cannot compensate for society'.

The tripartite system

The Butler Education Act (1944) introduced free secondary education for all (up to age 15 years). The Act resulted in a **tripartite system** of secondary schools and the introduction of an intelligence quotient (IQ test) known as the 11+. This test embodied the concept of equality of opportunity: all school children took it at the age of 11. The test was supposed to sift, sort and select children and allocate them to one of three types of schools according to ability:

- grammar schools for those deemed academic
- technical schools for those deemed scientific or creative
- secondary moderns for those deemed non-academic.

Why the tripartite system failed

- Few technical schools were built. In many areas, the system was bipartite rather than tripartite.
- Middle-class students dominated grammar schools because they were more likely to pass the 11+.
- Working-class students dominated secondary moderns.
- The 11+ IQ test was not culture-fair. Critics argued it mainly benefitted those students with access to economic and cultural capital (see page 35) and penalised those who experienced material deprivation (see page 34).
- Secondary modern schools (students left at the age of 15 years with a 'school certificate') were seen by employers and parents as inferior to a grammar school education.

Now try this

1 Which theories of educational underachievement inspired Educational Priority Areas?
2 Why do you think Marxists might have been critical of the tripartite system?

Comprehensive schools

In 1965, the Labour government replaced the tripartite system with the **comprehensive school system**. Selection at age 11 was abolished and all children living in a particular area would go to the same type of school. Comprehensivation was built on the concept of 'equality of opportunity'. It was meant to be more meritocratic than the tripartite system.

Theoretical views on comprehensive schools

✓ **Functionalists:** comprehensives promote social integration, social solidarity and meritocracy (see page 26) by bringing students from very different backgrounds and abilities together.

✗ **Marxists:** equality of opportunity and meritocracy are ideological myths. Streaming mainly benefits students from middle-class backgrounds. Working-class students are more likely to be found in bottom sets or streams and to leave school with fewer qualifications.

Views

✗ **New Right:** inner-city comprehensives suffer more truancy, indiscipline and poorer standards of teaching.

✓ **Liberal feminists:** comprehensives have worked hard to reduce gender stereotyping. Consequently, girls today are achieving better exam results than boys.

✗ **Radical feminists:** comprehensives are patriarchal institutions. They reproduce patriarchal power in the economy by funnelling girls into stereotypical subject choices. This results in low-status and low-paid careers.

Catchment areas

Urban areas are rarely socially mixed because people tend to live alongside others from similar social backgrounds.

For example, inner-city areas contain a disproportionate number of poor people, while the suburbs contain a disproportionate number of middle-class people.

Consequences of a deprived inner-city catchment may include a predominantly working-class intake from poorer families who may not be able to educationally support their children compared with middle-class parents. As a result, schools may become 'failing' and may then struggle to attract teaching staff.

Selection by mortgage

A good school can considerably raise house prices in catchment areas, causing working-class parents to be priced out of the housing market.

Gewirtz (1995) argues that middle-class parents may use their **economic, social and cultural capital** to get their children into top-performing comprehensives. Achievement levels and success rates in these schools are therefore likely to be high.

Evaluation of comprehensive schools

👍 Working-class children have the opportunity to pursue the same qualifications as middle-class children.

👍 More working-class students now enter higher education.

👍 Less bright students do better because of the greater range of courses and qualifications.

👍 The exam results of the top comprehensives compare well with the private sector.

👎 **Hargreaves** (1967) and **Ball** (1981) argue that the comprehensive ideal is undermined by streaming or setting. The allocation of children to streams or sets is often based on social class or conformity to rules rather than ability.

👎 Some local authorities continued with the grammar school system.

👎 Comprehensive schools in suburban areas achieve better exam results than those in inner-city areas, therefore reproducing class inequality.

Now try this

Explain how 'selection by mortgage' undermines equality of opportunity.

Educational policies, 1979–1988: marketisation and parentocracy

After 1979, educational policy shifted away from a Social Democratic emphasis on equal opportunities to a New Right emphasis on marketisation, parental choice and selection.

Timeline of UK educational policies, 1979–1988

The Conservative government under Margaret Thatcher focused on offering choice for parents.

1979
Conservative government under Margaret Thatcher takes power.

1980s
A range of schemes known as 'new vocationalism' are established.

1988
The Education Reform Act (ERA) introduced the national curriculum, Standard Assessment Tests (SATs), league tables, new types of schools (e.g. City Technology Colleges and grant-maintained schools) and Ofsted inspections.

Marketisation

The 1988 ERA encouraged **marketisation**. This was the idea that education could be run like a business. Schools would compete with each other for customers in the form of parents and students.

Two important changes to the administration of state education were introduced by the ERA. These aimed to help schools market themselves and compete with other schools:

1. **Open enrolment** – which allowed successful schools to expand to the limit of their physical capacity.

2. **Formula funding** – money given to schools was based on the number of students they attracted.

New Right educationalists argued that the more competition that schools faced, the more incentive there would be for them to improve. It was believed that such competition would lead to the expansion of successful schools measured by greater enrolment and the ability to recruit the best teachers.

In contrast, unsuccessful schools would have to improve or face the possibility of funding cuts and eventually closure. For more on the ERA, see page 18.

Parentocracy

Before the ERA, students were allocated to schools by the local education authority. However, the ERA symbolised a power shift from local education authorities to **parents**. This was because, in theory, the marketisation encouraged by the ERA aimed to transform parents into consumers in the educational marketplace by giving them the ability to choose a school that best suited the needs of their child. The concept '**parentocracy**' refers specifically to the fact that the ERA gave greater power to parents to shape their children's educational future by giving them the right to choose which school their children should attend.

Now try this

1 Define the term 'parentocracy'.
2 What was the main aim of encouraging competition between schools?

Educational policies, 1979–1988: The ERA

In addition to marketisation, the ERA encouraged **competition**. It also introduced 'new vocationalism' to deal with the skills crisis.

How the ERA worked

The ERA endorsed marketisation, **competition**, **parental choice** and **selection**.

Testing: children were tested at the age of 7, 11 and 14.

League tables: this resulted in ranking schools in terms of SATs, GCSE and A-level performance.

Ofsted: school inspections were published and reported on the quality of the teaching and learning experience in specific schools.

Selection: schools were allowed to select a proportion of their students.

ERA measures

National curriculum: the introduction of a national curriculum (1988) was hailed as meritocratic because all students were taught the same knowledge, and experienced the same SATs and exams such as the GCSE.

City Technology Colleges: these were introduced in some inner-city areas to try to improve educational standards and offer choice.

Diversification: in order to give parents more choice of schools (and to reduce local authority control of schooling), a greater variety of schools began to be introduced. Existing schools could 'opt out' of local authority control to become directly funded by central government. The managers of these 'grant maintained schools' had the freedom to make decisions about marketing, enrolment and selection.

New vocationalism

In the 1980s, New Right politicians argued that youth unemployment was caused by a skills crisis. A range of educational schemes, known collectively as the new vocationalism, was introduced to deal with the skills crisis. These included:

- **YTS:** a one-year training scheme combined work experience with education for unemployed school leavers.
- **The General National Vocational Qualification (GNVQ):** these were taught in schools as an alternative to academic courses. They aimed to prepare students for work by teaching job-specific skills in the classroom and placing students into the workplace for work experience.

In 2013, it was announced that vocational qualifications were to be dropped and no longer included in league tables.

Evaluation of the ERA

- Concerns were expressed over the damaging effects of frequently testing children.
- The validity of such testing was undermined by schools 'teaching to the tests'.
- The educational market was not a truly competitive market because parents were not paying for education and selecting schools on the basis of price.
- Schools often excluded students to improve their image.
- Popular schools quickly filled up, which restricted parental choice.
- The ERA failed to address inequalities caused by the existence of private schools (**Kynaston**, 2008).

Evaluation of new vocationalism

Marxists such as **Finn** (1987) argue that:

- it was the lack of jobs rather than inadequate skills that was the real cause of youth unemployment
- the hidden function of YTS was to produce a pool of low-skilled cheap labour
- such schemes legitimated class inequality as middle-class youths were educated to university standard, while working-class youths were merely trained for manual work.

Now try this

Why did the New Right claim that the national curriculum was meritocratic?

Evaluating marketisation policies

New Right policies on education – particularly those encouraging **marketisation**, selection and **parentocracy** – have been heavily criticised.

A two-tier education system?

There is some evidence that the 1988 ERA created a two-tier state education system in which schools at the top end of league tables were able to select the best students, leaving schools lower in the league tables with students not wanted by the top schools.

Critics such as **Bartlett** (1993) and **Whitty** (1998) point out that this produced a self-fulfilling cycle of success and decline.

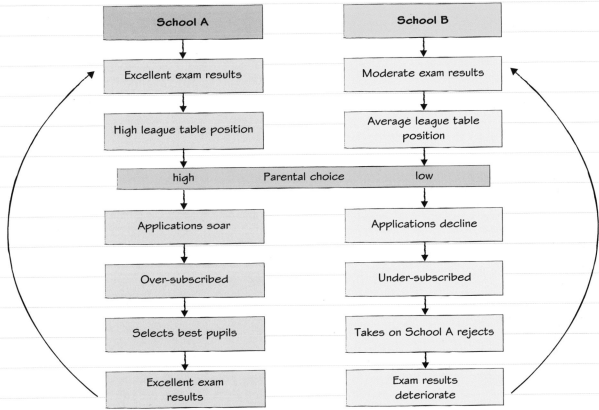

Ball (1994) argues that marketisation actually reproduced and even increased social class inequalities within education because the high-achieving schools tended to select the 'cream' of middle-class academic students and were less likely to admit students with learning difficulties.

Evaluation of marketisation and parentocracy

- 🗨 **Gewirtz** (1995) studied 14 London schools and found that parentocracy is a myth because parental power is not equally distributed across all parents. Middle-class parents have more power than working-class parents to choose schools because they are able to use their economic, cultural and social capital to ensure their children enter the 'best' schools.

- 🗨 Parents who fail to get their children into their schools of choice actually have limited choices in practice. Many of them have no choice but to accept a place for their child in either failing or average schools.

- 🗨 It created and reinforced inequalities between schools in middle-class and working-class areas in funding, facilities and the recruitment of teachers.

Now try this

1 What advantages do middle-class parents have over working-class parents in their choice of schools?

2 Outline how school league tables might be self-fulfilling.

Labour educational policies, 1997–2010

The educational policies of the New Labour governments of Tony Blair and Gordon Brown (1997–2010) were influenced by both New Right and Social Democratic ideas (see pages 17–18). Labour retained and modified New Right policies such as marketisation and encouraged some privatisation of aspects of the educational system. However, it also aimed to improve working-class opportunity (see page 21).

Timeline of UK educational policies, 1997–2010

1997 Education Action Zones (EAZ) introduced.

1997 Primary school class size reduced.

1998 Free pre-school nursery provision.

1999 Sure Start.

2001 City academies introduced.

2004 Aimhigher.

1997 Tony Blair's Labour government takes power. More **specialist schools** set up.

1997 **Educational Maintenance Allowance (EMA)** introduced.

1998 New Deal for Young People.

1998 University tuition fees introduced.

1999 EAZ replaced by Excellence in Cities.

2002 Young **Gifted and Talented initiative.**

The influence of the New Right

The New Right influence on Labour can be seen in Labour's focus on the following.

- **Choice and selection**: Labour expanded the Conservative policy of specialist schools. In 1998, it made it possible for such schools to select up to 10% of their intake based on aptitude in the existing specialisms of sport, the arts, modern languages and technology. New specialisms were added in 2001, and by 2002 nearly one-third of secondary schools were specialist schools. The aim was to extend the programme to 50% of secondary schools by 2005. The 2006 Education and Inspections Act gave schools greater freedom to be selective by setting their own admission arrangements.
- **Diversity**: until 1997 the only faith schools funded by the state were Christian (Anglican and Roman Catholic) and Jewish. The 2006 Act expanded faith schools to other religions.
- **Parental choice**: parents were given the right to request new schools for their children.

Privatisation

Labour initiated the **Private Finance Initiative (PFI)**, which involves private contractors and the state jointly funding the building of new schools and colleges. Exam boards and SATs testing, as well as some Ofsted inspections, are also now in private hands. This has led to some critics suggesting education has become a commodity to be bought and sold for profit.

Competition and raising standards

- Labour retained school performance tables. All schools were set targets to raise performance in national examinations.
- Failing schools, often in low-income communities, were closed because they failed to meet targets. As part of the 'Fresh Start' programme, they were re-opened as city academies in partnership with local employers. They had new head teachers and often new staff, new names, uniforms and sometimes buildings. The key objective of Fresh Start was to improve educational standards, particularly in disadvantaged communities.

Evaluation

💬 **Chitty (2014)** criticises New Labour for opening up the public sector of education to greater privatisation. PFI was more costly than anticipated, which led to some local authorities having severe financial difficulties.

💬 **Chitty** also criticises the inefficiency of private contractors, which often failed to deliver services on time or at a lower cost than local authorities.

💬 **Ball (2007)** notes that a significant **Education Services Industry (ESI)** now exists alongside the public sector of education. He argues that education has become increasingly **commodified** and profit-orientated. He suggests the strong possibility that the state will no longer be the main provider of education in the future.

Now try this

Identify **two** New Labour education policies that were influenced by the New Right.

Labour's social democratic policies

New Labour's educational policy was a paradox. While it took influence from the New Right, it also aimed to ensure **equality of opportunity** – the poorest sections of society should be fairly served by education.

Reducing inequality

1 Free pre-school nursery provision.

2 Primary school class sizes were reduced in low-income communities.

3 Some disadvantaged communities were identified and designated **Education Action Zones (EAZ)**. Here, Labour opened **Sure Start children's centres**, which aimed to give young children a better start in life. Sure Start brought together a range of educational and other services to support poorer parents in order to tackle cultural and material deprivation (see pages 33–34), which placed working-class children at a disadvantage before they even started school.

4 The **New Deal for Young People** aimed to help the young unemployed gain qualifications to improve their chances of finding work.

5 The **Aimhigher** initiative aimed to widen participation in higher education particularly among students from working-class and ethnic-minority backgrounds.

6 The **Gifted and Talented** initiative was introduced in 2002 to identify the top 5% of students aged 11–18 in inner-city secondary schools and provide them with extra study supports.

7 The **Apprenticeship scheme** and vocational educational qualifications were expanded.

8 The **Educational Maintenance Allowance (EMA)** aimed to increase the number of young people, especially working-class students, studying A-levels and applying to university.

Some of New Labour's policies aimed to increase opportunity.

Evaluation

👍 **Ball** (2013) suggests that, under New Labour there were overall increases in the proportion of students getting five or more GCSEs at grade C, and improvements in achievement for some ethnic minorities.

👎 Boys' achievement continued to lag behind that of girls' during Labour's term of office.

👎 **Ball** (2013) observed that the class divide in achievement between working-class and middle-class students persisted throughout New Labour's term of office.

👎 **Tomlinson** (2005) observed that, although the number of working-class students in HE has increased, class inequalities in HE have actually widened. This is because the number of middle-class students applying to university has increased at a faster rate than the number of working-class applicants.

👎 Labour was criticised by **Tomlinson** for deterring bright students from going to university by introducing tuition fees for HE and for replacing means-tested maintenance grants with loans to be paid back with interest after graduation.

University tuition fees

In 1998, as part of the Teaching and Higher Education Act, Labour introduced tuition fees across the UK for undergraduate and postgraduate certificate courses at university. In England fees have risen to up to £9,000 per year (and £3,800 in Northern Ireland). Scotland charges no fees for HE.

Now try this

Why do some critics argue that the Labour government's policy attempts to get more working-class students into university were contradictory?

Educational policies, 2010 onwards

The Conservative and Liberal Democrat Coalition government led by David Cameron (2010–2015) and the Conservative government (2015–present day) led by both David Cameron and Theresa May have further added to a complex British education system.

Timeline of UK educational policies, 2010–2016

2010 **Academies Act** introduced.

2011 **Educational Maintenance Allowance (EMA)** is abolished in England and Wales.

2013 School leaving age raised to 17.

2015 School leaving age raised to 18.

2016 Grants to help the very poorest through university are abolished.

2010 Conservative–Liberal Democrat Coalition government takes power under David Cameron.

2010 Aimhigher programme ended.

2011 Education Minister Michael Gove announces that over 300 schools will be rebuilt using Private Finance Initiative (PFI) funding.

2014 **Pupil premium** introduced.

2015 Conservative Party under David Cameron win the election.

The Coalition, 2010–2015

1. The **Academies Act** (2010) allowed all existing faith and state schools that had achieved an 'outstanding' grade in Ofsted inspections to become **academies**. It also encouraged further **privatisation** of the education system, because it positively encouraged businesses to invest in and run academies.

2. The **Academies Act** (2010) authorised the creation of **free schools**. These were a type of state-funded school controlled by parents, educational charities and religious groups, rather than local authorities. By 2014, 331 free schools had been opened or approved. Both academies and free schools are able to set out their admission policies. Therefore they are able to practise **selection**.

3. Reforms were made to the curriculum in 2013 stressing traditional, more rigorous teaching styles.
For example, primary school students now have to read Shakespeare plays in full. New, more rigorous A-levels were established.

4. The value of vocational qualifications were downgraded, so that schools could no longer use them to boost their league table position.

5. EMAs were scrapped. The cap on HE tuition fees rose to £9,000 per year in 2010.

6. Between 2010 and 2012, more than 500 Sure Start centres were closed down.

7. In 2004, the Liberal Democrats introduced the 'student premium'. Schools with high numbers of students eligible for free school meals were given extra educational resources to spend on further support for disadvantaged children.

The Conservatives, 2015 onwards

The Conservative government continues to support and increase levels of marketisation, privatisation and selection by encouraging more free schools to be set up in partnership with private companies.

In January 2016, higher education grants for the very poorest students were scrapped and replaced with loans. This may mean that fewer bright students from disadvantaged families will apply to university, while those who do will encounter greater levels of debt.

In 2016, Theresa May announced plans to re-introduce selective grammar schools (see page 15), which she argues are 'engines of social mobility'.

Now try this

What Coalition policy was aimed at improving educational opportunity for poorer students?

The Conservatives and privatisation

The Conservative government continues to support and increase levels of **privatisation** in education.

Privatisation

Privatisation involves moving functions previously provided by government into the private sector, to be run by businesses for profit.

For example, between 2010 and 2016, some aspects of the educational system such as careers services, catering and Educational Psychology services were contracted out to private providers.

Some academies operate in chains run by businesses.

Supply teachers provided by agencies.

Private Finance Initiative.

Exam tuition provided privately.

Software and student-support websites, e.g. getrevising.co.uk

The private company Capita was given a contract in 2004 to manage the strategy to improve literacy and numeracy.

Private provision of education

Educational conferences for teachers and students.

A US firm (Educational Testing Service, ETS) was given a contract to manage SATs testing for 11 and 14-year-olds.

Vending machines in schools; branded coffee and fast food outlets on college and university campuses.

Ofsted inspections contracted out in 2013 to three private companies: Tribal, SERCO and CfBT.

Management of some local educational authorities, e.g. education in Islington is run by a private contractor, Cambridge Education Associates.

Evaluation of education policy, 2010–present day

👍 New Right sociologists see privatisation as a good thing because they argue that state services are often inefficient and wasteful. They claim only private companies competing in an unregulated market can provide cheap educational services to a high standard and meet the variety of educational needs.

👎 Critics argue that privatisation will eventually mean that education will no longer be seen as a human right that should be available free to all; it will be a commodity to be bought and sold. The 'best' education will be too expensive for ordinary and poorer people.

👎 **Wintour** (2013) observes that the removal of EMAs (page 21) has lowered staying-on rates in further education (FE) for students from poorer backgrounds.

👎 **Ratcliffe** (2014) claims that the student premium (see page 22) is being used by schools to plug the gap left by austerity cuts rather than for the benefit of disadvantaged children as intended.

👎 Marxists see the privatisation of educational services as yet another example of the spread of the logic of neo-liberal capitalism, which sees public services such as the NHS and education as ripe for transformation into profit-making businesses.

👎 Critics of free schools claim they have brought in selection through the back door and are failing to meet the needs of the most disadvantaged children.

Now try this

Identify a Conservative policy that may further increase class inequalities in education.

Had a look ☐ Nearly there ☐ Nailed it! ☐

The impact of educational policies

Use this page to help you re-cap the impact of social and educational policies.

Class and increased opportunities for disadvantaged students

Fresh Start schools – New Labour 1997 (see page 20).

Student premium (2014) – Liberal Democrats under the Coalition government (see page 22).

The comprehensive system – Labour 1965 (see page 16).

New Deal for young people – New Labour 1998 (see page 21).

Social policy and class: positive

Education Action Zones – New Labour 1997 (see pages 20–21).

Education Maintenance Allowance – New Labour 1997 (see page 20).

Aimhigher – New Labour 2004 (see page 20).

Sure Start centres – New Labour 1998 (see page 21).

Class and increased inequalities

Academies and Free schools – Academies Act 2010, Coalition government (see page 22).

Marketisation and parental choice benefit the middle-class – **Gewirtz** (1995) (see page 19).

University tuition fees – New Labour and Coalition governments (see pages 21–22).

Social policy and class: negative

The tripartite system – 1944 Butler Act (see page 15).

Giving some state schools the power to select students – Academies Act 2010, Coalition government (see page 22).

The scrapping of EMA, Aimhigher and HE grants – Coalition government (see page 22).

Ethnicity and the impact on opportunities and outcomes

Marketisation and privatisation – negative impact on poorer ethnic minorities.

Young, Gifted and Talented programmes – **Gilborn** (2008): white students are twice as likely to be selected (see pages 20 and 45).

Teacher training to raise awareness of racism.

Social policy and ethnicity

Educational Action Zones – targeted inner city areas, often with higher proportions of ethnic minorities (see page 21).

Education Maintenance Allowance – New Labour 1997 (see page 21).

However this has since been cut, impacting on disadvantaged communities.

Aimhigher – New Labour 2004 (see page 21).

Sure Start children's centres – New Labour 1998 (see page 21).

Gender and the impact on opportunities and outcomes

Removal of sex stereotyped language, images and examples from textbooks.

The national curriculum – boys and girls must take the same core subjects.

Teacher training to raise consciousness of sexism.

Social policy and gender

Policies aimed at raising female participation in science and technology – such as GIST and WISE (see page 38).

Equal opportunity laws (see page 39).

Coursework-based GCSEs – girls perform well at coursework; since changed under new educational reforms from 2015.

Now try this

Identify **two** pieces of education policy that aim to improve the opportunities of ethnic minorities within British education.

Globalisation and educational policy

At its simplest, **globalisation** means that the world we live in now feels smaller and more accessible than it was a decade ago because of: developments in digital technology such as the internet; and the growth in movement of people, ideas and businesses.

Defining globalisation

Waters (2001) defines globalisation as a social process in which the constraints of geography on economic, political, social and cultural arrangements have declined. At a micro-level, for individuals this means that distance and time zones are no longer important due to the instant interaction of digital technology. At a macro-level, societies that were once distant, independent and very different from one another, are now increasingly globally intertwined economically and culturally and inter-dependent.

The impact of globalisation on educational policy

Education in the UK is partly shaped by global factors.

 The British economy operates in a global market. Skilled and qualified workers are needed so that British companies can compete successfully with foreign businesses.

Kelly (2009) argues that, in the past 30 years, British educational policy has become increasingly geared to global economic competitiveness. Governments argue that education has to produce workers who are able to compete in a global economy by having skills that will be valuable in a global market. Politicians often refer to England's position in various international league tables in order to justify claims that the country's schools are 'underperforming'.

For example, Michael Gove justified his changes to the primary and secondary school curriculum in 2013 on the grounds that Britain had dropped down the Programme for International Student Assessment (PISA) world rankings for educational performance in maths, reading and science.

 Education is impacted by the flow of ideas globally. This has led to both a more multicultural curriculum and the introduction of educational ideas and practices such as free schools, which have supposedly worked in other societies.

Examples of globalisation and UK education

- Former Education Secretary Michael Gove claimed that his new curriculum combined the best of global educational practices from Hong Kong, Massachusetts (USA), Singapore and Finland.
- **Ball** (2012) points out that British public schools and universities increasingly market themselves to a global audience, by setting up overseas branches in countries such as China, Russia and Singapore.
- British exam boards offer International GCSEs and A-levels to students in over 160 countries.
- Many British students study for the International Baccalaureate (IB) global diploma rather than domestic A-levels.
- English students (about 8500 in 2010–2011) are increasingly attracted to the 1800 undergraduate courses taught in English at cheaper European universities. Many also elect to study in the USA.

Evaluation

- **Ball** (2012) is critical of the globalisation of educational services. He sees this as the result of neo-liberal philosophies and practices that treat education as a business rather than a human right to be provided free of charge by the state. He argues that students are increasingly seen as commodities to be bought and sold for a profit.
- However, **Holborn** (2016) suggests that globalisation may have positive effects on the British educational system. Increased migration has led to a more **multicultural curriculum**, thus promoting understanding of other cultures and racial and ethnic tolerance. It may also lead to an increased emphasis on equality of opportunity as governments seek to capitalise on the talents of every individual to make the country more competitive in a global marketplace.

Now try this

Explain how increased global migration to the UK might influence educational policy.

Functionalism and education

Functionalists see the **education system** as a part of the wider social system. They see **socialisation** and value consensus as essential components of social order.

Socialisation

Functionalists such as **Émile Durkheim** (1903) see schools as secondary agents of **socialisation**. Generation by generation they transmit and reproduce shared cultural values such as: achievement; competition; individualism; belonging to society; equality of opportunity; and morality through both the **hidden** and **academic curricula**. This is known as **social reproduction** and helps to ensure value consensus and social order.

Social solidarity

Durkheim (1903) believed that education functions to bring about **social integration** and **solidarity**. He suggested that subjects such as history, language and religious education link children to society, past and present, and affirm to them a sense of belonging to society.

In Wales, for example, the Welsh language is compulsory in schools in order to remind children of their Welsh heritage.

Defining curriculum

- The **academic/formal curriculum** refers to the knowledge that is taught in schools for the purpose of exams and qualifications.

- The **hidden curriculum** refers to the informal learning processes that occur in schools. It is a 'side-effect' that serves to transmit messages to students about values, attitudes and principles.

For example, **Jackson** (1968) described the hidden curriculum as the 'unpublicised features of school life' in which students learn to accept the distribution of power in school and society, and that formal or informal rules about behaviour underpin most aspects of social life inside and outside of school. The hidden curriculum also teaches students how and when to accept criticism and praise.

School as a social bridge

Talcott Parsons (1961) argued that the main function of education was to act as a **social bridge** between the family (which loves its members regardless of talent and ability) and wider society in which people are judged purely on **merit**. He saw the classroom as a microcosm of society where children would be exposed to different cultures and, therefore, learn tolerance and how to integrate.

Defining meritocracy

An ideal **meritocracy** is a society or institution that practises equality of opportunity and in which people are rewarded solely on the basis of merit. In other words, on the basis of talent, ability, hard work and effort.

Functionalists argue that schools are generally meritocratic institutions because children are objectively evaluated through examinations and the awarding of qualifications.

Criticism of social reproduction

- It ignores aspects of education that might be dysfunctional or harmful to particular individuals and society. For example, some schools may be allocated less funding than others.
- It neglects conflict that exists within schools. The fact that some schools have had to go into special measures because of disruptive students, or exclude students who do not conform to school rules, suggests schools may not be entirely successful in teaching consensus and solidarity.
- The fact that some social groups – such as those in private education – enjoy greater educational opportunities than others undermines equality of opportunity and meritocracy.
- Marxists argue that the hidden curriculum functions to ensure working-class conformity rather than success.
- **Wrong** (1961) argues from a social action perspective that functionalists over-simplify the process of socialisation by seeing children as the passive puppets of society (see page 7). Wrong argues that the teacher–student relationship (see page 36) is not a one-way process. It is more complex than this.

Now try this

1 Why are British schools seen as meritocratic institutions by functionalists?

2 Explain how the teaching of history and languages promote social integration and solidarity.

Functionalism, education and the economy

Functionalists see education as functional because it teaches the **skills** required by a modern industrial society, produces **human capital** and allocates people to their most effective role in the **economic system**.

Skills provision

Functionalists argue that an important function of education is to produce a **skilled workforce** to meet the needs of industry and therefore the economy.

 1 The 1870 Education Act (see page 15) introduced mass compulsory education to raise numeracy and literacy skills so that the UK could compete with competition from the USA and Germany.

2 As the economy required more complex skills, in the 1960s more colleges and universities were built to provide degrees in subjects such as computer technology.

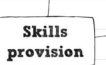 **Skills provision**

3 New Labour expanded the Apprenticeship scheme, introduced specialist schools and raised the school leaving age in order for Britain to remain competitive in the global marketplace (see page 21).

4 In the 1980s, vocational education and training was introduced to increase young people's skill levels (see page 18).

Human capital theory

Human capital is the stock of knowledge, skills, habits, values and creativity embodied in the ability to perform work that produces real economic value. The theory argues that economic investment in people is similar to investment in technology in that it will produce more effective workers.

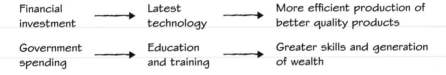

Financial investment → Latest technology → More efficient production of better quality products

Government spending → Education and training → Greater skills and generation of wealth

Role allocation

Davis and Moore (1945) believe that:

- education sifts and sorts students using exams and qualifications, and allocates them to a future job that best fits their abilities
- the most functionally important jobs are allocated to those who display the most ability, effort and flexibility
- those with lower grades end up with lower skilled jobs
- role allocation ensures a more efficient economy.

Evaluation

- New Right educationalists believe that state schools are not producing the right sorts of workers required for the British businesses to successfully compete in the global economy.
- The best jobs may not necessarily go to those who are best qualified. Other factors such as being privately educated, male or white may have more influence.
- The numbers going to university do not match the number of jobs available. An over-qualified workforce is therefore being produced. Over-qualified people are potentially less efficient because they are easily bored or disaffected because the job they are doing is neither interesting nor challenging.
- **Woolf** (2002) questions whether more government spending on education will automatically lead to economic growth.

  For example, Switzerland has relatively low education spending but high economic growth.

Now try this

1 Why do functionalists believe that role allocation produces a more efficient economy?

2 Outline the relationship between role allocation and meritocracy.

3 Why is an over-qualified workforce a problem?

Neo-liberal or New Right perspective

Neo-liberal (also sometimes called New Right) perspectives have had a great influence on British educational policy in recent years (see pages 17–18 and 20).

Functionalism and neo-liberalism

There are similarities between functionalism and neo-liberalism.

education should keep pace with ever-evolving economies and produce workers with the appropriate skills.

education systems need to respond to globalisation.

education should promote social integration and national identity.

Functionalism and neo-liberalism agree that ...

the most talented and skilful members of society deserve higher rewards than the less-skilled.

education systems should be meritocratic.

the state interferes too much in people's lives and should, instead, only play a minimal role in society; state education is often inefficient and a drain on a country's resources.

Neo-liberals also believe that ...

high government spending on education and other services is seen as undesirable because it requires high taxes.

education is best provided by the free market; therefore, neo-liberals believe education is a commodity or product (marketisation).

providers of education, such as schools, should be encouraged to compete with one another like businesses, because free market competition drives up standards and drives down costs.

consumers, such as parents and students, need to be empowered; they need more choices and a greater say in education decision-making.

John Chubb and Terry Moe (1990)

Chubb and Moe are American New Right educationalists who argue that state education in the USA has:

- generally been unresponsive to the needs of students, parents and the economy
- generally provided a low standard of education, especially for disadvantaged groups
- failed to produce workers with the sort of skills required to compete in a global economy
- resulted in high levels of unemployment as a result of its failure.

For example, workers in the West are increasingly losing their jobs to skilled workers in the developing world because Western educational systems are failing to provide children with the skills they need to compete with children in rapidly developing societies such as Singapore.

In contrast, privately funded education in the USA has to please its customers in order to survive; therefore, its standards of education provision are very high.

The free market puts constant pressure on private providers of education to maintain high standards or to improve their product. If they fail to do this, their consumers (parents and local communities) will choose to buy their education elsewhere.

Chubb and Moe recommend that parents should be given educational 'vouchers' to spend on a school of their choice. Schools would have to compete with each other to attract parental spending. Schools that had 'failed' in the past would have to improve their product or go out of business. This is '**parentocracy**' (see page 17).

Now try this

How might education become more efficient according to neo-liberals?

Neo-liberal or New Right influence

The New Right has exerted great influence over British educational policy.

Influence

1 In the 1980s vocational education was reformed to help ensure young people were equipped with the 'right' **skills** and attitudes in order to reduce youth unemployment (see page 18).

2 The 1988 **Education Reform Act (ERA)** introduced the concepts of marketisation and parentocracy into state education by:

- changing the **funding formula** (see page 17) so that popular schools obtain more funding, while funding for unsuccessful schools was reduced

- introducing **league tables** so that schools could compete with each other; students and parents could make informed choices about which school would benefit their child (see page 19).

3 The New Labour government of 1997–2010 introduced new types of schools – **academies** – some of which were run wholly or partly by private businesses (see page 20).

4 The Coalition government of 2010–2015 continued the **privatisation** of British education by allowing parents to set up **free schools** (see page 22). The **Education Services Industry (ESI)** has grown dramatically in the last 10 years; it owns exam boards (for example, the publisher Pearson owns Edexcel), while private companies are in partnership with the state in the building of schools (see page 23).

In Islington, for example, all 70 schools once run by Islington Education Authority are now run by a private company – Cambridge Educational Services. Failing schools are often taken over by private academy chains.

National curriculum

New Right sociologists, like functionalists, are keen to ensure the state continues to supervise the transmission of knowledge that helps to establish, and maintain, a shared cultural British identity and cultural identity. This was one of the main motivations behind the introduction of the **national curriculum** by the 1988 ERA (see page 18).

Educational initiatives promoted by Michael Gove, the Secretary of State for Education (2010–2014) highlighted the role of schools in promoting British values and citizenship. However, this New Right emphasis has been criticised for neglecting cultural diversity and the fact that the UK is a multicultural society.

The teaching of history, in particular, was supposed to promote national pride with its emphasis on British achievement.

Evaluation of the New Right perspective

- 👎 Marxists have observed that parental choice merely reproduces class inequality because middle-class parents use their economic, cultural and social capital to ensure their children get into the best schools.

- 👎 Evidence from both the UK and USA does not support the view that the privatisation and marketisation of education drives up standards. Many academies and free schools have been accused of providing poor-quality education.

- 👎 There is evidence that both academies and free schools discriminate against disadvantaged children.

- 👎 Vocational education in the 1980s was accused of preparing young people to passively accept a future of exploitation and low pay.

- 👎 Marxists argue that privatised education will always put profit before the wellbeing of students.

Now try this

Give **two** examples of the Educational Services Industry.

Marxist theory of education

Marxists argue that education, although a state institution, is an important component of the **superstructure** of **capitalist society** (see page 10). Consequently, it mainly serves the interests of the capitalist class rather than its students or society in general.

Louis Althusser (1971)

Althusser argues that the education system is an ideological state apparatus that aims to perform the following functions on behalf of the bourgeois or capitalist class.

1 Education functions to maintain, legitimise (justify) and reproduce **social class inequality** across the generations.

2 Education claims to be **meritocratic** (see page 26); however, this is a myth because schools actually discriminate in favour of privately educated and middle-class students.

3 Middle-class students have access to **economic and cultural capital** (see page 35). This gives them an unfair advantage over working-class students.

4 Education functions to deliberately engineer working-class failure because capitalism requires an unqualified factory workforce.

5 Private education prepares the children of the elite for future positions of power.

6 Education encourages students to uncritically accept capitalist values such as competition, individualism and private enterprise as normal and natural.

7 Teachers are agents of capitalism who funnel middle-class students towards success and 'persuade' working-class children to accept educational failure.

8 The organisation and content of education is shaped by a **hidden curriculum** (see page 26). This functions to assist middle-class achievement and to deter working-class achievement, thus reproducing class inequality.

9 The **hidden curriculum** encourages working-class students to conform and to accept hierarchy and inequality.

10 The **hidden curriculum** lowers the ambitions of working-class children and encourages them to accept the blame for their failure.

The correspondence principle

Marxists **Bowles and Gintis** (1976) argue that education 'stands in the long shadow of work'. This means that education corresponds with, or mirrors, work in order to prepare working-class children for their future as manual workers. The **correspondence principle** is transmitted via the **hidden curriculum** – the day-to-day expectations and rules that underpin classroom management such as queuing outside the door, or standing when the head teacher enters the room. Marxists argue that the hidden curriculum programmes students to uncritically accept failure, rules, hierarchy and inequality, thus preparing them for the factory or office. Bowles and Gintis claim that the characteristics schools prize most in students are obedience and punctuality. These are also the characteristics the capitalist system most prizes in workers.

School	Work
Students work for qualifications, not satisfaction.	Workers work for wages, not satisfaction.
Students have no control over what is taught.	Workers have no control over what is made.
Students have to obey teachers.	Workers have to obey bosses.
Some students deserve more status than others.	The skilled deserve more status than the unskilled.
Students learn discipline.	Workers who are ill-disciplined are sacked.
Students learn that school routine is boring.	Workers accept that work is boring.

Examples of the correspondence principle.

Now try this

1 Outline why Marxists view the hidden curriculum so negatively.

2 Give **two** examples of how schooling corresponds to work.

3 What determines educational success or failure according to Marxists?

Evaluating Marxist approaches

The Marxist theory of education has been criticised by a range of sociological perspectives including **neo-Marxists**, **Social democrats** and the **New Right**.

① Neo-Marxism

Neo-Marxists such as **Giroux (1984)** reject the idea that working-class children passively accept their lot and become compliant workers. He suggests that the existence of anti-school subcultures (see page 37), truancy, exclusion and industrial action show that both the hidden curriculum and the correspondence principle (see page 30) are failing in practice. Marxists also fail to see that gender, ethnicity and religion often combine with class to produce success or failure.

 Key study **Paul Willis (1977)**

Willis, a neo-Marxist, studied a group of 12 working-class boys (the 'lads') during their last 18 months at school and their first few months at work (see page 58). He found that they:

- rejected the hidden curriculum and teacher labelling
- chose to reject qualifications because the manual jobs they wanted did not require them
- saw their schooling as a success because they had redefined its aims as 'having a laff' with their mates.

Willis' 'lads' were neither conformist or docile.

② Social democratic

The social democratic perspective believes that Marxists exaggerate the effect of the education system on working-class achievement. **Halsey, Floud and Martin** (1873) point out that government intervention in the form of the comprehensive system, the expansion of university places and welfare policies has dramatically improved the chances of working-class people to escape being allocated to manual labour and factory work.

③ New Right

New Right thinkers believe that Marxists fail to consider that some people are naturally more talented than others. **Saunders** (1996) claims that middle-class educational success is due to genetic differences in ability. He argues that middle-class children possess genetic advantages from their parents in the form of talent whereas working-class children inherit a genetic deficit in regards to intelligence and ability.

④ Neo-liberals

Neo-liberals argue that Marxists fail to see that state intervention in education has actually failed all social groups, not just the working class. **Chubb and Moe** (1990), for example, state that education is inefficient and wasteful in its use of resources. It has failed to equip *all* students with the skills needed to be successful in the global marketplace.

⑤ Postmodernist

Postmodernists argue that Marxists fail to see that modern schools reproduce diversity rather than inequality. Moreover, postmodernists such as **Morrow and Torres** (1998) claim that students actively construct their own identities. They point out that postmodern societies are characterised by **individualisation**. This means people are no longer constrained by traditional structures like social class. In postmodern societies, students are now free to make their own choices about identity.

Consequently, Marxists exaggerate the influence of social class on student identity because it may also be influenced by factors such as gender, sexuality, ethnicity and religion.

In 2016, for example, it was reported that British schools were having to cope with an increasing number of trans students.

Now try this

1 Explain why Giroux and Willis are critical of the idea that schools are responsible for reproducing and legitimising working-class failure.
2 Why do postmodernists criticise Marxists for over-emphasising the influence of social class?

External factors: social class and education

Since the introduction of compulsory state education in 1870, the educational level of the average UK citizen has dramatically improved. However, at all stages of education – primary, secondary, further and higher – there is differential educational achievement, with students from middle-class families generally doing better than their working-class peers.

Working-class underachievement

Working-class students are more likely to:
- fall behind in reading, writing and maths
- be placed in lower sets or streams
- get fewer GCSEs or lower grades
- leave school at the age of 16.

They are less likely to study A-levels and go to university.

External vs internal debate

There are two broad **sociological explanations** for educational success and failure.

 Some sociologists blame factors **external** to the school, which mainly revolve around the idea that working-class students are denied access to types of capital which are taken for granted in middle-class homes.

 However, other sociologists blame **in-school (internal)** factors, especially teachers and the organisation of schools. For more on internal factors, see pages 36–37.

The influence of external factors on educational achievement

Private education. —

Cultural deprivation (see page 33). —

Educational success or failure

— Material deprivation (see page 34).

— Cultural and social capital (see page 35).

Private education

A very clear social class distinction can be seen in educational outcomes between state schools and private schools.

- A Durham University study in 2016 found privately educated children are two years ahead of students in the state sector by the time they reach the age of 16.

- According to the Sutton Trust, in 2014 an average of just 11% of state school students went to the leading 24 universities in the UK compared with 38% of independent school students.

- One in 20 students from private schools went on to study at Oxford or Cambridge University in 2011 compared with only one in 100 from state schools.

Critics of private education claim that such schools undermine equality of opportunity because the statistics suggest that the products of these schools experience positive discrimination in terms of job allocation. Most of these schools, and therefore their advantages, are out of the financial reach of most working-class families.

Private education does not, however, solely explain the class differences in achievement that exist within state schools.

Only 7% of children are educated in elite private schools, which are known as public schools.

Rodeiro and Zanini (2015)

A Cambridge University study conducted by Rodeiro and Zanini in 2015 found that, despite class disparities in university admissions, state school students are more likely to gain a first class degree than independent school students with similar A-level results.

Now try this

1 Identify **two** reasons why middle-class parents might send their children to private schools rather than state schools.

2 What sorts of advantages might a public school education equip a child with?

External factors: cultural deprivation theory

Cultural deprivation theory focuses on class differences in achievement within state schools. It essentially blames working-class parents and culture for depriving working-class children of the essential cultural skills and attitudes needed for academic success. Consequently, working-class children do less well than middle-class children because they are supposedly culturally deficient.

Cultural causes of underachievement

Cultural deprivation theory argues that working-class children are 'failed' by their parents in three crucial cultural respects:

1 They do not teach their children to speak or think in a way that suits the classroom.

2 They subscribe to values that impede educational success.

3 They lack interest in their children's education.

Parents are role models for their children.

1 Language

Bernstein (1975) argued that middle-class parents socialise their children into an 'elaborated speech code'. This means they can confidently use language that is abstract and complex. The language level is similar to that used by teachers and found in textbooks and exams. In contrast, working-class parents socialise their children into a simplistic and inferior '**restricted speech code**' that fails to fully convey meaning. They consequently fail to understand teacher or textbook explanations as quickly as their middle-class peers. Bernstein argues that this linguistic deprivation is responsible for their educational failure.

2 Working-class culture

Some cultural deprivationists blame working-class culture for the educational underachievement of working-class children. **Sugarman** (1970) argues that working-class culture generally sees the world as an insecure place. As a result, working-class children are encouraged to seek only short-term goals and immediate pleasure. They are therefore more likely to enter paid work than go into higher education. Sugarman argued that middle-class cultural values which stress being aspirational, the value of long-term planning, and the willingness to sacrifice immediate pleasure for higher future rewards, were more likely to bring about educational success.

3 Parental attitudes

Douglas (1964) claimed that working-class parents are less interested in their children's education. Consequently, their children are poorly motivated and less ambitious. He measured parental interest by counting the number of times parents visited schools for parents' evenings.

Feinstein (2008) argued that middle-class parents are more child-centred than working-class parents. This is reflected in greater personal investment in their children.

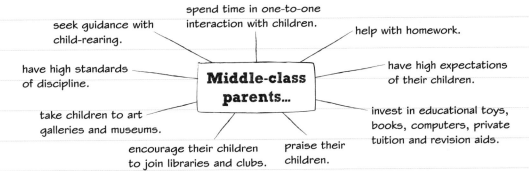

seek guidance with child-rearing.

spend time in one-to-one interaction with children.

help with homework.

have high standards of discipline.

Middle-class parents...

have high expectations of their children.

take children to art galleries and museums.

invest in educational toys, books, computers, private tuition and revision aids.

encourage their children to join libraries and clubs.

praise their children.

Now try this

1 Explain why working-class children underachieve according to Bernstein.
2 Identify **four** reasons why cultural deprivation theory believes middle-class parenting is superior to working-class parenting.

External factors: material deprivation

Some sociologists argue that the academic underachievement of the working class is the product of **material deprivation** or poverty rather than cultural deprivation.

Criticism of cultural deprivation

Material deprivation theory is critical of cultural deprivation theory because:

- it stereotypes all working-class parents as inadequate
- it is ethnocentric – it implies middle-class parental culture is superior
- working-class parents are less likely to visit schools, as they work long or irregular hours
- it particularly neglects the impact of poverty. **Peter Robinson** (1997) argues that tackling child poverty is the most effective way to tackle working-class underachievement.

The effects of poverty on schooling

- **David Bull** (1980) argues that so-called free education comes with hidden costs. Children from poor families often miss out because there is a lack of money for educational supports such as computers, books and trips.

- Families in poverty are more likely to be located in deprived areas where 90% of schools are failing. They cannot afford houses in areas with good schools due to their low wages.

- Poor housing means overcrowding and a lack of quiet space to study, and also more illness.

- An inadequate diet – for example, no breakfast – means difficulties in concentration.

- **Emily Tanner** (2016) found that children from poorer families are less likely to attend after-school clubs/sports because of the costs of fees, transport and kit.

- Parents cannot afford to support children through FE and HE.

A study by the Sutton Trust in 2013 found that teenagers from working-class backgrounds are up to three times less likely to attend a top university than their better-off classmates.

Only 11% of students at Oxbridge come from working-class backgrounds.

Poorer students are more likely to attend local universities and to continue living with their parents.

Quinn et al. (2005) found that white working-class men were more likely to drop out of university.

Forsyth and Furlong (2000) found that students from poor backgrounds are wary of 'elite' universities because they feel they will not fit in.

Working-class students are more likely to combine studying for a degree with working part-time.

Nearly four-fifths of middle-class university students receive financial support from their parents compared with only two-fifths of poorer students.

Callender and Jackson (2005) found that many bright working-class teenagers do not apply to university because of fear of debt.

Research focus **Alisdair Forsyth and Andy Furlong (2000)**

Forsyth and Furlong used both quantitative and qualitative research methods (see page 64) to research why bright, working-class students were less likely to go to university. Around 500 students in a secondary school completed a questionnaire and a follow-up postal questionnaire nine months later. Next, 44 unstructured interviews were conducted with students identified as coming from poorer backgrounds. Finally, a postal questionnaire was sent to a sample of the parents of those who took part in the follow-up questionnaire. They concluded that working-class students experienced a number of barriers to higher educational success. These included: lack of familiarity with HE (which meant they often enrolled on inappropriate courses), a lack of funds (which limited their choice of institution and the length of time in HE), a fear of debt (which deterred them from going to university) and a fear of cultural isolation (which lowered their morale and commitment to HE).

Now try this

Outline what factors support the view that poverty may reduce the number of working-class students applying to university.

External factors: cultural capital

Pierre Bourdieu (1984) acknowledges that **economic capital** or **financial help** is important in ensuring middle-class educational success, but he argued that **cultural capital** is just as influential.

Cultural capital

Cultural capital refers to the knowledge, tastes, language, values and behaviours transmitted by middle-class parents to their children, giving them the ability and confidence to interact with teachers.

Marxist thinkers often claim **Bourdieu** as one of their own because he argues that cultural capital leads to **cultural reproduction**: the children of middle-class professionals will also become middle-class professionals.

There is some evidence that the **marketisation** (see page 17) of both state and private schools focuses on educational experiences that might appeal to students with cultural capital.

For example, enrichment opportunities such as extra-curricular activities and preparation for Oxbridge interviews.

Educational capital

Bourdieu claimed that middle-class parents and students had access to educational advantages.

Graduate parents often take it for granted that their children will go to university. This means that money, time and effort will be spent enabling their children to achieve this goal. In contrast, working-class parents are less likely to have experienced HE and so are less likely to convey its benefits to their children.

Pierre Bourdieu (1984)

Bourdieu suggested the following:

1. Middle-class parents encourage cultural experiences, such as visits to museums and art galleries.

2. Middle-class parents encourage an interest in books.

3. Middle-class parents stress the importance of education, especially university.

4. Schools value children with high cultural capital because schools are middle-class environments.

5. Working-class children experience a **cultural deficit** – they lack cultural capital through no fault of their own.

6. '**Habitus**' refers to a set of attitudes and values held by the dominant class. These permeate to middle-class parents who 'naturally' see the need to invest time and money to 'conserve and increase' cultural capital.

7. Schools reflect a middle-class habitus. Teaching and learning ethos values middle-class ways of thinking while devaluing working-class tastes and behaviour.

8. Middle-class children acquire '**symbolic power**' at school. Their ways of speaking, tastes and preferences are seen as having greater value than those of working-class children.

9. The dismissal of working-class culture as having less value than middle-class culture is a form of '**symbolic violence**' that contributes to their underachievement.

Social capital

Putnam's (1995) concept of social capital refers to membership of social networks that can bring about particular benefits. Middle-class parents are more likely to know the 'right' people to advise on how their children can gain access to good schools, universities and work placements.

If a middle-class child is denied access to the parents' choice of school, then contacts who have been through the appeal process or who are teachers may prove useful in constructing a successful appeal.

For example, such parents are more likely to join a church in order to get their child into a high-achieving church school.

Research focus Alice Sullivan (2001)

Sullivan researched Bourdieu's concept of cultural capital via a questionnaire survey of 465 students approaching school-leaving age. The questionnaire operationalised and measured cultural capital by asking students about their tastes in books, television and music, and visits to theatres, concerts, art galleries and museums. She concludes that cultural capital is transmitted within the middle-class home and that it does have a significant effect on GCSE performance although she is critical of Bourdieu's concepts of 'habitus' and even 'cultural capital', which she describes as 'unhelpfully vague' and therefore difficult to operationalise. Also, Bourdieu does not account for individual agency and choice. Sullivan claims that although cultural capital has some impact on differential rates of educational success and failure, it only partly explains the social class effect.

Now try this

What is the relationship between poverty and educational capital?

Internal factors: school-based factors

Further possible explanations for the underachievement of working-class students focus on what goes on internally in schools. Studies of what goes on in classrooms have highlighted the role of teacher–student interaction, and particularly the labelling of students by teachers.

The teacher–student relationship

Interactionist sociologists are interested in how the day-to-day interaction between students and teachers can shape educational success or failure. **Becker** (1971) argues that teachers operate in the classroom with an 'ideal student' stereotype in their head, which they use to judge and **label** students either positively or negatively.

For example, middle-class teachers may erroneously judge working-class students from council estates or one-parent families as potentially troublesome. They may judge on appearance because working-class students may not conform to uniform rules, or because they have had a negative experience with their older sibling in the past.

Becker suggests these judgements and resulting negative labels have little to do with the intelligence or ability of the student.

Research focus: Pygmalion in the Classroom by Rosenthal and Jacobson (1968)

Rosenthal and Jacobson carried out a social experiment to test the validity of the self-fulfilling prophecy. They told teachers they had used an IQ test that had identified 20% of a class as especially bright (the 'bloomers') – but this was a lie. In reality, the 20% had been randomly chosen. A year later, Rosenthal and Jacobson found that the chosen 20% had made significantly more progress than the other 80%. They claimed teachers had responded to the 'bloomer' label, giving these students more attention and encouragement than the other students. The 20% reacted to this positive interaction by working harder. For an evaluation of this study, see page 71.

Labelling and the self-fulfilling prophecy

Becker suggests that teachers see middle-class students, especially girls, as closest to the 'ideal student' in terms of performance, conduct, attitude and appearance. Working-class students, especially boys, are seen as furthest from the 'ideal'. Becker claims that teachers' interaction with students is based on these labels and results in a **self-fulfilling prophecy**.

For example, middle-class 'ideal' students may develop a positive self-image. This motivates them to work hard because interaction with the teacher suggests the teacher believes they are bright. The teacher makes it clear they trust the student to work independently. There is also verbal praise accompanied by positive teacher behaviour such as smiling. In contrast, negatively labelled working-class students may develop a negative self-image from their interaction with the teacher. This may mainly consist of being frequently criticised and disciplined. Teachers may verbally convey their distrust and insist the student can only work under their supervision. This negative interaction and labelling may ultimately de-motivate them.

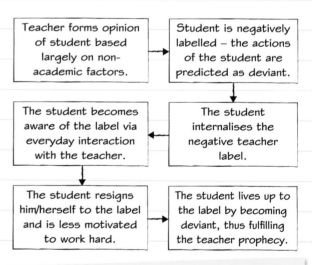

Teacher forms opinion of student based largely on non-academic factors. → Student is negatively labelled – the actions of the student are predicted as deviant.

The student becomes aware of the label via everyday interaction with the teacher. ← The student internalises the negative teacher label.

The student resigns him/herself to the label and is less motivated to work hard. → The student lives up to the label by becoming deviant, thus fulfilling the teacher prophecy.

The prediction contained in the label eventually comes true because the teacher–student interaction is shaped by the label.

According to Rosenthal and Jacobson, the tendency to give more one-to-one attention and encouragement may benefit some students more than others.

Now try this

1 Outline the ethical problems that Rosenthal and Jacobson's (1968) research suffers from.

2 Identify what Becker means by the 'ideal student'.

3 Explain how the self-fulfilling prophecy works.

Streaming, identity and subcultures

Most schools separate students into different ability groups called **sets** or **streams**. Interactionist sociologists view streaming as a form of **institutionalised labelling**.

Ray Rist (1970)

Rist studied a US primary school class. He found that the teacher used information gleaned from the children's home background to segregate them by placing them on particular tables.

- **Tigers** were neat and tidy middle-class kids, regarded as 'fast students' by the teacher who seated them closest to her desk. They were frequently praised for their efforts.
- **Cardinals** were mainly working-class children of middling ability.
- **Clowns** were working-class children whom the teacher defined as those who would not and could not learn. They were placed on a table furthest from the teacher and were expected to be 'troublesome'.

These labels became fixed as the children moved into their second year of schooling.

Educational triage

'Triage' refers to nurses ranking and sorting patients. **Gillborn and Youdell** (2001) claim that schools 'triage' students into three streams.

1. Middle-class students are labelled as potential university students and placed in top streams.
2. Some middle- and working-class students are seen as C–D borderline and given extra help.
3. Mainly working-class students are labelled as 'hopeless' and placed in bottom streams.

Class identity

Many students in bottom streams deliberately adopt particular dress codes. These attract respect and status from other like-minded students, but bring them into conflict with the school authorities.

For example, **Archer** et al. (2010) argue that some working-class students deliberately chose to break school dress rules by embracing a street style of appearance and behaviour focused on high-end sports brands and working-class TV celebrities.

Streaming

Ball (1981) found that grouping by ability leads to greater social class inequalities. His study of Beachside Comprehensive found that students were placed in bands on the basis of information supplied by their primary schools. The first band contained the most-able students and the third the least able. Non-academic factors had influenced where children were placed. He found that working-class students were disproportionately placed in bottom streams and that they experienced this as demeaning. They had low self-esteem, were apathetic about education, and were often disruptive in and out of class.

Keddie (1971) examined the effects of streaming in a London comprehensive. She was interested in the ways streaming affected how teachers transmitted subject knowledge to students. She found that highly valued abstract knowledge was conveyed to those in the top stream because teachers regarded them as 'bright' enough to handle it. The same knowledge was denied to those in the bottom stream because less was expected of students in terms of ability. Keddie observed that the very real commonsensical street knowledge and experience of students in the bottom stream was often dismissed as 'irrelevant' by teachers.

Anti-school subcultures

Studies by **Ball** (1981) and **Mac an Ghaill** (1994) found that those in the bottom streams react to their perceived inferior status by forming delinquent or **anti-school subcultures**. These award status to their members on the basis of anti-school activity, such as being disruptive or disobeying rules.

Students who develop a negative self-image may turn to deviant subcultures in compensation, confirming their failure in the school's eyes.

 Young (2012)

Young conducted a survey of 3000 15-year-old students in 22 Scottish schools and found evidence of a working-class subculture called **Neds** (non-educated delinquents). Neds generally thought schools were a waste of time and often truanted. They came from deprived areas in which there was little prospect of finding work. Some students chose the Ned identity because they were proud to be working class. The Ned label was also regarded as 'cool' and consequently attracted peer respect.

Now try this

What is the relationship between educational triage and streaming?

Gendered inequality

Until the late 1980s, boys performed better than girls at school, college and university. Since the 1990s, this **gender balance** has been reversed. You need to know the reasons for the **differential educational achievement** of boys and girls and why it has changed.

The trends

Official sources (ONS, JCQ, HEPI) have reported these trends:

1 At **GCSE** (2016), girls outperformed boys in gaining grades A*–C by 8.9 percentage points.

2 At A-level (2016), 79.7% of girls achieved A*–C grades compared with 75% of boys.

3 Women are 35% more likely to go to university than men (2015). Men who do are more likely to drop out.

4 Women outperformed men in terms of class of degree: 73% of women gained a 2:1 or above, compared with 69% of men (2015).

Evaluating the trends

👍 Recent **Joint Council for Qualification (JCQ)** figures (2016) suggest that boys' achievement has improved in recent years, especially to those with A-levels. Since 2006 the achievement gap has narrowed.

👎 The gender gap is still wide between boys and girls from working-class white, African-Caribbean and Pakistani/Bangladeshi backgrounds.

👎 The gender gap is wider in comprehensive schools compared to those with selective admission procedures – such as academies.

Subject choices

According to JCQ figures for FE and HE, boys' and girls' subject choices are very gendered.
- At A-level (2016), only 10% of computer science and 22% of physics students were female.
- In 2015, females were twice as likely as males to take A-levels in French, drama, English, and health and social care.
- HEPI reported that, in 2015, males dominated engineering and technology, physical sciences, computer science, architecture and mathematical science degree courses. More females than males embarked on degree courses in nursing, teaching, medicine and languages.

Reasons for gendered subject choices

1 **Colley** (1998) stresses the influence of **socialisation** by the family and influential peers who subscribe to **gendered stereotypes**. For example, research by **Edwards and David** (2000) indicates that parents believe certain toys, games and activities are suitable only for particular sexes. This may result in some females being 'steered away' from courses traditionally dominated by males, and vice versa. Colley observes that these cultural pressures are less likely to be influential in single-sex schools or are compensated for by positive female role models in the form of teachers and peers.

2 Students may be influenced by the choices of their peers. If a particular subject is dominated by girls, this may put boys off – and vice versa.

3 Changes to the educational system may influence male and female subject choice. Female take-up of science increased after the Girls Into Science and Technology (GIST) social policy initiative was introduced into schools in the 1970s, and WISE in the 1980s.

4 **Kelly** (1987) argued that girls were put off doing science because of its masculine characteristics. She noted that most science teachers in comprehensives in the 1980s were males, textbooks mainly focused on male scientific achievements, science laboratories were seen by boys as a masculine environment while scientific and technical equipment was monopolised by boys.

5 In 2013, the Institute of Physics found that girls in single-sex schools were 2.5 times more likely than those in comprehensive schools to study physics and maths at university.

6 The Institute of Physics (2013) suggests non-science teachers and career advisers often subscribe to traditional gender stereotypes. This can negatively influence female aspirations to study physics, as can the lack of female physicists on television.

Now try this

Outline **three** reasons why girls at comprehensive schools are less likely to study physics compared with girls at single-sex schools.

Girls succeeding: external influences

Girls' achievement once lagged far behind that of boys. However, these days girls are more likely to succeed while boys are more likely to fail. There are a number of **external** and **internal** explanations for this. For more on internal explanations, see page 40.

External influences

Liberal feminists argue that external influences, such as economic and social policy changes, led to changes in the aspirations of girls and women.

- Changes in the economy from the 1960s onwards increased the number of jobs and careers available to females.

- Social policies in the form of equal opportunity and pay laws improved the educational and employment options of females.

- The rise of the dual-career family (see page 97) meant that working mums became positive role models for their daughters.

- **Wilkinson** (1999) argues that feminist ideas emphasising equality between the sexes and women having careers filtered down to girls via the media in the 1980s and 1990s (despite the fact that girls might not be conscious or openly supportive of such ideas today).

- **Beck** (1992) argues that Western societies became increasingly **individualised** in the latter quarter of the 20th century. As a result, the aspirations of girls became more self-orientated compared with previous generations of women.

- According to surveys carried out by the Liberal feminist **Sue Sharpe** (1976), girls no longer prioritise traditional pathways of marriage and motherhood. Instead, they prioritise education, career and less reliance on men.

- Interviews conducted by **Francis and Skelton** (2005) found that the majority of primary and secondary school female students see having a career (rather than marriage or being a mother) as the most important influence on their future identity as a woman.

- **Edwards and David** (2000) suggest that gender-differentiated primary socialisation gives girls an initial advantage in both primary and secondary schools because:

  o girls may have better language skills than boys (mothers talk to baby girls more frequently than baby boys); as a result, girls are more experienced at talking and listening by the time they get to secondary school

  o girls are taught by their parents to conform to more formal standards of behaviour than boys, so they are less likely to misbehave in the classroom. By the age of seven, girls are more likely than boys to pay attention in class.

- **Burns and Bracey** (2001) found that secondary school girls generally work harder and are more motivated than boys. On average, girls put more effort into their work and spend more time on homework.

Evaluation

👎 Despite 30 years of gender equality in education, employment remains deeply segregated in terms of men dominating particular types of jobs (e.g. science and engineering), top jobs and pay, while the majority of low-paid and part-time workers are women (2016).

👎 Radical feminists argue that most of the changes to the education system are largely cosmetic because, regardless of improvements in girls' education and achievement, the glass ceiling is still firmly in place. Job opportunities for females are still limited by patriarchal assumptions that men should be the main breadwinners and a woman's place remains in 'the home'.

👎 The fact that working-class girls underachieve, and still follow traditional gender paths into low-paid, low-skilled jobs and early motherhood, suggests social class may be more important than gender as a differentiator.

Now try this

What is the relationship between Beck's concept of individualisation and girls' academic success?

Girls succeeding: internal influences

There are a number of **school-based** or **internal** explanations for why girls are more likely to succeed today.

School-based internal influences

- Equal opportunity policies have raised the consciousness of both teachers and female pupils and created a more girl-friendly environment in schools, which has positively encouraged female achievement both inside and outside of school.

- The national curriculum, introduced in 1988, was gender neutral. It encouraged boys and girls to study the same subjects.

- **Arnot** (1998) argues that most girls prefer open-ended, process-based tasks – especially project and source-based work such as coursework.

- **Gorard** (2005) argues that the introduction of coursework into GCSE curricula in 1989 benefitted girls because they are more conscientious and have better organisational skills than boys. The recent reduction in the coursework component at both GCSE and A-level may be partly responsible for the recent narrowing of the gender gap in educational performance in these exams.

- An increase in females in senior teaching and leadership roles created more positive role models for female students to emulate.

- Educational initiatives such as GIST (see page 38) encouraged more girls to study science.

- **Weiner** (1995) argues that gendered stereotypes were removed from classrooms and textbooks.

- Some studies, such as **Fuller** (2009), suggested that teachers see some girls (especially middle-class girls) as 'ideal students' and interact with them in a positive way, improving their self-esteem, motivation and success rates (see page 36).

- The marketisation of education (see page 17) may have benefitted females because girls may be seen by academically successful schools as better recruits than boys. This is because they are perceived as more hard-working and less likely to be disruptive.

Evaluation

💬 **Sue Johnson** (2014) notes that women's history still has a very low profile in many schools.

💬 **Fiona Terry** (1989) found a lack of women's history skewed students' understanding of the subject, marginalised women and ensured they had low status.

💬 **Fuller's** observations of classes and interviews with students in a single-sex school found mixed evidence with regard to the influence of teacher labelling and the self-fulfilling prophecy. Working-class girls had low expectations in terms of jobs. This meant they chose not to push themselves and often left school as early as possible. Middle-class high achievers largely accepted teachers' judgements about their ability. However, they still believed they could succeed – even when teachers were less positive about their progress.

💬 The fact that working-class African-Caribbean girls generally do better than white working-class girls suggests ethnicity is just as important as gender as a differentiator. Women's low status in some ethnic groups suggests gender differences in education, jobs and power might be the result of powerful cultural and/or religious beliefs about the role of women.

Now try this

Give an example of evidence that suggests gender is not the only influence on whether girls succeed or underachieve compared with boys.

Failing boys

Boys seem to do less well than girls in education. That said, the reality is that boys are doing better in terms of gaining qualifications compared with 20 years ago. There are a number of sociological explanations that stress both **external** and in-school (**internal**) reasons why boys under-perform in schools compared with girls.

External influences

- **Edwards and David** (2000) argue that boys mature more slowly than girls because primary socialisation in the family encourages boys to be more boisterous and attention-seeking. This may lead to a lack of concentration in classrooms. They also observed that parents read less to boys.

- **Burns and Bracey** (2001) found that the socialisation of boys may lead to over-confidence. They found that boys are often surprised when they fail exams and tend to put their failure down to bad luck, not lack of effort.

- **Frosh** (2001) found that boys' behaviour is often shaped and policed by their peer group. He found that many boys regarded schoolwork as 'feminine' and 'unmanly'; they engaged in hyper-masculine behaviour such as bullying the more academic boys.

- **Mac an Ghaill** (1994) argues that boys' underachievement is due to a 'crisis of masculinity'. He argues that working-class boys feel they are unlikely to occupy the traditional male role of 'breadwinner' because they can see that globalisation has resulted in the decline of British industry. This and the feminisation of the economy and workforce mean there are fewer job opportunities for males – and perhaps even long-term unemployment. Consequently, many working-class boys may view education and qualifications as irrelevant.

School-based internal influences

- Schools may be guilty of neglecting boys' learning needs because they have become too girl-friendly or feminised, and this is putting boys off education.

- Educational policy has been mainly aimed at improving girls' educational opportunities at the expense of boys' education.

- Boys do less well in coursework-based subjects because they are less organised than girls.

- **Becky Francis** (2001) claims that teachers are less likely to see and label boys as 'ideal students'. They have lower expectations of them and are more likely to label them as disruptive (see page 36).

- **Mitsos and Browne** (1998) suggest that teachers: have lower expectations of boys; expect their work to be late, rushed and untidy; and expect them to be disruptive. These expectations may have a self-fulfilling effect, which consequently depresses their educational achievement.

- **Jackson** (2006) found that the labelling of boys leads to a self-fulfilling prophecy, as some boys react to teacher labelling by turning to anti-school subcultures (see page 37) that view academic achievement as both uncool and feminine.

- There may be a self-fulfilling prophecy as a result of these processes as boys are excluded from school.

Evaluation

- 💬 Globalisation has mainly affected manual jobs, which do not require qualifications.
- 💬 Gender differences have narrowed in recent years.
- 💬 Social class may be more important than gender.
  For example, middle-class boys do better than working-class girls.

Now try this

1 What aspects of early childhood socialisation in the family might give girls an educational advantage over boys?

2 Why do you think it might be a problem for boys to be 'overconfident'?

Ethnicity and external factors: 1

Britain has an ethnically diverse population. Some minority ethnic groups out-perform white British ethnic groups in education, but others do less well. Some sociologists look for the cause of both ethnic academic achievement and underachievement in **external factors**, including material and **cultural deprivation**. For more on the role of cultural deprivation, see page 43.

The trends

1 African-Caribbean students are generally low achievers in terms of GCSEs and A-levels compared with other ethnic groups.

In 2014, only 47% of African-Caribbean students achieved 5+ A*–C GCSEs compared with the national average of 56%.

2 Black male students are the group most likely to be excluded from school.

3 Chinese and Indian students out-perform every other ethnic group at GCSE and A-level.

In 2014, 74.4% of Chinese and 72.9% of Indian students attained 5+ A*–C GCSEs.

4 Pakistani students perform the most poorly among Asian ethnic groups.

In 2014, only 51.4% of Pakistani students achieved 5+ A*–C GCSEs.

5 Gypsy/Roma students are the lowest achievers in terms of GCSEs compared with other ethnic groups.

In 2014, only 8.2% achieved at least five A*–C GCSEs.

6 White boys, especially those on free school meals, generally make less progress in school compared with other ethnic groups.

7 In 2016, research by the Centre Forum found that, while ahead at age five, white students slip to 13th place behind those of Chinese, Indian, Asian and black African heritage by the time they sit GCSEs at age 16.

8 Girls in all ethnic groups do better than boys.

The role of material deprivation

Material deprivation theory considers the **role of social class** and **poverty** in ethnic-minority students' experience of school.

- Ethnic minorities in the UK are more likely to be in poverty because they are more likely to be unemployed or in low-paid jobs.
- They are more likely to live in poor housing in economically depressed areas, which experience severe social problems.
- Children's experience of this deprivation as well as racism undermines their educational performance.

Supporting studies

✓ **Guy Palmer** (2010) found that nearly half of ethnic-minority children live in low-income families compared with a quarter of white children.

✓ **The Equality and Human Rights Commission** (2010) found that white British, Bangladeshi and African-Caribbean boys who qualify for free school meals (FSM) are half as likely than other groups to get good GCSE results; they are twice as likely to be permanently excluded from school.

✓ **Ireson and Rushforth** (2005) found that ethnic-minority parents from higher socio-economic backgrounds can afford to hire private tutors for their children.

Evaluation

👎 **Stokes et al.** (2015) observe that gaps in educational achievement by ethnic groups have narrowed considerably over the last 20 years. The fact that ethnic-minority students from poor backgrounds now perform better than white boys from similar backgrounds challenges the view that external factors such as cultural or material deprivation are responsible for the educational performance of ethnic-minority children. However, **Gillborn** (2015) challenges the view that white children are the main victims of educational inequality. He observes that white children in poverty measured by the number who claim FSM are three times more likely to achieve five GCSEs compared with Gypsy and Roma children.

👎 Gender may be more important than social class because girls generally achieve better results than boys regardless of ethnicity.

Now try this

What gendered trend can clearly be seen in educational statistics relating to ethnicity?

Ethnicity and external factors: 2

Another external influence on ethnic academic achievement or underachievement is **cultural deprivation**.

The role of cultural deprivation

Cultural deprivation theory focuses on the home background of ethnic minorities.
- Asian, Chinese, African families: children benefit from cultures and parents that value education.
- African-Caribbean families: young males underachieve because of a lack of positive adult role models and the negative influence of a hyper-masculine peer culture encouraged by rap music and street gangs, which puts pressure on boys to be anti-school.

Supporting studies

 Louise Archer and Becky Francis (2005) – Chinese parents see education as a 'family project', have high expectations of their children, and invest lots of time and money in their education.

 Tehmina Basit (1997) – Asian parents view education as a type of capital that can transform the lives of their children and so offer their children lots of support.

 Tony Sewell (1997) – African-Caribbean boys brought up by single mums lack the discipline provided by fathers and may be attracted by gang culture, which rejects academic values.

 Bereiter and Engelmann (1966) – black children suffer from verbal deprivation. They claim that children from lower-class black American families are unable to use complex vocabulary or engage in abstract thought. Instead, they communicate in gestures, and use shorter words and fragmented phrases.

 Ruth Lupton (2004) – Asian children, especially those from Muslim backgrounds, are well-behaved at school and work hard because their parents expect children to be respectful towards adults. As a result, parents are always generally supportive of school behaviour policies and sanctions.

Evaluation

🗨 Material deprivation or poverty may be more important than cultural deprivation in explaining differences in achievement between ethnic groups because Indian children are less likely to be in poverty compared with children from Pakistani and Bangladeshi backgrounds.

🗨 **William Labov (1972)** challenges the notion of verbal deprivation and argues that black children do not necessarily have inferior mothers, language or experience. He argues that teachers are to blame for any educational underachievement experienced by black children because they fail to understand that black inner-city culture is different, rather than deficient. Teachers make little attempt to understand the language of young urban black people, which Labov terms Black English Vernacular (BEV). He argues BEV is just as capable of articulating complex abstract ideas as the Standard English taught in schools. Labov argues that the problem lies with the school system and teachers, which unfairly discriminates against black culture and language.

🗨 Cultural deprivation ignores racism both within schools and in wider society as a possible cause of black underachievement.

🗨 Cultural deprivation does not explain why girls from all ethnic groups out-perform boys.

🗨 **Burgess (2015)** found that ethnic-minority teenagers consistently demonstrated higher educational aspirations than white students.

👍 **Gillian Evans (2006)** argues that the underachievement of white working-class boys living in poor families in inner cities is more of a social problem than ethnic underachievement, which has actually lessened in recent years. She points out that white boys' achievement has actually got worse in comparison and that they often have lower aspirations than their ethnic-minority peers. She argues that educational success is often not valued by a working-class street culture shaped by both poverty and violence.

Now try this

Which ethnic group is most likely to be excluded from school?

Ethnicity and internal factors

Some sociologists claim that **in-school** or **internal factors** such as teacher labelling or institutional racism may be more responsible than family or poverty for **ethnic-minority underachievement** in British schools.

Labelling of black students

Interactionists claim that teachers rarely label black students as 'ideal students'. Rather, they suggest that some teachers are guilty of racist labelling of black students, especially boys.

- **Gillborn and Youdell** (2000) argue that white female teachers have low expectations of black boys' potential academic performance and classroom behaviour. They were often dismissed as 'no hopers'. African-Caribbean boys were more likely to be given detentions than other groups of students, because teachers often interpreted their dress and speech as challenging their authority.

- The labelling of black boys as 'less academic' is translated into the organisation of teaching and learning. These boys were put into lower streams or sets.

- **Connolly** (1988) found that black girls were often labelled as potentially disruptive but good at sport, which meant that teachers often did not focus on their academic ability.

Labelling of Asian students

Evidence regarding teacher labelling of Asian students suggests that their experience of teacher expectations is more mixed than black students.

- **Gillborn** (2008) argues that white middle-class students, as well as the 'model' minorities such as Chinese and Indian students, are labelled as 'ideal students' because of their positive attitude towards school.

- Various studies suggest teachers label Asian girls as 'passive' and Asian boys as 'immature'. **Wright** (1992) found that some teachers openly labelled Asian culture as inferior to British culture. They often assumed that Asian children had a poor grasp of English. As a result, Asian students felt that they were not being allowed to participate fully in discussion and classwork.

Student responses and identities

There are a variety of student responses to teachers labelling ethnic-minority students.

Black boys may respond by withdrawing into **anti-school subcultures** characterised by hyper-masculinity and a desire to be more disruptive (see page 37). This is an example of a **self-fulfilling prophecy** (see page 36). However, it is important to understand that there are several student responses to labelling and not all of them result in failure:

- **Tony Sewell** (1997) argues that despite teacher stereotyping, most black boys are not a problem at school. They are friends with students of other ethnicities, generally obey school rules and leave school with a good set of qualifications.

- Ethnic-minority students may become anti-school but **pro-education**.

  For example, **Fuller's** (1984) study of black girls found that they valued academic success but this did not mean that they liked their teachers. Their anger at teacher labelling actually motivated them to work harder in order to prove them wrong.

Evaluation of labelling theory

- 👍 It is often based on observation of classroom interaction and usually backed up by qualitative interview data (see pages 73–74).

- 👍 Interactionists aim for high levels of validity by getting inside the head of the protagonists in order to see the world as they see it.

- 👎 Observation may produce artificial rather than natural behaviour (see page 57).

- 👎 Students might use teacher racism as an excuse for their own shortcomings.

- 👎 Widespread racism among teachers is highly unlikely, as teachers subscribe to professional ethics that forbid them from expressing such views. Racist comments are likely to attract peer disapproval and sanctions from school managers. It is also against the law.

- 👎 **Sewell** (1997) argues that the real causes of black boys' educational achievement lay outside schools, including living in poverty-stricken families, the lack of father figures or conformist male role models and peer pressure to find status as members of gangs.

Now try this

How might the labelling of black students lead to a self-fulfilling prophecy?

Institutional racism

Another **internal factor** that might be partly responsible for black underachievement in schools is institutional racism.

> **Institutional racism**
> The hidden, unconscious and unintended discrimination embedded in admissions and opportunities policies, the marketing of the school, the curriculum and staffing. Each in turn may not offer the same quality of service and opportunity to all ethnic groups. This may lower the self-esteem of ethnic-minority students and undermine academic performance. **Gillborn** (2008) suggests this produces a form of deep-rooted and 'locked-in' discrimination and inequality which is self-perpetuating.

Marketisation

Selection and admission process in schools may be biased in favour of white students. Increased **marketisation** (see page 17) has led to an 'A to C economy'. According to **Gillborn and Youdell** (1999), this creates a rationing of education. Teachers neglect students labelled as 'no-hopers' and 'high achievers' to focus on the borderline students. Many black students are often unfairly judged as belonging to the 'no hoper' group. **Tikly** (2006) found that teacher decisions to enter students for either Higher or Foundation GCSE exams resulted in ethnic inequalities in achievement.

Ethnocentric curriculum

Coard (2005) argues that what is taught in schools mainly reflects white culture. Black culture, music and art are largely ignored. Black students may view the knowledge taught in schools as irrelevant or insulting and consequently switch off.

Staffing

There may be a lack of positive ethnic-minority role models (teachers) in schools. **Sewell** sees this as the main in-school cause of the underachievement of black boys.

Examples

- **UCAS** (2015) suggested that white students with similar A-level results are more successful than ethic minority students at gaining places at university.
- **Gillborn** (2008) claimed that white students are twice as likely to be selected for 'gifted and talented' programmes than black students.
- **Moore and Davenport** (1990) found selection procedures in US schools often resulted in a form of racial stratification as they favoured white children.

Examples

- Little attention is paid to ethnic-minority language and literature in schools.
- Only lip service is paid to black history.
- **Tikly's** (2006) study found that African-Caribbean students were aware of their invisibility in the curriculum and were frustrated by the focus on white people and Europe.

Examples

- 17% of students in the UK are from black, Asian and ethnic-minority backgrounds, but only 7% of teachers are.
- **Ranson** (2005) says school governing bodies are disproportionately white, middle-aged and middle class.

Evaluation

👎 The educational achievements of some ethnic-minority groups – for example, Chinese and Indian students – are well above the national average.

👎 Girls in nearly all ethnic groups perform better than boys.

👎 There is little evidence that ethnic-minority children experience low self-esteem.

👎 Social factors outside school such as family background, poverty, racial discrimination by employers, policing and so on might be more important.

Now try this

1 Identify **two** examples of alleged institutional racism in schools.
2 Explain how marketisation and competition between schools might result in institutional racism.

Exam skills 1

These exam-style questions use knowledge and skills you have already revised. Have a look at pages 24, 39 and 42–45 for a reminder about social policies, girl's achievement and ethnic-minority achievement.

Worked example

1 Outline **two** factors from outside the education system that have resulted in improved educational performance for girls.   **(4 marks)**

According to Wilkinson, one factor external to the education system that has contributed to the improvement in girls' educational performance was the feminisation of the economy and the workforce that occurred in the 1980s and 1990s. This economic change meant that the opportunities for qualified women to have careers and economic independence considerably improved in this period, which probably motivated girls to view education very positively.

Secondly, Sue Sharpe has documented how girls' attitudes in the 1990s differed enormously from previous generations of females who tended to see marriage and children as their main priority. Sharpe found that the main priorities of teenage girls in the 1990s were educational achievement and careers. Sharpe speculates that these girls viewed their own working mothers as positive role models.

2 Outline **three** ways in which educational policy may have contributed to ethnic-minority educational achievement.   **(6 marks)**

- First, the introduction of the Educational Maintenance Allowance (EMA) gave bright adolescents from poorer ethnic-minority backgrounds the economic support to stay on at school or college to study A-levels in order to apply for higher education study.
- Second, both the Aimhigher and Gifted and Talented programmes targeted bright students from ethnic-minority backgrounds to encourage them to work to the best of their ability.
- Third, the decision by the Coalition government to abolish the EMA and the Labour government to introduce fees to study for university degrees probably contributed to ethnic-minority underachievement, as fear of debt may put off bright students from poorer ethnic-minority backgrounds applying to university.

Spend 15 minutes only on these two questions and give your answer in two and three clear paragraphs. No introduction or conclusion is required.

In each paragraph, start by **describing** (outlining) your reason in the first sentence.

Another factor you could consider is increased availability of contraception, leading to young women being able to plan their education and careers around having a family.

In each paragraph, aim to include at least one study and describe its findings with regard to the question.

Command word: Outline

You need to set out the main characteristics and then develop each reason more fully. In doing so, you should show knowledge and understanding of key concepts, theorists and evidence. This must be applied to the question and analysed (explain fully).

'Outline' questions require you to describe. You must also show that you can apply your knowledge to this issue, so make sure you make clear the link between educational policy and ethnic-minority underachievement. Avoid being vague.

You could bullet-point your response to this type of question to help you focus on the need for three distinct reasons. Each 'way' should be reasonably detailed and use examples of social policy and clearly make the link between the policy and the achievement or underachievement of ethnic-minority students.

Exam skills 2

Have a look at pages 36–37 for a reminder about labelling and anti-school sub-cultures.

Worked example

3 Read **Item A** below and answer the question that follows.

> **Item A**
>
> Interactionists argue that the labels applied by teachers shape pupil attitudes towards education, their behaviour in the classroom and consequently their educational performance. However, critics of this view ague that disruptive anti-school subcultures actually have little to do with teachers and are the product of factors outside the school.

Applying material from **Item A**, analyse **two** reasons why some pupils form anti-school subcultures. **(10 marks)**

- As observed by Item A, Interactionists argue that anti-school subcultures are often formed by working-class or ethnic minority pupils who feel aggrieved at the way some teachers negatively stereotype and label them. Becker, for example, argues that teachers often have 'an ideal pupil' stereotype in their heads. They use this to judge and positively label middle-class pupils and to negatively judge working-class and black pupils, who are allocated to bottom or low-ability sets and streams. They may also be entered for lower-status exams compared with middle-class students. For example, Hargreaves found that teachers expected pupils in the bottom streams to be 'delinquent'. Keddie argues that pupils in the bottom streams often do not receive the high-quality teaching and knowledge that top streams take for granted.

  This negative interaction between teachers and bottom-stream pupils can lead to confrontation, hostility and grievance if pupils feel they are being unfairly treated. Pupils may react to the perceived denial of status by forming anti-school subcultures that reject the value system of the school. Hargreaves calls this 'reaction formation'. Hargreaves argues that pupils who belong to anti-school subcultures may compensate for the negative treatment they receive from teachers by gaining status from their peers for being disruptive or for talking back to the teacher. In this way teacher labelling and its institutional equivalent – streaming – has a self-fulfilling prophecy effect.

- Secondly, Item A suggests that anti-school sub-cultures may have little to do with in-school processes ...

Command word: Analyse

You need to set out the reasons for anti-school subcultures methodically and develop a **logical** and detailed chain of reasoning. In so doing, you should show knowledge and understanding of key concepts, studies/ evidence. These must be applied to the question and **analysed** (explain fully).

Spend 15 minutes on this 10-mark question and give your answer in two clear paragraphs. No introduction or conclusion is required.

You could bullet-point your response to this question to help you focus on the need for two distinct reasons.

Each 'reason' should be reasonably detailed and use examples of studies of anti-school subcultures to support your points. Make sure you make a clear link between reasons and the anti-school subculture.

Note that this part of the response clearly applies the first part of the Item.

This response uses lots of relevant interactionist studies. Three are used in some detail.

This response uses concepts accurately and explains their relevance.

The second part of this answer needs to focus on non-school factors that might lead to anti-school sub-cultures. There are three possible options. First, you could consider the Marxist explanations of Willis and Corrigan. You could also consider how the concept of a 'crisis of masculinity' might lead to anti-school subcultures. Equally, with regard to black pupils, the work of Sewell could be considered.

Exam skills 3

Allocate your time effectively. You should be spending about 45 minutes on this question.

Worked example

Item B

The educational performance of both girls and boys has improved significantly over the past twenty years, but there is still a significant gender gap in achievement between boys and girls. For example, girls now outperform boys in most subjects and at most levels of education, especially at GCSE where 9% more girls than boys achieve five or more A*–C grades in 2016.

Some sociologists claim that gender differences in achievement are the result of changes in wider society, particularly changes in social attitudes. Other sociologists claim feminist ideas about having a career and being independent have influenced female educational achievement. However some sociologists argue that the gender gap in exam success has been caused by changes in the economy, bringing about higher demand for female labour and a decline in the demand for male labour.

In contrast, others argue that in-school factors are more important suggesting, for example, that the education system has become feminised and a lack of male primary school teachers means that boys have fewer male role models who might inspire them in the early years of schooling. Some sociologists claim that boys are negatively labelled by teachers leading to their educational underachievement.

4 Applying material from **Item B** and your knowledge, evaluate the claim that gender differences in educational achievement are primarily the result of factors that originate inside rather than outside of school. **(30 marks)**

Item B clearly shows a gender gap in educational achievement. The evidence shows that at all levels of the educational system females achieve better results than males.

Item B also notes that two groups of explanations exist. The first stresses the influence of factors that originate outside the school and lists three possible external causes of the gender gap in achievement: changes in the economy resulting in demand for female labour; changes in female attitudes; the impact of feminist ideas.

In contrast, Item B identifies a number of in-school factors that may be contributing to the gender gap in educational achievement...

For a 30 mark question, try to develop your evaluative points more and show more depth of knowledge. You can also use certain words to show that you are being evaluative. For example: however, although, whereas, despite, furthermore, nonetheless, in addition, and so on.

Command word: evaluate

This is an essay question. If a question asks you to **evaluate** a particular view, it wants you to:

👍 Outline the 'view' in the title in as much detail as you can using sociological terms, concepts and studies whenever possible.

👍 Make sure you use the material in the Item and your own knowledge to illustrate your points.

👍 Outline strengths and weaknesses and any opposing or contrasting views of which you are aware.

👍 Come to a reasoned conclusion.

Highlight those parts of Item B you might use in your response. Here the introduction uses the Item indicating good application.

This introduction should act as a plan for the rest of the essay and mention themes to be explored and developed.

The essay now needs to explore and describe the following developments in order to compare and contrast internal and external factors.

1 Internal factors identified in Item B.

2 Support for internal factors: the findings of sociologists (e.g. Frosh, Francis) who suggest teachers negatively label and its self-fulfilling effect; Mitsos and Browne (2011): teachers have lower expectations of boys.

3 The school as a feminised environment; coursework; studies which suggest boys view schools as feminine and learning as not masculine, lack of male primary school teachers leading to fewer role models.

4 Support for external factors (e.g. Wilkinson and Willis) changes in the economy and the demand for male and female jobs, the impact of male unemployment on boys' educational aspirations; the impact of varied female jobs on girls' education ambitions.

5 Studies looking at changes in women's attitudes towards family, work, etc (e.g. Sue Sharpe).

6 The role of feminism – to inform girls that they have a wide choice of futures via female role models and social media.

7 Feminist studies of education, such as Kelly on science, Spender, Stanworth.

8 Draw a conclusion based on the evidence you have provided.

Exam-style practice

Before looking at these exam-style questions, it would be useful to have revised theories of educational underachievement that blame external factors such as home background and cultural factors, along with theories of institutional racism. You will find answers on page 213.

1 Outline **two** cultural factors that might influence the educational performance of ethnic-minority pupils. **(4 marks)**

2 Outline **three** ways in which some children may express their rejection of the education system. **(6 marks)**

3 Read **Item A** below and answer the question that follows.

> **Item A**
>
> Some sociologists have suggested that pupils from different ethnic minorities are discriminated against by white teachers. Others have argued that the British educational system is guilty of institutional racism. Institutional racism occurs not because of the attitudes of individuals, but because of the systems, cultures, policies and/or structures of the organisations themselves. This results in organisations such as schools, failing to provide the same quality of service and opportunity to all ethnic groups.

Applying material from **Item A**, analyse **two** reasons why some sociologists believe that the British educational system is institutionally racist. **(10 marks)**

4 Read **Item B** below and answer the question that follows.

> **Item B**
>
> According to some sociologists, cultural factors are the most important cause of social class differences in educational achievement. In their view, there are important cultural differences between working-class and middle-class parents. For example, they argue that some working-class parents have lower expectations of their children, place less emphasis on constant improvement and do not reward academic success. In contrast, middle-class parents encourage their children to be achievement-oriented and to express themselves in ways approved by teachers. It is also argued that some working-class children are not taught to use the elaborated speech code supposedly used by middle-class families and preferred by schools and teachers.
>
> Bourdieu, although not a cultural deprivationist, argues that the superior standard of living and income enjoyed by middle-class families equips their children with cultural capital, which schools and teachers welcome as a necessary resource to achieve academic success. However, critics of cultural deprivation claim that material factors such as income, wealth and poverty, and schools themselves are far more important than cultural factors in shaping educational success and failure.

Applying material from **Item B** and your knowledge, evaluate the view that working-class underachievement in education is the result of home circumstances and family background. **(30 marks)**

You should spend no longer than 15 minutes on questions 1–2.

Use two clear paragraphs and In each paragraph, start by **describing** (outlining) your reason in the first sentence. Make sure you show your knowledge of key concepts and theories.

In each paragraph, aim to include at least one example which illustrates each 'way'.

In question 2, use three bullet-points so that your answer clearly outlines or describes three very distinct ways.

Spend 15 minutes on this 10-mark question and give your answer in two clear paragraphs. No introduction or conclusion is required. Make sure your answer is logical and the links are clear.

Each 'reason' should be reasonably detailed and use examples of studies of institutional racism. You could discuss the idea of an ethnocentric curriculum and policies of marketisation and selection.

You should spend around 45 minutes planning and answering question 4.

For question 4, you need to adopt an essay format: **Introduction**; **outline the argument** given in the question (cultural deprivation theory); **illustrate** with studies and/or Item A; **evaluate** that theory; outline **alternative theories**; give a reasoned **conclusion**.

In question 4, use the item to help you plan and organise your answer. Highlight those bits of the item that you might use in your answer and use it to illustrate or evaluate the view contained in the question. You can also use your own sociological knowledge to give examples to support your points. Try to make at least two direct references to the Item in your essay.

Research context and characteristics

In Paper 1, you will need to **apply** your knowledge of sociological research methods to the study of education. Look at the Research methods chapter to remind yourself of the different research methods (see pages 64–78).

Focus of research

Most educational research has focused on:

- causes of achievement and underachievement
- external influences on success and failure
- classroom relationships
- student behaviour and misbehaviour
- gendered educational performances
- contrasting the educational performance of different ethnic groups
- subject choices
- the effect of educational policy on schools.

Research groups and settings

Educational researchers tend to focus on:

Schools: organisation, discipline and marketing.

Teachers: attitudes towards gender, ethnicity and social class.

Students: deviancy, conformity, subcultures and identity.

Research groups

Parents: attitudes and support.

Classrooms: teacher–student interaction.

For example, a useful way of identifying children from poor families in schools is to focus on those who are eligible for free school meals (FSM) or those with special educational needs (SEN).

Access issues

Gaining access to a school to conduct research on students is not straightforward. Permission and informed consent need to be obtained from:

- local education authorities (LEAs)
- governors
- the head teacher
- parents – especially if pupils are very young
- students themselves.

By law, the researcher will also have to undergo a Disclosure and Barring Service (DBS) to check their suitability if the research involves spending one-to-one time with students.

Sampling

Schools have ready-made sampling frames which might include:

- lists or registers of present-day students divided into year groups, subjects and exam entry
- lists of past students and last-known addresses
- student lists that can be subdivided by gender and ethnicity
- the names and addresses of parents, past and present (these details are normally confidential but a school may support sociological research by writing to parents asking for their cooperation)
- a list of PTA members
- a list of staff and subject responsibilities.

Practical Practical issues in researching schools

The many different school types in the UK (comprehensives, academies, free, grammar and private schools) may undermine the representativeness of any sociological sample.	Schools are data-rich environments – they have a legal obligation to produce statistics on a range of processes in which sociologists are interested.
Finding similar schools to compare may be difficult – no one catchment area is the same.	Some school data may be unavailable due to confidentiality (e.g. relating to 'students at risk' or with special needs or to personal problems the student and/or parents are experiencing).
Sociologists may be excluded from some school settings, for example, management meetings.	
Governors and heads may deny permission for sociological research if they suspect that the findings may result in criticism or bad publicity.	Some schools – for example, prestigious private schools – have more power to say no to sociological research.

Now try this

What is meant by 'schools are data-rich environments'?

Researching parents and teachers

The Methods in Context question may be focused on researching parents or teachers using **questionnaires** or **interviews** (see pages 53–55). This page identifies some of the issues that you might consider in your discussion of their strengths and weaknesses.

Issues in researching parents

Sociologists may research parents to find out how home background influences achievement or subject choice. They will use questionnaires or interviews because it is impractical to observe interaction between parents and children (but parent–teacher interaction could be observed at parents' evenings or open days).

Practical Access to parents is more difficult because they are not concentrated in one place.	**Theoretical** Parental response to a questionnaire asking about educational supports may be uneven, thus undermining its representativeness.
Practical Parental addresses may be supplied by the school; the sample selected may be unrepresentative because such lists are unlikely to identify their social class, ethnicity and so on.	**Theoretical** Some groups of parents may enthusiastically over-respond because they are involved with the PTA; others may fail to respond because they feel that the questionnaire is implicitly critical of their efforts.
Ethical Some parents may only give informed consent for themselves or their children if they can see the benefits of the research.	**Theoretical** Some parents may attempt to manage the impression the researchers have of them by exaggerating their support or interest.

Issues in researching teachers

Questionnaires or interviews are used because it is impractical to observe interaction between teachers or teachers and managers (but interaction in a staffroom could be covertly observed).

Practical Teachers are accessible, once permission has been gained, because they are concentrated in one place.	**Theoretical** Teachers may engage in impression management and be unwilling to admit to certain types of 'negative' behaviour, such as stereotyping or labelling students, because they fear being judged as unprofessional.
Practical Teachers are constrained by timetables, the need to prepare lessons and marking, so may lack the time and enthusiasm to take part in research.	
Ethical It is essential to assure teachers of confidentiality because they may be anxious that managers may use the data against them.	**Theoretical** Teachers who volunteer or who are selected by the head teacher to take part in the research may be unrepresentative of teachers in the school.

Issues when researching classrooms

Direct or **non-participant observation** (see pages 57–58) is the most common method used to research classrooms.

Practical The closed setting means the researcher can exercise more control over observing particular interactions and relationships.	**Theoretical** Teachers may associate observations with inspection of their ability and may attempt to manage the researcher's impression of them by constructing an unrepresentative lesson, so their observed behaviour may not be high in validity.
Practical The teacher's awareness of the observation may mean their interaction with students becomes less natural.	
Practical **Ethical** There may be some scope for covert participant observation if the sociologist takes on the role of a supply teacher or teaching assistant (although there are ethical issues with this).	**Theoretical** Student behaviour may be unrepresentative as some may be subdued by the presence of a stranger, while others may be tempted to 'play up' to the researcher's presence ('**observer or Hawthorne effect**', see page 75).

Now try this

1 Why might observed student behaviour be low in validity?

2 Explain why it is unlikely that a sociologist will take on a role as a covert observer, as a supply teacher or teaching assistant, for example.

Researching students

The Methods in Context question may be focused on researching students using **questionnaires**, **interviews** or **observation** (see pages 53, 57–58). This page identifies some of the issues that you might consider in your discussion of their strengths and weaknesses.

Practical issues in researching students

Practical Students are relatively easy to access because they have to legally attend school.	**Practical** Questionnaire design and wording needs to consider the age and ability of the child.
Practical Representative samples can be taken from school sampling frames (registers) in terms of age, gender, ethnicity, ability and so on.	**Practical** Researchers can use children who are claiming free school meals as samples of children from poorer families.
Practical Some children may not be in school because they are persistently truant or have been suspended or excluded.	**Practical** Children may be reluctant to admit to behaviour (e.g. bullying or using racist language) because they associate the researchers with authority.
Practical Children who have had a 'difficult' time at school and/or are members of anti-school subcultures are less likely to cooperate with researchers.	**Practical** Researching children can be time-consuming and therefore potentially expensive.

Ethical issues in researching children

Ethical Children are generally regarded as a vulnerable group that need to be treated very sensitively.	**Ethical** Research must not damage or undermine a child's educational progress.
Ethical Some groups of children (special needs or at risk) may be less available for research because they need more protection than other children.	**Ethical** Although confidentiality is important, a researcher must report any evidence of abuse to the authorities.
Ethical Researchers, especially interviewers, will need to be vetted by officials to ensure that they are suitable to have close contact with children.	**Ethical** Children lack power and may find it difficult to turn down a request from an adult researcher, therefore undermining informed consent.
Ethical Researchers should obtain informed consent from children, but a young child is less likely to understand the aims of the research.	**Ethical** Researchers must ensure children suffer no emotional or psychological harm or distress because of their research.

Theoretical issues in researching children

Theoretical Interpretivist sociologists have suggested that power differences between children and adult researchers can undermine the validity of data.	**Theoretical** If interviewing is being used, children may respond in a limited and less valid fashion if they interpret the interviewer as 'threatening' or teacher-like.
Theoretical Children may act unnaturally when observed in the classroom.	**Theoretical** In group interviews, some students may undermine validity by insisting on hogging the limelight.
Theoretical If questionnaires are being filled in as a group, peer pressure may undermine the validity of the responses.	**Theoretical** Children may feel less threatened by research based on group interviews because the presence of their friends makes them feel 'safer'.

Now try this

1 Why might students feel less 'threatened' by researchers in group interviews?

2 Briefly explain why children might be reluctant to state views to researchers that challenge their teachers or head teacher.

3 Why is it a good idea for interviewers to make interviews with children as informal as possible?

Questionnaires and education

Questionnaires are often used by sociologists to research aspects of education. They can be targeted at students, parents, teachers and head teachers (see page 72 for more on questionnaires).

Aimed at students

Useful for collecting **quantitative data** (see page 64) about gender differences in attitudes towards homework, exams and coursework.

Used to collect quantitative data about the impact of material and cultural deprivation on educational performance.

Uses of questionnaires

Aimed at parents

Useful for collecting **quantitative data** about class and ethnic differences in levels of parental support offered to children.

Useful for counting the number of interactions between parents and teachers.

For example, the number of times parents attend parents' evenings.

Evaluation: student questionnaires

👍 **Practical** Closed questions with tick-box responses are student friendly because they do not require much effort.

👍 **Theoretical** Questionnaires avoid the problems linked with status differences, such as interviewer bias because the researcher is usually not present when they are completed.

👎 **Practical** They traditionally have lower response rates than other methods unless supervised by teachers.

👎 **Practical** Questionnaires need to take account of students' level of literacy and ability as well as their age to be successful.

👎 **Theoretical** Some students may fear that written responses may be used against them and so be partial with the truth.

👎 **Theoretical** There is no universal agreement about how material and cultural deprivation should be defined and measured using questionnaires.

👎 **Theoretical** Supervision by teachers could mean that questionnaires may be associated with authority.

👎 **Theoretical** Students may not have the knowledge to complete questionnaires (e.g. their parents' job, income or educational background).

Evaluation: parent questionnaires

👎 **Theoretical** Parents may view questionnaires as judgemental and react defensively by exaggerating or misleading researchers about the levels of support they give their children.

👎 **Theoretical** Some questionnaires can suffer from the **imposition problem**. This means the researchers have already decided upon the questions and pre-set answers, but these may not represent the experience of either parents or students. This can undermine the validity of the data collected.

🔍 Key study Bicknell (2014)

Bicknell used questionnaires to investigate parents' contribution to the education of their mathematically gifted children. Parents were asked to 'strongly agree', 'agree', 'disagree' or 'strongly disagree' with a number of statements. These operationalised and measured their role as 'motivator', 'resource provider', 'monitor', 'maths content adviser' and 'maths learning counsellor'. The research found that many of the parents identified their child's propensity for mathematics at an early age. Results indicated that parents played key roles as motivators, resource providers and so on that were just as important as their child's maths teachers.

Now try this

1 Briefly explain why asking parents about how often they turn up for parents' evenings might not be an effective way to operationalise parental interest in education.

2 What is the imposition problem?

Interviewing teachers and parents

Structured and **unstructured interviews** have been used to collect data from teachers and parents (see pages 72–73 for more on interviews).

Access to parents

Sociological access to **parents** can usually be obtained using school records, although parents might also be approached at the school gates while picking up their children or at parents' evenings, school open days or PTA meetings.

Access to teachers

Teachers are more easily accessed because most can be found during the school day within their workplace. A staff list might be used by a sociologist as a sampling frame. However, teachers are seen as the representatives of their schools, so a researcher would probably need to obtain the permission of a head teacher to involve teachers in their research.

Structured interviews

If the researcher requires **quantitative data** they may use **structured** (formal) or **semi-structured** interviews, which give respondents a choice of options to tick or to agree with. These can be conducted fairly quickly on large samples and usually produce lots of quantitative data that can quickly be analysed, compared and correlated (see page 57).

 Key study **Ruth Lupton (2004)**

Lupton conducted in-depth interviews with head teachers and teachers in four schools that served economically deprived neighbourhoods. Her aim was to test the hypothesis that schools with lots of children from economically disadvantaged backgrounds inevitably became 'failing' schools.

The data from her interviews, however, clearly show that teachers and schools work hard to help their students overcome the barriers to achievement that emanate from living in poverty. Consequently, these schools did not inevitably fail.

Unstructured interviews

Unstructured or informal interviews produce **qualitative data** (see page 64). This type of interview is flexible. It allows the interviewer to probe the reasons why parents and teachers behave the way they do. Teachers and parents can also express ideas in their own words and issues can be explored in greater depth.

Most interviewers use a non-directive, neutral and objective form of interviewing during which the interviewer offers no opinions of their own and does not express approval or disapproval of the responses of those being interviewed either in their tone of voice or facial expression. **Positivist** researchers argue that if respondents are not aware of the views or values of the interviewer, it is more difficult for them to give the answers they think the interviewer might want to hear.

Interpretivists prefer unstructured interviews because they avoid the imposition problem (see page 53) and sometimes throw up unexpected findings.

For example, if an interviewer asks a student, parent or teacher what they like about a school, they might express likes for things that the sociologist may not have considered, such as the quality of school dinners or the dedication of the staff.

 Key study **Howard Becker (1970)**

Interpretivist sociologist **Becker** used a style of interviewing that he terms 'aggressive' in which statements by interviewees were frequently challenged. He claimed that this style of interviewing produces more valid data because it gets closer to people's real opinions and feelings.

Using this interrogative style with Chicago school teachers, he claimed he uncovered racist feelings among some teachers which he argued would have remained hidden had he not been so confrontational in his interviewing technique.

Now try this

Outline what Becker means by 'aggressive interviewing'.

Issues with interviewing teachers and parents

Both positivist and interpretivist sociologists aim to achieve validity in their research. However, achieving this when interviewing teachers and parents can be problematic.

Issues with interviewing teachers

Practical Interviewers may face the very practical problem of fitting interviews into teachers' busy timetables and workloads. Teachers may be reluctant to give up their precious free time to take part in long interviews.

Theoretical Head teachers may only allow interviews with staff who share their vision of how the school should be run. The data collected from these teachers may lack validity because of their bias.

Theoretical Interview data may lack validity because teachers are unlikely to admit to unprofessional behaviour, such as racism or sexism, that may result in disciplinary measures being taken against them.

Theoretical Teachers' responses may be affected by the fact that their classroom performance is frequently scrutinised via management observation of lessons and Ofsted inspections. Consequently, they may be more cautious and reluctant to express their real feelings in interviews, which may undermine the validity of the data collected.

Theoretical Interpretivist sociologists observe that people often lack self-awareness of their behaviour.

For example, some teachers may not be aware that they are behaving in particular ways, so interviews are unlikely to uncover the reasons for that behaviour. They may genuinely believe that they treat all students equally and that they do not engage in the negative labelling of students (see page 36).

Issues with interviewing parents

Practical Some parents may be easier to access than others.

For example, it may be easier to approach some parents at the school gates or while they are attending PTA or parents' evenings. Other parents may be less agreeable to the requests for interviews because of their working hours or because they also have very young children to look after.

Theoretical Some parents may experience an 'interviewer effect' – they may feel 'threatened' by the status of the interviewer.

When **Bhatti** (1999) interviewed Asian parents, for example, she deliberately employed Asian female interviewers who could speak and interview parents in Urdu or Punjabi in order to make them feel more comfortable and trusting of the interviewers, thus increasing the validity of the data collected.

Practical It can be difficult for interviewers to judge the social class of parents without asking intrusive and unwelcome questions about income, which some parents may not wish to answer.

Theoretical Parents' responses to interviews may be affected by their social class, gender or ethnicity.

For example, some interviewers may prefer to interview parents separately rather than together because the presence of a husband or wife can bias the response of the other and reduce validity.

Theoretical Parents who manipulate the school admission system by making the most of their social contacts to get their children admitted to the best state schools are unlikely to admit to such unethical behaviour to interviewers.

Theoretical Feminists do not like males interviewing female respondents because such interviews reflect patriarchal inequality. They argue that female interviewers are more likely to elicit valid responses from female subjects.

Theoretical Some parents may interpret interview questions as critical of their parenting style and react by being partial with the truth and/or by exaggerating the supports they offer their child in order to manage the impression the interviewer has of them.

Now try this

How did Bhatti reduce potential interviewer effect when interviewing Asian parents about their children?

Interviewing students

A range of **interview** types have been used in educational research to collect data from students (see pages 73–74 for more on interviews).

Uses of interviews

- Researchers prefer to use informal **semi-structured interviews** for one-to-one interviews with students. Informality puts students at ease and the interviewer can respond flexibly to what students say and probe reasons for their answers.
- Well-trained empathetic interviewers should be able to establish trust between themselves and students, so increasing the probability of **validity**.
- Students may be more willing to vent their feelings about school and teachers to younger interviewers.

Language

The **language** of interviews has to be kept simple because students have less-developed language skills than adults.

For example, interviews with young children may have to be kept short because they cannot concentrate for long periods.

Evaluation: group interviews

👍 **Theoretical** They can draw out shared group values that, individually, students might be reluctant to express.

👍 **Theoretical** Some students may feel safe, more comfortable or confident within a small group environment rather than in a one-to-one interview with an adult who may be interpreted as an authority figure.

For example, **Willis (1977)** used group interviews to question non-academic working-class boys about their attitudes towards school and boys in the top sets.

👎 **Theoretical** Some students may be reluctant to express their true feelings because they fear how the group will react. They may fear being bullied.

👎 **Theoretical** Some students, especially boys, may be tempted to give invalid responses 'for a laugh' to impress their peers.

👎 **Ethical** Heads may not welcome group interviews with students that invite criticism about teachers or school rules because they do not view students as competent enough to judge teachers. Such interviews may be seen as undermining the relationship between teachers and students.

Issues with using one-to-one interviews

Ethical They require informed consent from parents and head teachers. Heads may refuse permission if they feel the research will reflect badly on the image of the school or negatively affect recruitment.	**Theoretical** Children may associate adult interviewers with authority figures (e.g. teachers). So some students may be less willing to cooperate with interviews if they have had a negative experience of education.
Ethical Researchers need to undergo a DBS check if they intend to spend time alone with children.	**Theoretical** Some students, for example truants, may not be available for interviews.
Ethical Researchers cannot guarantee confidentiality to students – they must disclose to the authorities any information they are given by students that suggests they are the victims of possible abuse.	**Theoretical** The interview schedule or questionnaire used by the interviewer may suffer from the 'imposition problem' (see page 53).

🔍 Key study   Frosh (2002)

Frosh interviewed teenage boys in the early years of secondary school to find out what masculinity meant to them and how it affected their daily lives. He recruited young male interviewers in order to minimise power differences and maximise validity. Interviewers were given a list of topics and possible questions to guide them through the interviews. All of the answers were recorded and transcribed (qualitative data), and common themes relating to masculinity were identified. The boys talked openly about their relationships with parents and friends, hardness, homophobia and football, and the importance of youth style, race and ethnicity.

Now try this

Briefly explain how Frosh minimised power differences between his interviewing team and the teenage boys being studied.

Observation and education

Observation can be **participant**, **non-participant** or **covert** (see page 75). Educational researchers mainly use **non-participant observation** to study teachers and students in the classroom.

Uses of non-participant observation

Non-participant observation is most often used in the classroom. It has been used by feminists to study the way teachers interact with girls – for example, **Spender** (1982), **Stanworth** (1990) and **Reay and Mirza** (2001). However, some sociologists, such as **Willis** (1977) and **Corrigan** (1979), have observed students in their free time – in the playground and in the 'private' spaces in which they congregate in school. For more on Willis and Corrigan's studies, and uses of observation, see page 58.

Non-participant observation is often used in the classroom.

Evaluation of non-participant observation

👍 `Theoretical` **Naturalistic:** it studies first-hand the everyday environment of students and teachers.

👍 `Theoretical` **Interpretivist** sociologists argue that the data has high **validity** because it reflects reality.

👍 `Theoretical` **Replicable:** the observations can be easily replicated using the same schedules on similar classes.

👍 `Theoretical` **Real behaviour:** it may uncover behaviour that people may not admit in interviews, for example, teacher labelling caused by prejudice (see page 36).

👍 `Theoretical` **New ideas:** it may uncover unexpected behaviour and generate new hypotheses.

👍 `Theoretical` **Environment:** it allows researchers to see behaviour from the point of view of the social actors – the teachers and students in the classroom.

👎 `Practical` **Invisible school processes:** observation is not suitable for observing all school processes. It is impossible to observe why students choose the subjects they do, for example.

👎 `Practical` **Time:** it is time-consuming and can be difficult to organise with busy teachers and if students are studying for exams.

👎 `Practical` **Social factors:** observation cannot measure the influence of external social pressures, for example, poverty or family life on student behaviour.

👎 `Ethical` **Access:** some social settings in schools are off-limits to observers, for example, the staffroom, meetings with parents, teacher meetings to discuss 'at risk students'.

👎 `Theoretical` **Data:** gathered data may be superficial because it does not generate insight into people's motives for behaving the way they do.

👎 `Theoretical` **Presence:** the group's knowledge that they are being observed may affect their behaviour which may become unnatural. Children may 'act up' and teachers may act more 'formally' than they would normally.

Covert observation

Covert observation is rarely used in educational research because:

✓ it is seen as unethical for researchers to mislead teachers and children

✓ it is difficult for researchers to adopt a covert educational role

   For example, researchers are usually too old to pose as students and do not have the qualifications or experience to pose as teachers. They will need a DBS check. Playing such a role may negatively affect the academic progress of students.

✓ head teachers are unlikely to give permission for such research

✓ it often fails to obtain informed consent from those being observed.

Now try this

What school spaces are off-limits to most sociological observers?

Observation in education

Sociological researchers have used both participant and non-participant observation to research educational matters.

 Key study **Participant observation in education**

Paul Corrigan (1979)

Corrigan's study *Schooling the Smash Street Kids* used covert observation to study how students, especially truants, viewed education and teachers. Corrigan misled both students and teachers in a comprehensive school in Sunderland by presenting himself as an author doing research for a novel based in a school. He deliberately blanked teachers because he did not want students to associate him with any sort of authority and because he wished to obtain the total trust of the students. By talking to students and observing them in their own space, he came to the conclusion that truancy was a response to the compulsory nature of school. Kids truanted because they resented the fact that the state forced them to go to school.

Paul Willis (1977)

Willis followed 12 working-class boys throughout their school, as well as in their leisure time for two years. He sat in their classes and observed how they interacted with teachers and other students. He even accompanied them on a school trip. He also spent time observing them in their workplace after they left school. He found that the 'lads' in his study defined 'success' in quite a different way from teachers and boys in the top sets, who saw success as equalling qualifications. In contrast, the 'lads' defined success as 'having a laff' because the jobs they wanted did not require qualifications.

 Key study **Non-participant observation in education**

Becky Francis (2001)

With permission from head teachers and parents of students, Francis carried out observation in three mixed-sex London secondary schools to record gendered classroom interaction and student behaviour. Students were asked about their opinion and interpretation of that interaction. A top-set and a lower-set lesson in each age group were observed, so four lessons were observed at each school (12 classes in all). The class teacher explained Francis' presence in the classroom. Francis felt that covering a large sample of students in different schools was more important than spending a longer amount of time with a smaller sample. However, she concedes that the small amount of time spent observing each class was a limitation. She also found it difficult to faithfully record all the interaction because of the noise levels in some of the classes. She found that boys got more attention from teachers than girls, but this attention was often negative in that boys were told off more than girls.

Colin Lacey (1970)

Lacey got permission from the Chief Education Officer and the head teacher to access the Hightown Grammar school. He spent two months familiarising himself with the staff and students. He talked to them about why he was in the school, which was to try to explain the underachievement of working-class boys in grammar schools. Lacey observed at least one lesson by every member of staff over a period of 12 weeks and engaged both staff and students in informal conversations. He taught classes for 12 hours a week, went on several school trips and ran the school's cricket team. Lacey found that despite working-class boys being perceived as bright because they had passed the 11+, they were more likely to be placed in middle or bottom streams than middle-class children. This streaming experience often engendered feelings of inferiority.

Now try this

1 Give **three** reasons why Corrigan's method of observation might have generated data high in validity.

2 Why can Lacey's methods be described as participant observation?

Official statistics and education

Schools now have to market themselves to parents. Consequently, schools and the **Department for Education (DfE)** produce **official statistics** on aspects of education (see page 76 for more on official statistics).

Uses of official statistics

Schools and the DfE produce facts and figures for educational attainment. These are often broken down into gender and ethnic categories. The DfE also produces statistics pertaining to truancy and exclusions. Schools produce their own statistics relating to attendance and lateness.

Evaluation of using official statistics

👍 **Practical** **Accessibility**: most DfE statistics are easily accessible via the internet and involve little or no cost.

👍 **Practical** **Trends**: DfE statistics are useful for examining long-term trends over time and for making comparisons between males and females as well as different ethnic groups.

👍 **Ethical** **Ethics**: using DfE statistics is unlikely to cause harm, so there are no ethical concerns involved.

👍 **Theoretical** **Positivist** sociologists are in favour of DfE statistics because they are the result of standardised data collection techniques that are objective, reliable and representative.

👎 **Practical** **Statistics** are not always available in the form that sociologists need.

For example, the DfE does not differentiate exam results by the social class of students. Instead, some sociologists have used DfE statistics for the number of students eligible for free school meals to identify students from deprived backgrounds.

👎 **Practical** **Limitations**: little or no statistical data is available about students in private, fee-paying schools or about the career trajectory of ex-students of schools and colleges.

👎 **Ethical** **Schools**: some head teachers may deliberately manipulate or distort some statistics to either secure funding or for marketing purposes.

For example, they may not accurately record absences or truancy and fail to enter students for particular exams to improve their league table position.

👎 **Theoretical** **One-dimensional**: many DfE statistics describe rather than explain.

For example, DfE statistics may show schools doing well or badly but they do not give much insight into why.

👎 **Theoretical** **Subject choice**: statistics on gendered subject choices give us little insight into the reasons for those choices.

🔍 Key study Equality and Human Rights Commission (EHRC) (2010)

The EHRC carried out a study in order to investigate whether the UK was really a meritocratic society. The study used official statistics from a range of government sources including the Higher Education Statistics Agency relating to class, gender and ethnicity, and the Labour Force Survey. The report concludes that although attitudes towards equality have radically changed over the past 30 years and many types of prejudice are now unlawful, what happens in the real world in the 21st century still falls short of the ideals of equality. This is because too many people continue to be trapped by the accident of their birth – their futures are still determined by social class because they are born into families without the material or social capital to give them the right start in education and life.

Now try this

1 Why are sociologists attracted by official statistics if they are researching education?
2 Identify **two** limitations of the use of official statistics to study aspects of the education system according to interpretivists.

Documents and education

A wide range of public documents relating to education and specific schools are available to sociologists including Ofsted inspection reports, publicity brochures, prospectuses and the minutes of governors' meetings (see page 78 for more on public documents). **Non-official documents** include autobiographies and books from ex-students and teachers, blogs and even text messages.

Uses of documents

Public documents are often used in conjunction with **primary research methods** to construct in-depth case studies of specific schools or aspects of the education system. Some sociologists have examined **non-official documents** such as the notes that students pass in class and the school reports of individual students. Schools are increasingly using social media – websites, subject-based Facebook and Twitter accounts – to assist students' knowledge, learning and revision.

Evaluation of using public documents

👍 (Practical) **Saves time, effort and money:** public documents are readily available to researchers at little or no cost. **Gewirtz (1995)** used school brochures and prospectuses to study how schools marketed themselves.

👍 (Practical) **Comparative value:** documents are often used in conjunction with other primary research methods.

👍 (Practical) **Historical comparisons:** public documents are vital for studying long-term social changes.
For example, Hansard records Parliamentary debates and can reveal why governments felt the need to make major changes to education in 1870, 1944, 1965, 1988 and 2010.

👍 (Practical) **Personal documents**: these may be the only way to gain insight into the daily workings of UK public schools which often deny researchers access to their teachers, students and practices.

👍 (Ethical) **Public domain:** public documents rarely focus on individuals and, consequently, there are no ethical consequences when they are used.

👍 (Theoretical) **Positivists** prefer public documents because they are based on evidence that has been systematically collected in a standardised, objective and reliable way.

👎 (Practical) **Personal documents:** the availability of diaries and autobiographies of students and teachers is patchy. Where they are available, there may be issues of authenticity. Consequently, relatively little research has been done using these sources.

👎 (Theoretical) **Distortion:** some school prospectuses may distort reality by glossing over poor attendance, poor classroom behaviour and truancy in order to maximise funding and/or to positively influence inspection.

👎 (Theoretical) **Bias:** school marketing documents may be biased because they focus only on the positive attributes of the school experience.

👎 (Theoretical) **Objectivity:** most public documents are written with the audience in mind.
For example, school brochures are trying to attract the attention of parents rather than providing a reliable and objective picture of all aspects of a school experience.

👎 (Theoretical) **Unrepresentative:** if official documents exclude views that the government disagrees with or that it does not want to be a matter of public discussion, they may be unrepresentative.

🔍 Key study — Valerie Hey (1997)

Hey carried out an ethnographic study of girls' friendships in schools by using the notes girls passed to each other in class as well as diaries, interviews and observations of female friendship groups. Some critics claimed Hey acted unethically because she did not obtain consent from the students who wrote the notes, which she often fished from bins without their knowledge. Hey concluded that these notes suggest that girls form feminine subcultures in school that are often suppressed, but which serve to help them cope with and survive school and their everyday experience of sexism found within their families, classrooms and relationships with boys.

Now try this

Identify **two** reasons why sociologists have to be careful about using the content of public or official documents.

Experiments and education

Experimental research has been used to investigate a range of topics in the education system, including the labelling theories of education and the effects of teacher expectations upon student's educational performance. For more on types of experiments, see pages 70–71.

Issues with using experimental research

Practical Experiments to 'prove' a link between teacher expectations and students' academic performance (due to internalisation of teacher labels by students) are a long-term process and therefore unlikely to be investigated.	**Theoretical** Interpretivists argue that it is not the introduction of the independent variable that changes behaviour but the experiment itself. If subjects know they are in an experiment, this produces artificial behaviour and reduces validity.
Practical If teachers know they are part of a scientific experiment to show them unfairly labelling students, they are unlikely to behave unprofessionally in front of researchers.	**Theoretical** It is very difficult to control all variables in social or field experiments. Changes in student performance might be due to other variables outside the school such as home life.
Ethical Researchers find it difficult to obtain permission to conduct experiments on young children. Laboratory experiments are usually confined to studying older students.	**Theoretical** Social experiments are difficult to replicate in order to verify results and so have low reliability.
Ethical There are ethical problems in conducting social experiments. **Rosenthal and Jacobson** (1968) were heavily criticised because their social experiment involved deception. See page 71 for an evaluation of their research.	**Theoretical** What counts as a positive or negative teacher action or label is a matter of interpretation – not all researchers are going to interpret these in the same way.

 Key study **The Sutton Trust (2014)**

On behalf of the Trust, **Becky Francis, Merryn Hutching** and **Philip Kirby** used the natural experiment approach in their study of academy schools. They compared different academy schools (especially those run by chains) with schools in general. They examined official statistics with regard to the number of disadvantaged students (identified by eligibility for free school meals and qualification for the student premium) achieving five GCSE grades, including English and maths, the degree of progress made by younger students in English and maths, and the proportion of students obtaining the International Baccalaureate (IB) diploma. They also compared the different types of academy chains to see whether any type tended to have more success than the others. They found that one in five academy chains achieved below average results and failed to improve the educational performance of their poorest students. However, they also found that the best chains (7 out of 39) delivered outstanding results.

For example, the ARK chain, which ran 34 primary and secondary schools, raised the achievement levels of both their disadvantaged and affluent students.

Harvey and Slatin (1976)

Harvey and Slatin used photographs of students from different social classes and asked teachers to rate their likely performance in education. Students from higher social classes were seen as more likely to be successful than students from lower social classes, suggesting that labelling on the basis of appearance does take place.

Now try this

Why does asking for informed consent create problems of validity for experiments?

Exam skills

This Paper 1 exam-style question uses knowledge and skills you have already revised. Spend about 30 minutes planning and answering this question.

Worked example

Item C

Investigating the effect of material deprivation on educational achievement

Some sociologists claim that material deprivation is the main cause of educational underachievement. 'Material deprivation' refers to a lack of material resources in the home background, such as low household income, poor housing and a lack of workspace in the home.

Some sociologists use official statistics to investigate the nature and extent of material deprivation. As researchers usually want to know the general impact of a factor like material deprivation, official statistics are useful because they are often produced by large-scale research. However, official statistics may not tell us much about the way students actually interpret and respond to material deprivation and whether it affects their attitudes to education or how parents may attempt to compensate for it by spending more quality time with helping children with their schoolwork. The ways in which material deprivation are defined and measured in official statistics may also be different from the definitions and measurements used by the sociologist.

---

1 Applying material from **Item C** and your knowledge of research methods, evaluate the strengths and limitations of official statistics for studying the effect of material deprivation on educational achievement.
(20 marks)

Official statistics refer to quantitative data collected by the state or other large-scale organisations. For example, the state produces lots of statistical data about poverty or material deprivation as well as education. An example would be league table data based on exam results. This is a type of secondary data because it is not collected by sociologists themselves. Positivist sociologists see official statistics as having particular theoretical strengths because, as shown in Item C, they are often the result of large-scale research that uses scientific, standardised, reliable and objective measuring tools such as questionnaires and structured interviews. Also, the use of official statistics means that the research is unlikely to run into ethical problems because it does not involve researchers interacting with people who may attempt to manage the impression the sociologist has of them.

Official statistics also allow sociologists to compare trends and patterns over a period of time and observe correlations between factors such as material deprivation as measured by children eligible for free school meals and educational achievement. Another way of using official statistics to study the effect of material deprivation on educational achievement might be to compare the exam results of schools in deprived areas with schools in more affluent areas...

The fact that this question is worth 20 marks indicates that you need to write in an organised essay-form: introduction; strengths; weaknesses; other methods; conclusion. Use examples from the item and your own knowledge to support your points.

This question is not just about the research method. It is about the **merits of using the research method to research a particular aspect of education** – in this case the effect of material deprivation on educational achievement.

Always deal with the strengths of the method before the weaknesses, and think about **practical, ethical** and **theoretical** factors.

The answer begins with a definition of the method, with an example. If the question mentions a specific group, identify how sociological research might sample that group (e.g. students).

Note how this answer incorporates Item C material into the body of the essay and focuses on the link between material deprivation and educational achievement.

• Next, discuss practical strengths such as cost, accessibility, currency and the benefit of these to sociologists.

• To complete this answer **discuss the weaknesses** of the method in researching material deprivation and educational achievement, using both those shown in the Item and your own knowledge. For example, you could explain why interpretivists are not keen on using official statistics. **Evaluate the merits** of other methods in researching this area, then come to a **conclusion** about the suitability of using official statistics. For example, you could conclude that a primary research method might be more suitable because sociologists can exercise more control over what aspects of material deprivation they want to focus on.

Exam-style practice

Practise for Paper 1 with this exam-style question. You will find the answer on page 215. Before looking at this question, it would be useful to have revised research methods as well as theories of educational underachievement that blame external factors such as the home background of children.

Item C

Investigating the role of linguistic deprivation in educational underachievement

Linguistic deprivation is a lack of the language skills needed for educational success; some sociologists see it as resulting from inadequate socialisation. They regard it as the main cause of underachievement among the working class and some ethnic minorities, who they claim often have negative feelings about education. However, critics argue that this view is unfair because it blames the home background of students for their own educational failure rather than material factors such as poverty or the middle-class value system of the school and teachers.

Some sociologists have used self-completion questionnaires to investigate the role of cultural factors in contributing to underachievement. These can allow children and their parents to anonymously answer questions about personal issues such as family life or their experience of education. Students may take questionnaires for completion at home, which removes the need for working-class respondents to interact with middle-class researchers. However, some parents may use a questionnaire to positively manage the impression that the sociologist has of their parenting skills and consequently may mislead or exaggerate the support they claim to give their children.

Applying material from **Item C** and your knowledge of research methods, evaluate the strengths and limitations of using questionnaires to investigate the role of parents in educational achievement.

(20 marks)

Spend around 30 minutes planning and answering this question.

This question demands an essay response: introduction. **Outline** the method given in the question; **illustrate** with studies and/or Item C; **evaluate** by outlining arguments for and against its use in this context; consider **alternative methods**; give a reasoned **conclusion**.

You are told to use the material in this item to illustrate or evaluate the view contained in the question, so make sure you do this.

Always remember that this is a Methods question first and foremost. You are only using Education to illustrate points you are making about the strengths and limitations of questionnaires.

Before you begin, read through the item and highlight the parts of the passage you will use in your answer. Try to make at least two direct references to the item in your essay. You can also use examples from your own knowledge to support your points.

Use the item to help plan your answer. Look at the strengths and then the weaknesses of using questionnaires in this context. The item identifies two strengths of using questionnaires to investigate parental involvement in education, but you need to use your knowledge of research to add some more. Use PET to do this as well as your knowledge of the drawbacks of researching students and parents as a social group, e.g. some students may not be fully aware of the extent of their parents' help or some parents may feel the questionnaire implicitly criticises their parental skills and will refuse to cooperate with the research.

The item also identifies a major potential weakness of using questionnaires to research parents. Use your knowledge of research methods to examine other potential weaknesses of using questionnaires to investigate parents' involvement in their child's education. PET again could be used to organise your response. You might also want to consider the merits of alternative methods that might be better suited to examining the role of parents in their children's education such as interviews.

63

Types of data

All research is based on collecting evidence or data about the organisation of the social world (society). You need to know the difference between **primary** and **secondary data**, and between **quantitative** and **qualitative data**.

Sources of data

Research methods aim to gather data about the **social world**. Such data may be descriptive. Alternatively, it may provide evidence to show how different elements of society – for example, education and poverty – relate to each other. Most sociologists aim to use this data to construct theories to explain social events or phenomena – for example, why education functions in the way that it does.

Common sense vs data

Sociologists collect data in an **objective**, **rigorous** and **methodical** way. Common sense, on the other hand, is:

- subjective
- based on limited experience
- often coloured by bias or prejudice
- accepted at face value and often not subjected to testing from other sociologists.

Primary data

Primary data is collected by the social researcher themselves. Research methods include experiments, survey questionnaires, interviews and participant or non-participant observation.

Secondary data

Secondary data is information that has been compiled by others. It includes: state-produced official statistics; personal documents such as letters, diaries and autobiographies; and media content such as television and radio programmes, newspapers and websites.

Quantitative data

Quantitative data is numerical data. It usually comes in the form of statistics or percentages. It is most often presented in graph, table or pie-chart form.

With education, for example, it might include league tables, the numbers of students excluded from school or the percentage of university students from working-class backgrounds.

Quantitative data may be produced from primary research methods such as a social survey, where results are often presented in numerical form, or extracted from secondary sources such as official statistics on truancy.

Qualitative data

Qualitative data is **non-numerical data**. It usually comes in the form of words and/or images.

For example, a researcher may use historical documents (secondary sources) to describe education in the early 20th century. A researcher carrying out primary research may use quotes from students taken from interview transcripts (word-for-word accounts of what was said during an interview).

Qualitative data may be produced from primary research methods such as unstructured interviews and participant observation, or extracted from secondary sources such as diaries and autobiographies.

Correlations

Sociologists often look for **correlations** – a relationship between social events or phenomena – when they gather data.

For example, there seems to be a relationship between educational achievement and social phenomena such as class, ethnicity and gender.

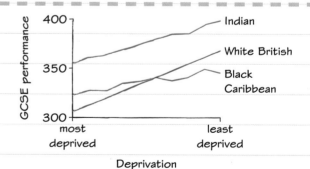

The relationship between GCSE performance and deprivation for different ethnicities.

Now try this

1. Identify **two** sources of secondary data.
2. What is a transcript?

Research design

Social research needs to be well-designed to be effective. Sociologists therefore aim to achieve five key goals when carrying out social research: **reliability**, **representativeness**, **generalisability**, **validity** and **objectivity**.

 Reliability

A research design and process is **reliable** if another sociologist, who repeats the research using a similar sample and the same method, consistently obtains the same or very similar results. This replication aims to check and **verify** the scientific **accuracy** of the way evidence or data is gathered. Sociologists often carry out **pilot studies** before the main research to ensure reliability by checking that all those who take part interpret the questions in the same way as the researcher.

 Representativeness

Most research uses a smaller **sample** of the **research population** – the group that the research is focused on. For example, it is not possible to investigate the classroom experience of every student or teacher in the UK. It is important that the sample is a typical cross-section of the wider group and that key groups – social classes, males and females, age groups, ethnic groups – are **represented** in the same proportion as they are in the overall population of students and teachers.

 Generalisability

Most researchers want to **generalise** from the data they have collected. They wish to say that the behaviour or attitudes found in the sample are typical of the wider population. So what is true of the smaller group is also true of the larger group.

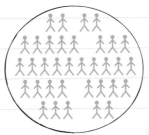

research population

sample

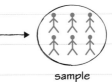

The larger the sample, the more likely it is to be representative of the research population, or even generalised to the whole population.

 Validity

Validity generally refers to whether the research findings give a true picture of what is being studied. That is, it should reflect the reality of the persons or groups being studied.

Validity can be difficult to achieve. For example, teachers may not admit to negatively labelling students (even though they actually do this) because they may fear that the sociologists may view them as unprofessional. The data collected from the teachers is therefore in danger of being invalid or untrue.

 Objectivity

Objectivity (also called **value freedom**) is the idea that all sources of personal or ideological **bias** (prejudice in favour or against something or someone) have been eliminated from the research process. This might be achieved by:

- using a random sampling technique
- ensuring questions used in a questionnaire or interview are neutral so that they do not lead research subjects into giving particular responses
- training interviewers not to bias responses by betraying their feelings during interviews
- encouraging observers and interviewers not to get too friendly or emotionally attached to their research subjects
- avoiding the temptation to be selective when analysing and evaluating their data so that only evidence that suits the hypothesis is used.

Now try this

1 Define what is meant by 'validity'.
2 Why is reliability important?
3 What is meant by 'bias'?

Practical and ethical factors

Sociologists need to take into account certain practical and ethical considerations that may influence their choice of topic, what method(s) to use and the conduct of the research.

Topic choice

Topic choice is influenced by a number of practical factors.

Academic debate: the researcher may wish to enhance their academic reputation by researching a 'hot' or fashionable topic.

Access: some groups of people have the power to shut out sociologists or they may be suspicious of authority and not wish to have their activities monitored.
For example, anti-school subcultures.

Practical factors

Source of funding: the subject matter may be shaped by those who control the purse strings. For example, governments may avoid funding research that sets out to be critical of educational policy.

Interests, values and politics of the researcher: they may feel the need to highlight some injustice or inequality.

Research method

The choice of research method is influenced by a number of practical factors.

Size of sample: if a large number of research subjects are required, questionnaires or structured interviews are most suited to generating data from lots of people.

Cost: some methods can be expensive. For example, unstructured interviews and observation tend to be more costly than postal questionnaires or secondary data.

Time available: some methods are more suitable if sociologists only have a limited time period in which to carry out the research.

Type of data required: quantitative or qualitative or a mix of both?

Practical factors

Subject matter: if it is sensitive or potentially embarrassing, this may rule out face-to-face methods.

Social characteristics: the age, social class, gender and ethnicity of the researcher(s) and the research subjects may mean that certain methods may not work.
For example, black students may not cooperate with white, middle-aged interviewers.

Ethical factors

The British Sociological Association (BSA) has issued a set of professional ethical guidelines that should be followed when designing and conducting research.

Honesty: researchers should avoid deceit and be honest about the purpose of their research.

Informed consent: researchers should seek informed consent from their research subjects or their parents/guardians.

Confidentiality: researchers need to protect the identity and privacy of their research subjects by ensuring anonymity and confidentiality.

Avoid harming people: researchers must avoid doing any harm to their subjects. They should not encourage criminal or immoral behaviour.

Ethical factors

Researchers should not engage in disreputable activities in the pursuit of their research. They have a duty of care to their research team.

Now try this

1 How might the aspirations of a young sociologist shape his or her choice of research subject?
2 Which primary research method is best employed if the sociologist only has a few months in which to carry out the research?

Theoretical factors

Another important influence on the choice of topic, the research method and the conduct of the research is the theoretical position held by the researcher. Some researchers may be positivists; others may be interpretivists (see pages 7 and 13).

Methodology

Positivists and interpretivists hold different beliefs about how societies are organised which influences their research methodology.

Positivist approach	Interpretivist approach
Social behaviour: the result of **social facts** – things that originate in the structure, institutions and culture of a society, which affect or shape the attitudes and behaviour of individuals. So an individual's behaviour is not the result of choice or free will.	**Social behaviour:** the result of how people interpret their interaction with others and social institutions. People exercise free will and construct their own social reality by freely choosing to interact with others and by applying meaning to other people's behaviour.
Society: people are the 'puppets of society'.	**Society:** people are the 'architects of society'.
Topics: macro/top-down approach to research how large-scale structures (education system, economy) relate to each other or how they shape the behaviour of individuals.	**Topics:** micro/bottom-up approach to research how individuals interact with one another and how they interpret each other's behaviour.
Methods: scientific methods should be used.	**Methods:** they do not have to be scientific.
Research design: a scientific logic known as the **hypothetico-deductive model** should underpin how the research process is designed and practised: observation → hypothesis → evidence → verification → theory	**Research design:** **validity** underpins the research process and practice. Validity is best achieved by establishing trust and goodwill between researcher and research subjects. The researcher should try to achieve **verstehen** – an empathetic understanding – that allows them to get inside the heads of their subjects and see the social world through their eyes.
Data: methods that are standardised, reliable, objective and produce **quantitative data** are preferred. Data is compared to establish cause and effect and/or to find correlations.	**Data:** methods that produce **qualitative data** are preferred, ideally describing the observed day-to-day activities of research subjects in their own words.

Positivist–Interpretivist research methods

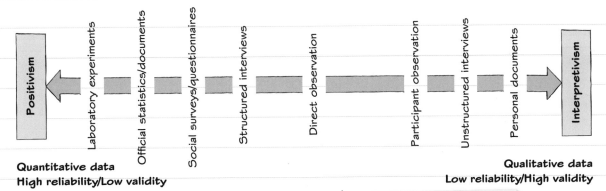

Positivism ← Laboratory experiments · Official statistics/documents · Social surveys/questionnaires · Structured interviews · Direct observation · Participant observation · Unstructured interviews · Personal documents → Interpretivism

Quantitative data
High reliability/Low validity

Qualitative data
Low reliability/High validity

Sociologists do not always exclusively follow these positivist–interpretivist pathways. They might use a mixture of methods in order to produce both quantitative and qualitative data.

Now try this

1 What is the relationship between verstehen and validity?
2 What is the relationship between positivism and science?

Stages in the research design

Once the research topic and method have been chosen, the research will need to go through eight design stages.

 Hypothesis

A hypothesis or conjecture is an informed scientific guess that something might be true. It is what the sociologist wants to test, and may be based on observation, previous research or the theoretical position held by the researcher.

For example, a feminist researcher may be interested in the aim of gender equality and construct a hypothesis to uncover gender inequality or discrimination.

A Marxist might construct a hypothesis that aims to show that the UK is a class-divided society.

An example of a hypothesis could be: Children from middle-class families are educationally successful because they have access to economic, cultural and social capital.

 Choice of method

The next stage is to choose a method, which will depend on practical, ethical and theoretical (PET) factors (see pages 66–67).

 Research population

The sociologist then selects the research population that best suits the hypothesis.

For the given hypothesis, the research population might be A-level students and/or their parents because:

- A-level students are 'educationally successful' because they have reached that particular level of education
- parents have insight into the help they have given their children during their education.

 Operationalisation

The hypothesis will then be operationalised. This means it is broken down into observable and/or measurable parts.

For the given hypothesis, using a survey questionnaire would involve deciding on sets of questions which define and measure:

- 'middle-class' status (as well as 'working-class status' as a point of comparison)
- educational success (and at what level)
- economic, cultural and social capital.

 Sampling

The researcher then finds a sampling frame – a list of names (and addresses) of people who might be willing to take part in the research process. The sampling frame is used to randomly select a representative sample from the bigger research population. Random sampling is often preferred because it means that everybody on the sampling frame has an equal chance of being included in the sample. For more on sampling techniques, see page 69.

 Pilot study

A **pilot study** is a dress rehearsal of the research. It is carried out on a very small sample (a sub-sample) and aims to ensure that the research design is reliable and the data collected is likely to be valid or true to life.

For the given hypothesis, a pilot study can check that:

- the sampling frame is composed of people relevant to the research
- participants are interpreting the questions in the same way as the researcher
- the questions do not lead the participants
- the data collected closely reflects the reality of the research subjects.

 Research

The research is now carried out in full.

 Report writing

Once the research is completed, the researchers write up a report in order to present their findings. Most reports will contain explicit details of the research design and process so that other researchers can replicate and therefore verify the findings. Interpretivist sociologists are very keen on **reflexivity**. They often keep a detailed day-to-day diary critically documenting the research process, and how their own beliefs and opinions about the research topic may be affecting their relationship with the research sample and their analysis of the data.

Now try this

Outline the stages of the research process.

Sampling techniques

The **research population** is the group of people that a sociologist is studying. In some cases, it may be possible to survey every member of the research population because it is a small group, for example, a single class of students. In the majority of cases, however, it is impossible to study every individual so a **sample** is drawn to represent them.

Sampling frame

A representative sample is often achieved by randomly sampling names from a list of potential research subjects known as a **sampling frame**.

For example, school registers or staff lists when researching education. For other research, the electoral roll or the Postcode Address File®.

It is not always easy to find a suitable sampling frame.

For example, if researchers were looking at deviant groups, there is no sampling frame for truants or anti-school subcultures.

Random sampling

Random sampling means that every member of the research population (if their name appears on a sampling frame) has an equal chance of being included in the sample.

Random sampling aims to achieve objectivity and to eliminate the possibility of bias in the choice of those who take part in the research. There are two main types of random sampling techniques used by sociologists: **systematic** and **stratified sampling**.

Systematic sampling

In systematic sampling, the researcher picks people according to a system.

research population

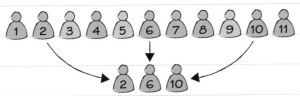

sample (every 4th)

For example, if there are 1000 people on the sampling frame, a number between 1 and 4 is randomly selected and every fourth name on the frame after that number is selected to take part in the research, thus producing a working sample of 250.

Stratified sampling

Stratified sampling involves dividing the frame into groups that reflect their presence in the larger group and then randomly selecting from those groups in a systematic way.

research population

strata

stratified samples

For example, a researcher interested in the experience of A-levels might subdivide his overall sixth-form group into Years 12 and 13, and males and females.

Non-random sampling

If a sampling frame is unavailable, researchers are forced to use non-random sampling techniques. However, all these techniques are likely to produce biased and unrepresentative samples.

Quota sampling: the researcher approaches a number of people (quota) who exhibit particular characteristics. However, quota sampling allows researchers some discretion and this may create the potential for bias. For example, researchers may only approach well-dressed men aged 25–40 years old in the street or city centre.

Non-random sampling techniques

Opportunity sampling: the researcher goes to a place that he or she knows will contain the type of person needed for the research. For example, a church for religious people or a sixth-form college for A-level students.

Snowball sampling: the researcher asks research subjects to identify others who might take part in the research, creating a snowball effect. For example, there is unlikely to be a sampling frame of heroin addicts so the researcher is dependent on any heroin addict they might encounter introducing them to other addicts.

Now try this

1. Why are non-random sampling techniques likely to produce unrepresentative samples?
2. Give examples of other sampling frames, apart from school registers.

Laboratory experiments

Social scientists use two types of experiment to collect **primary data** (see page 64): the **laboratory experiment**, preferred by positivists; and the **social** or **field experiment** (see page 71), preferred by interpretivists. The data is usually **quantitative**.

Variables

The laboratory allows scientists to manipulate, control and isolate possible causes or **independent variables (IV)** that result in particular effects or **dependent variables (DV)**.

For example, New Right sociologists aim to show that educational standards (DV) can be raised by increasing competition between schools (IV) and improving parental choice (IV).

Experimental and control groups

Experiments involve the setting up of two groups that are alike in every way. The **experimental group** is exposed to possible IVs and then compared to the **control group**, which is left to its own devices. Any difference (as measured by quantitative data) between the two groups is seen as a possible effect of an IV.

Evaluation

Positivists approve of the laboratory experiment because:

👍 **Practical** Hypotheses can be tested under controlled conditions.

👍 **Practical** Possible causes of events can be manipulated in turn and eventually isolated.

👍 **Practical** It is reliable and objective because it is repeatable and personal bias is excluded from the research process.

👍 **Practical** It produces lots of statistical data that can be compared for correlations.

👎 **Practical** It is impossible to get experimental and control groups of people who are exactly alike because people do not interpret things in the same way.

👎 **Practical** The **Hawthorne effect** – the presence of researchers – may result in the research subjects unconsciously changing their natural behaviour and behaving artificially.

👎 **Ethical** It is unethical to experiment on people without their knowledge or informed consent.

👎 **Theoretical** **Interpretivists** argue that social life is complex and probably cannot be reduced to variables that can be isolated or manipulated in a laboratory.

Laboratory experiments in educational research

Laboratory experiments have been carried out to investigate teacher expectations (**Harvey and Slatin**, 1976) and the use of technology in the classroom (**McGowan and Gunderson**, 2010). For more information, see page 61.

McGowan and Gunderson (2010) used a randomised experiment to investigate the use of clickers in undergraduate teaching.

Evaluation

👎 **Practical** It is difficult to reproduce the 'natural' conditions of the classroom and teacher–student interaction under laboratory conditions.

👎 **Practical** It is impossible to control all of the conditions in which education takes place because these often include external factors such as class, gender, ethnicity, parents, educational policy and so on.

👎 **Ethical** There are potential ethical problems.
For example, what if an experiment on teacher expectations results in student underachievement?

👎 **Theoretical** Interpretivists point out that it is difficult to distinguish whether what is being observed is natural behaviour or a reaction to the laboratory set-up. This is known as the '**Hawthorne effect**' after an experiment in a factory conducted by **Elton Mayo** in 1949.

Now try this

1 Why do positivist sociologists like laboratory experiments?

2 Outline how informed consent potentially undermines the reliability of the laboratory experiment.

3 Why do interpretivist sociologists dislike the laboratory experiment?

Social experiments

Social or field experiments are also used to collect **primary**, qualitative data (see page 64).

Characteristics of social experiments

Social experiments are carried out by **interpretivist** sociologists 'in the field' or natural environment (for example, a school playground or classroom) rather than under controlled laboratory conditions. The researcher manipulates a particular variable (the IV) and observes the reactions (the DV) of the group being studied. This group is usually unaware that a social experiment is taking place – the investigation is covert (see page 75). No control group is recruited. The researcher merely compares the behaviour of similar groups operating in a similar environment as the experimental group – for example, other students of the same age or teachers in a similar type of school.

The comparative method

The **natural** or **thought experiment** (also known as the 'comparative method') was first used by **Durkheim** (1897) as part of his classic study of suicide. It can also be used in an educational context.

For example, examination results from several schools could be compared in order to identify IVs crucial to success or failure such as class sizes, catchment areas and teaching methods.

Evaluation

👍 **Practical** It can be used to study the past.

👍 **Ethical** This type of experiment does not directly involve people, so there are no ethical concerns.

👎 **Theoretical** Some interpretivists are critical of this method because it fails to appreciate that statistics are socially constructed.

Evaluation

Interpretivists are in favour of social experiments for these reasons:

👍 **Theoretical** They can uncover the meanings or interpretations that underpin social behaviour – for example, why teachers treat students in the way that they do and how students react to teacher labels or stereotyping (see page 36).

👍 **Theoretical** They are carried out in the real world and so are more likely to measure natural, everyday behaviour.

👍 **Practical** They are more likely to produce qualitative information that is high in validity.

👎 **Ethical** They are often carried out without people's knowledge, which is unethical because it is deceptive.

👎 **Ethical** The experiment might have unethical results.

For example, social experiments on students might damage their confidence or alienate them from school, teachers or learning and produce failure.

👎 **Practical** The list of potential variables in any social situation is huge. The sociologist can never be quite sure whether the variable(s) they have 'isolated' are the cause of the behaviour/event.

Social experiments in educational research

Rosenthal and Jacobson (1968) examined the effects of teacher labelling on students in their study Pygmalion in the Classroom (see page 36). Their experiment has been heavily criticised.

Evaluation

👎 **Ethical** It is ethically suspect because the covert nature of the experiment meant they had not sought consent from teachers or parents of students.

👎 **Practical** They failed to verify their results (that the 20% of students labelled 'most intelligent' had reacted to this positive interaction by working harder) by carrying out any observation of classroom interaction between the teachers and the students.

👎 **Practical** It also failed to take account of other factors external to the school such as the home background of students and/or the role of economic and cultural capital on their education.

Now try this

1 Why are statistics criticised for being socially constructed?

2 Outline **three** ways in which the study of Rosenthal and Jacobson was 'ethically suspect'.

Survey questionnaires

Questionnaires are the main **primary method** for collecting extensive quantitative data (see page 64) from a large number of people in a relatively short period of time.

Questionnaires

Questionnaires consist of a list of questions, which can be distributed through the post, by hand, email or via mass media, for example magazines and on social media sites. A questionnaire may also be used in a formal or structured interview (see page 73).

Two types of questions are asked:

- **Closed** questions: respondents are invited to choose from a list that the researcher has compiled. The answers to these questions are easily quantified.

- **Open** questions: respondents are invited to answer as they wish in their own words. The answers to these questions will be qualitative.

Most questionnaires are made up of a combination of closed and open questions.

Questionnaire design

When the researcher designs a questionnaire, it is important that they minimise bias by avoiding certain types of questions, such as:

- **loaded or emotional questions** that elicit a predictable and invalid response.
  'Do you bully your fellow students?'

- **leading questions** that reflect the biases of the researcher are unlikely to elicit positive answers from teachers.
  'Do you think teachers often behave unfairly in the classroom?'

- **technical or complex questions** that use terms or concepts that only a sociologist would understand.
  'Do you think your chances of educational success were improved because you have access to cultural and social capital?'

Evaluation

👍 **Practical** Questionnaires can be distributed to large representative samples, including nationally.

👍 **Practical** A quick, low-cost and customer-friendly method because it is not time consuming.

👍 **Ethical** Little contact between the researcher and subjects so there are fewer ethical issues.

👍 **Ethical** Anonymity and confidentiality can be ensured.

Positivists like questionnaires for these reasons:

👍 **Theoretical** It is easy to quantify data and look for patterns and correlations.

👍 **Theoretical** The method is scientific – standardised, reliable and objective.

👎 **Practical** Response rates can be low (if postal).

👎 **Practical** People may misinterpret some questions or the wrong person might complete it.

Interpretivists dislike questionnaires because:

👎 **Theoretical** The responses may be invalid if people are economical with the truth.

👎 **Theoretical** Responses may be distorted by a desire to please the researcher or to seem respectable.

👎 **Theoretical** There is often a gap between what people say they do and what they actually do.

👎 **Theoretical** The **imposition problem** (see page 53) – the use of closed questions – limits choices and reduces validity.

Longitudinal studies

These surveys study the same group of people over a period of months or years.

The National Child Development Study has followed the same 40 000 children since 1958, collecting information on everything from educational development to social participation.

Evaluation

👍 **Theoretical** Researchers can establish trust with the research subjects, improving validity.

👍 **Practical** They can observe how long-term social factors such as class impact on people's lives.

👍 **Practical** Hypotheses can be changed or modified as the research progresses.

👎 **Theoretical** The researcher may get too friendly with research subjects, creating bias.

👎 **Practical** The sample may become unrepresentative as original members die, move away or drop out.

👎 **Practical** The research team may change or lose sight of their original goals.

Now try this

Why is a poor response rate a problem?

Structured interviews

Social scientists also carry out **interviews** to collect **primary data** (see page 64). There are different types of interview: **structured, semi-structured** and **unstructured interviews; group interviews** and **focus groups**. For more information on unstructured and group interviews and focus groups, see page 74.

Structured or formal interviews

Structured or formal interviews are preferred by **positivists**. The researcher sticks rigidly to reading out the same set of mainly closed questions, in the same order, from a questionnaire (known as an interview schedule) to each interviewee and records their responses. This may be simply ticking boxes or multiple-choice answers, or writing down, word for word, the interviewee's answers. The data collected is usually quantitative.

Structured interviews are preferred by positivists.

Semi-structured interviews

Many interviews are semi-structured – a mix of closed and open questions that collect both quantitative and qualitative data. Open questions allow the interviewer some flexibility to ask for clarification of vague answers.

For example, they can invite a respondent to expand on their answer and ask them to give examples.

The reliability of semi-structured interviews has been questioned by interpretivists because an interviewer might find that some interviewees need more probing than others. This may mean that every interview is different and data may not be comparable.

Demand characteristics

Demand characteristics refer to the interviewees' attempts to interpret the researcher's motives or aims, and in doing so changing their behaviour. Interpretivists argue that the validity of data collected by interviews can be badly affected by demand characteristics.

For example, interviewees may:
- exaggerate behaviour to impress the researcher
- work out what answers would please the researcher
- over-report 'positive' behaviour (e.g. giving to charity) or under-report 'negative' behaviour (e.g. smacking children) to manage the researcher's opinion and impression of them.

Evaluation

👍 **Practical** An interviewer can ensure that the right person responds to the questions.

👍 **Practical** They can explain the aims of the research and clarify what questions mean.

👍 **Practical** Interviews are better for people with low literacy skills.

👍 **Practical** They achieve a better response rate than questionnaires.

👍 **Practical** They can be conducted with large numbers of people.

👎 **Practical** Training interviewers can be expensive.

Positivists like interviews for these reasons:

👍 **Theoretical** They produce lots of quantitative data.

👍 **Theoretical** They are scientific – repeatable and therefore reliable.

Interpretivists dislike interviews for these reasons:

👎 **Theoretical** They suffer from the imposition problem (see page 53).

👎 **Theoretical** Structured interviews are inflexible – validity is undermined because the researcher cannot follow up interesting responses or ask probing questions.

👎 **Theoretical** Interviews are an artificial device – people may respond to them with suspicion and give false information.

👎 **Theoretical** Interview bias may cause people to respond negatively to the status or characteristics of the interviewer. Teenagers, for example, may associate researchers with authority and be reluctant to talk.

👎 **Theoretical** Social desirability – over-reporting of desirable behaviour and under-reporting of undesirable actions.

Now try this

1 How might interviewees respond negatively to the status of the interviewer?
2 What sort of behaviour might be over-reported because interviewees see it as 'desirable'?

Unstructured and group interviews

Unstructured and group interviews are used to collect **primary**, qualitative data (see page 64).

Unstructured or informal interviews

This type of interview is preferred by **interpretivists**. It resembles an informal conversation in which the interviewer asks open-ended questions of respondents. Interviewers are trained to be skilled in building trust and rapport with their interviewees by acquiring listening and empathetic skills.

Group interviews and focus groups

Group interviews: researchers interview several people at the same time	Focus groups: a variation on the group interview
They are often conducted with children who might not be willing to open up to an adult in a one-to-one interview. The presence of other children, especially friends, may increase their confidence in speaking to an interviewer.	A panel of adults is introduced to an issue or debate via some sort of stimulus (a short film or image) and is encouraged to discuss this as a group. This group conversation is recorded.
The interviewer directly questions the group but many of the questions asked will be flexible and highly dependent on the responses given to previous questions by the children. The sociologist will probe responses and ask members of the group whether they share the same meaning as each other in terms of attitudes or behaviour.	The sociologist does not directly question the group but focus group members are encouraged to question each other.
This type of interview produces qualitative data because the data is often expressed in the words of the children.	Observation and analysis of the focus group's interaction produces lots of qualitative data in the form of the transcript (see page 64).
The validity of the data may be undermined if some children are too shy or fearful of bullying to respond honestly.	However, the validity of the data may be undermined if one or two strong personalities dominate and influence other participants' opinions.

Evaluation

👍 **Theoretical** The interview is not restricted by a schedule; the researcher can follow up responses and probe for further details, which improves the validity of the data.

Interpretivists claim the following:

👍 **Theoretical** Trust and rapport are established through use of empathy and good listening skills, thus increasing validity.

👍 **Theoretical** Validity is established through involvement – authentic qualitative data is obtained by getting close to people's experiences and interpretations of reality.

👍 **Theoretical** The data generated often result in unexpected findings, and the hypothesis can be modified as the research progresses.

👎 **Practical** Time consuming and expensive compared with questionnaires and structured interviews.

👎 **Practical** If people are unaware of how they behave, trust and rapport will make no difference to the quality of responses.

👎 **Practical** Demand characteristics may undermine interview results (see page 73).

Positivists claim the following:

👎 **Theoretical** The method is unscientific and unreliable as interviews are not standardised, controlled or repeatable.

👎 **Theoretical** Trust and empathy may undermine the objectivity of the research.

👎 **Theoretical** Qualitative data is difficult to analyse.

👎 **Theoretical** This type of research is less representative because fewer people take part in it.

Now try this

1　Why are demand characteristics less likely to be a problem with unstructured interviews?

2　Why are unstructured interviews regarded as unscientific by positivist sociologists?

Observation

Participant and **non-participant observation** are **primary methods** of research. They generally produce **qualitative data** (see page 64), often in the words of those being observed.

Participant observation

Participant observation (PO) involves the researcher taking an active part in the daily lives of the group being studied. It can be **overt** or **covert**.

Overt participant observation

Overt PO involves the researcher participating in the same activities of the group being researched and openly observing their everyday lives. Overt means that the group being studied knows that the researcher is observing them.

Covert participant observation

Covert PO involves the researcher taking on a false identity and infiltrating a social group without their knowledge. The researcher therefore has to 'act' a role and convince members of a group that they are genuine.

Non-participant observation

In some studies, the researcher simply observes a social group without participating in their activities. Non-participant observation can also be overt or covert.

Overt direct observation

The researcher is given consent to observe a group, for example students in a playground or classroom. They use an observation schedule – a coding sheet specifying the categories of behaviour or events to be observed, and under what circumstances. Observations should therefore be standardised and easily replicated. However, this may produce an observer effect (also known as the Hawthorne effect), where the presence of the researcher may result in the group unconsciously changing their natural behaviour and behaving artificially.

Covert direct observation

The researcher watches a group without their knowledge, for example via CCTV. As the researcher's presence is unknown, there should be no observer effect among the group being observed. The researcher should be detached and objective as their job is to simply quantify types of behaviour. However, covert observation is often criticised for ethical reasons because it involves deceit, there is no informed consent and it may involve the researcher observing or being involved in deviant activities.

Evaluation

Interpretivists claim the following:

👍 (Theoretical) This method has high validity because it is an ethnographic approach – the sociologist spends time in the everyday natural world of the respondent and sees social action as it unfolds.

👍 (Theoretical) Achieves verstehen (see page 67).

👍 (Theoretical) It gets the researcher closer to the behaviour being studied than any other method.

👍 (Practical) Covert PO is often the only way to get data about closed environments or deviant groups.

👍 (Theoretical) It avoids the pitfalls of questionnaires and interviews because the sociologist can see what people really do as they do it.

👍 (Theoretical) Observation may result in behaviour the sociologist did not expect, so hypotheses can be modified as the research progresses.

👍 (Theoretical) Observations can be cross-checked by asking questions of the group, increasing validity.

Positivists claim the following:

👎 (Theoretical) There may be an observer or Hawthorne effect and so behaviour may be artificial.

👎 (Theoretical) The sociologist may 'go native' and become too attached to the group, thus losing their objectivity and being biased.

👎 (Theoretical) Observations are often the subjective views of the researcher.

👎 (Theoretical) The method is unscientific because it lacks reliability – it cannot be repeated for verification.

👎 (Theoretical) The qualitative data gathered is very difficult to quantify and analyse.

👎 (Practical) It can take years to complete and consequently is a very expensive method.

👎 (Theoretical) Observation studies are usually small-scale and therefore unrepresentative.

Now try this

1 Suggest why positivists might dislike participant observation.

2 What is covert observation?

Official statistics

Official statistics are **secondary sources** of **quantitative data** (see page 64). They are mainly gathered by state agencies. However, other agencies – political parties, trade unions, charities, businesses and think-tanks – also produce statistical data. Official statistics are often used by sociologists in conjunction with primary research methods.

Statistics and science

Positivist sociologists see official statistics as **scientific** because they are often the product of well-planned and organised surveys such as the **Census**.

The UK Census

The UK Census, which began in 1801, is a 10-yearly survey questionnaire carried out by the government. Every household in the UK is sent a questionnaire to fill in. Failure to fill in the Census can result in legal prosecution. Thus, the response rate for the 2011 Census was 94%.

The UK Census produces masses of statistical data on most aspects of British social life including size of household, occupational status, religious affiliation, educational qualifications, car ownership and so on.

Types of official statistics

There are two types of official statistics:

1 **Hard statistics** are facts that, once certified, cannot be changed. They are the product of accurate and objective counting processes undertaken by the state.

For example, births and deaths have to be officially registered; marriages and divorces are legally registered; A-level exam results are the product of objective examinations.

2 According to interpretivists, **soft statistics** are not facts because they are the product of subjective decisions and choices made by particular powerful individuals.

For example, crime statistics depend on a victim coming forward to report the crime and a police officer recording their situation as a crime or not. Schools are meant to record 'racist' incidents. Some may be rigorous in collecting such data, while others may deal with racist incidents informally and not record them.

The problem of social construction

Interpretivists are critical of some official statistics, such as for crime and suicide, because they believe they are socially constructed – the statistics tell us more about the values and priorities of the people involved in their collection than they do about the people surveyed. Such statistics are therefore not objective or value-free (see page 65).

For example, some statistics produced by schools and used in their publicity materials may reflect the need of schools to positively market themselves to parents. So, some heads may choose to construct definitions of what counts as 'attendance' and 'truancy', choosing to define these activities in a very narrow way compared with other schools.

Evaluation

👍 **Theoretical** Positivists see official statistics as scientific – they are reliable, representative, valid, generalisable and objective.

👍 **Practical** Statistics are easily accessible (through the internet) and cheap.

👍 **Practical** They are usually up to date and cover trends over time and large populations.

👍 **Practical** They can be used comparatively (exam results of boys and girls).

👍 **Theoretical** They allow researchers to see correlations (see page 64).

👎 **Practical** Official definitions of an event or trend may differ to those used by sociologists.
For example, they may each define poverty differently.

👎 **Practical** They may be biased or partial because they have been gathered for political purposes.
For example, 'unemployment' statistics may be manipulated by changing its definition.

👎 **Theoretical** According to interpretivists, statistics tell us very little about people's experiences, attitudes and feelings.

Now try this

1 Give **one** example of a 'hard' statistic and **one** example of a 'soft' statistic relating to education.

2 What is the UK Census?

Personal documents

Personal documents (sometimes called 'expressive documents') are **secondary** sources of qualitative data (see page 64). They include diaries, letters, memoirs, photos, emails and blogs, which may express the experiences, feelings, attitudes and motives of particular social groups.

Life documents

Personal documents are also known as **life documents** because they subjectively record stages in a person's life. **Interpretivists** believe they can reveal the social meanings that shape behaviour and give insight into how certain individuals and groups interact and interpret social reality.

Scott (1990) argued that if sociologists intend to use personal documents, especially historical ones, they need to ask four key questions:

1 Is the document **authentic**, for example is there proof of authorship?

2 Is the content of the document **credible** or plausible, or does it contain inaccuracies?

3 Is the document **representative** of the social group the sociologist is investigating?

4 Is the **meaning** of the document clear?

Scott points out that documents are easily forged, that authors tend to write such documents for selfish rather than sociological reasons and, consequently, it is common for sociologists to misinterpret what the author is saying.

Diaries

Research subjects are sometimes asked to keep diaries about how they spend their time (time budgeting) and how they feel about certain activities. Diaries are secondary data because they are written or recorded first-hand by the research subjects rather than by the researcher.

Diaries have been used by feminist researchers to make visible the experiences of marginalised groups (e.g. housewives and pregnant women).

Oakley (1974) asked housewives to keep a record of how they felt about the everyday experience of being responsible for housework and childcare.

Researchers may ask those they are observing to keep diaries in order to achieve **respondent validation** – the diary can verify data collected by primary research methods. Researchers may also keep a journal documenting the social process of research so that they can be **reflexive** – they can comment on how they interacted with research subjects and be vigilant for any potential bias.

Evaluation

Interpretivists like personal documents for these reasons:

👍 **Theoretical** They are highly valid sources of data because they document how people interpret daily life.

👍 **Theoretical** They are usually **ethnographic** because they document the natural environment and period in which the research subject lives.

👍 **Practical** They can be used alongside primary research methods to give a more rounded picture of what is being studied.

👍 **Ethical** They may be the only source of data for past events, especially if what they describe is too dangerous, sensitive or unethical for sociologists to research.

👍 **Practical** It is a cheap source of data compared with primary research methods.

👍 **Practical** Diaries are suited to longitudinal studies (see page 72) – the diarists can comment on events as they unfold over a period of time.

👎 **Ethical** Permission to use particular letters and diaries might be denied because of their confidential content.

Positivists dislike them for these reasons:

👎 **Theoretical** Few people voluntarily and consistently keep diaries – they are not a representative source.

👎 **Practical** Their authenticity and/or credibility might be questionable.

👎 **Theoretical** They are unreliable because their content cannot usually be cross-checked and verified.

👎 **Theoretical** The content may lack validity because the writer is only giving their version of events.

👎 **Theoretical** They are a subjective rather than objective source and lack scientific status because they are not standardised, reliable or quantifiable.

Now try this

1 What is respondent validation?

2 Define 'reflexivity'.

Public and historical documents

Public documents are **secondary** sources of both qualitative and quantitative data. They are produced by government departments or state agencies such as Ofsted, as well as companies, charities and other organisations. Public documents may be contemporary or historical.

Types

There are several types of public documents, some of which may overlap with official statistics (see page 76).

Major reports by governments such as White Papers, or reports produced by public enquiries.
For example, the investigations into the police response to the Hillsborough disaster and the murder of Stephen Lawrence.

Documents that report on the specific activities of individual organisations such as Parliament (Hansard records verbatim all parliamentary debates) and schools (Ofsted reports).

Many organisations – e.g. schools, colleges and universities – produce written **publicity materials** for marketing purposes aimed at parents and prospective students.

Types

Media reports in all their varied forms, including newspapers, magazines, adverts, films, radio and television programmes.

Internet content such as Facebook groups, learner chatrooms, blogs, Wikipedia and Reddit forums. Many organisations maintain websites that contain information about their services.

Uses

It is rare for documents to be the exclusive focus of sociological research, although media reports may be subject to **content analysis** – a primary quantitative technique for systematically describing the content of documents (qualitative secondary sources). However, a study of documents may form part of:

- the **background research** – they can be quite helpful in helping the researcher formulate a hypothesis
- a **triangulation approach** – documents might be used to check the reliability and validity of primary research methods (questionnaires, interviews and observations – see pages 72–75)
- a **plural approach** aimed at adding another layer of understanding.

For example, looking at school publicity materials as well as interviewing parents and observing classes to assess the impact of a particular school on a particular group of students.

Evaluation

Positivists like public documents for these reasons:

👍 (Theoretical) They are usually the product of standardised and reliable research methods.

👍 (Theoretical) They aim to provide an objective overview of events or social phenomena.

👍 (Practical) They allow sociologists to access the past and document historical change.

👍 (Practical) They are often easily accessible via government websites.

👍 (Practical) Their use saves time.

👍 (Practical) They are cheaper to use than primary research methods.

👍 (Practical) Their use avoids the potential bias involved in contact with research subjects.

👍 (Theoretical) They provide qualitative insight into how their authors see or interpret social reality.

Interpretivists dislike them for these reasons:

👎 (Theoretical) The authenticity of historical documents can sometimes be questioned.

👎 (Theoretical) It is difficult to check and verify the credibility of historical documents.

👎 (Theoretical) Documents may be biased because they may reflect the political and ideological biases of their source.

👎 (Practical) Official documents may be censored so that they exclude 'sensitive' information.

👎 (Practical) Public documents may not exist for subjects that interest sociologists.

👎 (Practical) Their content may be misinterpreted because the author is not available to clarify it.

👎 (Theoretical) There is no guarantee that documents are representative (historical) or reliable (internet).

Now try this

1 What is content analysis?
2 Outline **two** problems in using reports taken from the internet.

Functionalism: consensus theory

It is important to be able to illustrate knowledge and understanding of the functionalist theory of society in some depth. Functionalists believe that societies evolve and run by consensus.

Society as a system

The functionalist sociologist **Talcott Parsons** (1970) sees three similarities between society and the systems of biological organisms, summed up by the acronym **SSNF**.

S **System**: society and biological organisms (such as the human body) are systems comprised of inter-dependent parts, which function for the greater good of the whole.

SN **System needs**: organisms have needs that must be met. Social institutions have evolved in order to meet society's needs.

F **Functions**: each part of a biological organism has developed in order to function for the greater good of the organism, and would not exist without a need for it. Social institutions have evolved functions which benefit society as a whole.

Durkheim (1912) argued that all religions functioned to socialise people into moral codes of behaviour and to bring communities together.

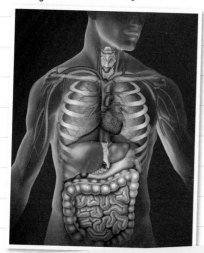

Functionalists view society as working like the human body.

Functional prerequisites

From the organic analogy, the method of functional analysis has developed to explain why institutions exist in terms of the **function** they perform for society. **Parsons** (1951) suggests that there are four basic needs (or functional **prerequisites**) that all societies have to satisfy.

1 **Goal attainment** (the political function): societies must develop ways of setting goals and making decisions about how power and economic resources should be allocated.

2 **Adaptation** (the economic function): every society has to provide an adequate standard of life for the survival of its members.

3 **Integration** (social harmony): each institution in society develops in response to particular functions. However, there is no guarantee that the different institutions will not develop elements that conflict. Specialist institutions therefore develop that seek to limit conflict and to bring about consensus or agreement on common values. Education, mass media and religions are often responsible for encouraging a sense of belonging to society.

4 **Latency**: this refers to the unstated consequences of actions (the stated purpose of education is to transmit knowledge and skills but its latent or hidden function may be to promote a sense of belonging to society). Parsons claims that there are two types of latency:

Pattern maintenance: the young are socialised into believing in the same sets of values and patterns of behaviour as older members of society.
The family is the primary agent of such socialisation.

Tension management: society can be very stressful for individuals - this tension needs to be managed by social institutions such as the family in order to prevent potential disorder and dysfunction.

Social roles

Functionalists argue that the functions of each social institution within the wider social system can be explained in terms of these functional prerequisites. Each institution has certain **social roles** (positions associated with particular socially expected norms of behaviour).

For example, the family includes the key roles of husband and wife who perform instrumental/economic roles and expressive/emotional roles respectively.

The existence of shared roles and norms results in societies that are relatively ordered because they are underpinned by consensus or agreement. (See page 171 for the functions of crime according to Durkheim.)

Now try this

Identify the **four** functional prerequisites, or basic needs, that must be met by the social institutions that make up the social system or society.

Functionalism and social change

Talcott Parsons' (1961) theory of social change is an important aspect of the functionalist theory of society. However, Parsons has been criticised both by fellow functionalists (**Merton**) and by conflict theories.

Social change and structural differentiation

Societies do not stay static – they undergo **social change**. Parsons argues that some societies are based on traditional values and roles of **pattern variables (PV)**. However, they evolve into more complex PVs and consequently 'modern societies' via a process of **structural differentiation**. Traditional societies rely on two institutions to carry out most functions: religion and families. In contrast, modern industrial societies develop new, more efficient specialist institutions in response to new functions or needs. For example, schools, colleges and universities take over the educational functions from families.

Traditional societies: pattern variables	Modern societies: pattern variables
Status is **ascribed** at birth.	Status is **earned or achieved** through hard work.
Diffuse relationships – usually with kin to satisfy a large range of general needs. E.g. mother and child.	**Specific contractual relationships** with individuals to meet **a specific need**. E.g. employer and employee.
Particularism – people may receive special treatment because they are a member of a particular group. E.g. tribal members will show loyalty to one another.	**Universality** – everybody is treated in the same way. E.g. everybody is equal before the law.
Affectivity – people aim to satisfy their needs immediately.	**Affective neutrality** – people defer or postpone their need for gratification. E.g. studying rather than earning to qualify for a job later.
Collective orientation – people put the needs of the group first.	**Self-orientation** – people selfishly put their own needs before the group to which they belong.

Merton's internal critique of functionalism

Robert Merton (1968) suggests that Parsons failed to realise the distinction between:
- **manifest** or intended functions
- **latent** or unintended consequences of the actions of social institutions – these may not always be functional or beneficial; they may even be dysfunctional or harmful.

Merton says that this makes any analysis of society much more complex than Parsons' simple model.

For example, religion has the manifest function of bringing people together. It also has latent functions: comforting people in times of need (positive) or encouraging people to see unbelievers as a threat (dysfunctional).

Theoretical critiques of functionalism

Sharrock et al. (2003) argue that there are several main criticisms of functionalism:

👎 Marxists and feminists argue that it overemphasises the level of consensus in society and fails to account for how conflict may result in social change.

👎 Similarly, Parsons seems to ignore differences in power. Yet these can have a strong impact upon the form that society takes and what interests it reflects.

👎 **Wrong** (1961) criticises the determinism of the Parsons' positivist model of society from a **social action** or interpretivist perspective (see page 13). He claims that Parsons views people like puppets having their strings pulled by all-powerful societies. Parsons therefore fails to appreciate that people are much more 'reflexive', making choices and socially constructing their own lives.

👎 The organic or biological analogy may be over-stated because society is a concept which has no natural lifecycle or form.

👎 Functionalism confuses effects with causes. It claims to explain why social institutions exist, but actually only explains the effects of those institutions. **Holborn** (2016) observes that the fact that something is needed does not explain how and why it developed in the first place.

👎 Postmodernists claim functionalism does not account for the diversity and instability within societies today, such as why different types of family meet basic needs as well as the nuclear family.

Now try this

Identify **two** ways in which pattern variables must change if a traditional society is to evolve into a modern society.

Neo-Marxism: conflict theory

Neo-Marxism developed in the 20th century from classical Marxist theory. There are three types of neo-Marxism: humanist Marxism, the Frankfurt School and structuralist Marxism.

Types of neo-Marxism

1 **Humanistic Marxism** overlaps with social action theory to argue that workers are active agents who can use their free will and choose to resist capitalism. The ideas of the neo-Marxist 'New Criminology' (see page 177) are influenced by this.

2 **The Frankfurt School** of Marxism is associated with **Marcuse** (1964) and **Adorno** (1991) who criticise Marx for being an economic determinist (for believing society is mainly determined by the economic system). They argue that workers' ideas and motivations are more important than Marx acknowledged.

3 **Structuralist/scientific Marxism** mainly focuses on the superstructure of capitalist society.

1 Humanistic Marxism

Antonio Gramsci (1971) rejects the traditional Marxist idea that economic forces or the infrastructure mainly determine the workers' experience of capitalist society.

Ideology

Gramsci focused on the role of the superstructure and, particularly, **ideology**. He argued that the capitalist state could not impose its will on the population. Rather, it needed the **consent of the people** to rule and this depended on its ability to persuade through the use of ideology.

Cultural hegemony

The bourgeoisie have won consent to rule from society because the agencies that make up the superstructure (especially the education system and the mass media) have:

- successfully persuaded society of the legitimacy of ruling-class ideology, so achieving cultural domination or hegemony
- offered concessions such as the Welfare State to the population.

However, this consent is not easily won or guaranteed. It has to be constantly readjusted and renegotiated.

Ideas and social change

Workers have a **dual-consciousness**. The daily experience of exploitation at work means that the working class is able to see through ruling-class ideology and develop their own ideas. Such ideas may challenge inequality in capitalist societies, force concessions from the dominant social class and even bring about social change.

2 The Frankfurt School

Three important ideas can be seen in the work of the Frankfurt Marxists.

Instrumental reason

Marx failed to explore people's motivations for accepting capitalism and consumer goods. It was wrong of Marx to dismiss this as '**false-consciousness**'. People work hard to have a career and earn money, so it is important to understand why workers rationally choose to work in conditions which they recognise as exploitative (**Adorno**, 1991).

Mass culture

Marcuse (1964) stresses the role of mass or popular culture in the exploitation of the working-class. He argued that the mass media replaced religion as the main means of maintaining ruling class power. The role of popular entertainment was to distract the working-class from inequality and to discourage critical thinking.

The media's focus on trivial entertainment such as television soap operas and football distract working-class attention away from inequality and injustice.

The oppression of personality

The personalities and desires of workers are controlled and directed to the benefit of capitalism. Advertisers encourage workers as consumers to pursue 'false needs'. Sex is also now used to sell a wide range of products. Our wants and desires are manipulated by capitalists in the interests of profit (**Marcuse**, 1964).

Now try this

Outline **three** ways in which hegemony is achieved by the ruling class.

Structuralist Marxism and evaluation

Structuralist/scientific Marxism mainly focuses on the relationship between the **infrastructure** and **superstructure** of capitalist society.

③ Structuralist/scientific Marxism

Louis Althusser (1969) argued that capitalist societies were made up of four components.

The **economic system** or infrastructure is responsible for the manufacture of goods and is also the source of inequality. It exercises control over most aspects of society.

The superstructure or **ideological state apparatuses** such as education and the media. These disseminate ruling-class ideology, which aims to reproduce and legitimate class inequality (see diagram on page 10).

Capitalist society

The **political system** or state is the most important part of the superstructure. It can choose to exercise ideological or repressive power.

The **repressive state apparatuses** – the ruling class sometimes has to use force such as the police or military to impose its will on the people.

Althusser's ideas are neo-Marxist because he did not believe that the **superstructure** (the political and ideological systems) solely functioned to justify the inequality and exploitation found in the economic system. Althusser believed that both politics and the ideas produced in the superstructure could be '**relatively autonomous**', meaning that political movements and ideas critical of capitalism could develop.

Like Humanist Marxism, structural Marxism concludes that the capitalist class chooses to rule by **consent** rather than repressive force or coercion because ideology is so persuasive in convincing the working class that capitalism is both a just and legitimate system.

Structuralist/scientific Marxism:
- sees itself as **scientific** because it aims to discover the laws that underpin capitalism
- is a **positivist** approach because it sees structural forces – particularly those that originate in the ruling class ideology produced by the superstructure – as largely determining or shaping individual thoughts and actions.

Evaluation of the three types of neo-Marxism

👍 Humanistic Marxism has influenced studies of working-class 'lads' in education, such as **Willis** (1977) and **Corrigan** (1979), as well as **Taylor, Walton and Young** (1973) in the field of crime and **Maduro's** (1982) idea that religion may play a progressive role in the political struggles of the oppressed classes.

👍 Structuralist Marxism has also influenced studies of education, most notably the work of **Bowles and Gintis** (1976) and **Bourdieu** (1986).

👎 Humanistic Marxism may be accused of understating the influence of economic factors and overstating free will and choice. Workers may have no choice but to consent to rule by the bourgeoisie if the alternative is starvation or poverty for their families.

👎 Humanistic Marxism may underestimate the resolve of the bourgeoisie to use the coercive powers of the state to impose their will on workers or those who rise up against them. For example, using the police against striking workers in the UK.

👎 Although Althusser rejects the economic determinism of Marx, he has merely replaced it with **structural determinism** – people's thoughts and actions are now shaped by ideological state apparatuses. People are still the puppets of society.

👎 Marxism may be undermined by globalisation (see page 86). Evidence suggests that people in the UK who occupy precarious zero-hour jobs do not define themselves in terms of their work in the same way as previous generations who expressed tribal loyalty to their social class and their class representatives, such as trade unions and the Labour Party. There are signs that this tribal loyalty to a working-class consciousness may be at an end and other forms of identity (gender, ethnicity, religion, sexuality, age) may now be just as important as social class in determining how people choose to act with regard to their social position in modern societies.

Now try this

Why do some critics see little difference between Marxism and Althusser's neo-Marxism?

Triple systems theory and postmodern feminism

It is important to be able to illustrate a sophisticated and detailed knowledge and understanding of the **conflict perspective of feminism** for the two-year A Level course. See also pages 11–12 for more on feminism.

Triple systems theory

Sylvia Walby (1992) has attempted to draw together the three broad ideas of liberal, Marxist and radical feminism. She argues that patriarchy intersects with capitalism and racism to produce a triple form of gender inequality which is underpinned by six key patriarchal social structures.

P A T R I A R C H Y

(2) Family: the distribution of housework and childcare tasks within families disadvantages females.

(4) The state: acts in the interests of men, particularly with regard to taxation and welfare. Laws protecting women from abuse or discrimination are weakly enforced.

(6) Violence: some men use a variety of violent techniques (domestic violence, threat of violence, rape) to control women.

(1) Economy: when women enter work, they generally experience lower pay and status than men. There is evidence that employers discriminate against women.

(3) Mass media: represents females in a narrow range of social roles. For example, as sex objects or as mothers, wives and girlfriends rather than as people in their own right.

(5) Personal relationships: a double-standard exists with regard to sexual relationships. Men are encouraged to be sexually active whilst women are negatively labelled if they behave in the same way as men.

Evaluation

🗩 **Walby** (2007) criticises post-structuralist perspectives for being too academic, overly concerned with language and irrelevant in terms of suggesting practical solutions to women's problems. Walby accepts that there are differences between groups of women, but observes that there are more similarities in how women generally experience patriarchy.

For example, older women, poorly qualified young women and single parents all suffer similar patriarchal disadvantages.

🗩 Post-structuralists pay little attention to the use of violence by all classes of men to control women.

Essentialism and ethnocentricity

Essentialism is the idea that women have a universal experience of patriarchy and this is similar the world over. This is seen as a weakness of the three forms of feminism.

Western feminists may be guilty of **ethnocentrism**. They have evaluated the experience of women in other cultures according to their own cultural experience of patriarchy and have failed to appreciate the global diversity of women's oppression.

Postmodern or post-structuralist feminism

Postmodern feminism rejects essentialism. It emphasises differences between groups of women based on a whole range of characteristics.

For example, the divisions between lesbian and heterosexual women, different classes and ethnic groups, and different ages.

Post-structuralist feminism highlights the importance of language and performativity in the production of patriarchal society. It argues that **discourses** (ways of seeing, thinking or using language) underpin debate about the way less powerful groups are perceived and treated. Some groups can be disempowered by the dominant language used about them.

For example, assertive or ambitious women can be disempowered by using words like 'hysterical' or 'pushy'.

Cixous (1993) describes language as **phallocentric** – male-dominated and reflecting a male view of the world. Post-structuralism argues that significant social changes can result from changing the way language is used.

Judith Butler (1990) focuses on how language and **performativity** (everyday body gestures and movements) contribute to the social construction of gender and sexuality, and the idea that there are essential and fixed differences between men and women and between heterosexuals and gay people. She argues that society needs to adopt a broader, more fluid definition of what constitutes gender identity. For example, UK Facebook users can choose from 71 gender options.

Now try this

Outline how postmodern feminism differs from post-structuralist feminism.

Social action theory: phenomenology

In many ways, **Max Weber** was the founding father of social action theory because he was the first sociologist to focus on the subjective meanings that people attach to their actions.

Max Weber (1905)

Weber observed that there were different sets of social meanings that helped to account for social action. He categorised different types of social action according to the social meanings that underpinned them.

1 **Instrumental actions** are underpinned by rational social meanings. The individual has calculated the benefits of their actions and weighed them up against their possible costs. This idea influenced **Cornish and Clarke's** (1986) cost–benefit analysis of crime (see page 181).

2 **Affectual actions** are underpinned by emotional or irrational meanings such as unconditional love and loyalty to family, religious fervour and devotion, belief in radical political ideology and actions initiated by feelings such as passion, hate, anger and grief.

Phenomenology

Phenomenology emphasises that all information about the social world is the product of the human mind. It therefore sets out to understand the shared social meanings that people use to make sense of the social world around them. Phenomenologists therefore aim to study how people experience social action and how, in order to make sense of their world, they organise elements of it into social categories called **phenomena**.

Phenomena

Phenomena are things which are held to have characteristics in common according to our senses.

For example, our ability to see allows us to construct the category of 'dog', which includes a range of animals with different characteristics (such as Alsatians and Yorkshire terriers).

Schutz (1972) calls these shared categorisations '**typifications**'. We use our commonsense interpretations to categorise all of these breeds under the typification or category 'dog'.

The emphasis is on the subjective nature of the categorisation. For example, when we look at a hamster, we do not think 'dog'.

Purpose of phenomenology

How the world is categorised is a matter of human choice rather than an objective process. The purpose of phenomenology is to understand the essence of phenomena – the essential characteristics which lead to something being placed in a particular mental category. Phenomenologists believe that research should be faithful to the phenomenon as it is lived, which means observing and understanding it in the natural context of the person or group being researched.

For example, the reason why certain people are categorised by journalists and the general public as 'welfare dependents' and 'scroungers' whilst other people with similar characteristics are not.

The phenomenological view of suicide

Steve Taylor (1988) applied a phenomenological analysis to suicide. He suggests suicide victims mentally categorise the phenomenon of suicidal action into two broad categories.

1 **Purposive:** the victim is certain he or she wants to die because they interpret their circumstances as irrevocably negative and suicide is perceived to be the only way out.

2 **Ordeal suicides** stem from a profound sense of psychological uncertainty. This is usually an attempt by suicidal individuals to gauge how important they are to significant others. Ordeals are therefore suicidal acts of uncertainty.

Now try this

How do phenomenologists define 'phenomena'?

Ethnomethodology and structuration

Ethnomethodology is closely related to phenomenology and is mainly associated with **Garfinkel** (1988). Some sociologists, notably Giddens, have increasingly tried to combine the **structural** and **social action approaches**, arguing that both aspects of society must be considered for a full understanding of how societies work.

Ethnomethodology

Ethnomethodology is a specialised interpretivist approach that aims to analyse how people construct and make sense of routine social activity by uncovering the commonsense rules that govern all social interactions and situations. People unconsciously share complex unwritten rules using this commonsensical knowledge.

Reflexivity

Garfinkel believes that the social meanings that people share cannot be taken for granted because they are potentially unclear. He was interested in what he called **reflexivity** – the way that two individuals in a social interaction will mirror each other's behaviour and talk in such a way that the interaction makes sense to the pair of them.

For example, a typical opening exchange might include sharing general information about the weather.

Investigating social meaning

Ethnomethodologists believe that we only become aware of these rules and their social meaning when they break down. Garfinkel has used two methods to illustrate these ideas.

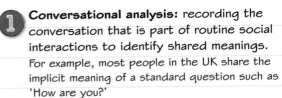 **Conversational analysis:** recording the conversation that is part of routine social interactions to identify shared meanings.

For example, most people in the UK share the implicit meaning of a standard question such as 'How are you?'

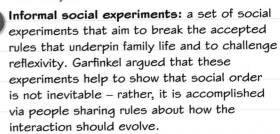 **Informal social experiments:** a set of social experiments that aim to break the accepted rules that underpin family life and to challenge reflexivity. Garfinkel argued that these experiments help to show that social order is not inevitable – rather, it is accomplished via people sharing rules about how the interaction should evolve.

Evaluation of ethnomethodology

👍 It challenges the idea that people are the puppets of society. It suggests that all social behaviour is socially constructed and depends on the unconscious sharing and mirroring of commonsensical rules about how interaction and conversation should be conducted.

👎 Many sociologists dismiss ethnomethodology as self-indulgent, mainly because its findings are interpreted as too trivial, especially by structuralist sociologists.

👎 Structuralists argue that all everyday reality is still influenced by social forces such as social class, patriarchy and power structures, which are beyond the control of most individuals.

Structuration theory

Giddens' (1984) theory of structuration argues that **structure** and **action** are two sides of the same coin and neither can be examined in isolation – structures make social action possible.

For example, political leaders require the structure of the state in order to put their actions into effect.

The duality of structure

These structures are produced, reproduced and maintained through the repetition of social actions by the individuals who make up social institutions. Structures therefore facilitate actions, which in turn reproduce structures; they are part of the same process. Giddens calls this the **duality of structure**.

Societal structures and institutions are reproduced through people's actions; if their actions change, the structures and institutions must change too.

For example, **globalisation** (see page 86) has had a profound effect on economic structures. The transfer of manufacturing to developing countries has led to a change in the UK both in the nature of work and in social-class identity. Many sociologists argue that work is now interpreted differently. It is no longer a source of pride, solidarity and loyalty, and consequently manual workers cannot be guaranteed to abide by traditional class loyalties. As such, their actions have been changed by changes in the social structure of employment.

Critics of Giddens, such as **Archer** (1982), argue that he puts too much emphasis on people's ability to change society by acting differently, and he underestimates the social constraints under which people operate.

Now try this

1 Define what ethnomethodologists mean by reflexivity.
2 What **two** methods are preferred by ethnomethodologists?

Postmodernism: globalisation

Globalisation means that the world we now live in feels smaller and more accessible than it was in the 1990s.

Globalisation

Postmodernists argue that globalisation has transformed modern societies:

- **Albrow** (1996) defines globalisation as all of those processes by which the people of the world have been incorporated into a single society.

- **Waters** (1991) observes that it is a social process by which the constraints of geography on economic, political, social and cultural arrangements have been reduced.

At a **micro-level**, **Martell** (2010) observes that for individuals, both geographical distance and time zones are no longer important. Digital technology has erased distance and substituted virtual space for physical space. Global digital-interconnectedness means that people can occupy the same online space at the same time.

At a **macro- or societal level**, globalisation means that goods, money, people, services, culture, crime, disease, news and ideas are crossing national borders on an extraordinary scale and at great speed. Societies that were once distant and independent are now increasingly globally intertwined and interdependent.

The macro and micro are also interwoven in that the local lives of ordinary people are increasingly shaped by events, decisions and actions that take place thousands of miles away.

Baudrillard (1983) claims that postmodern societies are hyper-real societies. They have become dominated by **simulacra** (simulations or signs of reality) embodied in theme parks, adverts, films and TV soap operas. These simulacra have become more real than reality itself. Baudrillard claimed the media is responsible for the inability of people in the postmodern world to distinguish between image and reality.

The causes of globalisation

1 **Technological change:** particularly advances in digital technology.

2 **Economic change:**
- ownership/control of the world's digital communications is now concentrated in the hands of a few transnational corporations (TNCs)
- there is now a 24-hour financial market
- an international division of labour has emerged in which the production and marketing of cultural products such as films, music, fashion, news and sport are often scattered across continents.

3 **Political change:** many TNCs have greater economic power than governments and can impose their agenda on states and political elites.

4 **Global movement of people:** brought about by cheap air travel, mass tourism and migration. This has led to changes in indigenous cultures and new forms of identity.
- Globalisation has created new global hybrid styles such as in fashion, food and lifestyle.
- Postmodern societies provide their members with a greater diversity of choice in terms of the availability of mass media, religious, political and philosophical beliefs, and in terms of how they construct their social identities.
- Cultural diversity has become the global norm.

Postmodernists therefore see globalisation as a **positive phenomenon** because it has created a new class of global consumers, in both the developed and the developing world, with a greater range of choices from which they can construct a **hybridised** global identity.

Marxism and postmodernity

Marxists argue that capitalism has engaged in global practices such as colonialism and global trade for hundreds of years and so globalisation is not a new phenomenon. The world is merely experiencing a further stage in the evolution of capitalism, which has always sought greater profits in the postmodern arena.

Harvey (1990) develops a Marxist analysis within a postmodern framework. He argues that capitalists have sought new sources of profit through the creation of new areas of commerce, which he calls **flexible accumulation**. This involves:

- using global markets to encourage changes in the consumption of brands and customised products
- using global production (such as factories in the developing world) to make rapid switches from one product to another
- the commodification of all aspects of cultural and social life
- using global media to persuade people to constantly reinvent themselves and their identities by buying new products and services, thereby feeding capitalism for example, via social media platforms such as Facebook.

Now try this

Outline **two** ways in which Marxists disagree with postmodernism.

Late modernity

Not all sociologists believe that modern societies have evolved into postmodern societies. **Giddens** (1990) and **Beck** (1992) argue that modern societies have moved into a state of 'late' or 'high' modernity. Late modernity is merely the latest phase of modernity rather than a completely new type of society or postmodern society.

Theories of late modernity

Giddens identifies two features which define periods of late or high modernity.

1 **Disembedding:** impersonal forms of communication such as emails and social media are replacing face-to-face interactions. Consequently, individualistic ideas and practices focused on looking out for ourselves rather than for others are fast replacing duty and obligation to other people. People are increasingly abandoning civil and ethical guidelines in their dealings with others.

A good example of this is the anonymous abuse and threats aimed at people in online forums.

2 **Reflexivity:** because we are less likely to take notice of tradition in our interactions with others, we often have to think and behave spontaneously when reacting. This involves constantly evaluating and judging the behaviour of others and modifying our actions accordingly (see page 85). Giddens argues that reflexivity means that we are more likely to challenge the ideas and behaviour of others.

Giddens observes that late-modern societies are characterised by:

- economic, political and cultural instability
- social change, as traditional ways of thinking and acting are challenged
- risk, particularly environmental risks to both individuals and the future of humanity.

  For example, through terrorism and global warming respectively.

Risk society

According to Beck, late modernity has a number of unique features:

- **Risk:** it is subject to a range of 'risks' that no other historical period has ever had to face. However, these are not natural risks but complex manufactured risks due to new technology. Beck argues that technology is creating risks that are becoming too big or complex for humans to control.

- **Subject to global influence:** risks such as diseases, pollution, radiation and terrorism can no longer be limited to any one country. Beck also argues that being wealthy no longer insulates the rich from these global risks.

- **Lack of class difference:** class differences are no longer important. Beck refers to class as a 'zombie' category because he argues that there is no life left in the concept.

- **Reflexivity:** members of society are now more reflexive – they engage in self-evaluation and are more open to adopting alternative ways of living. They no longer place their trust in leaders and 'experts'. The growth of reflexivity has resulted in people questioning modernity and particularly the idea that science always leads to progress. People are now more aware of risk and seek ways of minimising its presence in their lives. Risk and risk avoidance are therefore central to late-modern cultures.

- **Individualisation:** people's choices about lifestyle and identity are no longer constrained by tradition, family and community. They now make such choices on the basis of self-interest.

Evaluation of theories of late modernity

👎 Beck has been strongly criticised for arguing that social class is no longer important. **Skeggs** (2015) argues that rising inequalities in income and wealth have meant that class has more rather than less impact on the opportunities people experience from different backgrounds.

👎 **Elliot** (2002) argues that Beck's work fails to recognise differences in power. Elliot argues that rich and powerful groups are able to limit risk and to have greater influence on the context in which the risk occurs.

For example, they can live in areas with little pollution and far away from nuclear power stations.

👎 **Rustin** (1994) argues that capitalism and its emphasis on profit rather than technology is responsible for an increased risk to humanity.

Now try this

1 What is a zombie concept according to Beck?
2 What is the main cause of risk according to Beck?

Is sociology a science?

This topic focuses on debates about the **nature of science** and the extent to which sociology can or should be regarded as scientific. Whether sociology is a science or not depends on what definition of science we adopt.

The positivist definition of science

Positivists believe that sociology is a science – the science of society. They believe that just as there are natural laws governing the behaviour of the natural world, so too there are **social laws** governing human behaviour found in the social world. Positivists believe that sociologists should use the logic and method of the natural sciences. This scientific approach or method is known as the **hypothetico-deductive (H-D)** model (sometimes called verificationism). It is composed of a number of logical stages.

Observation → Hypothesis → Deduction from data/ evidence collection → Theory

The scientific characteristics of positivist sociology

Positivists believe that the research method used to collect evidence should have a particular set of scientific characteristics.

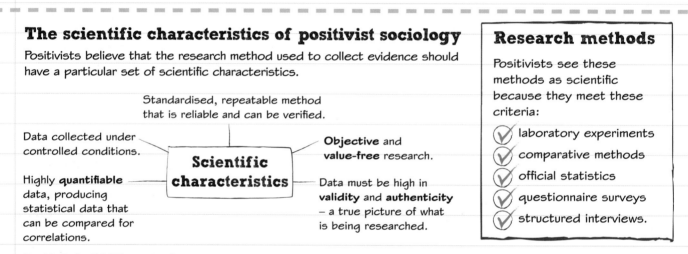

Standardised, repeatable method that is reliable and can be verified.

Data collected under controlled conditions.

Scientific characteristics

Objective and **value-free** research.

Highly **quantifiable** data, producing statistical data that can be compared for correlations.

Data must be high in **validity** and **authenticity** – a true picture of what is being researched.

Research methods

Positivists see these methods as scientific because they meet these criteria:

- ✓ laboratory experiments
- ✓ comparative methods
- ✓ official statistics
- ✓ questionnaire surveys
- ✓ structured interviews.

Durkheim's (1897) study of suicide is the best example of sociological science in action.

Sir Karl Popper's definition of science

Popper (1963) does not believe that sociology is a science. He claims that the H-D model assumes that if enough evidence is collected, it proves a hypothesis correct. However, he argues that good science is not about proving hypotheses right – it is about **proving them wrong** (false). Popper argues that scientists can never be conclusively right, they can only be conclusively wrong, so there is no such thing as 'truth' or 'absolute knowledge'.

Popper used the example hypothesis 'all swans are white' to illustrate his point. The H-D model would assume that 1000 observations of white swans would be enough to deduct that the hypothesis is right. However, the appearance of one black swan would conclusively prove the hypothesis wrong. The 1000 observations and the time and effort involved would be rendered redundant by just one observation.

Conjecture and refutation

Popper argues that his '**conjecture and refutation**' model is the true scientific model. The scientist forms a conjecture (or hypothesis) based on an observation, then looks for evidence to refute it (prove it wrong). Good science is about being sceptical and keeping an open mind as contradictory evidence might appear at any time.

Popper is reluctant to accept that positivist sociology, especially Marxism, is scientific because:

- positivist research uses the H-D model when analysing the data collected by experiments and social surveys
- sociological theories like functionalism and Marxism are too theoretical and rarely engage in scientific research aimed at proving themselves wrong
- Marxism makes predictions about the future (for example, that the working class will become class conscious and engage in revolutionary action to overthrow the bourgeoisie) which Popper claims is unscientific because the future cannot be proved wrong.

Now try this

1 What is the difference between the hypothetico-deductive model and Popper's conjecture and refutation model?
2 What makes a research method reliable?

Defining sociology as a science

The realist definition of science suggests that sociology can be viewed as scientific, although both **Thomas Kuhn** (1962) and interpretivists are sceptical about sociology's scientific status.

Criticisms of scientific models

Feyerabend (1965) argues that both Popper and the positivists exaggerate the notion of a scientific logic. He argues that there is no such thing as a universal scientific logic or method which is followed by all scientists. Scientific logic is a myth that exists to convince the non-scientific general public that scientists deserve their high status and rewards.

Research by **Kaplan** (1975) supports Feyerabend's observations. He found that a great deal of scientific discovery has nothing to do with logic. Rather it is the product of accident, luck, inspired guesses and imagination.

The realist definition of science

Scientific realists like **Andrew Sayer** (2000) reject the view that science needs to focus on observable phenomena. He suggests that many sciences are '**open sciences**' – they often hypothesise about events or things that are difficult or impossible to observe, detect and measure.

For example, the Big Bang cannot be directly observed by scientists but they are sure that this occurred.

Sayer defines science as an attempt to explain the effects of underlying and often unobservable structures and processes. So sociology is an open science because sociologists observe the effects of invisible social forces such as consensus and integration.

The paradigmatic definition of science: Thomas Kuhn

Kuhn argues that science should be defined as a **paradigm** – a body of knowledge that dominates a particular field of science and which sets out: **a)** what scientists should believe and **b)** how scientists should conduct research. Kuhn argues that science only progresses when scientists present evidence that **contradicts** the paradigm. Eventually the contradictory evidence becomes so numerous that the original paradigm loses credibility and is overthrown in a period of '**scientific revolution**'. The new ideas form an alternative paradigm that comes to dominate scientific thinking and practice, until alternative ideas and evidence again accumulate.

For example, early astronomy was dominated by a Catholic paradigm which stated that the earth was the centre of the universe and the sun revolved around it. When Galileo presented contradictory evidence, he was imprisoned and his data was suppressed. It took another 200 years before Galileo's data was accepted as fact.

Using Kuhn's definition, it is doubtful whether sociology is scientific. Sociology is made up of competing perspectives and theories, so there is no dominant body of knowledge or paradigm that all sociologists subscribe to: there is no **paradigmatic unity**.

Interpretivism or anti-positivism

Interpretivists reject the view that sociology is a science. They argue that it is wrong to treat human beings in the same way as the subjects of natural science because:

- people have consciousness and free will – the subject matter of physics and chemistry do not
- people are choice-making individuals who are actively engaged in the social construction of society and social reality
- behaviour is not shaped by social forces or laws over which people have no control; they are not the puppets of society.

Interpretivists argue that research should focus on collecting high-validity data by getting inside people's heads and seeing first-hand how they both construct and interpret the world around them.

Postmodernism and science

Postmodernists like **Seidman** (1991) reject the idea that science is about collecting facts to discover absolute truths about how the world works. They argue that:

- science is a meta-narrative (see page 138)
- science has no more claim to validity than any other meta-narrative (relativism, see page 14)
- science has become the dominant meta-narrative due to its relationship with capitalism, which has put society more at risk of exploitation, suffering and destruction
- science tends to represent the interests of powerful groups and is often engaged in the suppression of alternative views of the world.

Postmodernists, therefore, argue that there is no convincing reason why sociology should aspire to scientific status.

Now try this

1 According to Kuhn, what does a set of beliefs require in order for it to achieve scientific status?
2 Which theories deny sociology scientific status and why?

Subjectivity and value freedom

Some sociologists argue that a **value-free** (objective) sociology is impossible, whilst others claim that research should be driven by values because the point of sociological research is to change society for the better.

The value-freedom debate

There are a number of strands to this debate.

1. **Early positivists:** sociology should propose remedies for social and moral problems.

2. **20th century positivists, particularly functionalists:** sociological research should be underpinned by **value freedom**, which they dubbed 'objectivity through neutrality'.

3. **Critics such as Weber (1923), Alvin Gouldner (1964) and Gomm (2008):** values underpin all aspects of sociological research, including funding, decisions about what to research and what methods to use. Sociology is socially organised knowledge, so it reflects the subjective values of those who collect and organise it.

4. **Marxists and feminists:** sociologists should not be value free because their research should aim to improve society.

The early positivists

The founding fathers of sociology would have disagreed with the notion of value freedom.

- **Comte (1830)** believed that sociology was a new religion of scientific truth and that sociologists should be able to say objectively and with scientific certainty what was really best for society.

- Both **Charles Booth (1892)** and **Seebohm Rowntree (1899)** aimed not only to describe the extent of poverty in the East End of London and York respectively, but also to propose remedies based on their own values in order to rid society of poverty.

- **Karl Marx (1888)** believed sociological research could be used to reveal the truth of inequality to the working classes in order to motivate them to bring about revolutionary change and to transform unequal capitalist societies into communist utopias.

Objectivity through neutrality

Twentieth-century positivists argued that it was not the job of sociologists to fix society.

Summary of argument

1. Sociologists should be engaged in the objective and unbiased (value free) pursuit of knowledge and truth through their research.

2. Sociologists should aim to see facts as they are – not as they may wish to see them.

3. It is not the job of sociologists to fix society – that is the job of governments and social policy makers.

4. How the data provided by sociological research is used by those in power is not the sociologists' concern.

5. Sociologists should not worry about who employs them – they should just collect data in the most neutral way possible.

6. Sociologists should not let their personal prejudices, tastes and beliefs influence their research or the interpretation of their data.

Criticism of the concept of value-free funding

Gouldner (1964) was critical of functionalist sociologists who worked for big businesses and the military because they rarely criticised their paymasters for using the research to more efficiently exploit workers or train soldiers to more effectively kill their enemy.

Gomm (1982) concludes that value freedom in sociological research is virtually impossible because whoever controls the funding for research controls the values. He also observes that some sociologists may censor their own work because they wish to avoid upsetting those in power, who could harm their career prospects.

Weber (1919) rejected the idea of value freedom and argued that sociologists must take moral responsibility for the harm that their research might do.

For example, **Gonzalez (2009)** argues that the social scientists embedded within military units in Iraq and Afghanistan were engaged in identifying those likely to become insurgents or terrorists and may have been responsible for the subsequent deaths of people in the region.

Now try this

Outline **one** argument against value freedom.

Debates about value freedom

There are different views about whether sociology can and should be value free.

Values, bias and the research process

Derek Phillips (1977) claims that data collection is a social process in that it involves interaction between researchers and their human subjects and respondents. Values inevitably bias this interaction. For example:

- some respondents when faced with a questionnaire or interviewer may seek social approval and deny behaviour or attitudes that they perceive not to fit the value position of the researcher – poorly trained interviewers may inadvertently give clues about their own values via their facial expressions or body language

- those sociologists who use participant observation may 'go native' and end up over-identifying with the values of the group they are studying

- there is always the danger that the presence of the sociologist may influence the values of the group being studied

- the pursuit of **verstehen** (an empathetic understanding of the actions of their research subjects, see page 67) and the use of ethnographic methods may result in bias in favour of the group being studied – Interpretivists reject the idea of value freedom because they believe the closer a researcher can get to a group, the more valid the data collected will be.

Domain assumptions

Gouldner (1962) believes value-free sociology is a myth because it is impossible to separate sociologists from what they observe. Sociological knowledge is a social product – it is the result of human actions and values. He argues that all sociologists possess **domain assumptions** – a world view into which they have been unconsciously socialised by their culture and which may seep into their research. For example:

- male sociologists may unconsciously subscribe to the dominant value system of their patriarchal culture

  For example, **Parsons** (1970) believed that there were distinct gender roles within the family which were the product of biology (see page 79).

- functionalist sociologists believe that society is characterised by consensus and their research, therefore, is unlikely to look for conflict or to interpret the data they collect as evidence of inequalities brought about by powerful groups – this largely unconscious value position means that functionalists rarely criticise capitalist society or see inequality as a major problem

- new-right thinkers are generally critical of the poor and tend to argue that poverty is the fault of the individual or their culture – they rarely consider that poverty might be the fault of the unequal organisation of society or the wealthy

- sociologists who argue that crime is a working-class phenomenon rarely look at white-collar, corporate or state crime.

Political sociology

In the 1960s and 1970s, sociology was often accused of left-wing bias and of having a disregard for value freedom. This was an era when Marxist and feminist sociology dominated academic debate and research. They believe it is undesirable to be value free and are happy to take the sides of the poor and powerless.

Labelling theorists such **Becker** (1963), **Young** (1963) and **Stan Cohen** (1972) believed that sociologists should take the side of the underdog or 'outsider' against institutions such as the police and the media. These sociologists clearly did not believe in value freedom but that did not prevent them from carrying out highly regarded and objective social research.

Now try this

1 Identify **two** reasons why it is almost impossible to prevent values impinging on social research.

2 How do domain assumptions create bias?

Sociology and social policy

Social policy refers to attempts by governments to influence both how society is organised and social behaviour by bringing in new laws, guidelines and controls. It is often aimed at bringing about social change. There are a number of theoretical perspectives on the role of social policy.

Functionalism and social policy

Functionalists believe that the state and social policy work for the good of all who make up society. Laws and social policies reflect value consensus and therefore contribute to social order. Functionalists prefer social policies that bring about gradual social change – piecemeal social engineering – rather than sudden or major social change. They prefer to tinker with society because they believe that the way society is organised works well on the whole.

New right: social policies to fight crime

New right sociologists have suggested that certain social policies are required to fight crime. For example, **Wilson and Kelling** (1982) focus on encouraging communities to take responsibility for their locality in order to deter criminals. They also argue in favour of the social policy of zero-tolerance policing (see page 202).

New right sociologists argue that individuals and communities must 'design out' crime by making themselves harder targets through increased investment in alarms and CCTV (see page 182), thus reducing the need for social policy to reduce crime.

New right and social policy

New right sociologists are not keen on state interference in people's lives and, as a result, prefer that social policies be kept to a minimum. They believe that people should be independent and that the 'nanny state' undermines people's sense of responsibility and independence. **Murray** (1989) and **Marsland** (1996) believe an idle criminal underclass has appeared because welfare social policies such as benefits are too generous (see page 181). They believe that social policy should cut benefits in order to encourage people to look for work.

Feminism and social policy

Radical feminists see the state and social policy as largely patriarchal because they claim social policy mainly reinforces women's subordination, especially in the family. However, liberal feminists point out that the state has actually helped reduce patriarchy and has brought gender equality closer through social policies such as the Equal Pay Act and Equal Opportunity Act (see page 12). Educational social policy has also improved girls' educational performance (see page 39).

Perspectives in favour of greater social policy

This approach is aimed at improving opportunity, equality and justice, especially for poorer sections of society. It believes that more social policy is required in the form of spending on education and investment in inner-city areas in order to create jobs.

1. **Left realists** believe that inner-city crime can only be reduced by social policies that improve economic opportunities and reduce deprivation, poverty and inequality, as well as eradicating racism in the police (see pages 183–184).

2. **Labelling theory** is critical of the way the criminal justice system labels people as 'criminals', so preventing them from reintegrating into society. **Braithwaite** (1989) suggests that social policy needs to expand restorative justice schemes that focus on 're-integrative shaming' – labelling the act rather than the person so that people are not judged and written off as worthless (see page 179).

3. **Marxists** see the state and therefore social policy as working in the interests of the capitalist system and ruling class. They argue that the function of social policy is to hide or to justify exploitation and inequality by encouraging people to see individuals as responsible for any lack of economic success and, therefore, to scapegoat the poor. Social policy such as the NHS also functions to ensure that workers are fit and healthy so that they can be exploited at work. In summary, Marxists argue that social policies are a useful way of buying off working-class opposition to capitalism because they give the impression that capitalism cares about them.

   For example, social policy has given workers trade union protection and health and safety laws. However, Marxists claim that trade unions make workers easier to control whilst health and safety laws are very weakly enforced.

Now try this

Outline **two** examples of perspectives that are critical of social policy.

Exam skills 1

Questions on theory and methods will appear on both Paper 1 and Paper 3 of your A Level exam. Have a look at pages 90–91, 67, 72 and 88 for a reminder about value freedom, theoretical factors, survey questionnaires and whether sociology is a science.

Worked example

1 Outline and explain **two** arguments against the view that sociology should be value free. **(10 marks)**

Gouldner claims that sociology is culture laden rather than culture free. This is because all sociologists are influenced by their domain (the culture and context in which they study and research). This unconsciously affects how they view the world. For example, if it is the norm in a society that women stay at home and bring up children, then this norm may influence sociologists like Parsons who argues that women play an important expressive role within families. Similarly, some sociologists may be so influenced by their own culture that they unconsciously see it as superior to other subcultures. Rostow was accused of Western bias in his studies of development. He saw Westernisation as the goal that developing societies should set out to achieve and dismissed communism as a disease. Gouldner therefore argues that value freedom is impossible because of these domain assumptions….

2 Outline and explain **two** advantages of carrying out longitudinal sociological research. **(10 marks)**

Longitudinal research refers to research that is carried out over a long time span. It usually takes the form of a social survey, for example, questionnaires may be distributed and interviews conducted. Consequently, it is favoured by positivist sociologists. The Granada Television series Seven Up! has been following the lives of a dozen or so individuals since they turned 7 years old in 1963. The researchers have returned to the group every seven years. The advantage of this type of longitudinal study is that we can see how individuals from particular social backgrounds and genders progress. These case studies can support statistical patterns which show that social mobility for people from poorer backgrounds is blocked or limited. Another example is Farrington et al. who studied 411 males aged 8 who lived in a deprived area of London in 1961. They returned to them when they reached the ages of 10, 18, 32 and 48 years to assess the impact of a set of childhood factors on their chances of becoming a criminal. Such studies are therefore advantageous in determining patterns of behaviour and establishing cause and effect relationships…

Outline and explain

Question 6 of A Level Paper 1 and Question 5 of A Level Paper 3 will ask you to 'outline and explain' two arguments, strengths, advantages, weaknesses, disadvantages and so on, relating to **either** a sociological research method or a theoretical debate. You should:

- ✓ give a reasonably detailed answer, showing good knowledge and understanding

- ✓ use sociological terms, concepts and studies whenever possible – aim to include at least two examples/applications of relevant material

- ✓ think about different perspectives and viewpoints – for example, on particular research methods or debates.

Spend a maximum of 15 minutes on each of these questions.

This answer now needs to discuss a second argument, such as that of sociologists who argue that sociology should not be value free and instead should be used to rid society of inequalities.

Make sure that you focus on exactly what the question is asking you. In this case, it is the **advantages** of carrying out longitudinal research (not the disadvantages).

Develop your points by using examples to support what you are saying. Make a **point**, give an **example** or provide **evidence** and then **explain** your point.

You don't need to write an introduction. Begin with your first issue.

To complete this answer you would need to focus on a second advantage, such as how interpretivists view the use of longitudinal studies.

Exam skills 2

Paper 3 of your A Level exam includes a 20-mark theory and methods question. Spend around 30 minutes on this question. Have a look at pages 13, 84 and 85 for a reminder about social action theories.

Worked example

Read **Item C** below and answer the question that follows.

Item C

Social action theory sees society as being socially constructed: society is the net sum of people choosing to come together in social groups. Social action theory studies how people interact with one another and how people apply meaning to social situations or how they interpret the social world around them.

In contrast, structuralist sociologists such as functionalists and Marxists see society as the result of social forces or facts over which individuals have little control.

Applying material from **Item C** and your knowledge, evaluate the usefulness of social action theories in understanding society. **(20 marks)**

...Item C suggests that structuralist theories such as functionalism and Marxism do not agree that society is socially constructed via interaction and interpretation. In contrast, functionalists and Marxists see social behaviour as shaped by social forces beyond the control of individuals, such as consensus and social class respectively. Structuralist sociologists tend to be positivist (they see people as the puppets of society), whereas social action theory is interpretivist (it sees human beings as the architects of society)...

This extract makes a good evaluative point by using the item and the student's own knowledge to contrast structuralist theories with social action theory.

Highlight the sections of the item that might be useful when describing social action theories.

Evaluate

The command word 'evaluate' means that you must both **describe** and **critically discuss** the **strengths and weaknesses** of the social action theories of society. Try to create a debate and form a judgement about how useful social action theories are to an understanding of society. Use the item and your own knowledge to help you do this.

This question is about the strengths and weaknesses of particular **theories of society**, rather than theories of a specific topic (such as crime or education).

Using the item as a guide, the following might be a possible plan for this answer:

- **Define** 'socially constructed' to explain how social action theory sees society. Use Item C to help illustrate this – for example, 'people choosing to come together in social groups'.

- **Extend** the analysis by using the item and your own knowledge to show how crime, suicide and/or crime statistics are socially constructed by those in power.

- The item focuses next on 'interaction' so use this and your own knowledge to describe the theory of **symbolic interactionism**.

- **Describe other social action theories,** such as Mead's 'looking glass self', labelling theory and phenomenology. This will show knowledge and understanding as well as analysis and application.

- In line with Item C, show **evaluation** by contrasting social action theories with structuralist theories such as functionalism and Marxism.

- **Illustrate the difference** between social action and structuralist theories using the example of suicide, or their differing explanations of crime.

- Sum up and come to a **considered judgement** about the usefulness of social action theories in explaining how society works.

Exam-style practice

Paper 1 will include **one** 10-mark theory and methods question. Paper 3 will include **two** theory and methods questions: one 10-mark question and one 20-mark question. Look back at the core themes and the theory and methods chapters to remind yourself about structured interviews, the nature of science and feminist approaches. You will find answers to these questions on page 218.

Paper 1

1 Outline and explain **two** arguments for the view that sociology can be seen as a science. **(10 marks)**

Link your points back to the question, using the exact phrasing. This will show that you are applying your answer to the question.

Paper 3

2 Outline and explain **two** advantages of using structured interviews in sociological research.
(10 marks)

3 Read **Item C** below and answer the question that follows.

Use examples to support the points you make.

Make sure that you focus on exactly what the question is asking you. In this case, it is the **advantages** of using structured interviews (not the disadvantages).

Item C

Feminism sees most societies as patriarchal. Consequently, in these societies men occupy positions of power whilst women occupy subordinate positions. For example, in the home, they are mainly responsible for domestic and childcare roles. In the economic world there exists a glass ceiling through which talented women can glimpse the highly-paid top jobs but face cultural and discriminatory barriers in their attempts to obtain them. However, despite a universal belief in patriarchy, feminists are not united in their explanations of the source of patriarchy or in their strategies for removing patriarchal obstacles.

Be aware that the 20-mark question might also focus on the merits of a particular **method**.

Read through the item carefully and highlight those sections that might be useful when describing feminist approaches.

Applying material from **Item C** and your knowledge, evaluate the usefulness of feminist approaches in understanding society. **(20 marks)**

In your answer, you must include an **introduction** and a **conclusion** as well as **evaluating** the argument in the question. Once you have set out your arguments, using studies and concepts from each theory, make a judgement based on the evidence you have presented.

You can demonstrate your evaluative skills by making clear the differences between the three main feminist perspectives as well as by identifying their general strengths and weaknesses. You can also show that you are being evaluative by using words such as: however, although, whereas, despite, furthermore, nonetheless, in addition.

Question 3 tells you to use the material in the item, so make sure that you do this. The item contains clues as to what you should be discussing. Make sure you reference the concepts used in the item, such as patriarchy, politics, the glass ceiling, the domestic division of labour and so on.

Different family types

It is important to have a good knowledge of the range of family types that exist in the UK.

The nuclear family

The nuclear family is stereotypically seen as a two-generation family, with one adult male, one adult female and dependent offspring. It is seen as the norm and ideal by many sociologists, especially New Right and functionalist sociologists.

The nuclear family is widely believed to be the most stable unit in which to raise children.

The beanpole family

This is a new type of family, first identified by **Julia Brannen** (2003), which has been brought about by three factors:

1. More women are working and choosing to marry later in life, so they are having fewer children compared with their own mothers.

2. Falling birth rates mean that large families with lots of brothers and sisters are a thing of the past.

3. Falling death rates mean that some families may comprise four generations.

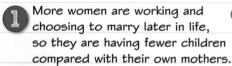
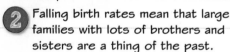

▲ male
● female

Beanpole family structure.

The beanpole family is essentially a type of nuclear family that is not part of a wider extended kinship network. This is because, over the course of the last 40 years, families have had fewer children, which means children have less extended kin in the form of uncles, aunts and cousins. However, children are likely to have strong relationships with their grandparents and even great-grandparents because of longer life expectancy.

The symmetrical family

The symmetrical family was first identified by **Willmott and Young** (1973). It is a form of nuclear family that is **privatised**, which means family members spend most of their time together in the home and have little contact with extended kin. Here, conjugal roles are supposedly more symmetrical. In other words, they are shared – joint equal.

The lone-parent family

Also known as the **single-parent family**. These are families headed by a lone parent. Around 90% of them are mother-headed because custody of children in the UK is usually given to women by family courts.

The matrifocal family

In matrifocal families, women are at the centre of the family, although they are not necessarily the head of the household. **Squire** (2003) defines a matrifocal or **matriarchal** family as one that is headed by a mother. They often consist of a woman with her dependent children and sometimes their grandmother. They are mainly found in low-income or poor communities.

In the USA, for example, about 30% of black families are matrifocal.

In the UK, they are associated with so-called 'baby fathers', a concept first used by **Augustus** (1999) who argued that some black men deliberately have lots of children with different women because this is symbolic of their virility and masculinity. Augustus controversially claims these men often feel no responsibility for the mothers or their children, but this has been criticised for racially stereotyping black men.

The extended family

This family unit contains relatives beyond the core of the nuclear family unit who may be living under the same roof, or in the same street or nearby locality. There are two broad types:

- A **vertical extended family** includes at least three generations (for example, grandparents, parents and children) living under the same roof or in the immediate neighbourhood. **Janet Foster** records examples of vertical extended families living in the East End of London in the 1980s.

- **Horizontal extended families** contain aunts, uncles and cousins living under the same roof. Sikhs in the UK tend to live in horizontal extended units.

Now try this

Briefly explain the main causes of the emergence of the beanpole family.

Defining more family types

You will need to have an understanding of the trends in contemporary family and household structures.

The reconstituted family

A reconstituted family is one in which one or both adults have been previously married, and the children are living with both a natural parent and a step-parent – and possibly step-brothers and/or step-sisters. The reconstituted family is sometimes called a **step-family** or a **blended family**.

Dual-career family

In a dual-career family, both parents in a 'nuclear family' are employed in paid work. The wife and mother has a career that is important to her self-development. The income of both husband and wife is usually essential to the family's standard of living. However, such families may be characterised by potential conflict because of the tensions between career and domestic arrangements, especially for women. Many working women find themselves with the dual burden of juggling work and domestic responsibilities.

Cereal packet family

This is an idealised nuclear family created by advertisers. It comprises a father, mother and two children (a girl and a boy). It was often portrayed in television commercials in the USA for breakfast cereals. In the UK, the most famous version of this family was found in a stock cube commercial, which featured the same family for over 20 years.

In this idealised version of the family, the father is portrayed as the breadwinner while the mother is the centrepiece of the home – preparing family meals, and making sure the home is hygienic and the family's washing is 'whiter than white'.

Empty nest families

In empty nest families, the children have grown up and moved out of the parental home.

The adult partners are left as a couple by themselves.

Cohabitation

A situation in which a couple lives together as man and wife, although they are not legally married.

- **Nubile cohabitation** refers to couples who cohabit before marriage.
- **Post-marital cohabitation** refers to couples who cohabit after being married before.

Cohabitation has become very popular in the last 20 years and is most common among widowed, divorced or separated couples, and the young.

Households

A household can be a single person living alone, or a group of people who live under the same roof or share the same address. A family is a household, but a household is not necessarily a family. The main characteristic of a household is shared residence.

A student household.

Now try this

What is the difference between a household and a family?

Functionalist theory of the family

You need to understand different sociological views of the family and its relationship to the wider social structures such as the economy and social change. This page looks at **G P Murdock**.

Murdock's theory of the family

G P Murdock (1949) is a functionalist sociologist who argues that the nuclear family is **universal**, meaning that it exists in every known society.

He defined the nuclear family as:

> *a social group characterized by common residence ... (which) includes adults of both sexes, at least two of whom maintain a socially approved sexual relationship, and one or more children, own or adopted, of the sexually cohabiting adults.*

Functionalists like Murdock see the family as the foundation stone of society. Using the human body analogy (see page 8), the family could be described as the heart of society. It is certainly the social institution in which most members of society will spend considerable time and energy. He also claimed that the nuclear family performed **four crucial functions** that are beneficial and necessary for the smooth running of society and for the personal development of individuals.

Crucial functions of the family

Murdock claims that the nuclear family meets some of society's most essential needs, particularly the need for consensus and order.

Family function	Benefit to society	Benefit to the individual
1 Procreation/ reproduction	All societies require new members to ensure their physical survival.	Children are seen as symbolic of a couple's emotional commitment to one another. In this sense, having children functions to stabilise both the marital relationship and family life.
2 Sexual	This ensures order in wider society, especially when reinforced by marriage, which sends out the message that the couple belong to one another and are not sexually available to others.	The sexual relationship between the couple reinforces their emotional commitment and fidelity to one another.
3 Economic	Paid work benefits the economic system. Parents economically support their children and encourage them to eventually take their place as good citizens and workers.	Children are physically and economically dependent on their parents for several years. In Western societies, parents agree to economically provide for their children in terms of food and shelter and to be legally responsible for their health and welfare.
4 Educational/ socialisation	Culture is reproduced and passed down through the generations via primary socialisation.	Children learn how to fit into society and how to conform by learning key values and norms and to obey laws from their parental role models.

Now try this

What does Murdock mean by the 'educational function'?

Evaluation of Murdock

Critics of Murdock suggest there are societies in which the nuclear family is absent (the Nayar). However, in support of Murdock, it can be found in most societies and attempts to abolish it in Russia and Israel failed.

Ubiquity of the nuclear family

👍 Murdock is probably right to stress the importance of the nuclear family. Although there are one or two exceptions (for example, the Nayar) most people in most societies are born into a nuclear family and most people marry, have children and start their own nuclear families.

The Nayar

Anthropological studies have found cultures in which Murdock's nuclear family does not exist.

In the Nayar community of south-west India, for example, girls were often married to several husbands but these men rarely lived with their 'wives' and children. The male had a 'visiting husband' role and some women had more than one husband. Inheritance was matrilineal – property was passed down the female line.

Are family functions effective?

👎 Reproduction – many women are now choosing not to have children.

👎 Sexual – attitudes towards sex have dramatically changed since Murdock's study. Sex before and outside marriage are now the norm, while alternative sexualities are becoming increasingly acceptable.

Dysfunctions of the family

👎 Murdock may put too much emphasis on the functional benefits of the nuclear family and downplay the dysfunctions of the nuclear family that produce social problems, such as domestic violence, child abuse and anti-social behaviour in children.

Failure to abolish the nuclear family

👍 There have been two attempts to abolish the nuclear family. Both have failed.

1 In the 1920s, the Russian government made divorce and abortion easier for women to obtain in order to free up women's labour. It gave women the same rights as men and set up state collectives to provide childcare, laundry and kitchen services. This attempt to abolish the nuclear family was quickly abandoned because it resulted in nearly 7 million homeless children and a dramatic rise in crime.

2 In Israel many people lived in communes (called **kibbutzim**). In these, children were raised in children's houses by carers and would only see their parents for a few hours each day. This failed because children often ran away to be with their parents or parents refused to cooperate with the aims of the children's house.

Children and carers at a kibbutz.

Family diversity

👎 Murdock's theory has failed to keep up with modern trends, such as:
- the feminisation of the workforce
- increases in life expectancy
- changes in fertility rates (women are now choosing to have fewer children).

Family life in the UK is now characterised by diversity. There are many versions of the family in the UK that effectively perform the functions identified by Murdock.

Is Murdock too prescriptive?

👎 Murdock's theory has been accused of **ethnocentrism** because it sees nuclear families as morally superior to other family types such as cohabiting couples, single-parent families, gay families and reconstituted families. These alternative family types are often dismissed as 'inferior'. Politicians may consequently discriminate against these alternatives because they see them as less 'ideal'.

Feminist critique of Murdock

👎 Feminists are critical of Murdock because he implies that women's main role is the nurturing of children. However, most families today are dual-career and the wife's economic contribution is just as important as the husband's. Women may now be playing less of a role in the socialisation of children – a function that has transferred to childminders, nurseries and grandparents.

Now try this

1 Define the term 'ethnocentrism'.

2 Identify **two** features that distinguish the Nayar family from the nuclear family.

Talcott Parsons

The functionalist **Talcott Parsons** (1951) believed that the **isolated nuclear family** has evolved historically as a result of changes to the social structure and economy to become the most common type of family today.

Functional fit theory

Functionalists such as Parsons argue that the family performs essential functions but these are dependent on the type of society in which the family finds itself.

Pre-industrial society	Industrial society
The extended family composed of nuclear families plus other kin such as uncles, cousins and grandparents is the norm.	The nuclear family is the norm because industrial society demands a workforce that is geographically mobile. The nuclear family is also more suited to the upward social mobility which is often the outcome of industrial society.
Extended families: self-sufficient agricultural units that functioned to produce their own housing, clothing and food.	**Nuclear families:** mainly live in urban areas and consequently are no longer self-sufficient. Their members are wage-earners. They have to buy housing, clothing and food produced by others.
Members of the family group felt a strong sense of duty and obligation to each other, and consequently have a collectivistic or group-orientated outlook.	Members of the nuclear family became isolated from wider kin. Members are more individualistic in outlook.

Structural differentiation: specialised agencies developed and took over many of the functions of the family – for example:

- manufacturing businesses took over the function of producing food, shelter and clothing
- state agencies took over the functions of health, welfare and education.

The nuclear family was left with two specialised 'basic and irreducible' functions:

- The primary socialisation of children into common agreed values, norms and so on.
- The stabilisation of adult personalities – the family soothes the stresses of its adult members. For example, parents de-stress by playing with their children.

The extended family was multi-functional: in addition to producing its own food, shelter and clothing, it also took responsibility for the education, health and welfare of its members because no other institutions existed that had the resources to do this.

Adult males and females perform similar roles. Older children and grandparents are responsible for housework and childcare.

Parsons sees males and females in nuclear families as equal but different:

- The female is the expressive leader responsible for both the socialisation and stabilisation functions.
- The male is the instrumental leader responsible for the economic upkeep of the family.

Extended family was functionally best suited to pre-industrial societies while nuclear families functionally fitted the demands of modern industrial societies.

Now try this

What does 'structural differentiation' mean?

Evaluation of Parsons

A number of general weaknesses of the functionalist theory of the family have been identified by New Right sociologists, historians, interpretivist and postmodernist sociologists.

Historical critique 1: Peter Laslett (1965)

👎 Social historian **Laslett's** study of British parish records suggests the most common family type in pre-industrial Britain was actually the nuclear family rather than the extended family that Parsons claims. This was because people married at a late age but died young.

Historical critique 2: Mike Anderson (1973)

👎 Historian **Anderson's** study of a British industrial town – Preston in 1851 – found that the most common type of family was the extended family rather than the nuclear family as Parsons claims. People sought out extended kin as part of a mutual support system – in order to pool low wages to pay high rents and share accommodation.

Historical critique 3: Pete Willmott and Mike Young (1969)

👎 **Willmott and Young** carried out a survey in Bethnal Green, London, in the 1950s and found that working-class people had organised themselves into extended families. Women were at the heart of these families, mutually supporting one another with regard to childcare, and men helped each other find work. This contradicts Parsons' view that the nuclear family best suits industrial societies.

👍 A later survey (1984) of upwardly mobile working-class people in the 1960s found that they had adopted a different family type – the **symmetrical family** – a **type of nuclear unit** that was **privatised** (see page 96). The unit spent a great deal of time in the home rather than with kin or neighbours and was **egalitarian** – husband and wife shared wages, housework, childcare, decision-making and leisure time. This type of nuclear family closely resembles the nuclear family of Parsons' industrial society. **Robert Chester** (1985) also observes that the nuclear family, which he calls the neo-conventional family, is the most common type of family in modern UK. He argues that most people, either as children or adults, will find themselves in a nuclear family at some point in their lives.

Family communities in Bethnal Green in the 1950s.

Ronald Fletcher (1969)

👎 The British functionalist **Ronald Fletcher** does not believe structural differentiation led to a loss of functions in the family. He argues that the nuclear family still carries out education, welfare and health functions, but is now assisted by the state.

For example, parents still teach their children to read and write and treat them for minor illnesses or injuries.

Interpretivist critique

👍 Interpretivist sociologists criticise functionalists for viewing children as 'empty vessels' or 'blank slates' that are filled up by parents with culture, values and so on. Interpretivist sociologists argue that socialisation is in fact a two-way process in which children can also influence the behaviour of parents, for example through pester power. See page 104 for **Evans and Chandler's** study on pester power.

Now try this

Briefly explain why Laslett and Anderson's findings are critical of Parsons.

New Right theory of the family

The New Right (which is closely associated with the Conservative political party) approach to the family is very similar to functionalism. It argues that the nuclear family is the ideal type of family in which to bring up children and that the adult members of the nuclear family perform biologically determined roles. New Right thinkers believe that politicians of all parties have not done enough to protect the nuclear family.

Three principles of the New Right

New Right thinking revolves around three central ideas.

1 There is too much state intervention in ordinary people's family lives. It is argued that state interference in the family and in people's personal and private lives has resulted in a **'nanny' state**, which attempts to govern our health, levels of fitness, weight as well as our eating and drinking habits.

2 The welfare state has resulted in **welfare-dependency** because welfare acts like charity and denies its recipients a sense of social worth. Instead, welfare has undermined people's ability to stand on their own two feet because it supposedly destroys the desire to escape from poverty and find work, and to live independently from the state.

3 The free market is better and more cost-efficient at delivering services than the state. This is known as **neo-liberalism**.

New Right view of equal opportunities

The New Right claim that legislation such as the Equal Opportunities Act (1970) and the Equal Pay Act (1975) have encouraged women, especially mothers, to give up their expressive domestic roles as full-time nurturers and, instead, pursue full-time careers. As a result, children experience maternal deprivation and are supposedly emotionally damaged by their mother's absence, thus producing social problems such as juvenile crime and anti-social behaviour. The New Right complain that there have been very few social policies such as tax incentives encouraging women to stay at home with their children.

The nuclear family under attack

With regard to the family, New Right sociologists recommend that:

- parents should be married
- mothers should stay at home
- families should not receive benefits.

They are implicitly critical of functionalist ideas because they believe that marriage and the nuclear family are in decline and under attack because state social policy:

- has encouraged women to abandon their family responsibilities by promoting equal opportunity and pay in the workplace
- has weakened family life by failing to counter what the New Right perceive as deviant or 'broken' family forms, such as cohabitation and one-parent families
- has undermined marriage by making divorce easier
- has resulted in too many families becoming dependent on benefits; these 'problem' families (often 'fatherless') are part of a **deviant underclass** – a segment of society that chooses to be jobless and is mainly found in impoverished urban areas;

  Murray (1990) claims that the underclass engages in 'deplorable' behaviour – committing crimes, having illegitimate children and failing to socialise its offspring properly, causing a rise in social problems such as juvenile crime and educational underachievement.

- has undermined morality by promoting sex education in schools, homosexuality (especially gay marriage) and adoption, as well as contraception for teenagers, which they believe should not be so freely available on the NHS
- should do more to encourage marriage and to discourage cohabitation.

The New Right critique of the 1997–2010 Labour government's family policy

The New Right were particularly critical of the Labour government (1997–2010), claiming that it had interfered too much in family life. They argued that Labour had given too many rights to children and was too keen on giving mothers the right to go back to work rather than encouraging them to stay at home and look after their children full time. However, the New Right were also very critical of the 2010–15 Coalition government's decision to legalise gay marriage.

Now try this

Why do New Right sociologists see social policies as negative?

Evaluation of the New Right theory of the family

New Right theory of the family has contributed heavily to a **family ideology** that dominates both popular culture and common-sense thinking about how families and their members should behave. However, New Right ideas and family ideology have been criticised on a number of fronts.

Has social policy damaged the family?

🗨 Some sociologists argue that social policy has not undermined the nuclear family as the New Right have argued. Rather, it is argued that social policy has largely supported both traditional marriage and the nuclear family. Examples include these:

o Tax and welfare policies have generally favoured the heterosexual married couple rather than cohabiting (unmarried) couples, single parents or same-sex couples.

o Government ministers frequently make reference to the idea that the nuclear family is the best possible type to bring children up in and that marriage is preferable to cohabitation.

o Payment of child benefit to the mother and the government's reluctance to totally fund free universal nursery care have reinforced the idea that women should take the main responsibility for children.

Some unmarried fathers are actually denied rights over their children. Hence the setting up of the pressure group 'Fathers For Justice'.

o The 'Child Support Agency' (CSA) reinforces the idea that fathers should be economically responsible for their children.

o The social policy for maternity rights reinforces the idea that women should be more responsible for children than men because women are granted more paid leave from work than their male spouse.

o Most council houses were built with the nuclear family in mind.

The New Right and familial ideology

👎 **Family** or **familial ideology** is mainly made up of a set of ideas about how family life should be organised, which dominate public and media debates about the best way to organise family life. Many of these ideas – for example, that the nuclear family is the most stable family type, single parents are a problem, divorce is too easy to obtain, women should stay at home and look after children – have originated in New Right ideas about family life.

However, familial ideology has come under attack from feminists who argue it is problematical because it:

o is patriarchal because it restricts women to the home

o over-idealises the nuclear family as 'too good to be true', which distracts from the 'dark side' of family life
For example, problems caused by divorce, violence, abuse, poverty.

o portrays divorce in a negative way

Bernardes (1997) argues divorce may be a lesser evil than an unhappy, abusive marriage.

o has led to the idea that the family is a private institution that requires little intervention from the state, but this idea has meant that problems such as child abuse were ignored for many years

o dismisses other types of family as deviant, wrong or broken and suggests they are the cause of a large number of social problems despite the evidence suggesting that these other types of family raise children just as well as the nuclear family.

Now try this

Define the term 'familial ideology'.

Marxist theory of the family

Marxists such as **Eli Zaretsky** are very critical of Parsons' theory of the nuclear family's evolution and its functions (see page 100). Zaretsky claims that the nuclear family's functions are ideological and benefit the capitalist ruling class rather than society as a whole.

Zaretsky's theory of the family (1976)

Zaretsky identified three functions that benefit capitalism.

 Socialisation of children

Zaretsky argues that children are **socialised into ruling-class ideological beliefs** such as blind obedience, respect for authority and acceptance of hierarchy. The nuclear family trains children into seeing inequality as 'normal' and 'natural' so that no one thinks to challenge ruling-class power or class inequality. Consequently, children grow up to become uncritical passive and conformist citizens. The family therefore transmits ruling-class values rather than common values. It keeps working-class people in a state of **false consciousness**.

 Stabilisation of adult personality

Zaretsky argues that rather than stable adults, the family produces **docile workers**. The family encourages them to focus on their families, home life and consumerism rather than think critically about their lack of job satisfaction, or the everyday exploitation and inequality they experience. Marxists argue that the focus on the family as a haven from a heartless working world is ultimately an illusion and is based on the exploitation of women's labour because they are expected to be responsible for the upkeep of the home.

 Nuclear family as a unit of consumption

Zaretsky believed that the family played a major role as a consumer in generating profit for the capitalist system. He points out that most marketing and advertising of consumer goods and services is aimed at the family unit.

For example, families are strongly encouraged to keep up with their neighbours in terms of their consumption of products for the home and garden.

Engels' theory of the family (1884)

Engels believed that as society evolved, so did the family.

> The earliest human societies were classless because property was communally owned. This was known as 'primitive communism'. In these societies, there was no such thing as 'family'. People lived in 'promiscuous hordes' – there was no marriage or other controls over sexual relationships.

> As societies developed and became capitalist, wealth and property were acquired by men. In order to legitimate the paternity of children and therefore male inheritance, monogamous marriage and the patriarchal nuclear family evolved. Engels noted that these developments led to the oppression of women.

However, there is no hard evidence for any of Engels' arguments. It is mere speculation that people once lived in 'promiscuous hordes'. He also implies that once capitalism disappears the patriarchal family will disappear too. Evidence from communist societies does not support this prediction.

 Evans and Chandler (2006)

Evans and Chandler collected qualitative data from 45 children (24 girls, 21 boys) ranging from 7–11 years of age. They used a range of methods: diaries completed over a weekend prior to the researchers going into the school; small group discussions; and an activity where the children had to rewrite the end of a story in which the central characters discussed how they might negotiate with adults to obtain commodities such as toys, games and clothing. Parents (14 mothers and 5 fathers) were interviewed at home or at work. Evans and Chandler found that children often successfully **pestered** their parents to buy them expensive consumer items. Their research supports Zaretsky's argument about consumption and observed that children's pester power was central to the family's role as a unit of consumption because they nagged their parents to buy them expensive consumer items such as computer games. They also found that this was used as an expression of love by parents.

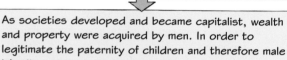

Now try this

Why does the nuclear family and monogamous marriage exist in capitalist societies according to Engels?

Marxist-feminist theory of the family

Margaret Benston (1989) argues that the nuclear family benefits men and the capitalist class rather than industrial society and all of its members respectively, as Parsons argues. Marxist-feminists particularly reject Parsons' idea that men and women occupy equal but different roles within the family.

The nuclear family and women

Marxist-feminists reject the functionalist idea that the nuclear family is beneficial for all. **Benston**, for example, argues that the nuclear family benefits the capitalist class and men but is negative for women for three reasons.

1 Women produce and nurture/socialise the future labour force; this is unpaid domestic labour.

2 Women's daily domestic labour – housework, which is also provided for free – maintains the health and efficiency of the current adult male workforce.

3 Women soak up men's frustrations with their jobs and capitalism in the form of domestic violence.

Reserve army of labour

Benston sees the nuclear family as a patriarchal institution which mainly serves the interests of patriarchal capitalism rather than all members of industrial societies. It does this by disseminating the ideology that women should derive most of their life or job satisfaction from motherhood and childcare. This benefits men by removing female workers from the job market. It benefits the capitalist class by turning mothers into a low-paid, low-skilled and often part-time **reserve army of labour** that can be recruited into work in times of economic boom and be made redundant during times of recession. The ideology 'a woman's place is in the home' legitimises this treatment.

Fran Ansley (1972)

Challenge to masculinity

Capitalism has stripped male workers of dignity, power and control at work. Surveys of factory workers suggest that many are bored by the tedious nature of their work. Many are alienated, meaning that they cannot identify with or bring themselves to care about the product they are producing. They feel powerless and consequently feel that their masculinity is being challenged.

Domestic violence

Ansley argues that this male frustration and alienation is often absorbed by the family and particularly by the wife in the form of **domestic violence**. She argues that problems such as domestic violence and child abuse occur because alienated men attempt to assert power, control and authority in the home to make up for their lack of power and control in the workplace. Wives therefore act as safety valves for capitalism. She argues that these men are not directing their anger at the real cause of their problems – the nature and organisation of capitalism.

Evaluation

👍 Marxist-feminists have shown how gender roles within the family may be created and perpetuated by the requirements of capitalist society rather than being 'natural' as functionalists argue.

👎 They ignore the everyday experiences and interpretations of women who choose to live in nuclear families because they enjoy and benefit from the experience of being a mother, wife, partner and so on.

👎 The nuclear family is also largely based on the rather dated model of the nuclear family of working husband and economically dependent full-time housewife. Many families no longer fit into this category because modern families are extremely diverse. Many nuclear families are now dual-career (see page 97).

Now try this

Outline **four** ways in which the nuclear family benefits the capitalist class according to Marxist-feminists.

Feminist theory of the family

You need to know about different feminist views on the family and their relationship to wider social structures.

Liberal feminism

Liberal feminists, such as **Jennifer Somerville** (2000), believe that the family is no longer the patriarchal institution it was back in the 19th century. Governments have since introduced **social policies** that have benefitted women and there have been profound changes in both men and women's social attitudes. **Somerville** argues that women's freedom to work and greater choice has enabled greater equality in marriage, though perhaps not in all areas (such as household work).

Social policies

1932 Women given the vote.

1970s The contraceptive pill became available on the NHS, allowing women to take control of their fertility.

1990s **Rape** within marriage was made illegal; police forces and the courts were encouraged to take domestic violence more seriously.

1870 Women given the same property and inheritance rights as men.

1970s The **feminisation** of the economy as married women entered the workforce in large numbers. Sexual Discrimination Act (1970) and the Equal Pay Act (1975) helped reduce employer discrimination against women.

1972 **Divorce Reform Act** Divorce became more accessible to all.

These social changes have not totally eradicated patriarchy in families. **Stanko** (2013) notes that domestic violence continues to be a major social problem. Motherhood also continues to be a major obstacle to upward mobility in the workplace.

Changes in social attitudes

Survey evidence shows changes in social attitudes.

- **Sharpe** (1976) suggests that teenage girls now see careers and educational qualifications as more important than marriage and motherhood. **Wilkinson** (1994) argues that these attitudinal changes between generations of women are now so significant that they constitute a 'genderquake'.
- Both men and women see divorce as a lesser evil than an unhappy marriage.
- The British Social Attitudes Survey (2013) suggests men now believe that they should contribute significantly to childcare.

Oakley: gender role socialisation and patriarchy

Liberal feminists believe gender role socialisation is the main reason why patriarchy is reproduced in families. According to **Ann Oakley** (1985), some parents are using gender role socialisation to teach their children that males are dominant and women are subordinate. Surveys of parents suggest that a significant number still stereotype some school subjects and careers as either 'male' or 'female'. For more on Oakley, see page 117.

Radical feminism

Radical feminist **Kate Millett** (1969) sees gender role socialisation in the family as the main source of patriarchal ideology. For example, boys see inequality between men and women as normal and natural. **Andrea Dworkin** (1976) also argues that men use their physical power and the threat of it to control women and keep them in a subordinate place in families. This is why domestic violence, child abuse and rape are still major social problems today.

Delphy and Leonard (1992)

Radical feminists **Delphy and Leonard** reject the functionalist idea that men and women perform roles of equal importance in the family. They argue that husbands exploit women in the home by making little contribution to housework and childcare. They argue that women are expected to be there for men – to flatter and emotionally maintain them. Women therefore occupy a subordinate role in many families while men assume the head of the household role.

Now try this

Briefly explain what the main source of patriarchal ideology is according to radical feminists.

Social policy

You need to know about the impact of social or government policy on the family and how different sociological perspectives view the impact of social policy on family life in the UK.

What is social policy?

A **social** or **state policy** is any attempt by the government to deal with a social problem (poverty, unemployment, domestic violence, child abuse or homelessness). Social policies are also set up to ensure that social needs (jobs, benefits and a happy family life) are achieved. A social policy is usually aimed at changing, improving or regulating social conditions to make sure they achieve a certain standard.

For example, social policy aims to make sure parenting is carried out to a good standard and that parents do not neglect or abuse their children.

Functionalism and family social policy

Functionalists see the state or government as serving the interests of society as a whole. **Fletcher (1969)** argues that social policies such as free compulsory schooling and free health care function to assist parents to successfully rear children.

For example, family social policy in the UK is generally underpinned by a set of traditional ideas about family life that would earn the approval of functionalist thinkers like Parsons, such as the idea that the nuclear family is the ideal family form, that males should be breadwinners and females should be nurturers.

New Right and family social policy

New Right commentators such as **Murray** believe that the state should play a minimal role in people's lives (see page 102) and that some social policies (e.g. legalisation of same-sex marriage) have damaged marriage and the nuclear family by promoting 'deviant' family types and lifestyles.

Feminism and family social policy

Liberal feminists such as **Sharpe** (1976) and **Oakley** (1985) argue that social policies relating to equal opportunities and work pay have helped many women to insist on more equality within the family. Radical feminists argue that social policy has generally reinforced patriarchy (see page 106). **Drew et al. (1995)** argue that if family social policy across Europe is examined, two types can be observed:

- Social policy that supports **traditional gender regimes** or the idea that males and females occupy very different roles in the family.
  In Greece and Spain, there is no free childcare to assist mothers in returning to work.

- Social policy that supports **individualistic gender regimes** or the idea that men and women deserve equal treatment.
  In Sweden, Denmark and Finland, free childcare is provided so mothers can work.

Marxism and family social policy

Marxists argue that the state generally serves the interests of capitalism. They see social policy as serving three purposes:

1. It aims to hide or disguise capitalist exploitation.

   For example, free health care suggests capitalism has a human caring face and that it cares about the sick and elderly.

2. It maintains the workforce.

   For example, the existence of the NHS means that the workforce is generally fit, healthy and productive.

3. It buys off working-class opposition to capitalism and prevents revolt or revolution by making social policy concessions to the working class, such as providing welfare benefits.

Donzelot (1979)

In 'The Policing of Families', Donzelot notes that familial ideology (see page 103) is part of a wider process of surveillance and social control that is operated by the state. He argues that family social policies are mainly targeted at 'controlling' problem social groups, such as the so-called underclass, and preventing and/or solving wider social problems, such as juvenile delinquency and crime. So, social policy is used by the state to keep potentially problematic individuals under surveillance. Family social policy is therefore focused on keeping families intact, supporting parents and producing children who are psychologically well adjusted.

Now try this

1 Give an example of a social policy that feminists would support and explain why.
2 What is the role of social policy according to Donzelot?

Changing pattern of marriage

There is evidence to suggest that the number of first **marriages** in the UK has been steadily declining over recent generations. It is useful to be able to explain some of the reasons behind this trend and to be able to understand the implications this decline has had on **family diversity** and **childbearing**.

Trends in marriage

↑ In 1972, 480 000 couples got married in the UK, which is the highest on record.

• Since this point, marriage has steadily declined in the UK.

↓ In 2009, only 231 490 couples got married in the UK, which is the lowest on record.

• The average age of a newly married couple in the UK is 32 for men and 30 for women.

• By 2015, 15 000 same-sex couples were married in the UK according to the ONS.

Same-sex marriage

In 2013, the **Marriage (Same-Sex Couples) Act** was passed to allow same-sex couples the opportunity to get married in the UK. Previously, same-sex couples were only able to obtain a civil partnership, which was seen as inferior to a married couple with regards to legal rights and societal acceptance.

Same-sex marriage was legalised in the UK in 2013.

Cultural differences in marriage

Arranged marriages are common in many Asian communities. They involve families assisting individuals to find a compatible partner, by searching for another family that has similar beliefs, values and goals, rather than relying on love as the main bond within the partnership.

Epstein (2011) claimed that these relationships tend to have more stability than marriages based on love because of this rational process of matchmaking.

Forced marriages involve no input from the couple involved and usually occur against their will. In 2013, 1302 forced marriages were allegedly conducted in the UK. However, the figure may be higher as many young couples may not report their families to the authorities.

Reasons for the decline in marriage

1 **Changes in attitude:** couples are choosing to marry later in life or not at all as marriage is not as significant in contemporary society. Couples may choose to cohabit (see page 109) for long periods of their relationship before eventually marrying.

2 **Secularisation:** the decline in religious influence on society allows couples to have more freedom with regards to their lifestyle choices.

3 **The cost of weddings:** due to the significant expense of a wedding (and the high cost of a possible future divorce), couples may choose to put the money towards buying their home or raising children instead of getting married.

Evaluation

👍 **New Right** theorists, such as **Morgan** (2000), believe that marriage is essential to society as it promotes morality and obligations. They are concerned with the decline in marriage in the UK. Morgan argues that statistics prove that married men are more likely to be employed, earn more money and live healthier lives than unmarried men. Morgan also rejects the development of same-sex marriage as she believes it undermines the influence of the Church of England and illustrates the state-sponsored moral decline that is occurring in the UK.

👎 **Feminists** believe that traditional views of marriage are **patriarchal** as women were expected to give up their careers to become a mother. A decrease in marriage allows women more freedom and independence to choose their own family experience.

👎 **Marxist-feminist, Barrett** (1988) argues that women are deceived about the positives of marriage during their childhood when, in reality, marriage traps women into a life-long expectation of doing the housework without recognition or reward.

Now try this

Outline the New Right view of marriage.

Changing pattern of cohabitation

In order to gain an understanding of contemporary family and household structures, you need to be able to explain the growing importance of **cohabitation**, the fastest growing household structure in the UK over recent generations.

Definition

Cohabitation refers to a couple who live together but are not married. Although viewed as immoral in the past, cohabitation is now the norm and is usually encouraged between young couples to test the compatibility of their relationship. However, couples may choose to cohabit for many different reasons and therefore should not be generalised.

Cohabitation is no longer seen as 'immoral' and therefore is a viable option for young couples.

Trends in cohabitation

- In 2015, the ONS stated that about 3 million heterosexual couples were cohabiting in the UK. This has grown from 2.3 million in 2004.
- In 2015 90 000 same-sex couples were cohabiting in the UK.
- Around one-fifth of couples who cohabit are 'serial cohabiters' as they have cohabited with someone else before, but the relationship was unsuccessful.

Evaluation

👎 The **New Right** believe that the increase in cohabitation is another sign of the moral decline in the UK as it is threatening the future of marriage. It is seen as a '**marriage-lite**' option by **Patricia Morgan** (2000), who believes that cohabiting couples are less happy and not as fulfilled as married couples.

👎 This is supported by **Murphy** (2007), who believes that children born outside of marriage are more likely to underachieve at school and develop serious illnesses.

👍 **Beaujouan and Ni Bhrolchain** (2011) believe that the rise of cohabitation in the UK is probably the reason for the decrease in divorce rates in recent years. This is because it tends to '**screen out**' weaker relationships as couples have the opportunity to test their relationship through a trial period before committing to marriage. They claim that around 80% of marriages in recent years involved couples who were already cohabiting.

👍 **Smart and Stevens** (2000) suggested that couples who cohabit are '**testing the water**' with regards to their relationship and therefore saw it as a temporary phase or precursor to marriage. Although the couples included in their study had separated, participants believed they were no less committed to each other compared with a married couple. However, they were grateful for the flexibility when the relationship didn't work out.

Cohabitation and childbearing

- The number of children who are born outside of marriage has significantly increased over recent years. According to the ONS in 2014, 47% of all children born in the UK were born in a cohabitation or to a single parent.
- The majority of births outside marriage are jointly registered by both parents.
- Women are also having children much later; the average age stands at around 28 which has increased by four years since 1971.

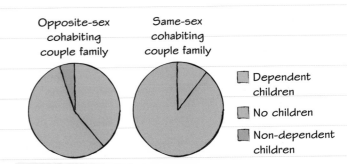

Opposite-sex cohabiting couple family   Same-sex cohabiting couple family

☐ Dependent children
☐ No children
☐ Non-dependent children

The number of children born to cohabiting couples in 2014.

Now try this

1 Define the term 'cohabitation'.

2 What did Smart and Stevens mean by 'testing the water' when referring to cohabitation?

Changing pattern of divorce

One of the main causes of family diversity is **divorce**. It is important to understand the trends surrounding divorce and to know some of the reasons for the increase in divorce over recent generations.

Distinctions and definitions

There are three different concepts that are applied to the breakdown of a marriage.

 Divorce: the legal ending of a marriage.

 Separation: the couple decide to live apart while remaining married.

 Empty shell marriage: an unhappy couple stay together due to financial reasons or for the sake of their children, even though there is no love left in their relationship.

Changes in divorce law since 1969

Before 1969, divorce was only granted if a **marital crime** such as adultery was proven in a court of law, which was often difficult and embarrassing to experience. The following helped to create change.

1969
The **Divorce Reform Act** allowed couples to legally obtain a divorce if they could prove that their relationship had experienced an 'irretrievable breakdown' if both partners consented after a period of separation.

1984
The **Matrimonial and Family Proceedings Act** reduced the time limit for divorce from three years to one year.

1996
After a surge of divorces, the **Family Law Act** increased the minimum time limit for divorce to 18 months and introduced a mandatory 'cooling-off period' in which couples were expected to attend marriage counselling.

2011
The government attempted to ease the burden on family courts by referring divorcing couples to mediation to sort out any differences and settlements of assets.

Trends in divorce

- Although possible before 1969, divorce was both expensive and complex.

- Spouses had to prove that their partners were guilty of a matrimonial offence, such as adultery.

- Divorce increased significantly after 1969 due to the changes made by the **Divorce Reform Act**.

- In 1993, 165 000 couples got divorced, which is a record high.

- Divorce has steadily declined since, despite some fluctuations.

Trends in divorce rates, 1960–2015

Y-axis: Number (0 to 450 000). X-axis: 1960 to 2020.
Lines: Divorces, Marriages. Source: Office for National Statistics

Social causes for the increase in divorce

1. **Thornes and Collard (1979)** believe there has been an increase in divorce due to the **changing expectations of family life**. According to the study, women in particular developed higher expectations of marriage. They were less willing to tolerate empty shell marriages. This may explain why 75% of divorces today are filed by women.

2. Social attitudes towards divorce changed so that it was no longer regarded as shameful because of the declining influence of religion in society.

3. The liberalisation of social attitudes meant that society saw divorce as a lesser evil than domestic violence or the psychological damage done to children by two parents in conflict.

Now try this

Outline **two** reasons for the increase in divorce since 1969.

Theoretical views of divorce

In order to successfully tackle an essay question on divorce, it is important to be able to apply your knowledge of theoretical perspectives to the debate.

New Right

- Divorce, according to the New Right, is one of the main causes behind the moral decline that has gripped the UK over recent generations.

- **Charles Murray (1990)** believes that an increase in divorce has led to a rise in **fatherless families** in which children are not being socialised into the correct norms and values by their mothers. Consequently, Murray claims that an **'underclass'** has emerged in which single mothers are claiming state benefits to live and pass on their **cultural deprivation** to their children (see page 102).

According to official statistics, more than one in four families (26%) are led by a single parent – usually a mother.

- **Rodgers and Pryor (1998)** agree by stating that divorce has a negative impact on children. When children are raised without a father figure, they are more likely to:
  - underachieve in education
  - engage in under-age sexual activity
  - be involved in crime
  - have addiction issues with drugs and alcohol.

Research has found a correlation between parental divorce and risk-taking behaviour in children.

Theories of late modernity

- **Beck and Beck-Gernsheim (1995)** argue that divorce is more common today because of an increase in **individualism** and **choice**, referred to as the 'Individualisation thesis'. Partners are more likely to prioritise their own interests and will leave a relationship if their needs are not met. Individuals also have more choice in contemporary society due to the decline of traditional pressures such as religion (known as **secularisation**). This decline could lead them to experiment with alternative lifestyles such as cohabitation, in order to find 'pure' relationships **(Giddens, 1993)** where individuals choose to stay together to meet their needs.

Functionalism

- Functionalist **Ronald Fletcher (1966)** believes that divorce is a very positive trend because it suggests that people have higher expectations of marriage. If the love within a relationship has eroded (known as an **empty shell marriage**) it is no longer functional. By breaking up and then re-marrying, individuals will have a happier experience of family life and therefore **perform their roles more effectively**.

Feminism

- Feminists **Duncombe and Marsden (1993)** argue that the increase in divorce illustrates the frustration of women who feel that their marriages are exploitative. This is because in addition to going out to work, they were expected by their husbands to take on most of the childcare and housework. Duncombe and Marsden refer to this as the 'Triple shift'. Many women also felt that their husbands were guilty of emotionally neglecting them. Duncombe and Marsden therefore argue that divorce can be positive for women who feel emotionally disconnected from their husbands. A similar view was taken by **Hart (1976)**, who claimed the increase in divorce since the 1970s was due to the frustration women experienced because they were still being held responsible for the majority of domestic tasks – even when participating in full-time employment.

Now try this

1 Why would an increase in individualism and choice lead to a rise in divorce?
2 What did Charles Murray mean by the 'underclass'?

Consequences of divorce

The two most common family structures that arise because of divorce are **reconstituted families** and **single-parent families** (see pages 96–97). The New Right and some other sociologists tend to have a negative view of these family structures.

Reconstituted families

Otherwise known as step-families, reconstituted families are usually caused when two previously divorced adults re-marry to create a new family. As remarriage is now common (due to serial monogamy), reconstituted families have become socially acceptable within contemporary society.

The actor Will Smith has a son from his first marriage and two children from his second marriage.

Evaluation of reconstituted families

🗩 **De'Ath and Slater** (1992) outline some of the struggles that can be experienced within a reconstituted family. Although every experience can be different, the study outlines how tensions may arise between step-parents and children or even between siblings and half-siblings if the re-married couple have a child of their own.

🗩 **Allan et al.** (2011) suggest the reconstituted family is a fairly problematic and complicated structure. Within this 'blended' family, the children involved are mixed together with new 'step' siblings who may conflict with each other. Additionally, Allen et al. discuss the complexities that occur with regards to authority and discipline within these family units as children often struggle to accept the authority of their step-parent, especially if they are still in contact with their 'natural' parent who has been replaced.

👍 **Ferri and Smith (1998)** believe that being in a reconstituted family can be very similar to a 'first family' in many ways. In particular, the bond between a step-parent and step-child can be positive and therefore it is important not to overgeneralise this family structure as they can be vastly different.

Single-parent families

In 2009, there were 1.9 million single-parent families in the UK. This equates to around a quarter of all family units. The vast majority of these units are headed by a woman (known as **matrifocal** families). Most are caused by divorce although some are brought about by a death of a parent and the decision of some mothers to raise children alone.

Evaluation of single-parent families

🗩 The New Right believe that the single-parent family structure has been endorsed and encouraged by the **'perverse incentives'** (benefits) that have been provided by the state over recent generations. As a result, young women are choosing to have children outside of marriage in order to gain access to a supposedly overgenerous benefit system.

👍 **Mooney et al.** (2009) are critical of the New Right analysis of single-parent families. Their study suggests parental conflict has more of a detrimental effect on child development than parental separation. Being raised by a single parent may therefore provide more stability than being raised by two unhappy parents who are in constant conflict with one another.

👍 **Burghes and Brown** (1995) conducted a qualitative study using unstructured interviews with 31 single mothers who were teenagers at conception. They found that most of these pregnancies were accidental. However, the teenagers decided to keep the babies due to strong anti-abortion views. Although the single mothers claimed that raising a child alone was 'hard work', they also found it an 'enormous joy'. Most of the mums preferred to stay at home and look after the children (most likely living off benefits). However, they all stated an ambition to return to education, training or employment once their children were in education. Interestingly, marriage was their long-term goal.

Now try this

1 What is meant by a 'reconstituted family'?
2 According to the New Right, what are 'perverse incentives'?

Personal life perspective

The **personal life perspective** provides a useful insight into the significance and extent of individual choice in personal relationships. This page outlines the main points of the theory, along with explaining particular views on **family diversity**.

The importance of 'personal life'

Smart (2007) recommends using the term 'personal life' instead of 'family' because the concept of family is too often associated with value judgements about 'ideal' or 'normal' types. **Smart** argues that the concept of 'personal life' is more neutral and flexible because it goes beyond marriage and biological kin to include newer types of relationships.

Allan and Crow (2001) agree with this sentiment as they believe that the life course has become far more complex in contemporary society. In the past, young individuals would have a fairly predictable path in that they would be single, then cohabit, get married and so on. These days, individuals have multiple paths which they can experience.

In many cases, the connections within these families can be just as strong as those that exist within traditional family units.

Critique of individualism

Although there is some agreement with theorists such as **Giddens** (1992) and **Beck and Beck-Gernsheim** (1995) about the increasing individualism of society, theorists from the personal life perspective believe that the extent of individualism has been over-stated.

Vanessa May (2013) believes that Giddens and Beck et al. only apply to white middle-class couples and that many couples do not enjoy the same level of choice and freedom because of economic or cultural constraints. Therefore people do not have as much choice as individualisation suggests.

Pahl and Spencer (2001) argue that the concept of 'family' is no longer useful to describe personal relationships in the 21st century. They argue that people no longer feel they have to maintain relationships with other kin out of duty or obligation. Instead people are now more likely to subscribe to 'personal communities' which are made up of a combination of relatives and fictive kin, such as friends, who are valued for their friendship and social support. **Tiper** (2011) found in her study of children's interpretations of what counted as 'family' that many saw their pets as an important part of their family unit.

The importance of family history in influencing identities

Misztal (2003) claims that throughout an individual's life course, their memories from childhood tend to shape their decisions and identities. These memories could be shaped by many things – such as parents divorcing, having a pet or losing significant relatives such as a grandparent.

According to Misztal, the memories of these events/people can tie people together for life, and can influence the decisions we make.

View of parenthood

With regards to parenthood, those who adopt the personal life perspective believe that biological bonds are not as significant as social or emotional ties. **Nordqvist and Smart** (2014) suggest that in cases such as adoption, parents are not biologically connected to their children. However, this does not mean that there is not a strong bond within the family.

Now try this

Explain the view of the personal life perspective with regards to the importance of biological ties in family units.

Family diversity: the debate

Due to a decline in marriage and a rise in divorce, it may seem evident that family diversity is occurring. However, some theorists still believe that the nuclear family is the dominant structure in our society. Here is an outline of a key theoretical debate – for and against family diversity – that you need to be familiar with.

Arguments for family diversity

If family diversity is occurring, the nuclear family is in decline.

 Rhona and Robert Rapoport

The **Rapoports** (1982) claim that due to changes caused by **globalisation** and the postmodern world, family diversity is the norm. They believe there are many different types of family diversity.

Here are five examples (remember **CLOGS**):

Cultural diversity – caused by migration. For example, matriarchal families, extended families.

Life-stage diversity – through an individual's life course, they are likely to experience a variety of different structures. For example, newlyweds, widows.

Organisational diversity – every relationship is different in the way that the couple separates the domestic tasks.

Generational diversity – depending on the era in which an individual is raised, they may have different views towards different household structures, divorce and so on.

Social class diversity – the income of a family can influence its structure. For example, middle-class women pursuing careers may choose to have children later.

Remember: CLOGS

 Giddens (1992)

Because of a decline in traditional pressures and an increase in divorce, family diversity is the norm. This acts as a positive as individuals are now free to form 'pure relationships' that bring happiness rather than being bound to empty shell marriages (see page 113).

Arguments against family diversity

If family diversity is not occurring, the nuclear family is still dominant.

 Radical feminists

Radical feminists argue that the patriarchal nuclear family in which women's labour is exploited by men is still the norm. Some radical feminists argue that women-only communes are the only way in which such exploitation can be avoided.

 **Functionalism**

Robert Chester (1985) suggests that society has been misled by claims of family diversity, as he believes the nuclear family is still dominant (see page 101). But he claims that the nuclear family, which he calls the neo-conventional family, has evolved. For example, it is now likely to be a dual-career family although even in this type of nuclear unit, women continue to be responsible for the expressive role. **Chester** acknowledges that diversity is on the increase but he points out that most individuals will experience a neo-conventional nuclear family at some point in their life course.

While women now work, they still carry out their expressive domestic role as carers.

3 **Marxist feminists**

The nuclear family still dominates family life because it is the family form best suited to meeting the needs of the capitalist system for reproducing the future workforce at a minimal cost and for maintaining the health and effectiveness of the current workforce. Capitalism has a vested interest in making sure that this family type continues to dominate.

Now try this

1 Define what is meant by the 'neo-conventional nuclear family'.
2 Identify **five** types of family diversity, outlined by the Rapoports.

Examples of family diversity

This page recaps on some of the other different examples of families/households that exist in the UK. For more on family types and households, see pages 96–97.

Singletons/lone person households

Around one-third of households are comprised of one person who lives alone. The reasons for this are varied, some people:

- may be young professionals who do not want to be in a relationship
- may be recently divorced or separated
- may be elderly widowed.

For the majority, singlehood (or being a singleton) is a temporary phase.

Living apart together

As a result of more young people being singletons, there has been a rise in the number of couples who choose to begin a relationship but continue to live separately. **Duncan and Phillips** (2013) refer to these couple as the **LATs** (those who live apart together). This illustrates how young couples prefer to maintain a level of individualism, even though they are in a relationship. In most instances, the LAT phase is a period of time that often leads to cohabitation, if the relationship is deemed to be successful at this early stage.

Some couples committed to each other choose to live in separate homes.

Extended families

Extended families have become increasingly common over recent years. However, their meaning has had to evolve over time. Generally speaking, the extended family refers to having close ties to family members who are not directly part of the nuclear unit, such as grandparents, aunts, uncles and cousins. In the past, this was more common as families would generally live close together within the same communities. This is also common in Asian families where around one-third constitute extended families.

Due to **internal migration** (movement of people within a country) and **emigration** (people leaving a country), family members are now becoming more dispersed. As a consequence, the extended family has had to evolve in order to survive. **Peter Willmott** (1988) claims that due to technology such as the internet and phones, families have been able to keep in close contact with members who have moved away and therefore maintain the strong support networks that are associated with the extended family.

Judith Stacey (1998) discusses a different evolution of the extended family known as the '**divorce-extended family**'. This could occur after a divorce in which women may decide to maintain strong connections with their former in-laws due to the strong bonds that may have been forged during their marriage.

House husbands

Due to the rise in female employment and flexible parental leave, it may make more sense for some men to become house husbands if their partners earn more money. Although some feminist studies suggest women still dominate domestic tasks, there is evidence to suggest some men are choosing to adopt the traditional expressive role.

Gray (2006) argues that there has been a clear shift in attitudes with regards to the role of men when it comes to childrearing. Gray found that dads emphasised a desire to play a more active role in their child's development and spend more time at home.

Same-sex relationships

As a consequence of policies such as the **Sexual Offences Act** (1967) and the **Marriage (Same Sex Couples) Act** (2013), same-sex relationships have become more socially and legally acceptable within the UK.

Gillian Dunne (1999) states that the lesbian household is the most likely to be truly **symmetrical** as opposed to traditional heterosexual couples. This is due to the lack of traditional assumptions made about the roles of each partner within the lesbian relationship and therefore the partners are free to decide for themselves which tasks they complete. For more on Dunne, see page 118.

Now try this

Explain what Duncan and Phillips mean by LATs.

Domestic labour

You need to know about **power relationships** within the family and different sociological views on this. **Conjugal roles** refer to the roles played by men and women within families, especially the distribution of **domestic labour** (housework and childcare).

 Key study **Elizabeth Bott (1957)**

Functionalists such as **Talcott Parsons** saw men and women as having 'different but equal' conjugal roles in the family, based on biological differences (see page 100). **Bott** carried out research on working-class and middle-class couples in the 1950s. She made two observations:

- **Working-class couples** were more likely to organise their domestic labour along **segregated** lines. Women took most responsibility for childcare and housework. Men were the main breadwinners and carried out only 'masculine' household tasks such as DIY. Bott argued that the relationship between a working-class husband and wife was shaped by their proximity to other family and friends.

- **Middle-class couples** had **joint** conjugal roles. They were more likely to share housework, childcare and leisure time. Middle-class couples were more likely to have experienced geographical mobility. They were less likely to be influenced by their extended family because they saw them less often. This meant they were more dependent on one another's company and more inclined to share tasks.

 Key study **'The Symmetrical Family', Young and Willmott (1973)**

Young and Willmott take a 'march of progress' view that argues modern couples have abandoned old-fashioned and unequal/segregated marital roles, and now have joint conjugal roles. Their research suggested that upwardly mobile young working-class couples and young middle-class couples were likely to be living in symmetrical nuclear families in which they shared income, housework, childcare, decision-making and leisure time (see page 101). They argued this progress was shaped by four major social changes in the 1960s and 70s:

1. **Slum clearance programmes in the 1960s** relocated many working-class families to council estates, fragmenting extended families. Couples were forced to rely on each other for social support and companionship.

2. **Greater educational and job opportunities** in the 1970s resulted in greater geographical mobility, isolating greater numbers of workers from their extended kin.

3. **Women went out to work in greater numbers than ever before in the 1970s** and made a significant economic contribution to the standard of living.

4. **Dual-career symmetrical families** could now afford to buy goods (such as televisions) and labour-saving devices (such as vacuum cleaners), making the home a more attractive place to be in for both husband and wife.

Evidence in favour of the symmetrical family

- **Gershuny** (1994) found that in families in which the wife works full-time, husbands carry out more domestic labour.
- **Leighton** (1992) found that the power to influence and make family decisions changes when males became unemployed; working wives often take charge of bills and spending.
- Studies by **Pahl and Wallace** (1981) and **Laurie and Gershuny** (2000) suggest that as women's earning power rises, so they are likely to experience equality in decision-making.
- **Beck** (2013) argues that Western societies have entered the 'age of the second modernity' – a globalised world characterised by individualisation, risk and uncertainty in which traditional identities such as 'worker' or 'breadwinner' have been fragmented.
  For example, fathers can no longer rely on jobs to provide them with a sense of identity and fulfilment.
- **Silver** (1987) and **Schor** (1993) observe that housework has been made easier for both husbands and wives because it has been increasingly commercialised.

Now try this

What is the difference between segregated and joint conjugal roles?

Critique of the symmetrical family

A host of studies, mainly carried out by feminist sociologists, have suggested that the concept of **joint conjugal roles** and the idea that marriage and the domestic division of labour is now symmetrical or egalitarian has been exaggerated by functionalists and by Young and Willmott.

Key study · Ann Oakley (1974)

The liberal-feminist Ann Oakley is critical of Young and Willmott because they do not distinguish between childcare tasks and responsibilities. She observes that Young and Willmott give equal weight to fathers playing with their children and mothers preparing meals and washing children's clothing. Oakley found that husbands saw housework and childcare as 'her work' rather than a joint chore. She observed that mothers are generally responsible for the day-to-day welfare and security of children, while most fathers only engage with the more enjoyable childcare tasks such as playing with children or reading to them at bedtime. Oakley therefore rejects Young and Willmott's conclusion that the modern nuclear family is symmetrical and that modern marriage is equal.

The dual burden

Many women have full-time jobs but still do more housework and childcare than their male partners. This is called the '**double shift**' or **dual burden**.

- **Ferri and Smith** (1996) surveyed 1589 families in which both fathers and mothers worked. They found that just 4% of fathers equally shared childcare responsibilities.

- **McKee and Bell** (1986) found that the dual burden existed in families in which the male was unemployed and spent most of his day at home. Unemployed men, who felt emasculated, resisted pleas from their wives to do more housework and childcare. Their wives, despite being at work all day, did most of the housework and childcare.

- **Man-yee Kan** (2001) found that many men pay only lip service to equality in the home while letting women do 75% of the household chores. She also found that educated women tend to do less housework than women who had left school at 16. Working women with degrees spent about two hours less on chores than working women in households where both partners had only GCSEs. Kan suggested this was because better-educated women had a more egalitarian or feminist approach to how much housework their men ought to do; they insisted that men do more.

Distribution of domestic labour

- Research by **Craig** (2007) found that women do between one-third and half more housework than men. She argues that this inequality begins when a couple move in together and before they have children. She calls this aspect of domestic inequality the '**partnership penalty**'. She found that when couples marry, the wife's unpaid domestic labour rises in volume while the husband does less compared with when he was single. She calls this '**the marriage penalty**'.

- **Ben-Galim and Thompson's** (2013) study challenges Young and Willmott's findings. They found that eight out of ten married women did more housework than men, while only one married man in ten did the same amount as his wife. They concluded that patterns of housework have changed only slightly since the 1980s (more than eight out of ten women born in 1958 said they did more laundry and ironing than their partner, compared with seven out of ten women born in 1970).

- A survey of 1000 men and women by the **BBC's** Woman's Hour in 2014 found that modern marriage is characterised by '**chore wars**' rather than equality. The BBC survey found evidence of persistent conflict between couples; two-thirds of the female sample admitted they regularly argued with their male partner over the amount of housework he did.

- **Man-yee Kan** (2016) surveyed 30 000 couples from a range of ethnic backgrounds; she found African-Caribbean and Indian men have more liberal attitudes towards housework than white men and do more around the home than their white peers.

Now try this

What are chore wars?

Criticisms of equality in domestic labour

Critics of the notion of **equality in domestic labour** have carried out studies of family decision-making and emotional work to show that distinct inequalities between males and females still remain in both marriage and the distribution of domestic labour.

Decision-making in families

Edgell's (1980) study of professional couples found that:

- very important decisions (finance, change of job or moving house) were either taken by the husband alone or taken jointly but with the husband having the final say

- important decisions (children's education or where to go on holiday) were usually taken jointly, and seldom by the wife alone

- less important decisions (home décor, children's clothes or food purchases) were usually made by the wife.

When the study was repeated by **Hardill** 17 years later, it was found that middle-class wives, even in dual-career families, still generally deferred to their husbands in major decisions.

Professional women and decision-making

Studies by **Pahl** (1989) and **Laurie and Gershuny** (2000) suggest that as women's earning power rises, they are likely to experience equality in decision-making.

Vogler and Pahl (2001) found that decision-making was shaped by income. In their study, only one-fifth of households were egalitarian decision-making units. Most household decision-making was controlled by men because they earned higher incomes.

These studies all show that equality in marriage does not really exist because men control rather than share domestic decision-making.

 Key study

Duncombe and Marsden (1993)

Duncombe and Marsden argue that few studies of domestic labour take account of the **emotional labour** carried out by women in families. In in-depth interviews with 40 couples they found that women work a 'triple shift' because: they take the major responsibility for the emotional wellbeing and happiness of their partners and children; they do paid work; they have responsibility for housework and childcare.

Consequences of the triple shift

- **Unequal leisure time: Green** (1996) found that wives usually interpret leisure time as time free from both paid work and family commitments, whereas husbands saw all time outside paid work as their leisure time.

- **Women's mental health: Bernard** (1982) found that husbands were more satisfied with their marriage than their wives – many of whom expressed emotional loneliness.

- **Divorce: Bittman and Pixley** (1997) suggest inequalities in the distribution of childcare, housework and emotional work are the main cause of divorce in UK society.

Domestic labour in gay and lesbian couples

Gillian Dunne (1999) argues that the traditional division of domestic labour continues because of deeply ingrained 'gender scripts'. These are the conventional social expectations that set out the gender roles of heterosexual men and women in relationships.

In her study of 37 cohabiting lesbian couples with dependent children, Dunne found that these gender scripts did not exist. There was evidence of symmetry and equality. Both partners gave equal importance to each other's careers and shared childcare. However, she did find that where one partner did more paid work, domestic work was likely to be unequally distributed.

Now try this

How might lesbian households or couples differ from heterosexual couples in terms of their approach to domestic labour?

Social construction of childhood

In contemporary UK society, **childhood** is a special time that is often taken for granted. Sociologists study how this phase of life is not a natural process and is actually **constructed** by the society in which it exists.

What is childhood?

Biologically speaking, childhood is a number of different stages that an individual experiences throughout early life.

Childhood stages include, for example, being classed as a baby from birth to 18 months or an adolescent from 13 to 17 years.

Childhood as a social construct

Sociologists look at childhood in a different way. **Wagg** (1992) argues that childhood is clearly a **social construct** (made by society) as it is not the same in every society. In the UK, it is a clearly defined stage of life, whereas in other communities it doesn't exist at all. For more on cross-cultural differences, see page 120.

From economic assets to a child-centred society

Aries (1960) claims that childhood in Western societies was created during the process of industrialisation. Through studying paintings of children across different centuries, Aries claims that experiences of childhood have significantly progressed to create the '**child-centred society**' that we currently live in and therefore believes that childhood is a 'social construct'.

Pre-industrial societies	Reason for change	Industrial societies
Children seen as '**miniature adults**' who were independent at the age of seven.	Concerns were raised about the safety of children with regards to prostitution, abuse and criminal activity.	Child protection policies, as well as an official 'age of sexual consent', were gradually introduced over the course of the 19th and 20th centuries. As a result, children came to be seen as innocent and in need of protection.
Families would tend to be large in size; therefore parents did not form close bonds with all of their children due to high levels of infant mortality.	Middle-class attitudes began to change as infant mortality rates fell for those who could access health care.	Families have fewer children as they are more likely to survive, and parents develop strong bonds with them. Aries refers to this as a '**cult of childhood**'.
As there was no state education system before 1870, children from poorer families were '**economic assets**' to their family as they were expected to work in order to help the family survive.	Due to injuries and deaths occurring in dangerous workplaces, children were banned from factories and mines.	Free state education was introduced in the late 19th century, then expanded into **secondary and further education**. Children now have to stay in education or training until the age of 18.

Now try this

1 What did Aries mean when he claimed that children used to be seen as 'economic assets' by their family?
2 Describe what is meant by a 'social construct'.

Development of childhood

Pilcher (1995) believes that childhood has become a specific life stage that is kept separate from the adult world. She refers to this as the **'golden age of innocence'**. This has been achieved through a variety of **social policies** that protect children from adult experiences.

Social policies and the development of childhood

1 **Children's Act (2004)** ensures that all professionals who work with children adhere to the five strands of the 'Every child matters' initiative.

be healthy   stay safe   enjoy and achieve

Children are encouraged to:

achieve economic wellbeing   make a positive contribution

The Every child matters initiative.

The state has introduced laws and social policies that monitor the quality of parenting and have defined child neglect and abuse as criminal acts.

Cross-cultural differences

In some pre-industrial countries, communities do not view children in the same way as Western countries.

For example, children are expected to work alongside the rest of their family.

This clearly contrasts with UK society as children are not allowed to work full-time until the age of 16 and those who do decide to take on part-time employment alongside their compulsory education have their rights protected by law to ensure their wellbeing.

2 **Censorship of the media: the British Board of Film classification** is responsible for restricting children's access to certain films; there is a 9pm watershed on television programmes that include adult content – regulated by **Ofcom**.

3 Social policies prevent children from gaining access to harmful substances. The state has also attempted to exercise moral control over children's activities pertaining to sex and marriage.

For example, the state has passed laws that make it illegal to have sex with minors (The Criminal Law Amendment Act of 1885) and does not allow marriage until age 16.

Child abuse

The state has implemented a series of policies to attempt to reduce the level of child abuse in society and therefore increase the level of protection for children in the UK.

In 2004, for example, it was classed as 'unreasonable' for a parent to smack their child if they left a mark such as a bruise or a cut on their body.

emotional

physical   sexual

Child abuse

bullying   neglect

The **NSPCC** outline five different forms of child abuse.

Punch's (2001) study of child labour in Bolivia found that children were expected to work from as young as five years old, in many cases in exploitative conditions.

 Key study **Donzelot (1977)**

Donzelot observed that the increasing level of state surveillance has led to a focus on the behaviour of parents towards their children. As parents are aware that state agencies (such as teachers, doctors and social workers) are indirectly watching for signs of abuse, parents have to regulate their actions when disciplining their children.

Now try this

1 According to the NSPCC, what are the five different forms of child abuse?

2 What did Pilcher mean by the 'golden age of innocence'?

The erosion of childhood

You need to know about different sociological views of childhood. There is an argument suggesting that the **'golden age of innocence'** may not be relevant to today's childhood. An approach, taken by some theorists, suggests that bad parenting and an irresponsible media are leading to the disappearance or **erosion** of childhood.

The 'sexualisation' of childhood

Unlimited access to music videos and celebrity culture is being blamed for children having access to 'adult' material that is inappropriate for their stage of life.

Postman (1994) believes that the media exposes children to all of the secrets of adulthood. This, in his opinion, is encouraging children to grow up too quickly. He claims that the distinction between adulthood and childhood is disappearing as children have access to the same leisure activities as their parents. He refers to this as **'social blurring'**.

Theorists such as Postman believe censorship needs to be much tighter on television, the internet and video games in order to protect children from this inappropriate content.

Supporting Postman's claims, evidence from surveys conducted by the **BBC** (2011) and by **Cambridge University** (2007) suggests children are increasingly becoming anxious about 'adult' issues such as terrorism and being victims of crime.

Studies like these have led to concerns about young people in the UK, as international league tables on obesity, self-harm, depression and teenage pregnancy indicate that the UK has high rates compared to other countries.

'Toxic childhood'

Palmer (2007) claims that children are being deprived of a traditional upbringing because their parents are not spending quality time with them. Instead, parents are using modern technology and junk food to appease their children, which is leading to an inadequate socialisation experience. Palmer refers to this process as **'toxic childhood'**.

Palmer argues that children are spending more time engaging with their friends and the media than they are with their parents.

Flight from parenting

Melanie Phillips (1997) believes that the culture of parenting in the UK is being undermined by the amount of rights children have been given compared to adults. As a result, children no longer accept authority and become deviant. Phillips suggests that children are forced to grow up too quickly as they fall into problems such as teenage pregnancy and therefore do not develop the 'emotional maturity' needed to succeed. Phillips also blames parents for using this as an excuse and therefore avoiding the responsibility of raising their own children. Phillips refers to this as the 'flight from parenting'.

Criticism of the erosion of childhood

The **postmodern** view of childhood suggests children are actually becoming more important to the family in terms of their bond with their parents and therefore criticises the views of theorists like Postman. **Jenks** (2005) believes that, due to the instability of the postmodern world and the ever-increasing individualised attitudes of parents, the bond between parent and child becomes more important. As relationships between parents become more unstable, adults see their children as a rare source of stability which encourages them to have stronger bonds with their children than they have with their spouse or jobs.

Now try this

1 What did Postman mean by 'social blurring'?
2 Briefly explain how the postmodernist view contrasts with Palmer's view of parenthood.

Conflict view of childhood

The structural approach of theorists like Postman may raise some concerns about how childhood has evolved since the 1950s, but it tends to view childhood as a shared experience for all within a Western society. However, some theorists take an alternative 'action' approach by studying the different experiences of children. They therefore believe that the views of theorists such as **Postman** and **Palmer** (see page 121) are too generalised.

The conflict view

The conflict view states that childhood is not a shared experience and can be negative for some children.

Ethnicity
Children from ethnic-minority backgrounds may suffer from racism in the education system and/or in wider society.

For example, **Jasper** (2002) claimed that white female teachers fear African-Caribbean boys and therefore ignore them in class while having low expectations of their academic achievement.

For more on ethnicity and achievement, see pages 42–43.

Emotional terrorism
Leach (1968) argued that families are the source of all our emotional discontents and prejudices because spouses demand too much of one another and children fail to live up to their parents' expectations

For example, **Cooper** (1971) argues that the family emotionally 'terrorises' children by teaching them to be blindly obedient to authority and intolerant of others.

Social class and poverty
Children from poorer backgrounds have different experiences to those from wealthy backgrounds.

For example, **Marilyn Howard** (2001) stated that children from materially deprived families are more likely to have poorer nutrition, lower levels of energy and therefore weaker immune systems than their middle-class peers.

Conflict view

Gender
Boys may have less parental supervision compared to their sisters and girls are generally subjected to more social controls over their behaviour.
See **McRobbie and Garber** below.

Child abuse
The **NSPCC** states that one child a week was killed by its parents in 2015, clearly indicating that some children have negative experiences of family life.
See **Gittens** below.

 Key study

McRobbie and Garber: Gender differences in childhood

McRobbie and Garber's (1976) bedroom culture study indicated that parents would much prefer their daughters to be day dreaming about their favourite pop stars from posters on their walls than being outside, where real dangers exist. The study also indicated that boys had a different experience as they were actively encouraged to go out with their friends rather than be stuck inside.

 Key study

Diana Gittens: Focus on child abuse

Gittens (1998) argues that it is not only women who suffer with patriarchy; children can also be victims of their father's need to dominate the family. She calls this **'age patriarchy'**. This concept uses the traditional definition of patriarchy: **'rule by the father'**.

Gittens observes that age patriarchy means that parents exercise control over children's time, daily routines and bodies, for example how they sit, dress and so on, as well as the speed at which they 'grow up'.

Now try this

Identify **two** ways in which it could be argued that childhood is not a shared experience.

An action approach to childhood

To further develop the critique of structural approaches to childhood (such as **Postman**, see page 121), the **personal life perspective** (see page 113) and **interactionists** believe that each child has a unique experience of childhood. Both approaches focus on how powerful children can be within families with regards to shaping their own experiences, rather than being completely subject to the environment around them.

The new sociology of childhood

There are two main points raised by the personal life perspective with regards to childhood.

1 Children have the power to determine their own concept of family.

Mason and Tipper (2008) claim that children have more power than other theorists suggest.

- Children are **active agents** of their upbringing and can therefore shape their own experiences of family life. In some cases, children may hold the balance of power in the household as parents revolve their lives around the demands of their children.

- Children have the power to determine who is part of their family and who is not. **Biological ties are not significant to children**. Therefore, anyone could be a family member in the eyes of a child.

2 Each child is unique.

Theorists from the personal life perspective suggest that all children are unique. Therefore, **their experiences should not be generalised**.

Womack (2011) observes that most state policies have aimed to improve childhood, based on the idea that if families are 'better-off' then children will be happier. However, she argues that there is no association between the reduction in child poverty and children's life satisfaction. Research suggests that few if any items included in the government's list of what is important to children – holidays, having your own bedroom by the age of 10 – make a real difference to children's lives.

 Interpretivist methods

Studies conducted by the personal life perspective use **interpretivist** research methods such as **unstructured interviews**, which allow children to express their thoughts and feelings so that a valid understanding can be obtained about their experiences. For more on unstructured interviews, see page 74.

Friends of their parents, pets and even memories of deceased family members can still have a big influence over an individual's childhood.

Evaluation

👍 In a similar vein to the personal life perspective, **interactionists** suggest that children can be influential members of their family in many ways. Their main focus revolves around the view that children can teach their parents just as much about society as their parents can teach them. As a result, socialisation is not as 'top down' as structural approaches would suggest. Instead, it is a **two-way process** that occurs through everyday interactions. Although children do not make the most important decisions in families, research conducted by **Morrow** (1998) suggests they are frequently involved in family discussions and believe they have a right to share decisions about their activities with their parents. However, as children grow, their desire for independence can lead to tensions with parents, especially when it comes to restricting certain freedoms such as social media activity and going out with friends.

Now try this

Outline **one** way in which the personal life perspective differs with other theoretical views of childhood.

Demographic trends: birth rate

This topic analyses the changes to the UK population from 1900 to present day. There are many factors that influence these changes such as birth and death rates, life expectancy and migration. You need to know key definitions, trends, reasons behind the trends and the consequences of each process. This page looks at birth rates.

Definitions

☑ **Birth rate:** the number of live births per 1000 of the population over a year.

☑ **Fertility rate:** the number of live births per 1000 women, aged 15–44 over a year.

☑ **Total fertility rate:** the average number of children women will have during their fertile years.

The most significant of these is the **birth rate**. However, the fertility and total fertility rates are useful references when discussing how family sizes have changed since 1900.

Trends in fertility rates

The UK fertility and total fertility rates have both generally declined. They have, however, fluctuated during the baby booms and are recently experiencing an increase.

- In 1900, the fertility rate was 115 live births per 1000 women aged 15–44, compared with only 63.6 in 2009. This figure has been on the rise over the last decade as in 2001 the fertility rate stood at 54.5.
- In 2008, the total fertility rate reached 1.96 per woman, but this has since declined to 1.83 in 2014.

The recent rise in fertility could be explained by a rise in immigrant families in the UK, who tend to marry younger and therefore have longer periods of fertility and larger families.

Birth rate trends

Overall, the UK population has grown from 38 million in 1901 to 64 million in 2014.

The trend has shown:

- a general decline since 1900 – the birth rate was 28.7 births per 1000 in 1900 compared to 12.2 births per 1000 in 2014
- fluctuations during the 'baby booms' after the First and Second World Wars, in the 1950/60s and late 1980s
- that since 2001, the birth rate has slightly risen again, reaching its highest rate since 1971 in 2012.

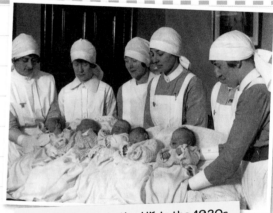

The baby boom in the UK in the 1920s.

Live births: UK 1900–2014

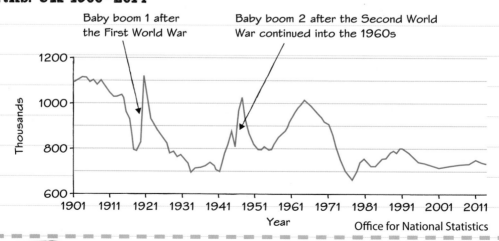

Baby boom 1 after the First World War

Baby boom 2 after the Second World War continued into the 1960s

Thousands
1200
1000
800
600

1901 1911 1921 1931 1941 1951 1961 1971 1981 1991 2001 2011

Year

Office for National Statistics

Now try this

What is the difference between the fertility rate and the total fertility rate?

Decline in the birth rate since 1900

Once you have gained an understanding of the trends in the birth rate, it is then important that you can explain the reasons behind the trends. This page covers why the birth rate has generally declined from 1900 to the present day, along with some explanations for the recent steady increase.

 Decline in the infant mortality rate (IMR) – the number of children who die before their first birthday: families choose to have fewer children because they have developed a stronger bond with their children who are now more likely to survive into adulthood compared with previous generations. This is due to improvements in both medical science and public health. These improvements mean that there is less need to replace children who have been lost to disease.
For example, in 1901, the IMR was 154 per 1000 babies born compared to 4.62 per 1000 babies born in 2012.

 Family diversity: as alternative lifestyle choices are now socially acceptable, some couples may choose to remain childless. Also, some couples may find it difficult to have children due to biological barriers (e.g. same-sex couples).

 Cost of raising children: the costs spiralled upwards in the 20th century and consequently parents may have chosen to have fewer children because they could not afford to raise a large family. It is estimated that the average cost of each child in the UK over the course of 21 years is £186,000, according to the insurance company Liverpool Victoria.

 Changing expectations of women: due to an increase in educational achievement, employment opportunities and the availability of contraception, women may choose to prioritise having a career rather than having a family. For women who do have children, they can now control how many children they have and when they have them. As a result, there has been an increase in women who are having children much later in life.

Reasons for the recent rise in the birth rate

Since the turn of the 21st century, the birth rate has begun to steadily increase. The reasons for this may include migration and the economy.

Increase in net migration	Economic recovery
As the majority of migrants are of childbearing age, the increase in recent migration has led to a rise in the birth rate in the UK. This trend can also be illustrated by studying the average family size of Asian, African, Polish and Irish-Catholic families in the UK, which tend to be much larger than the average white British family.	After the global recession of 2007 onwards, the economy began to stabilise post-2010, which coincided with an increase in the birth rate. Official statistics suggest that in 2007, 690 013 babies were born in the UK; in 2012, this increased to 729 674. This could have occurred because people may have delayed having a child until they felt more secure in their employment.

> ### Now try this
>
> 1 Identify **two** reasons behind the general decline in the birth rate since 1900.
> 2 Provide **two** reasons why some couples may choose to remain childless in today's society.

Decline in birth rate: implications

As the birth and fertility rates have declined since 1900, there have been some direct implications on family life, as identified by sociologists.

Family sizes have declined

Families are smaller due to parents having fewer children compared to the past where large families were the norm. The total fertility rate in 1964 was 2.95 children per woman compared to only 1.89 in 2014. This clearly indicates that women are having fewer children today. In 2013, 47% of nuclear families had only one child; only 14% had two children. However, ethnic-minority families tend to be larger (partly because parents are younger and more fertile).

There has been a significant decline in the number of women aged 24 or under who are having children, whereas there has been a major increase in older mothers aged 40 or over.

On average, Asian families have 4.6 children compared to the 2.4 children of the 'conventional' nuclear family in the 1980s.

Asian families

However **Westwood and Bhachu** (1988) observe that the decline in the birth rate does not apply to Asian families.

Increase in family diversity

The fall in the birth rate has had some effects on family diversity:

1. **Voluntary childlessness:** there has been an increase in the number of women voluntarily choosing not to have children. The Family Policy Studies Centre found that in 2000, one in five women aged 40 had not had children compared with one in ten in 1980. **Hakim** (2010) argues that voluntary childlessness is a relatively new lifestyle choice, which could only have been brought about by the contraception revolution.

2. **Dual-career family:** there has been a decline in full-time mothering and a rise in the number of dual-career families in which couples combine jobs and family life. About 60% of nuclear families are dual-career families. For more on the dual-earner family, see page 97.

Evaluation

👍 **Liberal feminists** generally support the decline in the birth rate because it allows women more freedom over their lives – to pursue, for example, a career (if they wish). **Helen Wilkinson** (1994) argues that there has been a ground-breaking shift in female expectations since the 1960s that have led to what she calls a '**genderquake**' in attitudes. Women no longer automatically consider motherhood to be an obligation compared with previous generations of women.

👎 The **New Right** would argue that the declining birth rate, caused by female employment and the availability of contraception, has a negative impact on our society. These changes are viewed by the New Right as partly to blame for the demise of the traditional nuclear family that is triggering an **alleged** moral decline.

Motivations for wanting to be 'child-free'

Gillespie (2003) identifies two potential motivational factors for voluntary childlessness. Some women are attracted by the **pull** of being child-free, especially the increased freedom and better relationships with partners that it may afford. A number of studies indicate that couples are happier without children. There may also be a '**push**' factor where some see parenting as conflicting with their careers or leisure interests. These women tend to express little interest in having children.

Now try this

Outline **three** different implications of the decline in the birth rate.

Demographic trends: death rate and life expectancy

Another possible reason for the growing UK population is the declining **death rate** and increasing **life expectancy**, which has led to an **ageing population**.

Definitions

- Death rate: the number of deaths per 1000 of the population over a year.
- Life expectancy: the average lifespan of each individual living in a particular society.

The **death rate** has steadily decreased since 1900. It was 19 per 1000 in 1901 compared to 9.0 per 1000 in 2014.

Life expectancy has risen from 48 years for men and 52 years for women in 1901 to 79.5 years for men and 82.5 years for women in 2014.

Reasons for the increase in life expectancy and decline in death rate

 1 **Improvement in living standards**
According to **McKeown** (1976) the 20th century has seen a dramatic improvement in living standards:
- Wage rises lifted many people out of poverty, meaning they could afford better housing and more nutritional food.
- The provision of well-ventilated social housing for the poor contributed to the near eradication of tuberculosis – a major killer of the poor in the 19th century.
- The introduction of public health initiatives such as clean water in the home and public sanitation/sewage schemes reduced the number of people dying from water-borne diseases such as cholera.

2 **Improved education** and knowledge of hygiene led to people taking more responsibility for avoiding health-threatening behaviour and adopting more hygienic, healthy lifestyles.

3 **The introduction of the Welfare State** – particularly access to the free medical care provided by the NHS, as well as social services and welfare payments – provided a safety net for those most at risk of ill health (for example, the elderly, the unemployed, and the long-term sick and disabled).

4 **Improvement of health care:** Life expectancy had increased before the introduction of the NHS in 1948, probably because of public health measures. However in 1958, the NHS introduced mass vaccination of all children under the age of 15 against diseases such as polio. Moreover new medicines and treatments are being created continuously with the aim of prolonging life as much as possible – for example, improvements in cancer treatments.

 Now try this

1 Outline the trends of both the death rate and life expectancy.
2 Briefly explain **one** reason for the decline in the death rate.

Implications of the ageing population

As there are now more people aged over 65 than under the age of 16, it is clear that the UK has an **ageing population**. With this trend come certain **implications** that are changing the nature of our society.

Implications

 Burden on public services and the dependency ratio

Evaluation

💬 **Concern with the dependency ratio.** The dependency ratio is the balance between the working population (who contribute to the state funding of pensions via taxation) and those dependent on the welfare state, such as pensioners. The government is concerned that the dependent elderly will soon outnumber tax-paying workers and that the state may not be able to afford to pay for the health care and pensions of an ageing population.

💬 **The Griffiths Report** (1983) indicated that the cost of elderly care will escalate in future years. This is because the 'baby boom' generation is predicted to retire around the same time, which could lead to unsustainable pension and health care costs. As a consequence, the Coalition government (2010–2015) increased the state pension age to 66 and there are plans of a future increase to 70 in order to cover the costs of this trend.

---

2 Increase in one-person households

Evaluation

💬 There has been an increase in elderly people living alone when their partner passes away. In 2013, 14% of all households consisted of an elderly person who lived alone. These are mostly women, as they generally have a longer life expectancy than men. **Chambers** (2012) refers to this as the '**feminisation of later life**'.

---

3 Increase in beanpole and extended families

Evaluation

👍 **Brannen** (2003) claims that the decline in birth rate and rise in life expectancy have combined to produce the **beanpole family**. As people live longer and have fewer children, so the relationships between grandparents, parents and children have become more significant. Families are now multi-generational as people tend to live long enough to have grandchildren and great grandchildren. Elderly relatives are useful because they can assist with childcare, which can allow their adult children to work longer hours. **Ross et al.** (2005) claim that the relationship between grandparents and their grandchildren has become significant because grandparents now play a major role in both the economic maintenance of nuclear families and the primary socialisation of children.

---

4 'Positive ageing'

Evaluation

👍 **Blaikie** (1999) observes that the growing number of empty nesters and more affluent retirees has brought about a change in how the elderly are viewed. There now exists an active but leisure-based '**third age**' in which the elderly are seen as a means of boosting the economy rather than a dependency problem as they have more disposable income than previous generations.

Now try this

How might family size be affected by the ageing population?

Migration

Another recent cause of the rising UK population is **migration**. Due to our increasingly globalised world, the movement of people has become a global process that is having a significant effect on society. Over recent years, **net migration** has hit record levels as more people enter the UK than leave it.

Different forms of migration

- **Immigration**: the number of people who enter the UK.
- **Emigration**: the number of people who leave the UK.
- **Net migration**: the difference between immigration and emigration over a period of time.
- **Internal migration**: movement within a country.

Trends in migration

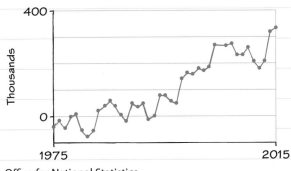

Office for National Statistics

There has been an increase in migration since the 1980s.

- The 2011 Census stated that 14% of the UK's population was made up of ethnic-minority groups compared to 6% in the 1991 Census.
- It is estimated by the ONS that 43% of the predicted future increase in the UK population will be due to immigration.

Reasons behind increasing migration

Legislation and border controls: some countries may reduce border controls and therefore encourage higher levels of immigration if they have a particular skills shortage within the economy.
In Australia, for example, there is a points-based immigration system that allocates a certain level of points to each immigrant application. If there is a shortage of a particular skill in their economy, a higher points score will be allocated to an immigrant who possesses attributes such as – for example – teachers, nurses and plumbers.

Push factors encourage people to leave a country.
Examples of push factors include war, poverty, lack of job opportunities or oppressive governments.

Pull factors encourage people to enter a country. Examples of pull factors include a generous welfare state, a reputable education system, a high standard of living, good job opportunities and weather.

Globalisation: it is now easier to move between countries due to transport and multi-national political organisations such as the EU allowing freedom of movement.
For example, evidence suggests that the UK vote in 2016 to leave the EU (Brexit) may have been partly caused by fears about the relaxation of such controls.

Now try this

1 Define what is meant by 'net migration'.
2 How has globalisation encouraged the increase in migration?

Implications of increased net migration

You need to know how increased migration affects families and households, and also wider society.

Cultural diversity in family structures

Certain communities are associated with different structures.

For example, **Berthoud** (2000) notes that over 50% of African-Caribbean families are headed by a single parent, whereas Pakistani and Bangladeshi families are most likely to be nuclear or extended.

African-Caribbean families

Chamberlain and Goulbourne (2001) researched African-Caribbean family structures. They argue there is an increasing trend of African-Caribbean women who choose to raise children independently from their child's father due to the struggles that men face with employment and the police. Chamberlain and Goulborne also discuss the importance of the extended family within the African-Caribbean community as single mothers have a wide support network that stretches beyond biological ties.

Gilroy (2003) argues that the promotion of the nuclear family is mainly influenced by what 'Western European' countries believe a 'conventional' family looks like. He uses the assumption that all families need a father to be effective at raising children. Gilroy believes that the 'matriarchal' nature of African-Caribbean families originates from the slave trade, which was essentially caused by the white population. Instead of being classed as inferior, African-Caribbean families should be seen as different; they are only deemed as inferior because they differ from the 'norm'.

Asian families

Asian families tend to be more traditional than other ethnic groups. **Berthoud** (2000) found that marriage is highly valued and therefore cohabitation and divorce are rare. There is also evidence to suggest that there is very little intermarriage between Asians and other ethnic groups. This could be due to the levels of arranged marriages within Asian communities.

Increase in dual-heritage and hybrid identities

Eriksen (2007) states there has been an increase in children who are born in the UK to parents where one or both are from another country. As a consequence, children form a unique identity that blends together their family heritage together with influences from contemporary UK culture.

African-Caribbean families

Platt (2009) claims that African-Caribbean people are the most likely community to marry someone from another ethnic group, specifically white people. In fact, only a minority of African-Caribbeans are married to each other. This has led to an increase in mixed race relationships and mixed race children to such an extent that only 25% of African-Caribbean children have two black parents.

Asian families

Modood (1997) discusses the tensions that can arise within different generations of the Asian community. As third- and fourth-generation Asian migrants have been raised in the UK, they may have different views from their parents and grandparents when it comes to religion and family diversity.

However, **Woodhead** (2001) claims that Muslim girls, in particular, are finding ways in which to stay true to their religion while also making a commitment to British culture by creating a 'hybrid identity'. Furthermore, **Eade** (1994) found that second-generation Bangladeshi Muslims in Britain created 'hierarchical identities' in that they saw themselves as Muslims first, Bangladeshi second and British third.

Third- and fourth-generation immigrants combine their heritage with British culture to create their own, unique 'hybrid identity'.

Now try this

1 What is meant by a 'hybrid identity'?

2 Which ethnic group is most likely to marry someone from a different ethnicity?

Exam skills 1

This Paper 2 exam-style question uses knowledge and skills you have already revised. Have a look at pages 119–123 for a reminder about childhood.

Worked example

1   Outline and explain **two** ways in which childhood is experienced differently, even in the UK.   **(10 marks)**

• Experiences of childhood in Britain may vary according to social class. Upper-class children may find that they spend most of their formative years in boarding at expensive private schools, with the superior facilities and smaller class sizes this provides. Middle-class children may be encouraged from an early age to aim for university and a professional career, and both are likely to receive considerable economic and cultural support from their parents. However, working-class childhood may be made more difficult by the experience of poverty. Howard notes children born into poor families in the UK are also more likely to die in infancy or childhood, to suffer longstanding illness, to be shorter in height, to fall behind in school, and to be placed on the child protection register. They may also lack the cultural and economic support available to middle-and upper-class children.

• Experiences of childhood in Britain may vary according to ethnicity and/or religion. The vast majority of white children are unlikely to be much affected by their parents' religious beliefs unless their parents belong to a Christian sect such as the Jehovah's Witnesses. For example, children whose parents belong to this sect may not be allowed to celebrate their birthday or Christmas. Some Christian parents who are regular church-goers may insist their children attend services such as mass or attend Sunday school, but because of secularisation this is increasingly unlikely. In contrast, there is evidence that Muslim, Hindu and Sikh children generally feel a stronger sense of obligation and duty to their religious community and their parents than white children. Generational conflict is therefore less likely or is more likely to be hidden. Girls may also experience more restrictions than boys in terms of how they can behave during childhood.

Command words: Outline and explain

👍 Here you need to show your knowledge of concepts, policies, theories and so on. However, you also need to apply what you know to the context in the question and weigh up the different arguments.

👍 Use studies and examples to support your points, and make sure you also use sociological terms and concepts.

Always make clear how the point you are making links to the question.

You could bullet-point your response to this type of question. Bullet points will focus you on the need for two distinct ways.

This response develops the point about the different experience of childhood based on class by analysing the effects of economic and cultural support.

This is immediately followed by an evaluative point backed up by sociological evidence (Howard).

You need to discuss the two ways in which childhood is experienced differently in some detail. Write two in-depth paragraphs using full sentences with good examples and references to sociological studies if possible to support your points.

Exam skills 2

Have a look at pages 98–107, 110 and 116–118 for a reminder about power relationships in modern families. Spend no more than 15 minutes on this question.

Worked example

2 Read **Item A** below and answer the question that follows.

> **Item A**
>
> Some sociologists argue that power is more fairly distributed between spouses in UK families because men and women now have equal access to divorce. Some sociologists also observe that increased participation by women in the labour market has also led to more equality in modern family life. However, feminists are cautious about drawing such conclusions because male abuse of power and control can still be seen in many family relationships today.

Applying material from **Item A**, analyse **two** ways in which power is now more fairly distributed between spouses in UK families today. **(10 marks)**

- Some sociologists have concluded that power is now more fairly distributed between spouses by carrying out surveys which quantitatively measure the number of hours a week that each spouse spends on childcare and housework tasks. For example, Young and Wilmott concluded in the early 1970s that nuclear families had become symmetrical because, as Item A observes, wives and mothers were entering the labour market in large numbers. According to Young and Wilmott this has led to a move to joint conjugal roles where husbands and wives share housework, childcare and leisure-time. These replaced segregated conjugal roles in which men and women occupy distinctly separate roles, such as men as breadwinners and women as mother-housewife. Young and Wilmott claim joint conjugal roles mean that men and women wield similar levels of power in UK families today. However a range of feminist studies suggest that women are still overwhelmingly responsible for both childcare and housework tasks and that Young and Wilmott's concept of symmetry is exaggerated. The evidence suggests that women often carry a dual burden of labour in that they often have paid jobs and are still doing most of the childcare and housework.
- Item A also suggests that changes in the divorce law have contributed to women having more power in families …

Command word: Analyse

These questions require you to analyse two ways, reasons, factors etc. Take each 'way' and explain logically how it proves the point in the question, here this is that power is more fairly distributed between spouses in the UK.

Link your points together, showing how each follows on from the next, providing examples to prove your point, and linking back to the question.

You could bullet-point your response to this question to help you focus on the need for two distinct points.

Each 'way' should be reasonably detailed and use examples of changes in family life and how these have supposedly contributed to power now being distributed more equally between spouses in families today.

Make sure you also refer to and use examples from the item in your answer, and support this by extending with your own knowledge and examples.

This response makes a very relevant reference to a sociological study which claims that a feminised economy and workforce was leading to more equality in the family. Note too the reference to sociological concepts such as 'joint conjugal roles', 'segregated conjugal roles', 'symmetrical families' and 'dual burden of labour'.

You don't need to come to a conclusion but do link your point back to the question to show that you are answering it.

The second part of this response should focus on divorce and how it has contributed to equality. Describe how divorce pre-1972 favoured men and show how the Divorce Reform Act led to 'more equal access' to divorce. Include references to feminists such as Hart who observes that women can now escape abusive empty shell marriages and that four out of every five divorces are initiated by women. Think too how you might make use of the final point in Item A.

Exam skills 3

This Paper 2 exam-style question uses knowledge and skills you have already revised. Allocate your time effectively. You should be spending about 30 minutes on this question.

Worked example

3 Read **Item B** below and answer the question that follows.

> **Item B**
>
> In Victorian times, it could be said that the family, whether middle-class or working-class, was truly patriarchal. In the 19th century, married women were generally excluded from paid work and the husband was often the only breadwinner. Violence by men against their wives was common and the existing divorce law favoured husbands who were granted divorce more than their wives. In summary, a married woman's status was not dissimilar to that of a child.

Applying material from **Item B** and your knowledge, evaluate the view that the patriarchal family is in decline in the 21st century. **(20 marks)**

A patriarchal family is one that is dominated by a male head of household. Item B observes that the patriarchal family dominant in Victorian Britain in both working-class and middle-class communities had a number of distinctive characteristics. First, men were expected to go out to work and support their families while women stayed at home as mothers and housewives. Women who worked met with severe social disapproval. Second, Item B suggests that domestic violence by men against women was commonplace. Third, divorce laws favoured males. Women found it extremely difficult to escape from unhappy violent marriages, whereas men found it relatively easy to divorce their wives. Fourth, property laws also favoured husbands according to Item B. When a middle-class woman with property married, her wealth and property transferred to his control. Finally, Item B concludes that the status of a married woman in the Victorian patriarchal family was second-class and not dissimilar to that of a child. ...

This introduction acts as a plan for the rest of the essay because it mentions five themes that can be explored and developed in more detail to show that families are now less patriarchal.

Command word: Evaluate

If a question asks you to **evaluate** a particular view:

👍 Outline the 'view' in the title in as much detail as you can using sociological terms, concepts and studies whenever possible.

👍 Use the material in the Item and your own knowledge to support aspects of the 'view' and illustrate your points.

👍 Outline any opposing or contrasting views.

👍 Identify any strengths and weaknesses of the view to create a debate.

👍 Draw an appropriate conclusion.

Define any key concepts used in the question – in this case, the patriarchal family.

Highlight the parts of the item that could be used in your response. The introduction uses the item and constantly refers to its use. This indicates good application.

The rest of the essay now needs to explore and describe the following:

1 **Describe** changes to the economy especially the feminisation of the economy and the workforce and demonstrate how this affected the family, for example, it turned the patriarchal nuclear family into a dual-career family.

2 **Use studies** that show the family is now less patriarchal – for example, **Young and Wilmott's** (1973) study of the symmetrical family. To show **evaluation** use feminist studies such as **Oakley** (1974) to question this view.

3 Examine characteristics of the Victorian family that have not disappeared – for example, domestic violence. Look at changes in official attitudes (the law and the police). However it is still the most common form of violence in society today. **Use examples and/or studies** to support your points.

4 Describe how divorce laws have changed, and how these benefit women today (for example, initiating divorce).

5 **Draw a conclusion** based on the evidence you have provided. For example, here it would be that women now generally enjoy the same rights as men and no longer occupy the same status as children.

Exam-style practice

Practise for Paper 2 of your A Level exam with these exam-style questions. You will find answers on page 221. Before looking at these questions, it would be useful to have revised the functionalist and postmodernist debates about of the family and family diversity, and power in family relationships.

1   Outline and explain **two** ways in which marriage could be described as more egalitarian compared with 50 years ago. **(10 marks)**

2   Read **Item A** below and answer the question that follows.

Item A

Functionalist sociologists such as Murdock argue that the nuclear family (father, mother and children) is the universal norm whilst Parsons argued that this type of family is best suited to modern industrial societies. However postmodernist sociologists argue that family diversity is the norm in the UK and that the concept of the 'family' should be abandoned and replaced either with the concept of 'life-course' or 'personal life'.

Applying material from **Item A**, analyse **two** changes in UK family life that have occurred in recent years according to postmodernist sociologists. **(10 marks)**

3   Read **Item B** below and answer the question that follows.

Item B

According to functionalists, industrialisation led to greater geographical mobility and loss of regular contact with extended kin. The wider family network was no longer required as wages and living standards improved. The state gradually extended welfare benefits to vulnerable sections of the population as the emotional and personal needs were met by the nuclear unit. However, a number of sociological studies of the 1950s and 1960s suggested that the isolation of the nuclear family from the wider family had been exaggerated. The study of Bethnal Green in London by Young and Wilmott (1957) found extended families with frequent and strong contact between kin.

Applying material from **Item B** and your knowledge, evaluate the view that industrialisation led to the decline of the extended family and the rise of the nuclear family. **(20 marks)**

In question 1, the command word 'outline' means you need to set out the main characteristics of the theory or trend being referred to by the question. The question is worth 10 marks so you should write two reasonably detailed paragraphs explaining how some aspect of marriage has become more egalitarian or equal. If relevant, sociological studies should be mentioned to support your points.

Spend 15 minutes on each 10 mark question. No introduction or conclusion is required.

In order to 'analyse' you need to set out the social changes methodically and develop a logical and detailed chain of reasoning. In doing so you should show knowledge and understanding of key concepts, studies/evidence. These must be applied to the question and analysed (explained fully).

If you bullet-point your response to question 2, it will help you focus on the need for two distinct points. Each 'change' should be reasonably detailed and use examples of sociological theories or studies and clearly make the link between the 'change' and postmodernism.

Question 2 instructs you to use the Item so make sure you do this. You need to identify and refer to two points from the item to help you answer the questions.

This question demands an essay response. It also clearly instructs you to use material in this item to illustrate or evaluate the view contained in the question. Before you begin answering the question, carefully read through the item and highlight the bits of the passage that you might use in your answer. Try to make at least two direct references to the item in your essay. Draw the examiner's attention to your use of material in the item by using phrases such as 'as can be seen in Item B'. You can also use your own knowledge of sociological theories and studies to give examples to support your points.

Definitions and types of religion

Sociologists argue that religion is a **social construct** as they believe that religion is a product of society. Consequently, it is not possible to produce a universal definition of religion because different societies and even groups within the same society interpret 'religion' in very different ways.

Substantive definitions

Substantive definitions aim to identify the core **characteristics** shared by major religions.

For example:

• There is a reference to a God, gods or a supernatural power that is able to influence the destiny of society or humanity.
• Beliefs and morality are collected in a sacred text, for example, the Bible, the Qu'ran, the Torah.
• Particular objects, places and people are revered as 'holy'.

Substantive definitions are **exclusive** in nature because belief systems can only be classed as religions if they have these particular features.

Max Weber (1905) defines religion in a substantive way. He claims that it is a belief in a **supernatural power** that cannot be proven scientifically.

Constructionist definitions

Interpretivists are mainly interested in how definitions of religion are constructed, challenged and fought over. **Aldridge (2007)** shows how, for its followers, Scientology is a religion despite the fact that several governments have denied it the legal status of being a religion and in some cases, such as Germany, have actually banned it. Interpretivists therefore conclude that whether a belief system is defined as a religion depends on who has power.

Functional definitions

Functional definitions analyse what a religion does for the society that it exists within. It may bring comfort to its believers, reinforce societal values or even maintain inequality. These definitions are criticised as being mainly **inclusive**, as any belief system can be classed as a religion if it performs certain **functions**.

Sacred canopy

Berger (1967) claims that religion acts like a **sacred canopy** to its believers as it protects them from all of the dangers in the world. Just like a jungle's canopy protects the life on the ground beneath, religion comforts its followers by answering the '**big questions**' they have about life's uncertainties, such as how the world was created and the afterlife.

Could football be a religion?

Types of religion

Theistic religions

• A belief in a higher power that could be one god (monotheistic) or many gods (polytheistic).
• This supernatural power is the source of the beliefs around which the religion revolves, and is therefore seen as sacred by its followers.
For example, Christianity (monotheistic) and Hinduism (polytheistic).

Animism

• A belief in spirits and ghosts that can positively or negatively impact the human and natural world.
• Animistic religions tend to be more prevalent in pre-industrial and non-industrial societies.
For example, paganism, and ancient religions associated with the Aztecs, Native Americans and the Azande people (see page 136).

Types of religion

New Age movements

• A spiritual rather than religious belief system, focused on self-development and fulfilment rather than a devotion to a higher, supernatural power.
• These movements are often based on Eastern religions like Buddhism and Confucianism.
• Postmodernists believe that New Age movements are on the increase (see page 154).
For example, Reiki.

Totemism

• A form of animism in which a community creates a **symbol** (usually an animal or plant) that represents them as a group. The symbol gains a **sacred** (holy or special) significance and is believed to protect the people it represents.
• **Durkheim (1915)** believed that many religions include elements of totemism, which forms the basis of his view of the functions of religion (see page 139).
For example, Australian Aborigines.

Now try this

1 What is the difference between inclusive and exclusive definitions of religion?
2 Explain what is meant by a New Age movement.

Religion as an ideology

Regardless of what form it takes, religion is an example of an **ideology**. It is a belief system which aims to provide an explanation for the way societies are organised, in terms of the distribution of power and inequality. However, religions are also **closed belief systems** because they tend to reject challenges to their core beliefs from other belief systems such as science, philosophy and competing religions.

Religion as a closed belief system

As many religions claim that they hold a **monopoly on the truth** (they see themselves as the true representative of God), they often do not tolerate challenge from their rivals or even their own believers. Consequently, it is argued that their beliefs are too conservative, inflexible and resistant to social change. Some sociologists believe that this has led to a decline in religious beliefs in some societies – a process known as '**secularisation**'.

Religion as an open belief system

Some religions have become open belief systems as they are having to adapt to social change in order to remain relevant. **Herberg** (1960) notes that some religions have also had to dilute some of their core beliefs in order to maintain their relevancy in the modern world. Herberg refers to this process as **internal secularisation**. It explains why religions such as the Church of England felt the need to push through the vote to allow women bishops in their hierarchy in 2015, as they were increasingly becoming out of touch with the rest of society. (The impact of such decisions will be analysed in later topics.)

Self-sustaining beliefs

Polanyi (1958) states that in order to protect themselves from challenge, closed belief systems, such as religions, tend to have specific tendencies.

 Denial of legitimacy – by completely rejecting the basic principles of their rivals, belief systems can convince their followers that they are the only possible answer.

For example, religions that believe in creationism (the belief that God made the world) demand the total obedience of their followers by rejecting all evidence attached to evolution.

 Subsidiary explanations – Polanyi claims that closed belief systems have a series of 'get out clauses'. If a religious leader is directly challenged, they then have a way of deflecting the focus of the argument.

An example of this would be the statement that 'God works in mysterious ways' in response to people who question why natural disasters occur.

 Key study   **Evans-Pritchard (1936)**

Evans-Pritchard, a functionalist, studied the Azande people of Sudan, whose animistic religion reflected the characteristics of a closed belief system.

Their view that witchcraft caused misfortune may have seemed irrational to non-believers, but the Azande people had been indoctrinated into their beliefs and they were not allowed to question them.

The Azande believe that individuals have no control over the witchcraft that exists within their stomachs. Therefore, an accusation that someone has cast witchcraft on another is very hard to prove or disprove. This could be problematic as it might lead to further conflict within the community. In order to deal with this issue, the elders (the most respected members of the tribe) would create a potion made of natural ingredients to be used as a form of oracle (the Azande call this a 'benge'). An elder would ask the benge if witchcraft had been cast by the accused person and would then feed the benge to a chicken. The belief was that if witchcraft had taken place, the chicken would die and therefore signal what had happened. As a consequence, the accused person would apologise and try to make up for the misfortune caused by their witchcraft in order to repair the relationship between them and the victim.

Now try this

1   What is meant by a closed belief system?

2   Explain the term 'monopoly on the truth'.

Science as an ideology

After the Industrial Revolution of the 1800s, **science** replaced religion as the dominant ideology in Western society. This period of time is known as the **Enlightenment**. However, just like religion, science is a socially-constructed belief system that is based upon some core principles (see pages 88–89).

Core principles of science

1 Science is the pursuit of **facts** that are supported by evidence.

2 It is **objective** (not biased).

3 Science studies the impact of **cause and effect** relationships based on **reliable** data that can be accurately tested.

The impact of science

The impact of science can be clearly seen in contemporary society.

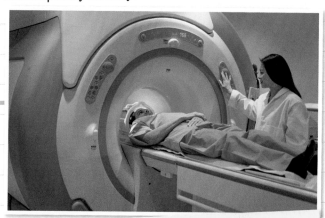

Scientific discoveries have led to technological and medical advances that have revolutionised our economy and everyday life, along with providing society with potential answers to questions about our existence.

Science as an open belief system

Sir Karl Popper (1959) believes that science has become the dominant belief system in the Western world because it can be challenged and has therefore grown as a discipline. He claims that the basis of science is built upon **falsification**, a process by which all scientists attempt to challenge pre-existing theories or knowledge with the aim of testing their findings. If a theory is proven wrong, another replaces it and therefore the knowledge within the discipline grows (see page 88).

Science as a closed belief system

However, science may not be as 'open' as Popper suggests. **Thomas Kuhn** (1970) believes that science as a discipline is actually a closed belief system due to the **paradigms** that dominate it. A paradigm shapes:

- how the discipline is defined and understood by those who operate within it and by others
- how research is conducted, i.e. by creating hypotheses and so on.

Kuhn argues that scientists generally work within a pre-existing framework that does not encourage creative freedom. Those who follow the guidelines tend to be rewarded, whereas those who question how science should work tend to be ridiculed and marginalised. In this view, science is in many ways similar to other ideologies as it denounces all beliefs that challenge its core principles (see page 89).

Robert Merton and the CUDOS norms (1942)

Merton, a functionalist, agrees with the sentiments of Popper's view of science by claiming that science has grown because of the following ethos, which is shaped by four specific norms.

Communism – scientific knowledge is shared with the whole community and therefore is not kept private.

Universalism – all scientists are regarded as equal and so it should be their work that is challenged, not their social characteristics.

Disinterestedness – scientists should be committed to truth and publish their findings honestly. There should be no fraud or subjective bias in their claims.

Organised Scepticism – all knowledge within science should be challenged and scrutiny should be encouraged by all scientists.

This ethos is known as the **CUDOS norms**.

Now try this

1 In your own words, explain what Merton meant by the CUDOS norms that have led to the growth of science as an ideology?

2 What is meant by a paradigm?

137

Theoretical views of ideologies

Both science and religion are **ideologies** as they are sets of beliefs based around core principles aimed at explaining why the world works in the way that it does. Within the field of sociology, there are different views on the purpose and relevance of ideologies.

Marxist view

All ideologies, including science and religion, are manipulated by the ruling class to maintain and reproduce inequality. They are in place to justify the principles of the capitalist system and prevent a working-class revolution.

With specific reference to science, Marxists argue that the majority of discoveries are motivated by generating mass profits, which only fuels the capitalist system further.

Michalowski and Kramer (1987)

An example of this Marxist view in practice is **Michalowski and Kramer's** study of pharmaceutical companies who produce vital medicines that are needed for society, but sell their product at prices that only the wealthy societies can afford. There have also been claims that some pharmaceutical companies have sold unsafe medicines to developing countries, which have not established stringent testing standards, in order to maximise their profits.

Feminist view

Ideologies like science and religion have promoted patriarchy for generations, for example by blocking women from positions of power or tainting them as weak or impure. These ideologies are responsible for the lack of progress made with regards to gender equality.

Ann Oakley (1972) argues that John Bowlby's theory of maternal deprivation (1951) is a good example of science acting as an ideology. This justified gender inequality in the workplace by claiming that the development of young children was 'damaged' by working mothers. It strengthened the patriarchal idea that only men should be breadwinners and that women should stay at home with their children.

Postmodernist view

Postmodernists such as **Lyotard** (1984) claim that religion and science are **meta-narratives**. These ideologies, which seek to explain 'truth', are no longer relevant due to the fragmentation of society. Because knowledge is relative to the individual, scientific facts and religious teachings are no longer automatically accepted as 'truth' in the postmodern world.

Karl Mannheim (1929)

Mannheim claims that all world views or ideologies (such as science, religion and sociological theories) are the product of theologians or intellectuals who cannot relate to the everyday individual, so their ideas reflect their own personal interests. Mannheim states that there are two types of world view:

1. **Ideological thought** – this style of world view attempts to justify tradition and the maintenance of society as it is, thus resisting change. This is probably because those who control the ideology personally benefit from the current state of society and are therefore trying to consolidate their position of power.

2. **Utopian thought** – this style of world view or ideology attempts to promote social change because the current state of the world does not suit those who construct utopian belief systems.

Mannheim argues that we need to detach subjectivity from these world views and instead create an objective world view that every individual can subscribe and relate to. Such knowledge, which would be free of ideology, can only be produced by free-floating intellectuals unattached to any particular value-position. He refers to this as a '**free-floating intelligentsia**'.

Now try this

1 What is meant by a 'free-floating intelligentsia'?
2 Why is science deemed to be a meta-narrative, according to postmodernists?

The functionalist view of religion

Theoretical debates with regard to the functions of religion tend to focus on whether it acts as a force for **social change** or maintains **social stability**. Functionalists have a structural view of society (see page 8) and believe that religion is a vital institution that reinforces social order. They believe that religion functions to provide stability to society and is therefore a **conservative force**, as it tends to maintain society as it is, rather than encouraging social change.

The sacred and the profane

Durkheim (1915) believed that the main purpose of religion was to clearly differentiate between things that were **sacred** or **profane** in our society.

Key definitions

Sacred: things that are special because they are the product of a higher being or supernatural power. Consequently they inspire, invoke fear, have power and are associated with rules and taboos. For example, buildings such as churches and temples are sacred.

Profane: things that are ordinary, average, and have no special meaning or purpose.
For example, buildings such as offices are profane.

Collective conscience

Through his study of the Australian Aborigines, **Durkheim** (1915) claimed that many religions are based on **totemism** (see page 135). To a community, their chosen sacred symbol represents the higher power that protects them and themselves as a society. By worshipping their god, therefore, they are also celebrating their own society.

Durkheim observed that worship was a collective activity, rather than something that was conducted on an individual level. He claimed that community worship provides people with a **collective conscience**, a shared understanding of the norms, morals, values and beliefs that promotes a sense of belonging to society, known as social integration.

Cognitive functions of religion

Durkheim believed that not only is religion a major agent of socialisation and a source of social integration, but that it also provides its followers with the intellectual capacity to understand the world. It achieves this by helping congregations to understand concepts such as time, space and causation along with classification when it comes to understanding status differences, such as God being more powerful than man. To Durkheim, therefore, religion was the beginning of human thought and reason.

Socialisation

As with all of the other social institutions, functionalists believe that religion acts as an agent of **secondary socialisation**, in that it teaches its followers the norms and values of society. By performing this function, religion reinforces the value consensus that underpins social order.

Talcott Parsons (1967) believed that, through sacred texts, religion elevates the values of a society into **sacred moral codes**.

For example, the ten commandments in Christianity generally underpin UK law and culture. By entrenching the same values into the national religion, the sanctions imposed for breaking those values (the afterlife) become more effective as a form of social control.

Another example of how religion underpins the law of a society could include processes such as taxation. By paying mandatory taxes, privileged citizens are helping those who are less fortunate, which is also a value that is encouraged within the Church of England.

According to Durkheim, the worship of the totem for the Australian Aborigines was a metaphor for the worship of their society.

Now try this

What is meant by a collective conscience?

Understanding the functionalist view of religion

The work of **Malinowski** (1948) and **Robert Bellah** (1970) can help to develop your understanding of the functionalist view of religion.

Psychological functions

In addition to the other functions that religion provides for society, **Malinowski** (1926) claims that religion also provides society with **psychological functions**. He claims that religion can help people overcome life-crises. It achieves this by creating '**rites of passage**', such as funerals, to help its believers to deal with the stress, anxiety and grief that they are experiencing so that they can return to normality as soon as possible. By minimising the level of disruption caused by significant life events, religion acts as a vital source of stability, which is beneficial to society.

Civil religion

Following on from Durkheim's belief that religion was more about social integration, **neo-functionalists** have applied this understanding to contemporary societies. **Robert Bellah** (1967) argues that the USA has its own civil religion known as '**Americanism**' that combines religious and national values.

Bellah points out that the USA is an immigrant society containing a vast amount of diversity and inequality. Americanism as a civil religion has developed in order to avoid conflict and to promote integration into American society. This is because the American notion of God is not associated with any particular religious group. Instead, God represents America, which is consequently viewed as 'sacred' – the promised land.

The study of Americanism as a civil religion suggests that religion is not just about a belief in a higher power. Instead, it is a tool that is used to integrate a population in order to promote social solidarity and stability.

 Key study

Trobriand Islands, Papua New Guinea

In his anthropological study, **Malinowski** (1948) observed how the Trobriand Islanders used religion to help them overcome the grief and uncertainty that was sometimes the result of their most sacred activities.

Malinowski studied how the Islanders participated in a ritual known as the '**kula**', in which they would exchange seashells with neighbouring islands to build and maintain friendship. However, the journey to the neighbouring islands was often dangerous due to the tropical seas that they had to cross. Consequently, the Trobriand Islanders used to pray to their gods before the journey due to the uncertainty of their loved one's survival. When people drowned, the Islanders would pray in order to seek comfort. Malinowski concluded that religion exists as a means of helping people cope with the uncertainties around death.

Trobriand men preparing the kula trading canoe.

As with other religions, the civil religion of 'Americanism' has its own sacred rituals, such as pledging allegiance to the flag (which acts as their totem) along with singing the national anthem at all sporting events.

Evaluation

👎 Whilst the functionalist theory of religion illustrates the many positives it may provide for society, it tends to ignore the negative effects of religion. **Hamilton** (1995) claims that religion also has **dysfunctions**, such as creating conflict and encouraging irrational thought, which do not benefit society and, in many ways, prevent positive change from occurring.

Now try this

How do rites of passage provide psychological functions for religious believers?

The Marxist view of religion

Like functionalists, Marxists believe that, by acting as a **conservative force**, religion is a source of **social stability**. However, Marxists believe that this only benefits capitalism, which is therefore negative as it reproduces and justifies class inequality. You can use this perspective to criticise the functionalist view.

Religion as ideology

Karl Marx (1844) believed that as religion was part of the **superstructure of capitalism**, its main function was to benefit capitalism through its power as an ideology. He claimed that it maintained capitalism in two ways:

 It suggests that inequality is God-given and therefore unchangeable.

 It teaches the poor that their poverty is a test from God, which will be compensated for in the afterlife if they accept their lack of power.

By convincing the proletariat to accept inequality, religion is succeeding in its purpose to promote **false class consciousness**, as the proletariat never become fully aware of how they are exploited by the capitalist system.

Christianity versus socialism

Engels (1895) claims that socialism and Christianity have some similar features. Both ideologies are targeted at the poor and provide a promise of a better life. The key difference between the ideologies is that while Christianity only provides its followers with salvation in the afterlife, socialism provides a better future in this life.

Marxists therefore believe that religion provides no help to the poor as it prevents real change from occurring. Upon the creation of a communist state, there would be no need for religion as there would be no inequality to justify.

The 'opium of the masses'

Marx saw religion as a way of comforting the proletariat about the **alienation** (lack of connection/feeling of distance from what they are doing) that they experienced in the workplace. Marx stated that religion was the **'opium of the masses'** as it dulls the pain of oppression by giving its followers a temporary 'high' through promises of a better afterlife in order to distract them from their exploitation. Religion therefore promotes social stability because it functions to prevent a working-class revolution.

Application of Marxism to Hinduism

The caste system of Hinduism (see page 6) is a good illustration of how religions justify inequality. Hindus believe that they are born into their caste (similar to social class) based on their actions in a previous life. If they are born into a lower caste, they are being punished by the gods; those born into the top castes are being rewarded. Consequently, Hindus in the lower castes are encouraged not to question their current exploitation in the hope that when they are reincarnated they will be rewarded in the next life.

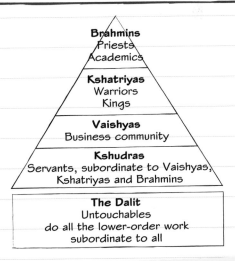

In Hinduism, each strata is differentiated by religious purity: the Brahmin caste is regarded as the most pure whilst the Dalits are regarded as the most impure.

Now try this

According to Marx, how does religion maintain a false class consciousness?

Evaluation of the Marxist view of religion

As part of your evaluation, you can use specific theorists who support or criticise the Marxist view of religion in addition to the use of wider theoretical perspectives.

Leach (1988)

👍 **Leach** claims that there is a strong connection between the powerful and the national religion that is imposed upon the public.

For example, the Queen of England is also the head of the Church of England. Also, only 13 per cent of bishops in the Church of England attended state comprehensive schools, which illustrates how it is dominated by the privately educated, wealthy elite.

Norris and Inglehart (2004)

👍 **Norris and Inglehart** agree with Marxists that the poor are often the most attracted to religion. Within their study of **existential security**, Norris and Inglehart believed that the most vulnerable people are more likely to be religious as they are less secure in predicting their own future existence. As a result, they turn to religion as the only source of comfort they will have in providing that security within this life, or the next. This may explain why Americans seem to be more religious than people in the UK due to their lack of universal health care and a restrictive welfare system.

Criticisms of the Marxist theory of religion

👎 Some sociologists claim that society has become more secular (less religious) and therefore question the influence that religion can have on exploiting the working class.

👎 Marx's analysis mainly focuses on the conservative nature of religion and therefore does not consider examples where religion has helped to influence positive change for the most vulnerable.

👎 Marx predicted that religion would cease to exist within a communist society. However, this has not occurred in some of the communist states that have emerged. It is predicted that China will become the most Christian nation by 2030.

Halevy (1927)

👍 **Halevy** argues that religions have a history of preventing revolutions and therefore act as a source of social stability. He discusses how the **Methodist Church** was influential during the 18th and 19th centuries in appeasing the workers' disconnection with the 'corrupt' Anglican Church in England.

Methodist leaders like John Wesley would often preach to large groups of mill and factory workers and encourage them to become part of a new form of Christianity that was tailored for them.

The Methodist Church aimed to appeal to workers by having simple undecorated chapels and more relaxed sermons that contained anti-establishment themes, which made the workers feel as though they were not conforming to the upper-class values represented by the Church of England.

Halevy concludes by stating that without the Methodist Church, there may have been a working-class revolution in the UK. Instead of taking to the streets in protest of their exploitation, the workers found another way to vent their frustration whilst continuing to participate in the capitalist system.

Now try this

Outline **one** study that provides evidence to support the claims of the Marxist theory of religion.

The neo-Marxist view of religion

Within the Marxist discipline, there have been theorists who present religion in a slightly different light. Although all Marxists agree that religion can exploit the poor, some believe that, in certain extreme circumstances, it can also **promote change** in order to help the most vulnerable.

The 'dual character' of religion

Ernst Bloch (1959) claimed that religion had a '**dual character**' as it had both a positive and negative effect on social change. In many ways, religion acted as a conservative force, however it could also be seen as a '**principle of hope**' that could inspire the proletariat to revolt in the most extreme circumstances.

Antonio Gramsci (1971) agreed with this analysis. He claimed that although the church played its part in maintaining the **cultural hegemony** (dominant set of beliefs) that benefitted the ruling class, it could also produce its own ideas that could inspire social change. This would often occur if clergy members from the lower parts of the church hierarchy felt that they could make a difference in their community, rather than persisting with the official messages of the church. This **individual autonomy** could, in some circumstances, override the ruling-class ideology that was promoted by the religion as a whole.

Religion's influence on social change and conflict

Otto Maduro (1982) agreed with Gramsci's ideas and argued that in some countries where protests were banned by dictatorships, the church could be the only **safe outlet of frustration** for the proletariat. In addition, religious leaders could be the charismatic figures that would inspire their congregations to achieve real social change. Maduro claims that they would be led by their conscience rather than sticking to the message of the religion. The religious leaders would also be seen as untouchable by the oppressive governments because they were seen as **sacred** by their followers. If they came to any harm, an uncontrollable uprising could occur. Maduro believed that if people could be inspired by religious leaders, they may begin a political movement that could influence positive social change (see Liberation theology below).

Emergence of the Pentecostal Church

🗨 Although neo-Marxists claim religion can influence change through instability and conflict, the **Pentecostal Church** has emerged as a dominant force in South America to instil greater stability. **David Lehmann** (2002) claims that instead of encouraging their followers to take political or, in some cases, violent action against oppressive governments, the Pentecostal Church challenges their followers to focus on taking charge of their own futures by working harder to progress out of poverty. This movement has become very popular in Brazil and tends to promote social stability rather than conflict and instability. It could also be said that by promoting the value of hard work, the Pentecostal Church is benefitting the capitalist system.

Liberation theology

In South America during the 1960s and 70s, for example, Catholic priests developed the **liberation theology movement** as a response to the failure of the Vatican to help its followers with the poverty and exploitation that they faced. The priests encouraged their followers to enforce change upon their society, even to use violence when necessary, in order to overthrow the dictators that oppressed them. The movement succeeded in its aim in Nicaragua as the dictator Somoza was overthrown by the Sandinista Revolution. By taking this action, the priests who were involved were excommunicated (excluded) from the Catholic Church.

Although the liberation theology movement has shown how religion can bring about change, it is often volatile and unstable.

Now try this

What do neo-Marxists mean when they claim that religion has a 'dual character'?

Max Weber

Max Weber (1905) believed that religion can help bring about change, as well as encouraging social stability, depending on the **theodicy** that dominates the belief system.

The role of religion

Weber believed that the role of religion was to meet the **social and psychological needs of the population** in order to make them feel more secure. This could have two possible outcomes:

- Religion could act as an ideology and justify a system of inequality.

- Religion could bring about much needed social change.

It would achieve this by attempting to explain why certain social groups experienced misfortune as opposed to those who seemed to benefit from a god's favour.

Theodicies

According to Weber, different social groups would create different religious ideas in order to understand and explain their experiences. He referred to these views as **theodicies**.

For example, the poor construct '**theodicies of misfortune**', which explain their poverty as a challenge or test. Their reaction to this test would prove their worthiness for reward in the afterlife.

Weber's ideas are similar here to those of Marx. However, Weber observes that Christian ideas can be and have been used to overcome injustices, such as slavery and improving the conditions of child workers in the 19th century.

Three forms of leadership

When it comes to religious organisations, Weber believed that there were three different forms of leadership.

1 **Charismatic leadership** – the individual inspires their followers through their **personal qualities** and ability to communicate effectively.

Reverend Martin Luther King Jr was a Baptist preacher and considered by many to be a charismatic leader in the American Civil Rights movement in the 1960s. For more on Martin Luther King Jr see page 146.

2 **Traditional leadership** – the individual holds power and influence because they preserve and support existing cultural norms and values that they wish to maintain.

3 **Legal-rational leadership** – the individual exerts authority because they have the support of the legal system.

The leadership of a religion would dictate its ability to achieve change. Weber claimed that **charismatic leaders** were the most likely to achieve social change because they could galvanise their followers to question those who were traditional leaders or who relied upon pre-existing laws for their power.

Examples of theodicies of fortune and misfortune

Through their study of American religious organisations, **Christiano and Swatos** (2008) found examples of Weber's theodicies. They found that the churches representing the mainstream, middle-class American, tended to preach '**theodicies of good fortune**'. These churches would encourage conservative values, promote social stability and approve of how society operated in its current condition. In doing so, they also supported social inequalities and justified them by suggesting that their successful congregation were receiving God's favour as a result of their actions.

Christiano and Swatos also studied the approaches taken by churches with poorer congregations, such as the **Pentecostal Church**. They found that these churches attempted to encourage change through promoting '**theodicies of misfortune**' and hoped to inspire their followers to reform elements of their character or behaviour in order to be successful.

For more on Martin Luther King Jr see page 146.

> **Now try this**

Outline the **three** different forms of religious leadership, according to Max Weber.

The Protestant work ethic

When discussing the potential of religion to encourage change through charismatic leadership, **Weber's** study The Protestant Ethic and the Spirit of Capitalism (1905) offers a prime example. Weber believed that the development of **Calvinism** was highly influential in creating modern capitalism.

Introduction

Before the emergence of Calvinism in the 1500s, Weber believed that capitalism existed in a different form to that which we understand today. Wealth was considered to be a sign of greed and it was therefore seen as a sinful activity to possess vast amounts of money. Consequently, wealthy people would make sizable donations to the Roman Catholic Church or to religious charities that helped the poor and those less fortunate than themselves. However, **John Calvin** (the founder of Calvinism) created his own denomination (offshoot) of the Protestant religion, in which he changed the way that wealth and work were viewed by his followers.

Beliefs of Calvinism

1 **Predestination** – Calvin preached that God had already decided who would enter the kingdom of heaven before birth and that his decision was unchangeable. Those who were chosen were to be known as 'the elect'.

2 **Divine transcendence** – no individual would have the power to rival God and be able to predict his wishes. The only source of information would be the bible itself. Even the priests within the Calvinist faith could not predict God's will.

3 **Asceticism** – Calvin preached that the followers of Calvinism should lead a life of abstinence, denying themselves all pleasure that could distract them from their devotion to their faith.

4 **The value of work** – Calvinists believed that the only way to glorify God was to devote themselves to their work. Although this would not influence God's decision on their experience in the afterlife, their devotion to hard work would honour him.

Outcomes of the Calvinist belief

Followers became anxious about whether or not they were part of 'the elect' but had no way of confirming their place.

⬇

To overcome their anxiety, Calvinists devoted themselves to their work, often acquiring massive amounts of wealth in the process. Weber noted that Calvinists took this wealth as a sign of God's favour, which may mean that they were part of 'the elect'.

⬇

Instead of squandering their money, Calvinists were driven by their work ethic to re-invest their hard-earned money into their businesses. The vast difference between the wealth of Calvinists and that of others caused greater inequality to emerge.

⬇

Weber believed that the emergence of Calvinism resulted in the '**Protestant work ethic**' and a '**spirit of capitalism**', in which the pursuit of profit was seen as a spiritual goal.

Karl Kautsky (1927)

👎 **Kautsky**, a Marxist, disagreed with Weber's analysis of the role that Calvinism played in influencing capitalism. In Kautsky's opinion, modern capitalism already existed before the emergence of the Calvinist belief system. Therefore, the only purpose of Calvinism was to justify the reasons why the ruling class controlled the means of production and thus to continue to support the myth that inequality was a sign of God's will.

Now try this

What did Calvinists mean by 'the elect'?

Steve Bruce: religion and social change

Like neo-Marxists and Max Weber, **Steve Bruce** (2003) also believed that in some circumstances religion could produce **social change**. However, although the aim of a particular religion might be to influence change, its actions and reputation can often determine its ability to succeed. Bruce compares two different American movements: one that has been successful in influencing change and one that, in his opinion, is currently struggling.

The American Civil Rights Movement

The Civil Rights Movement was notably active in the 1950s and 60s with the aim of ending racial segregation in America.

Bruce claims that the most important people in the movement were black clergymen, led by **Dr Martin Luther King**.

Martin Luther King attempted to influence change by gaining national support from all communities.

Although not everyone agreed with his sentiments, Martin Luther King used religion as an **ideological resource** in the way that he appealed to all Christians, regardless of ethnic background, in order to find common ground based on their Christian values.

Reasons for success in achieving change

Bruce claims that the Civil Rights Movement was successful because:

👍 it was a peaceful protest

👍 it achieved public support

👍 it negotiated with its opposition

👍 it shamed those who had prejudicial values that conflicted with the Christian message.

Bruce believes that the Civil Rights Movement is a good illustration of how religion can bring about social change. Although Bruce does not believe in God and religion himself, he acknowledges how it can have a positive influence by bringing communities together and transcending politics in order to obtain the moral high ground.

The New Christian Right

The New Christian Right began in the 1960s and is a fundamentalist movement that is conservative in nature.

The main aim of the New Christian Right is to resist the changes that have occurred in American social policy over recent generations in order to return to a system that reflects the values of the Bible.

In particular, the New Christian Right believe that the following activities are immoral and should therefore be criminalised:

👎 homosexuality

👎 divorce

👎 abortion

👎 teaching evolution and sex education in schools.

Reasons for failure to achieve change

1 **Negative tone of the message**
Bruce believes that an analysis of the mass media coverage shows that this group has been heavily criticised by the mainstream for opposing the liberal values of the majority.

2 **Lack of cooperation**
The New Christian Right don't cooperate with and tend to distance themselves from others who have similar common values, such as those on education and abortion.

The key to effecting change

Bruce suggests that the key to achieving social change through religion is being able to integrate into the population by promoting shared, liberal values. In contrast, religious organisations such as the New Christian Right tend to incite conflict and are therefore marginalised, and so fail to achieve mainstream cultural change.

Now try this

Summarise what makes a religious organisation successful in achieving change, according to Steve Bruce.

The feminist view of religion

Feminists believe that religion is a conservative social force because it is a patriarchal social institution that reinforces gendered inequalities. Feminists criticise functionalists and Marxists as 'malestream' because both theories ignore the fact that religion often justifies male power and women's subordination.

Religion is patriarchal

Feminists believe that the main function of religion is to maintain gender inequality. It achieves this by portraying male domination over women in a variety of different ways, such as:

- portraying God as a man
- restricting access for women to the top levels of the religious hierarchy
- depicting women as bad influences within the sacred text.

    For example, Eve in the garden of Eden, or Mary Magdalene.

Mary Daly (1978), a Christian feminist, suggests that the emergence of monotheistic religions (see page 135) has allowed men to control the idea that God is a man and is therefore the only supernatural being. She claims that the Christian faith has deliberately sought to eliminate polytheistic religions (see page 135) such as paganism that include powerful female gods. Daly concludes that we will never achieve gender equality in religion until we can consider that God could potentially be a woman.

'Second-class believers'

Simone de Beauvoir (1953) believes that religion successfully maintains gender inequality by tricking women into thinking that they are equal to men in the eyes of their god and that they will be compensated in the afterlife for any hardship. However, de Beauvoir claims that women are exploited by religion as they are raised to worship a male god from an early age and therefore are unconsciously encouraged to see men as superior.

In support of de Beauvoir, **Jean Holm** (2001) focuses on the segregation that occurs in many religious places of worship and, in particular, the way in which women are treated within the place of worship. In many mainstream religions, women are seen as 'impure' because they have periods. In Islam (and other religions), women can be denied access to the place of worship if they are currently at that stage of their menstruation cycle.

The 'stained glass ceiling'

Karen Armstrong (1993) studies how women are often blocked from positions at the top of the mainstream churches. She studied the Church of England, which she claims has a **'stained glass ceiling'**, meaning that women in the church have not been able to progress to the top of the hierarchy.

The Church of England has only recently voted to allow female bishops for the first time.

The vote to allow female bishops has proven to be a very unpopular move. Some traditionalists within the church are being very vocal in their opposition. This issue is not only confined to the Church of England as many other religions face the same response too.

El Saadawi (1980)

El Saadawi, an Islamic feminist, suggests that Islam is not patriarchal in nature. She claims that it is the male domination of Arab cultural institutions that has led to Islam's role in maintaining gender inequality. This is because men held the powerful positions within Arab culture and they were able to use this cultural power to dominate the interpretation of Islamic texts in favour of men.

For example, the Qur'an stated that both men and women should be given the same punishment for adultery. However, this was circumvented by Arab culture, which allows men to have more than one wife if they wish. Women, on the other hand, would face brutal punishments in some Islamic countries if they behaved in the same way as men.

Now try this

How does El Saadawi's view of religion differ to that of other feminists?

147

The postmodernist view of religion

Postmodernists believe that traditional religions have lost their significance in society and therefore lack the ability to encourage both social stability or bring about social change.

Recap of postmodernism

Due to **globalisation** and other social and economic factors, society has fundamentally changed over the past 40 years. As a result, theories that are associated with describing the modernist era have become irrelevant for two reasons.

1 **Knowledge is now regarded as relative to the individual**, therefore all generalised claims to the truth about society are dismissed as only one way of looking at the world.

2 **Identities have become fluid** – people's identities are no longer fixed for their whole life-time by family, class or religion. In postmodern societies, identity is fluid and is subject to change because of the importance of consumerism.

Religion as a meta-narrative

As traditional religions were part of the modernist era, they are seen by postmodernists to be **meta-narratives** (big stories). This is because they claimed a monopoly on the truth. However such claims are no longer acceptable within the postmodern world because postmodernists claim that there is no such thing as absolute truth within our increasingly **fragmented society**.

Hervieu-Leger (2000) believes that religion's reluctance to change has also led to its demise because there are now so many alternative world views to compete with its teachings. This has led to further scrutiny of the beliefs of the mainstream religions.

'Spiritual shoppers'

As **identities are fluid** within the postmodern world, individuals are constantly constructing new identities for themselves through consumption. This has been perpetuated by the rapid growth and influence of the mass media, which has also had an impact on religious belief. **Lyon** (2000) observes the emergence of a religious marketplace, which developed as religious leaders turned to the media to publicise their belief system in order to survive. As religions have evolved over time, hundreds of thousands of **denominations** (off shoots of mainstream religions) now exist, all competing for new followers. Consequently, individuals are no longer loyal to just one religion or movement. Instead, they become '**spiritual shoppers**', trying out new movements to see if it suits their identity.

The emergence of a religious marketplace saw religious leaders turn to the media to publicise their belief system (Lyon, 2000).

New Age movements

Because of the changes in society, postmodernists claim that traditional religions have been replaced by a range of **New Age movements** with a focus on spirituality rather than a devotion to God (see page 154.)

Evaluation

💬 Although the range of religious and spiritual movements has undoubtedly grown, **Steve Bruce** (2002) believes that postmodernists have over-exaggerated their importance and the demise of traditional religions. He claims that the New Age and religious movements that have emerged are more likely to be short-lived and do not compare with the influence of the worldwide religions, which have experienced significant longevity and impact.

Now try this

1 According to postmodernists, why would the fact that identities are fluid encourage a change in an individual's engagement with religion?

2 Explain why New Age movements may suit more modern views than more traditional religions.

Religious organisations

This section looks at different types of **religious organisations**, including their characteristics and explanations for their **growth** or **decline**. Some sociologists claim that religion has lost its influence on society – a process known as **secularisation**. Others, however, believe that although traditional religions may be losing their dominance, other religious movements are being created that are more relevant to today's society.

The secularisation cycle

Stark and Bainbridge (1985) believe that **religious belief** is always changing and are therefore critical of any theorists who suggest that religion no longer has an influence on society. Although periods of secularisation may occur, they are often temporary until new forms of religion are created that appeal to a population who will always desire a form of spiritual or religious experience.

Secularisation – *the decline in religious influence on society.*
Society experiences a decline in religious influence as rival ideologies dominate society's world view and tend to hold more relevance than pre-existing religious beliefs.

Religious decline – *previously dominant religious organisations begin to lose their relevance.*
Over time, the dominant religious views are challenged and criticised. Followers become sceptical and feel alienated (distanced) from the movement. Rival ideologies begin to provide alternative explanations that become more relevant to the everyday life of individuals.

Innovation – *the creation of new forms of religious organisation.*
After a period of secularisation, there is a demand for a spiritual or religious experience that other ideologies cannot fulfil. New forms of religion are created to meet the needs of the population. They attempt to tap into the situations of different communities to provide an alternative to the old religions that lost their relevance.

Religious revival – *the resurgence of religion as a dominant belief system.*
The new forms of religious movement become established and begin to influence the world view of communities.

Now try this

1 Define what is meant by secularisation.
2 Give **two** reasons that might explain secularisation.

Classifying religions

There are four types of religious organisation that you need to be aware of. These classifications focus on how these religions are **structured or organised** rather than on their beliefs.

Religious organisations: churches, denominations, sects and cults

	Churches As defined by **Troeltsch (1912)**	Denominations As defined by **Niebuhr (1929)**
Structure	Have a multi-layered hierarchical structure; have professional clergy.	Tend to originate as a sect but become successful enough to evolve into a larger movement; have professional clergy, although often require the assistance of volunteers.
Membership	Large, worldwide memberships (universal); have inclusive memberships meaning people are often born into these religions.	Relatively large memberships – can be international, national or regional; tend to attract those from within the poorest communities.
Lifespan	Long lifespans – often centuries or even millennia.	Large variety of different denominations, some have long lifespans (Methodist Church), whereas others are more recent (Pentecostalism).
Commitment	Few demands or restrictions on members; accept the social environment around them.	Rely on members for active involvement in their cause, such as converting others.
Example	Can be linked to the state. For example, the Roman Catholic Church in countries such as Spain.	Pentecostalism emerged at the start of the 20th century as a different form of Protestant Christianity; it focuses on the revival of members who can be 'born again' through baptism.

	Sects As defined by **Niebuhr (1929)**	Cults
Structure	Revolve around a charismatic leader who claims to have been chosen by a supernatural power; majority do not have professional clergy.	Usually have a loose structure and no professional clergy; often wrongly confused with sects by the media; rarely associated with a supernatural power.
Membership	Tend to have small memberships.	Have small memberships or clientele that buy into a service offered; tend to consist of people who consume the service but rarely meet as a group.
Lifespan	Short lifespan, especially if the leader dies (see page 152).	Varies with market demand.
Commitment	Often demand total dedication from their followers; can evolve into a denomination, if they gain wider popularity.	Rarely demand strong commitments and mainly attract people looking for spiritual fulfilment, through, for example, meditation or channelling positive energy.
Example	Daesh (Islamic State or ISIS) and the Moonies (see page 151).	Scientology was founded in 1954 by an American, L. Ron Hubbard (see page 151).

Three forms of cults

Stark and Bainbridge (1986) suggest that cults offer their members 'this-worldly benefits' as they feel they are suffering from some sort of deprivation (see page 153). They subdivide cults into three different categories:

1 **Audience cults** – usually transmit their ideas through the media to a large audience and therefore do not require specific membership, for example astrology or feng shui.

2 **Client cults** – involve a personal connection between a leader and their followers (known as 'clients'). This usually revolves around some form of teaching that is designed to enhance the lives of the clients.

3 **Cultic movements** – these may require specific commitment from their clients, for example paying for courses.

Now try this

Outline **three** different characteristics of sects.

New religious movements

Wallis (1984) developed the term '**new religious movement**' (NRM) when analysing the actions and beliefs of different denominations, sects and cults that have emerged over recent generations. He tends to categorise these movements into three different groups based on how they see the world.

World-affirming movements

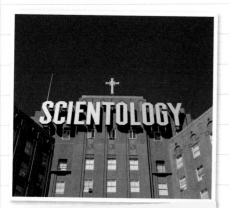

For example, Scientology, which involves the process of 'auditing'. This removes any traumatic memories (engrams) from the 'client' in order for them to progress to a 'clear state' of mind.

- Most are **cults**.
- They do not denounce other religions.
- They attempt to be optimistic and to enhance the lives of their followers.
- They are attractive for ambitious professionals who seek progression.
- They accept the world in its current state and do not seek societal change.
- Their members are usually seen as clients or customers rather than religious believers.
- They often charge fees for their services and teachings. In some cases, followers may be restricted from different levels of scripture without payment.

Another example is Transcendental Meditation, which uses techniques and knowledge for personal growth and problem-solving.

World-accommodating movements

For example, Subud was founded by Muhammad Subuh Sumohadiwidjojo in the 1920s. It is a denomination of Islam that originates from Indonesia. Subud provides its followers with 'spiritual exercise', which aims to cleanse their spirits.

- Usually **denominations** or offshoots of mainstream churches.
- Although not happy with the current state of the world, they wish to make the most of their situation to achieve salvation.
- These movements focus on improving the lives of their followers whilst still conforming to the way in which society operates.
- They are often popular with vulnerable communities as they can inspire a more determined work ethic or offer salvation in the afterlife.
- They can attract people who are unhappy with societal changes and tend to be conservative in nature. They tend to disapprove of abortion and divorce.

Another example is Pentecostalism (see page 150).

World-rejecting movements

For example, Jim Jones' People's Temple was founded in 1955. The movement is famous due to its dramatic end in 1978 when 918 members committed suicide.

- A vast majority are **sects**.
- They demand social change as they do not agree with the current state of the world.
- Members often leave old lives behind and create new identities and communities to cut themselves off from society.
- They are seen as '**millenarian**' movements as they focus on the intervention of a divine power to bring judgement on those who are sinful.
- They have a clear understanding of a god and focus on the literal truth of the sacred text. They are therefore fundamentalist in nature.
- They are often accused of brainwashing their members. Some have committed murder and mass suicide.

Another example is the Moonies (the Unification Church). Founded in 1954 by Sun Myung Moon in South Korea, they promote the sanctity of marriage by holding mass weddings ('blessing ceremonies').

Now try this

1. What is meant by a 'millenarian' movement?
2. Outline the difference between a world-accommodating and a world-rejecting movement.

The lifespan of sects

The **growth** of new religious movements is intrinsically linked with the formation of sects (see page 150) that break free from traditional churches.

Short lifespans

Niebuhr (1929) believes that sects rarely last longer than a generation for a variety of different reasons:

- The movement loses momentum when the leader dies.
- The children of sect members do not have the same intensity of belief as their parents and therefore the movement dies out in the second generation.
- The movement becomes successful and therefore evolves into a denomination by developing a professional hierarchy instead of relying on a charismatic individual.
- The movement begins to compromise with the outside world and therefore dilutes its beliefs.

The sectarian cycle

Stark and Bainbridge (1986) have similar views to Niebuhr on the short lifespans of sects. They suggest that sects usually progress through the 'sectarian cycle', which has the following five stages.

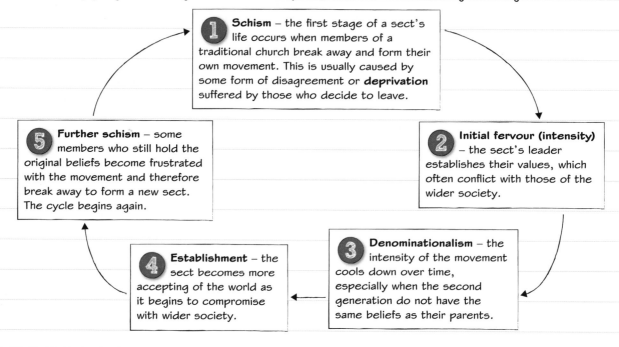

1 Schism – the first stage of a sect's life occurs when members of a traditional church break away and form their own movement. This is usually caused by some form of disagreement or **deprivation** suffered by those who decide to leave.

2 Initial fervour (intensity) – the sect's leader establishes their values, which often conflict with those of the wider society.

3 Denominationalism – the intensity of the movement cools down over time, especially when the second generation do not have the same beliefs as their parents.

4 Establishment – the sect becomes more accepting of the world as it begins to compromise with wider society.

5 Further schism – some members who still hold the original beliefs become frustrated with the movement and therefore break away to form a new sect. The cycle begins again.

Different categories of sects

Wilson (1970) argues that sects should not be generalised as they tend to be very different in nature. He outlines the following categories into which a sect could fall:

- **Introversionist** – they cut themselves off from wider society and are often viewed as threatening.
- **Conversionist** – they seek to save those in the outside world by converting them to their movement (e.g. Mormons).
- **Reformist** – they attempt to improve society through their teachings (e.g. Quakers).
- **Manipulationist** – they promote discipline and asceticism (e.g. Opus Dei).
- **Millenarian** – they believe that divine intervention from God is imminent and therefore judgment day will occur (e.g. Jehovah's Witnesses).

Established sects

In contrast to the ideas of Niebuhr as well as Stark and Bainbridge, **Wilson (1970)** claims some sects do not have a short lifespan. He suggests that some become **established sects** rather than denominations as the believers successfully socialise their children into a strong commitment to the movement as a result of being isolated from the mainstream. This ensures that the message remains pure, rather than becoming diluted by the compromise of popularity, for example Mormons.

Now try this

Identify the **five** stages of Stark and Bainbridge's sectarian cycle.

Growth of new religious movements

There are many reasons why new religious movements (NRMs) are said to be on the increase.

A response to marginalisation and poverty

Max Weber (1922) claimed that NRMs tend to attract individuals who do not belong to the majority within a community. These movements tend to preach 'theodicies of disprivilege', and provide the poor and the powerless with reasons that explain their unfortunate situations and allow them to gain access to a new community of people with similar experiences and beliefs.

Relative deprivation

Eileen Barker (1984) discusses a more recent trend of young, middle-class people being attracted to NRMs, such as the Moonies (see page 151). Barker notes that in some cases, middle-class children feel neglected by their career-orientated parents and therefore suffer from **relative deprivation** when they compare their experiences to peers who have strong connections with their parents. NRMs provide an alternative family for the individual due to the strong sense of commitment and the community that they create.

However, Barker argues that in many cases such membership for younger people may be only temporary as they lose the need for this alternative family as they grow older.

A response to social change

Increased religious participation

Wilson (1970) claims that in times of rapid social change, individuals often feel a sense of anomie (confusion) and anxiety. This has historically led to increased participation in current NRMs because they appease the anxieties of those individuals. To evidence his point, Wilson uses the example of how the Methodist denomination surged in popularity during the 18th and 19th centuries during industrialisation.

Increase in radicalism

In contemporary society, however, increasing globalisation and the pressure to accept a cosmopolitan (tolerance of all lifestyles) culture could be pushing certain groups within society to more radical NRMs. **Bauman** (1992) suggests that there has been a rise in fundamentalist religious movements (sects) due to the increased risk of living in the postmodern world. Traditional beliefs are being undermined and therefore the popularity of fundamentalist sects may symbolise a strong defence of conservative values. This is referred to as a **resistance identity**, according to **Castells** (2010), because individuals are attempting to prevent their traditional culture from being eroded.

The religious marketplace

Postmodernist **Hervieu-Leger** (2000) describes a process known as 'de-traditionalisation'. She claims that parents are now less likely to pass on traditional customs to their children and this is leading to **cultural amnesia** whereby religious norms, which were once central to a society's identity, are being lost and forgotten. As a consequence, children are less likely to be attracted by stale, traditional churches that resist change and claim a monopoly on the truth. Instead, individuals now prefer to engage in **spiritual shopping** within a **religious marketplace** to find a different religious or spiritual movement that best fits their identity at that time. This may mean that NRMs that use the media and other contemporary means to engage with people are seen as the more attractive option. (For more information on religious marketplaces, see page 163.)

Internal secularisation

To further develop Bauman's point, **Herberg** (1960) suggests that NRMs are benefitting from the **internal secularisation** that is occurring within traditional churches. In order to remain relevant, traditional churches are diluting their beliefs on conservative principles, such as acknowledging abortion and same-sex marriage. Herberg claims that this had led to some traditional followers feeling left behind by their religion and in search of a more fundamentalist movement that stays true to the sacred text. Sects therefore become a very attractive option.

Now try this

Define what is meant by 'de-traditionalisation'.

New Age movements

Whilst the emergence of new religious movements has catered for disconnected groups of people, some new religions have been labelled 'new age' because they offer a spiritual experience tailored to people's individual needs.

Defining a New Age movement

Often influenced by ancient Eastern traditions and customs (Chinese and Indian), New Age movements do not focus on the religious elements of spirituality. Instead, these movements promote **self-spirituality**, meaning that the individual can customise their own experience rather than be dictated to by an established hierarchy. They are sometimes called me-religions as a result.

Examples of popular New Age movements include Yoga, Reiki, Feng shui and Tai Chi.

Postmodern explanations

From a postmodernist perspective, **Drane** (1999) believes that New Age movements have increased due to the increasing fragmentation of society. As knowledge is now relative to the individual, people are less interested in 'absolute truth' provided by the traditional religions. As a consequence, individuals have lost faith in religious 'experts' such as priests and suffer from a **spiritual void** because they have no trust in the religious ideologies of the modernist era that used to shape their knowledge and identities. Instead, the postmodern individual now relies on their own ability to find a spiritual experience that is relevant to their own life.

The Kendal Project

Heelas et al. (2005) conducted research on the emergence of New Age movements within the rural community of Kendal in the Lake District. They chose Kendal because attendance for the traditional churches was twice the national average, suggesting that traditional churches were still influential in the area.

Heelas et al. conducted questionnaires and interviews with individuals who attended traditional religious services and people who were part of local New Age movements. They also undertook a random doorstep survey of 100 houses in the local area.

Although traditional church attendance was still the dominant religious experience (referred to as the 'congregational domain'), Heelas et al. suggested that they found a rapid increase in the levels of participation in a 'holistic milieu' of New Age movements. They claimed that New Age movements reflect the self-interested or individualistic nature of our society and are therefore more relevant to the contemporary individual, especially those who have distanced themselves from the high level of commitment required by the traditional churches. According to Heelas et al., this process signifies the increasing **subjectivisation** of spiritual belief.

Heelas et al. refer to this increase in New Age movements as a **spiritual revolution** and believe that if current trends continue, the 'holistic milieu' could overtake the 'congregational domain' in future generations.

Evaluation of New Age movements

The suggestion that New Age movements are becoming the new dominant form of religious experience has attracted criticisms from some sociologists.

- Studies like the Kendal Project by **Heelas et al.** (2005) indicate that the majority of those attracted to New Age movements tend to be middle-aged, middle-class women (around 80 per cent of practitioners) and therefore do not represent other social groups.

- **Steve Bruce** (2002) claims that although many people may 'dabble' in New Age movements, these movements rarely become essential to their identity and therefore tend to be a short-term interest rather than a life-changing experience.

Now try this

1 What did Heelas et al. mean by the 'congregational domain' and the 'holistic milieu' in their research in Kendal?

2 Give **one** explanation for the popularity of New Age movements in today's society.

Social class and religiosity

The work of classical theorists such as **Marx** and **Weber** has led us to assume that the poorest in a society will be the most religious. Current trends in the UK, however, may indicate that patterns have changed, but measuring the relationship between religion and social class is problematic. This page looks at the trends of **religious belief** and **church attendance**.

Religious belief

Evidence suggests that the working class is more likely to hold a permanent religious belief.

Recap

According to **Marx** (1844), the main function of religion is to benefit capitalism by fooling the proletariat into believing that inequality is justified. He claimed that religion is the 'opium of the masses' as it dulls the pain of oppression whilst providing followers with temporary highs to mask the exploitation that occurs within the capitalist system (see page 141).

Weber (1905) argued that religion can attract the poorest in society because it explained their poverty as a challenge from God that would be rewarded in the afterlife (see page 144). Religion can then offer them an alternative life through a change in their work ethic or mind-set.

Lifelong theists

In a similar vein, **Lawes** (2009) claims that working-class people are more likely to be **lifelong theists** – they will believe in God throughout their lives. However, these findings may be heavily skewed by ethnicity as many ethnic minorities are working class and tend to be more religious than the white majority. (To find out more about ethnicity and religiosity, see page 156.)

Lawes also found that the numbers of **lifelong atheists** (non-believers) were small. However, lifelong atheism tended to be more common in those with a university educated middle-class background.

Church attendance

Interestingly, church attendance figures seem to conflict with trends on religious belief.

Monitoring would suggest that churches in more affluent, rural areas tend to have higher attendances than those in urban, working-class areas. **Ashworth and Farthing** (2007) claim that individuals who are reliant on state benefits are actually the least likely to attend church services.

These findings are supported by a **YouGov** survey in 2015, which found that 62 per cent of regular church attenders came from middle-class backgrounds. Explaining these trends could be difficult, however **Voas and Watt** (2014) suggest that middle-class church attendance is a strategy aimed at making sure their children enrol at the best State schools. These are often affiliated with either the Roman Catholic Church or the Church of England.

The relationship between social class and religious organisations

Historically, trends seemingly suggest that middle-class people are more likely to feel attached to traditional churches, whereas working-class people are drawn more to new religious movements such as Pentecostalism. **Ahern and Davie** (1987) claim that the working-class mistrust traditional religions such as Anglicanism because they associate them with authority, the establishment and royalty. They argue that working-class people identify more with non-conformist religions like Methodism, which tend to be less judgemental and which provide practical solutions to their circumstances. This view is very similar to that of Weber (see page 144). Alternatively, according to **Martin** (1990), middle-class people may see church-going as an opportunity to network with members of the community and appear respectable in the eyes of their neighbours. This may explain why church attendance statistics are high but religious belief tends to be lower within middle-class communities.

Now try this

Explain the difference between 'lifelong theists' and 'lifelong atheists'.

Ethnicity and religiosity

Evidence suggests that in the UK, ethnic minorities are more likely to engage in religious beliefs and practices than the White British population.

The evidence

O'Beirne's (2004) research suggests that ethnic minorities tend to see religion as a central element of their **identity**. Muslims, in particular, indicated religion was as important as their family with regards to shaping their identity, whereas African-Caribbean participants ranked religion as the third most important aspect of their identity. In comparison, White British participants ranked religion lower than family, occupation, education, age, interests, nationality, gender, income and social class.

Official statistics from 2011 indicate that the difference between affiliation and membership figures clearly suggests a difference in the way that different cultures engage in religion. Of all White British people who affiliate with Christianity, only 32 per cent actively participate in their religion. This compares to 80 per cent of those from a Muslim background.

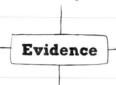

Evidence

The 2011 Census found that black people make up just over 3 per cent of the general population and yet around 10 per cent of the official church population.

Half of the Pentecostal churches that exist in the UK have predominantly black congregations. **Goodhew** (2012) estimates that around half a million black people are involved with Pentecostalism in the UK.

Declining attendance

Although their religious participation still remains higher than the White British majority, **Modood et al. (1997)** suggest that there seems to be an emerging **decline** in some ethnic groups who have been in the UK for multiple generations. He claims that the trends suggest that the more generations that exist within a community, the lower their rate of religious participation.

Reasons why ethnic minorities are more religious

Cultural defence

Steve Bruce's (2002) concept of '**cultural defence**' suggests that religion could be used as a way to unite a community against change or hostility from wider society (see page 160). Bruce's concept can be applied to ethnic minorities in the UK. For example, according to **Bird** (1999), many Anglican churches in the 1950s were largely white and did not welcome those from other cultures. In reaction to this perceived racism, many African-Caribbean Christians set up their own churches. This may partly explain the rapid rise of the Pentecostal movement in the UK.

Cultural transition

Bruce also suggests that ethnic minorities may use religion as a form of **cultural transition** to help them assimilate into British society (see page 160). Places of worship act as a communal meeting place and a support network for people from similar backgrounds, and therefore help integrate believers into the community. Bruce claims that as people integrate further into a community, they are more likely to leave religion behind. This may explain the trends behind **Modood et al.'s** findings.

Functionalists

Functionalists believe that ethnic minorities integrate into their society by adopting the key elements of the value consensus of the community. This can be applied to **Robert Bellah's** (1991) theory on **civil religion**, as religion was used to unite a diverse population under a common banner and therefore promote social solidarity (see page 140).

Marxists

As many ethnic-minority communities tend to be working class, Marxists would suggest that they would be more likely to be attracted to the teachings of religions that help them understand that inequality is natural and justified (see page 155).

Max Weber (1922)

New religious movements, such as Pentecostalism, attract ethnic minorities because they feel marginalised by society (see page 153). However, these religions are also attractive because they provide guidance on how to overcome their marginality and develop a 'protestant work ethic' that could lead to economic success.

Now try this

Explain Modood et al.'s findings on ethnicity and religiosity.

Age and religiosity

Statistics on religious belief and church attendance suggest that the **elderly** are more religious than other generations.

The trends

Brierley (2015) conducted research into church attendance for different age groups. He found the following trends:

- The only age group to show a recent rise in church attendance is the 65-plus age group.
- Since the 1980s, the number of under-15s attending church regularly has halved.
- By 2025, it is projected that only 2.5 per cent of regular church attenders will be 15–19 years old.
- Half of all English churches have no one under the age of 20 in their congregation.

Why are the elderly the most religious age group?

Voas and Crockett (2003) suggest that there are two different explanations behind the elderly's increased participation in religion.

1 **The ageing effect** – as people come closer to the end of their life, their interest in spirituality and religion increases. This may be due to a growing concern about the afterlife, or a desire to seek forgiveness for past sins or company within the church community. It may also explain trends which suggest that elderly women are more likely to attend church than men because they live longer. In this view, age would have a more significant impact on church attendance than gender.

2 **The generational or period effect** – the current elderly generation may be more religious due to their upbringing, which was less secure than that experienced by today's youth. They were more likely to suffer from poverty and lived through the Second World War. **Norris and Inglehart's** (2004) existential security theory (see page 142) could therefore be applied to this age group.

Why are the young less interested in religion?

1 **The virtual collapse of religious socialisation** – **Arweck and Beckford** (2013) claim that it is increasingly unlikely for parents to pass on their religious beliefs to their children. Also, traditional Sunday Schools, which used to be widespread (in the 1950s, around a third of all children attended), are now rare and so churches cannot recruit from them. Another factor that could lead to this 'collapse' is the increase in 'inter-faith' relationships where each parent has a different religious belief. **Voas** (2003) suggests that there is only a 25 per cent chance that a child raised in these circumstances will become a regular churchgoer as an adult, as there may be no strong encouragement to follow either faith as they grow up. These arguments could be applied to **Hervieu-Leger's** (2000) views on de-traditionalisation and cultural amnesia (see page 153).

2 **Church is boring** – **Brierley** (2015) found that 87 per cent of 10–14-year-olds claimed that church was boring and old fashioned. They felt that the traditional teachings didn't relate to their lives and so they avoided attending church if they could.

3 **Increasing individualisation** – **Collins-Mayo** (2010), a postmodernist, suggests that religion has become more of a personal choice rather than an expectation that is thrust upon today's youth. Even faith-based schools take a more liberal approach to introducing children to religious teachings and tend to focus more on the moral message of the faith, rather than the sacred fundamentals. This mirrors the general shift in UK culture of individualism becoming dominant over social pressures and traditions. The young therefore feel less obliged to affiliate themselves with religions compared to previous generations and would rather spend their leisure time on hobbies or interests than attending places of worship.

Islamic youth

Whilst the trends seem to suggest that the young are distancing themselves from religion, other sociologists believe that Islamic youth are a clear exception. **Samad** (2006) claims that for young Pakistani and Bangladeshi children living in Britain, being a Muslim is more central to their identity than their nationality. Being a Muslim transcends national borders and allows them to honour their heritage whilst also integrating into UK culture.

Now try this

Provide **two** reasons why the elderly may be more religious than the young.

Gender and religiosity

Although there is evidence to suggest that women are exploited within religion, statistics suggest that women are **more likely** to be religious than men. According to **Field** (2010), in 2005, 57 per cent of regular church attenders were female. There are many different explanations for this trend.

Gender role socialisation

- **Walter and Davie** (1998) claim women feel closer to God because they are involved in the creation of life. They are also more likely to be involved with death as carers of the sick, disabled and the elderly.

- **Miller and Hoffman** (1995) claim that females are socialised into values such as empathy, compassion, submissiveness and caring for others. These values are compatible with religious belief.

- **Miller and Hoffman** also argue that women worry more about the risks of not being religious, for example being damned for all time, compared with men.

- **Miller and Hoffman** argue that religion provides identity and roles for women in societies in which they traditionally have low status.

Wanting to be seen as a 'good mother'

- **Greely** (1992) believes that young women are not necessarily interested in participating in religion until they have a child, which then changes their outlook. To be seen as a '**good mother**', they feel that they need to raise their children with a strong sense of morality and ethics, which can be helped by taking their child to church every Sunday.

- According to **Abby Day** (2007), women may claim that they are a Christian, even though they do not necessarily believe in the religion. Their main motive is to appear to be a good role model to their children and to fit in with the majority. (For more on Day's study Believing in belonging, see page 160.)

New religious movements

Glock and Stark (1969) studied the rise in participation of women in new religious movements They argue that the increase is due to three types of **deprivation** suffered by women in society.

1. **Social and economic deprivation** – a lack of status in society, such as in employment.

2. **Ethical deprivation** – the sense that there has been a moral decline in society and therefore some women want a return to traditionalism – a strong set of core values that they can relate to.

3. **Organismic deprivation** – women are more concerned about their health than men and therefore may seek the comfort and healing that religions such as Christian Science claim to provide.

Evaluation

👎 **Linda Woodhead** (2004) criticises many of these explanations because they are dated. She argues that due to recent changes in the position of women in society, the way they engage in religion has changed. As a consequence, there are now three types of women with regards to religious participation.

1. **Home centred** – women who stay at home rather than work. Woodhead claims that these women are the most likely to engage with traditional religions as they subscribe to more conservative values. They may also require the support of religion because they lack status.

2. **Work centred** – women who work full time in demanding jobs. These women are more likely to be secular, according to Woodhead, because they don't have the time for religion and probably cannot relate to the way women are portrayed in the scriptures.

3. **Jugglers** – women who balance work with family life may still seek some form of spiritual experience or guidance. Woodhead suggests that these women are more likely to get involved in a range of New Age movements that are more individualistic, such as Yoga, and which require much less commitment than traditional religions.

Now try this

Outline what Linda Woodhead meant by 'jugglers'.

Defining and measuring secularisation

Wilson (1966) defines **secularisation** as 'the process whereby religious beliefs, practices and institutions lose their social significance'. He is referring to the decline in the importance of religion that he claims has been occurring in the UK since the 1960s. This page mainly focuses on Christianity, but remember that the UK is increasingly multicultural and so multi-faith.

Church attendance and affiliation statistics

Church attendance and affiliation statistics provide evidence that secularisation is occurring in the UK.

Church attendance statistics

- From the 1800s to the 1960s, Church of England attendance declined significantly: around 40 per cent of the population went to church before industrialisation, compared to only 15 per cent in the 1960s.

- In 2015, only around 5 per cent of the population regularly attended a church service on a Sunday.

- In 1971, 60 per cent of weddings took place in church. Since then, this number has halved, with only 30 per cent of weddings held in church by 2012.

- Fewer people are having their children baptised. In the Catholic Church, the number of baptisms has halved compared to those in 1964.

- **Penman** (2013) observes that there has been an increase in 'bogus baptisms' where atheist parents have their children baptised in order for them to enrol in high-achieving church schools.

Decline in the number of clergy

One of the biggest problems for traditional Christian churches in the UK is the declining number of professional clergy who work in the churches. Between 1965 and 2011, the number of Catholic priests fell by a third and similar trends are occurring in the Church of England.

The average age of the clergy is also increasing due to a lack of recruitment for younger replacements; only 12 per cent of the current Anglican clergy are under the age of 40.

Steve Bruce (2002) states that the Church of England can no longer claim to be an influential organisation in the future if these trends continue at the current rate. He predicts that by 2030 the Methodist denomination may be extinct.

Davies (2006) argues that secularisation has partly been caused by the decline of respect that the general public has for the clergy due to frequent allegations of child abuse especially by priests within the Catholic Church in recent generations.

Religious affiliation statistics

- In the 2001 Census, 72 per cent of the population in England and Wales stated that they were Christian but this had declined to 59 per cent in the 2011 Census.

- The 2015 British Social Attitudes survey suggested that half of all adults asked stated that they did not belong to any religion.

- The largest declines are seen within the Anglican Church (Church of England). Other forms of Christianity, such as Catholicism, have benefitted from increased migration from Eastern European countries since 2004.

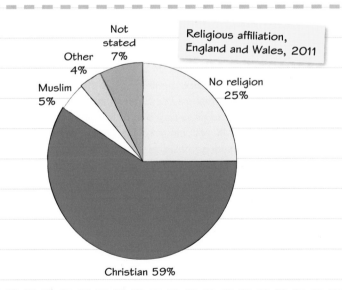

Religious affiliation, England and Wales, 2011

- Not stated 7%
- Other 4%
- Muslim 5%
- No religion 25%
- Christian 59%

Terry Sanderson (1999)

Terry Sanderson believes that the Church of England is losing its 'core business'; people who attend what he calls the 'hatching, matching and dispatching' services – christenings, weddings and funerals. People are now increasingly abandoning the church and pursuing civil alternatives that are secular in nature, such as naming ceremonies, celebration of life parties and humanist funerals.

Now try this

What did Terry Sanderson mean when he stated that the Church of England has lost its 'core business'?

Explanations for secularisation in the UK

Some theorists believe statistics indicate that the UK has increasingly become a **secular country**.

Rationalisation

Max Weber (1905) argued that the Enlightenment led to the 'disenchantment of the world' as science became the dominant belief system. As a consequence, the public do not believe in the 'sacred' qualities of religion due to the lack of evidence to support their claims. This process is also known as **desacralisation**.

Steve Bruce (2011) agrees with Weber's analysis, claiming that the public have developed a 'technological worldview' to explain misfortune. Instead of relying on religious myths to understand tragedy, they now seek scientific explanations that are supported by evidence to provide them with the answers they seek.

Privatised religious belief

Steve Bruce (2004) claims that secularisation has occurred because modern societies have undergone a process called **individualisation** and consequently religions no longer exert the same control over communities.

For example, religious teachings are no longer imposed upon society as they were in the Middle Ages when the Catholic Church was the dominant institution in Europe; the number of religious programmes on television such as Songs of Praise has fallen; there is a liberal multi-faith approach to religion taken by most schools; and wearing religious symbols in the workplace is often discouraged.

Being religious is now something that has been left to personal choice – Bruce refers to this as '**privatised religious belief**'.

Cultural defence and transition

Steve Bruce (2002) claims that people who still refer to themselves as religious are technically using it for secular purposes. Bruce believes that ethnic minorities and other marginalised people use religion in two ways.

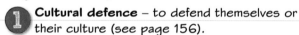 **Cultural defence** – to defend themselves or their culture (see page 156).

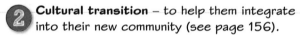 **Cultural transition** – to help them integrate into their new community (see page 156).

For example, Polish people who have come to the UK to work may attend local Catholic churches.

Believing in belonging

Abby Day (2007) also believes that the UK is becoming increasingly secular. In her study Believing in belonging, Day suggests that many people in the UK still claim to be Christian, even though they have no religious belief. A possible reason for affiliating to a religion revolves around people's desire to be a part of perceived 'British' culture. She found that if people believe being 'British' is important to their identity, they will claim to be a Christian.

Day identified three different types of Christians.

1. **Natal Christians** – people who affiliate because they were christened and therefore state that they are a Christian.

2. **Ethnic Christians** – immigrants who want to belong to British culture.

3. **Aspirational Christians** – those who want to seem moral and respectable.

For example, women who want to be seen by others as a 'good mother' (see page 158).

Religious pluralism and diversity

Peter Berger (1969) claimed that another reason for the growth in secularisation was the vast number of religious organisations that now exist. In the past, countries would be dominated by one religion, enabling that ideology to maintain a grip on a particular nation. As there are now many different religions operating in the UK, there has been a shift in attitudes. Berger suggested that this has caused a '**crisis in credibility**' for religion. Because religions claim a monopoly on the truth, they contradict one another and consequently no one knows what to believe.

It is interesting to note that in 1999, Berger distanced himself from this view by stating that religious competition and pluralism stimulates interest in religion rather than undermining it.

Disengagement

There is an argument that the decline in church attendance and affiliation can be explained by **disengagement**. This is the idea that the church no longer performs its traditional functions of socialisation and social solidarity due to the rise of other institutions, such as the government, education and the media, which perform them more effectively. This idea is rooted in **Parsons**' (1951) concept of structural differentiation.

For example, schools and the Welfare state have taken over some of the functions of religion such as promoting tolerance, charity and compassion for others.

Now try this

Why did Peter Berger suggest that there is a 'crisis in credibility' for religion?

Arguments against secularisation in the UK

Although there are many arguments for the decline of religious influence in the UK, there is evidence to suggest that religious belief is still relevant to contemporary life. **Glock and Stark** (1999), for example, claim that religion is more vibrant and relevant than it was in the past because of the rise of new religious movements.

'Believing without belonging'

Grace Davie (1994) agrees to an extent with Steve Bruce's claim that religious belief has become **privatised** (see page 160). However, she argues that this does not necessarily mean there has been a decline in personal religious belief.

Davie suggests that the nature of religious activity has changed. She argues that many people believe without feeling the need to belong to a particular religious movement.

Moreover, Davie argues that **vicarious religion** is now the norm, and it is the role of the **active minority** (the professional clergy and regular church attenders) to pray on behalf of the wider community. The true extent of religious belief can be seen when normality is interrupted – such as by a natural disaster or the death of a significant national figure – and church attendance spikes for a short period of time.

According to Davie, the use of church attendance statistics as evidence of a supposed increase in secularisation lacks **validity** because there is no quantitative method to measure personal religious belief.

Postmodernist critique of the secularisation debate

Although postmodernists believe that traditional religion is on the decline (see page 148), this does not mean that religious belief has become irrelevant. There has been a whole host of new religious and New Age movements that have reinvigorated religious belief within the postmodern world (see pages 153–154). **Hervieu-Leger** (2000) argues that this has created two new types of religious believer.

1. **The pilgrim** – people who seek religious movements that help them to achieve specific spiritual goals and with their personal development.

2. **The convert** – people who seek religious movements that provide them with a sense of community in response to the increasing fragmentation of the postmodern world.

(For more on postmodernist views, see Supply-led religion on page 163.)

Online religion

To develop the idea that people can still be religious without going to a place of worship, **Helland** (2000) discusses the importance of **globalisation** (see page 86) and the media in shaping the way that the public engages with religion.

According to Helland, the growth of the internet has changed the way in which the public can interact with the religious community. Religious beliefs have therefore become **disembedded** (removed) from places of worship and transported to a digital space online. Helland discusses two ways in which people engage with religion on the internet.

1. **Religion online** – when established religious movements use the internet to communicate messages to their followers. This method is often used by evangelical movements in America (see page 163).

2. **Online religion** – where like-minded people interact in forums to discuss their beliefs in an unstructured format. They may create online communities that do not exist in the real world.

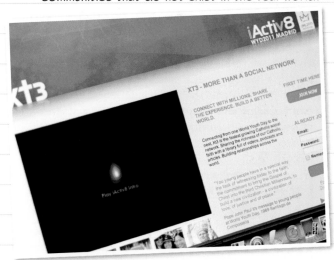

Online religious communities aim to bring people together so they can unite over shared spiritual beliefs.

Now try this

Define the term 'vicarious religion' and explain why this criticises the view that the UK has become a secular country.

Religious belief in the USA

There is an assumption that Americans are more religious than Europeans. This statement is heavily debated by theorists on both sides of the argument.

Church attendance analysis

Since the 1940s, 40 per cent of Americans, when asked, have consistently stated that they regularly attend church. As the American population is around 322 million people, we can assume from this statistic that churches in the USA should be well attended.

However, research by **Hadaway** (1993) has proved otherwise. Hadaway and his team attended a range of church services across the state of Ohio. They took a register at each church and compared their findings to the surveys. They then conducted their own interviews. They found that whilst many people stated that they went to church, in reality, many did not.

Hadaway's research clearly indicates that Americans want people to think that they attend church, when the reality is somewhat different. This study supports a claim by **Wilson** (1962), who suggested that religious belief in America had become 'superficial' and therefore secular in nature.

Hadaway found that many churches had much lower attendances than expected.

Secularisation from within

Steve Bruce (2011) argues that religion in America has become **secularised from within**, which has masked the decline in traditional religious beliefs.

In line with **Herberg's** (1960) view of **internal secularisation** (see page 153), Bruce claims that the Christian churches have had to compromise their beliefs in order to remain popular and competitive and therefore survive. Bruce claims that religion in America has become a commodity to sell like any other product and that American religions have had to tailor and adapt their product to attract consumers and customers through their doors.

Civil religion

To an extent, the views of Bruce and Wilson and the findings of Hadaway can be applied to **Robert Bellah's** (1991) study of Americanism (see page 140). Bellah claims that the religion of 'Americanism' transcended individual beliefs and unified the diverse population into belief in a common purpose and community, based on the view that God and America are much the same thing. This is similar to Durkheim's ideas (see page 139). **Day's** (2007) findings in the UK where people affiliate themselves to a national religion to appear to be part of the mainstream, rather than being truly religious (see page 160) are also similar.

Existential security theory

In contrast to the theories of secularisation, **Norris and Inglehart** (2004) believe that Americans are more likely to be genuinely religious than European nations such as the UK. They suggest that this is because Americans have less support from a welfare state and lack access to effective free healthcare. Consequently those who are less fortunate may feel less secure in their chances for survival and so turn to religion as an alternative security source (see page 142). This is further substantiated by the vast gap between rich and poor in America, in which poverty is experienced without the safety net of state support. **Weber** (1905) claimed that the poorest are more likely to be religious as it provides them with theodicies that explain and justify their poverty (see page 144).

Now try this

1 Why does Wilson claim that religion has become 'superficial' in America?

2 What does Bellah mean by 'civil religion'?

Religious market theory

The **religious market theory** (also known as rational choice theory) put forward by **Stark and Bainbridge** (1985) discusses how the nature of religion in America (along with other countries) is different to that of European countries.

Secularisation is Eurocentric

Stark and Bainbridge argue that the study of secularisation is **Eurocentric** and therefore heavily criticise the views of Bruce and Wilson who claim that it also applies to American society. They criticise secularisation theorists for fooling people into believing that there was a **golden age of religion** in the past and that this has since declined. Instead, Stark and Bainbridge believe that religious belief tends to flow through cycles, in which temporary periods of secularisation are followed by religious revivals which occur as a result of the creation of new religions and New Age movements (see page 149).

Religious market theory

According to Stark and Bainbridge, two assumptions about human nature influence the way that people engage with religion.

 People are naturally religious – there will always be a demand for some form of religion.

 All humans want big rewards for the smallest costs – humans make rational decisions about what benefits them the most.

What makes religion unique is that it can claim to provide supernatural rewards that other institutions cannot. Stark and Bainbridge refer to these as **compensators**. They believe that believing in religion has a small cost and barely any risk, and promises great rewards. It will therefore never cease to exist.

Supply-led religion

The key difference between religious experiences in America and Europe, according to Stark and Bainbridge, is that most European countries are dominated by one religion, which may not suit the needs of every citizen. Traditional churches monopolise religion in these countries and therefore become complacent in the service they provide. This leads to the religious experience turning stale and boring, which eventually leads to the public turning away from religion.

In America, there is a **supply-led** religious market in which there is a vast range of different religious organisations to choose from. The religious groups know they have to compete for survival and therefore ensure that their religious experience is the best it can possibly be. There are several examples of this.

Jesus in Disneyland

Postmodernist **David Lyon's** (2000) study, *Jesus in Disneyland*, showed how denominations were holding services in theme parks to attract new followers who were essentially seen as customers within a **sphere of consumption**. According to Lyon, **spiritual shoppers** are buying into religious experiences that attract them, which has brought back an element of magic to the experience that was supposedly lost after the Enlightenment. Lyon argues that this has led to the **re-enchantment of the world**, which can be used as a criticism of **Weber's** (1905) view that people no longer believe in the 'sacred' qualities of religion (see page 160).

Televangelism

Hadden and Shupe (1988) discuss the growth of **televangelism** as Christian denominations spend large sums of money on television advertisements and allow filmmakers access to their services in order to spread their message across the population. This has led to a surge in Evangelical Christian denominations in the USA, in which **mega churches** are being built to cope with the high levels of demand.

A US mega church with the capacity to seat 16 000 people.

Now try this

How could you use David Lyon's (2000) 'sphere of consumption' to criticise the views of Steve Bruce (2011) who believes that America has become secular?

Religious fundamentalism

Another argument against the view that religion is losing its influence in the UK and abroad is the rise of **religious fundamentalism**. Fundamentalism refers to the process of returning to the basics of a religion (the sacred texts) and belief in its **absolute truth**. Fundamentalist groups can emerge from any traditional religion.

Features of religious fundamentalism

Fundamentalists believe in the exact wording of the sacred texts and will often cite quotations to justify their actions and beliefs.

Hawley (1994) claims that fundamentalist groups tend to be patriarchal in nature, which is often inspired by their conservative value base.

Many fundamentalist movements are awaiting the 'end of days' due to a form of a divine intervention (**millenarianism**).

Features

Fundamentalists use modern technology to promote their message, which is ironic as they tend to resist most other forms of social change. They also recruit many of their followers online.

Fundamentalists have a world-rejecting attitude to wider society and therefore isolate themselves from the mainstream and others who have different views.

Fundamentalist movements tend to be sects in terms of their structure and claim a monopoly on the truth.

Fundamentalists attempt to shock the population through extreme views or acts of terrorism to gain public attention. For example, the Westboro Baptist Church, whose members believe that natural disasters are a sign of God's anger at the acceptance of homosexuality on Earth.

The influence of globalisation

Anthony Giddens (1999)

Giddens believes that **globalisation** has triggered the recent rise in fundamentalism due to the rapid promotion of cosmopolitan values. In all societies around the world, individuals with conservative values are feeling threatened by a more liberal world view that seeks to undermine traditional assumptions about gender differences, abortion, sexual activity, and so on.

Even traditional religions are diluting their own beliefs on traditional values due to their unpopularity, which is driving more conservative followers to greater extremes.

Bauman (1992)

Bauman, a postmodernist, agrees that the uncertainty caused by globalisation has led to a rise in fundamentalist movements. He claims that some individuals struggle to cope with the lack of absolute truth related to postmodernity and are therefore attracted to fundamentalism as one of the only sources of 'truth' around which they can build their identities.

Castells (2010)

Castells claims that postmodernity has led to two different responses.

1. A **resistance identity** – the individual turns to fundamentalist movements to protect their conservative values, which are now under threat.

2. A **project identity** – the individual attempts to embrace change by engaging with New Age movements or progressive environmentalist or political groups.

Evaluation

💭 **Beckford** (2011) is critical of Giddens and the postmodernists. He claims that they tend to be obsessed with fundamentalism and ignore the way that globalisation affects all forms of religion. He also criticises Giddens specifically for talking about fundamentalist groups as a whole when it is very clear that there are different forms of fundamentalist groups around the world.

Now try this

Provide **two** explanations for the rise in fundamentalist groups.

Types of religious fundamentalism

To an extent, **Bruce** (2008) agrees with Giddens (and others) that religious fundamentalism is mainly caused by individuals who feel under threat from the adoption of different beliefs as a result of globalisation (see page 164). However, Bruce claims that certain religions are more likely to generate fundamentalist movements than others.

Two types of fundamentalism

According to Bruce, polytheistic religions (that have more than one god) are less likely to generate fundamentalist movements than monotheistic religions (that worship one god). This is because monotheistic religions (such as Christianity and Islam) present their god as almighty and powerful, with the potential to be vengeful and authoritative. These religions are less open to interpretation and therefore have specific sacred texts that can influence radical followers.

By discussing monotheistic religions, Bruce is suggesting that Christianity and Islam are more prone to generating fundamentalist sects. However, unlike Giddens, Bruce attempts to differentiate between what he calls the two types of fundamentalism.

1 **Western (Christian) fundamentalist groups** are often reacting to changes within Western society such as secularisation. They are often attempting to battle with their own community in order to bring back traditional values that have been eroded due to cosmopolitanism.

2 **Third-world fundamentalists (Islamic)** are often reacting to external influences that are attempting to erode their way of life through secular and liberal values. They therefore use religion as a form of cultural defence to protect their belief systems and heritage.

Secular fundamentalism

Davie (2013) agrees to an extent with theorists who claim that religious fundamentalism has been triggered by increasing globalisation and supposed secularisation. However, Davie also claims that fundamentalism is not confined to religion as certain movements have emerged that have no connections with traditional religious teaching and yet have common themes with religious fundamentalism.

For example, there is increasing support for far-right political groups in Western societies who are 'protecting' conservative values that were once dominant but are no longer respected by the liberal majority.

In the UK, Davie's views could be used to explain the result of the recent EU referendum, which for many was a reaction to uncontrolled immigration.

The clash of civilisations

Huntington (1996) takes a different approach to other theorists when discussing fundamentalism. Huntington claims that, due to globalisation, there are seven different civilisations in existence that transcend national borders.

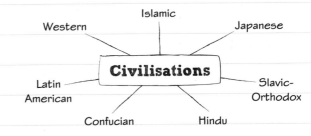

Each of these 'civilisations' are associated with a mainstream religion. Huntington suggests that civilisations often unite against a common enemy and therefore constantly attempt to generate an 'us and them' mentality. As religion is the major source of difference today, religious conflict becomes the battleground of the civilisations. According to Huntington, this is the reason for the rise in religious fundamentalism in Islam as Muslims attempt to fight against the dominance of Western Christian civilisation.

Now try this

1 How does Bruce differentiate between Christian and Islamic fundamentalist groups?

2 Give **two** examples of the kind of changes in society that groups from the right might seek to resist.

Religion and economic development

Some theorists who argue against the idea of global secularisation believe instead that religion may be playing a vital role in the **economic development** of previously disadvantaged communities. Many of these theories cite **Weber's** (1905) **Protestant ethic** as an influence (see page 145).

Hinduism and India

Meera Nanda (2008) studied how Hinduism has evolved to assist the rapid economic growth experienced by India over recent generations. Globalisation has brought a wealth of opportunities to India due to a surge in global demand for industries that India is reputable in, for example medicine and IT services. This has led to the emergence of a young, professional middle class. The expectation is that this class will become more secular, as their need for the traditional religion of Hinduism diminishes with their new-found prosperity. However, Nanda claims that the opposite has occurred.

The role of the tele-gurus

Nanda claims that this surge in popularity is due to the role of the **tele-gurus**, who have changed the way that Hinduism values wealth and prosperity. Traditionally, Hinduism denounced wealth as a sin, mirroring the views of traditional Catholicism in central Europe. Contemporary Hindu leaders now encourage a more progressive view of wealth by stating that it is seen as a sign of divine favour. This encourages young Hindus to pursue the opportunities that are available to them because of increasing globalisation without the guilt imposed by traditional Hinduism. By remaining relevant to its population, Hinduism has surged in popularity whilst also stimulating further economic growth.

Hinduism is reportedly more popular than ever before: 85 per cent of the Indian population affiliate themselves with the religion, making it statistically the most religious nation on Earth.

Ultra-nationalism

Nanda suggests many Indians believe that their Hindu values have stimulated their economy and success in the global market. As a result, Hinduism is creating a sense of **ultra-nationalism** by generating a worship of Indian culture rather than just a focus on the gods. In this sense, parallels can be drawn between Hinduism and the **civil religion** that **Robert Bellah** claims can be found in America (see page 140).

Pentecostalism in South America

Berger (2003) believes that the rapid spread of Pentecostalism across South American countries such as Brazil has had a similar impact to that of Calvinism in central Europe (see Weber on page 145). Berger suggests that Pentecostalism has become a strong rival to Catholicism in the region as it encourages its followers to better themselves by working their way out of poverty rather than awaiting salvation in the afterlife. This in turn stimulates economic growth by inspiring followers to adopt a dedicated work ethic, similar to the Calvinistic Protestant work ethic that is playing a role in its country's economic development.

Adapting to local identities

Lehmann (2002), having analysed the way that Pentecostalism is rapidly expanding across countries like China and South Korea and appearing to be attractive to people of different cultures, agrees with Berger's findings. Lehmann argues that whilst all Pentecostal denominations preach similar messages on a global scale, they tend to 'tap in' and adapt to local concerns and traditions in order to appeal to their new followers. In so doing, Pentecostalism develops a local identity in each society that it penetrates, which boosts its popularity and impact.

Now try this

How can Weber's study of Calvinism be applied to the impact of Pentecostalism in South American countries?

Exam skills 1

These questions will help you to revise for Section B of your A Level Paper 2 exam. The 'Beliefs in society' unit is the second optional module of Paper 2, which is entitled 'Topics in Sociology'. There are 40 marks available for this section spread across three different questions. It is advised that you spend around 60 minutes on this section of the exam in total. Before you look at the question on this page, remind yourself about the growth of new religious movements on page 153.

Command words: Outline and explain

You need to set out the main characteristics and then develop each reason more fully. In doing so, you should show knowledge (Outline) and understanding (Explain) of key concepts, theorists and evidence. This must be applied to the question and analysed (explained fully).

Worked example

1 Outline and explain **two** reasons why women are more likely to be religious than men. **(10 marks)**

One reason why women are more likely to be religious than men is due to the socialisation process. Miller and Hoffman (1995) claim that women are socialised to be more nurturing whilst requiring more emotional support than men, which is provided by religion. The comfort of knowing that they are loved by a higher power is attractive to women, according to Miller and Hoffman, and tailors to their 'risk averse' nature as the promise of a secure afterlife eases their anxiety. In addition, due to their role as housewives, women have far more time to attend church services than their husbands who work full time. This view is supported by Greely (1992) who claims that women will often attend church to assist the nurturing of their children by providing them with a sense of morality. Greely suggests that a woman is much more likely to engage with religion after they have children for this reason. Therefore, it is claimed that women are more religious than men due to the socialisation process...

 Spend 15 minutes on this 10-mark question and give your answer in two clear paragraphs. No introduction or conclusion is required.

 In each paragraph, start by **describing** (outlining) your reason in the first sentence.

In each paragraph, aim to include two different theorists and **explain** their research using key terms and specific examples.

 At the end of each paragraph, link your point back to the question, using the exact phrasing. This will show that you are applying your answer to the question.

To complete the answer, you need to add a **second reason** in the same style as given here. You might focus on different forms of deprivation (Glock and Stark and Heelas et al's Kendal project).

Assessment objectives

AO1: Knowledge
Demonstrate knowledge and understanding of sociological theories, concepts and evidence.

AO2: Application
Apply sociological theories, concepts and evidence to the question/issue and the item.

AO3: Analysis and evaluation
Analyse and evaluate sociological theories, concepts and evidence in order to present arguments, make judgements and draw a conclusion.

Exam skills 2

This question will help you to revise for Section B of your A Level Paper 2 exam. Spend around 15 minutes on this question. Before you look at this question, remind yourself about secularisation in the UK on pages 159–161.

Worked example

2   Read **Item A** below and answer the question that follows.

> **Item A**
>
> Wilson defines secularisation as 'the process whereby religious institutions lose their social significance' and claims that this has been occurring in Western countries, such as the UK. There are many potential forms of evidence to support this claim, including the analysis of declining church attendance for the Anglican Church and the increasing rationalisation of society after the Enlightenment.

Applying material from **Item A**, analyse **two** sociological explanations that suggest that secularisation is occurring in the UK. **(10 marks)**

Item A states that one sociological explanation which suggests that secularisation is occurring in the UK is the declining church attendance of the Anglican Church. Although 59 per cent of the UK population claimed that they were Christians in the 2011 Census, only around 5 per cent regularly attend Sunday church services, which suggests that the religion has lost its 'social significance' (referring to Wilson's definition of secularisation in Item A). Abby Day (2007) agrees with this view as she claims that individuals affiliate themselves with Christianity in the UK for non-religious reasons. Day claims that the main motivation for doing so is that people believe that being a 'Christian' is central to the 'British' identity and therefore feel as though they identify themselves as being Christian in order to belong to the White British majority. Furthermore, not only has regular church attendance been on the decline, so have the amount of baptisms, weddings and funerals that used to form what Terry Sanderson (1999) refers to as the church's 'core business'. Sanderson claims that the church has survived for generations from these services, however, due to the vast range of secular alternatives, the population is no longer using the church for these purposes. Arguments that solely focus on church attendance are open to criticism as theorists such as Grace Davie (1994) suggest that the population in the UK tends to 'believe without belonging' and therefore practise religion in a private way without attending church services. This does not necessarily mean that secularisation is occurring in the UK...

Command word: Analyse

Here, you need to look at different evidence and theories for secularisation and examine each in turn. You need to use information in Item A as well as your own knowledge.

Read the item carefully and highlight anything that seems important. Before writing, figure out how you are going to use the item and which studies you are going to cite.

All three assessment objectives will be credited (see page 167). Show that you have 'sound and detailed' knowledge by using at least two well-explained studies in each paragraph. Make sure you explain how each suggests that secularisation is occurring (or not).

To show application, link to the item directly in the first sentence and provide an outline of the point you are going to analyse. Attempt to find other uses for the item and make it obvious when you do so.

Here, the answer has provided a good evaluation by using two studies (Abby Day and Terry Sanderson) to support the claim that secularisation is occurring in the UK and a further study (Grace Davie) as a counter-argument.

To complete this answer, you need to analyse a second sociological explanation for the occurrence of secularisation in the UK. You could use rationalisation or privatised religious belief as an effective theme for the paragraph. Remember, attempt to use two studies to support your claim and then criticise the point with some brief evaluation towards the end of the paragraph.

Exam skills 3

The last question will be a 20-mark essay. Spend around 30 minutes planning and writing this question. Remind yourself about the theories of religion, gender and religiosity, and new religious and New Age movements.

Worked example

3 Read **Item B** below and answer the question that follows.

Item B

Sociologists have a view on whether or not religion promotes social change. Functionalists, Marxists and feminists generally believe that religion prevents change and therefore acts as a conservative force. However, there are disagreements between these theory groups on who benefits from this process. Other theorists believe that religion promotes social change.

Applying material from **Item B** and your knowledge, evaluate sociological explanations that suggest that religion acts as a conservative force. **(20 marks)**

As item B suggests, functionalists believe that religion prevents change and therefore acts as a conservative force. By preventing radical change, religion is beneficial to society as it provides stability and maintains social order. Durkheim (1915) claims that religion provides society with a 'collective conscience' by transmitting and reinforcing the vital norms and values that underpin the value consensus that is passed down from generation to generation. Furthermore, Malinowski (1954) claims that religion acts as a conservative force as it assists its followers with 'psychological functions' as they seek comfort during times of crisis. By providing 'rites of passage', religion ensures that all followers can return to normality as soon as possible to ensure that the specialised division of labour is not disrupted. Overall, functionalists believe that religion, as a conservative force, is beneficial for society. However, functionalists are often criticised for not acknowledging the influence of secularisation and how this may undermine their claims that religion is effective in preventing change...

...To conclude, whilst classical theories like functionalism and Marxism suggest that religion acts as a conservative force, there is sufficient evidence to suggest that religion can influence change in certain circumstances. The views of theorists such as Max Weber (1905) and Bloch (1959) therefore seem to have the most validity as they identify that religion can influence change and act as a conservative force, depending on the social situation.

Command word: Evaluate

You must include an introduction and a conclusion as well as evaluating the argument in the question. Once you have set out your arguments, using studies and concepts from each theory, make a judgement based on the evidence you have presented. All three assessment objectives will be credited (see page 167).

You must refer to Item B in your answer. Select the studies and concepts from each theory that make the most impact (see the Essay plan).

Essay plan

1 **Introduction** – define 'conservative force' and outline the argument; use Item B.

2 **Functionalists** (link to question/item) – use **Durkheim** (1915) and **Malinowski** (1954).

3 **Marxists** (link to question/item) – use **Marx** (1844) and **Engels** (1895). Use the caste system to develop your point. Show contrast with functionalism.

4 **Neo-Marxists** (link to question/item) – use **Bloch** (1959), **Gramsci** (1971) and **liberation theology**. Contrast with Marxism.

5 **Max Weber** (link to question/item) – use the **Protestant ethic** (1905) as the main focus and show contrasts with Marxism.

6 **Feminists** (link to question/item) – use **De Beauvoir** (1953) but evaluate with **El Saadawi** (1980) and **Linda Woodhead** (2004). Link to **new religious** and **New Age movements**.

7 **Conclusion** – make a judgement whilst linking directly to the question. Which theory has the most validity in this argument?

For each paragraph, ask yourself:

✓ Have I used key concepts and sociologists as evidence to support my claims?

✓ Is it clear how this point is relevant to the question?

✓ Can I apply this point to the item?

✓ Have I explained each point in enough detail?

✓ Could this point be evaluated by another study or point?

Exam-style practice

Practise for Section B of Paper 2 of your A Level exam with these exam-style questions. There are answers on page 224. Some questions require more extensive prose and more thought and application of knowledge. Try to keep these answers strictly timed. You will always get the most marks by attempting every question on the topic.

1 Outline and explain **two** reasons why ethnic minorities are more likely to be religious than the White British.　　**(10 marks)**

Spend 15 minutes on this question. Use two, well-structured paragraphs and get straight to the point – you do not need an introduction or a conclusion, nor do you need to include any evaluation.

You could use Max Weber (see pages 144 and 153) to explain the link between poverty, religion and ethnic minorities. Durkheim (see page 139) considered how ethnic minorities used religion to help them integrate into new societies.

2 Read **Item A** below and answer the question that follows.

Write two, well-structured paragraphs to answer this question. Aim to use two studies in each paragraph. Link directly to the question at the start and end of each paragraph.

Item A

Since the Enlightenment, it is believed that science has become the dominant belief system. Some theorists suggest that this is due to Western societies developing a 'rationalised' world view where logic and the pursuit of evidence are used to explain world events. Others suggest that the 'open' nature of science has led to its dominance as religion is traditionally described as a 'closed' belief system.

Applying material from **Item A**, analyse **two** explanations that suggest that science has replaced religion as the dominant belief system.　　**(10 marks)**

Your answer should use the suggested material in the item and link to it in both paragraphs. Evaluation is credited in these questions so aim to include some form of strength of critique.

Key works to consider in your answer to question 2 include Max Weber and Steve Bruce, who explain rationalisation and technological world view respectively (see page 160). Sir Karl Popper and Robert Merton look at science as an open and closed belief system (see page 137).

3 Read **Item B** below and answer the question that follows.

Item B

The evidence suggests that religious fundamentalism is on the rise in both the Western and the developing world. Many theorists suggest that this is due to the rapid growth of a cosmopolitan world view that has spread due to globalisation.

Applying material from **Item B** and your knowledge, evaluate the view that the growth in fundamentalism is primarily due to globalisation.　　**(20 marks)**

Spend 30 minutes answering this question. Use the item wherever possible; link to it directly using statements like 'as suggested in the item'. Think about how your paragraphs connect together – will the answer flow well?

Ensure that all of your points are supported by evidence with reference to specific studies conducted by sociologists. As the command word asks you to evaluate, you must show alternative points of view within your answer. For information on religious fundamentalism, (see pages 164–165). Also consider using the reasons for the rise of new religious movements (see page 153) for further options.

Functionalist perspective on crime

Functionalists such as **Durkheim** (1893) argue that crime and deviance can only be explained by looking at the way societies are socially organised – their **social structures** – and that crime is caused by society rather than by the circumstances of the individual. Functionalism is therefore a **structuralist theory** of crime.

Definitions

Deviance is behaviour that lies outside of the social norms of a social group. Its abnormality attracts social disapproval.

Crime is deviant behaviour that breaks laws.

Mechanical solidarity

Durkheim argued that traditional societies had little crime and deviance because of the existence of strong social controls. He saw **traditional** societies as underpinned by **mechanical solidarity**:

- Powerful agencies such as the family and religion socialised members into a clear consensus about right and wrong.
- Those who strayed beyond the consensus faced severe and often public forms of punishment.
- Individuality was regarded as deviant and was suppressed. Loyalty and duty to the group was paramount.

Traditional societies include medieval British society, Islamic societies, and communist dictatorships.

The functions of crime

Durkheim argued that crime existed in all societies. This universality suggests it has **positive functions**.

1. **Boundary maintenance** – punishment by the courts for breaking a law reaffirms value consensus and public faith in social controls. The boundary between acceptable and deviant behaviour is clear, discouraging offending.

2. **Functional rebellion** – some 'deviance' may enable much-needed social change.
   The Suffragettes aimed to change laws that denied women the same rights as men.

3. **Social cohesion** – horrific crimes such as terrorism may create public outrage and draw diverse communities closer together.

4. **Early warning system** – deviance may act as a warning that a social institution is not working properly.
   High numbers of suicides in prison may indicate an issue with the prison system, prompting changes to the way prisons are run.

5. **Safety valve** – some functionalists argue that relatively minor crimes may act as a safety valve because they prevent more serious crimes.
   Polsky (1967) controversially suggested that pornography may prevent more serious sexual offences; feminists take issue with this idea.

Social control

Most sociological theories of crime aim to explain why particular social groups commit crime. However, some focus on '**social control**' and look at why most people do not commit crime. Theories of social control examine the process of persuading and enforcing conformity to cultural values, norms and laws.

Organic solidarity

Durkheim saw **modern** societies as underpinned by **organic solidarity**:

- Agencies (the family and religion) are less influential and members of society are exposed to ideas that challenge tradition and authority.
- Consequently there is no longer clear agreement about what constitutes right and wrong behaviour.
- Formerly deviant acts become socially acceptable.
- Punishments for crime and deviance grow weaker and no longer deter.

Durkheim suggests that in modern societies like the UK and USA, crime has risen because of a weakening of social controls, which has undermined consensus and led to '**anomie**' (instability resulting from moral uncertainty about rules and values). Some societies no longer have the power to deter or socially control individuals from committing criminal or deviant acts.

Evaluation of Durkheim

👍 The concept of anomie has been very influential and inspired a range of theories of crime, such as those by **Robert Merton** (1949, 1968) (see page 172) and **Albert Cohen** (1955) (see page 173).

👎 Marxists argue that crime is caused by inequality and conflict, which are the natural outcomes of capitalist thinking and practices rather than a weakening of consensus.

👎 Durkheim neglects the effects of crime on its victims. How can crimes such as rape benefit society?

👎 Marxists argue that Durkheim neglects the role of the powerful in shaping or fixing the consensus about crime so that their activities are not defined as criminal.

Now try this

Why has crime increased according to Durkheim?

Strain theory

The functionalist thinker **Robert Merton** (1949, 1968) aimed to explain why most crime was committed by poorer sections of society in capitalist societies such as the USA.

Crime as a consequence of strain

Merton argued that in the USA, cultural institutions, such as the mass media and education, socialise individuals to:

- believe in the American Dream – prosperity and upward mobility is available to all who work hard
- achieve shared goals (financial success, home ownership)
- achieve these by approved means (working hard to gain qualifications and well-paid jobs).

The institutional means of achieving prosperity (education and jobs) are usually provided by the **social structure**. However, Merton argued that these structural means were not fairly distributed across all social groups. He concluded that a gap or **strain** existed between the dominant cultural goal and the structural means of achieving that goal.

Strain theory

Merton believed that this strain led to the poor experiencing a state of **anomie** – a form of moral frustration and disenchantment. This potentially undermined their commitment to consensus and order and they may respond by adopting one of five types of behaviour.

Type of behaviour	Cultural goal	Structural means	Example
Conformity	✓ Strong belief	✓ Accept means	The majority response – most work hard and take responsibility for failure.
Innovation	✓ Strong belief	✗ Reject legitimate means – they see that the means to success are blocked	A minority choose criminality to achieve the goal of prosperity. For example, gangsters and drug dealers.
Ritualism	✗ Weak belief	✗ Accept means but lack ambition	Someone in a low-level job who takes comfort in following their daily routine and the avoidance of risk.
Retreatism	✗ Reject goal	✗ Reject means	Gives up and drops out of society. For example, a drifter or drug addict.
Rebellion	✗ Reject all goals ✗ Substitute alternative goals	✗ Aims to tear down and replace the existing social means	Violent revolutions and terrorism. For example, the French Revolution (1789) or the Islamic Revolution in Iran (1979).

Merton concludes that the behaviour of both criminals and non-criminals are shaped by the same material desires and goals.

Evaluating Merton

👍 He clearly shows capitalist social structure as the cause of crime. **Sumner** (2004) and **Young** (2007) claim that he has uncovered the main cause of crime in modern societies – the capitalist cultural emphasis on material success.

👍 **Savelsburg** (1995) used strain theory to explain the explosion in crime rates in ex-communist societies like Russia when they embraced capitalist practices and cultural goals in the 1990s.

👎 Merton does not explain why individuals choose the responses that they do.

👎 He fails to explain crimes that are not economically motivated.

👎 **Valier** (2001) argues that Merton exaggerates the importance of monetary success in people's lives. Goals such as helping others and job satisfaction may be more important than prosperity.

👎 Merton underestimates the amount of crime committed by the upper and middle classes who are not affected by the strain between goals and means.

👎 Marxists like **Box** (1983) claim that Merton fails to acknowledge that the powerful benefit from the capitalist system and, in particular, the laws that underpin it.

Now try this

What type of crime does Merton fail to explain?

Cohen's subcultural theory

Crime committed by adolescents is known as **juvenile delinquency**. Subcultural theory tries to explain why juvenile delinquency has a collective or subcultural character – it is often committed as part of a larger group or gang.

Juvenile delinquency

Albert Cohen (1955) was influenced by Merton and was interested in the fact that Merton had not addressed juvenile delinquency.

Cohen observed that delinquency is often malicious in nature and not linked to material or financial goals: for example, vandalism, recreational drug use and gang violence.

Delinquent boys

According to Cohen, juvenile delinquency is caused by a strain between cultural goals and the institutional means of achieving them. He argues that young people's main cultural goal is the desire for status and respect:

- Middle-class boys usually attain this through their parents and educational success.
- Working-class boys are denied this by wider society – their parents don't equip them with the necessary skills and they are placed in bottom sets at school.

Status frustration and the subcultural response

Cohen's theory suggests that poor access to good education and job opportunities left working-class juveniles frustrated with their inability to achieve status. They experienced a form of anomie, which he called '**status frustration**'.

They responded to this frustration by developing **delinquent subcultures** of like-minded boys, who reversed the norms and values of the dominant culture and awarded one another status on the basis of anti-school and delinquent behaviour.

The interactionist critique

Matza (1964) suggests that there are problems with all subcultural theories. The assumption is that delinquents are different from others, but their values are actually similar to those of mainstream society. Matza observed that delinquents:

- are often outraged by crime
- often express regret and remorse when caught offending
- use techniques of **neutralisation** to 'normalise' their behaviour as acceptable or to justify it as an exception to the social norm.

  For example, 'everybody does it' or 'I had a rough childhood'. They rarely justify their criminality by pleading loyalty to a gang or deviant subculture.

Matza argues that:

- only a minority of working-class youth actually get into trouble or join gangs
- youths tend to drift between orthodox and delinquent behaviour, but eventually grow out of delinquency when they reach adulthood
- all members of society subscribe to 'deviant' or **subterranean** values – such as craving excitement, thrills, aggression and risk-taking – but they express these in a socially acceptable fashion through leisure activities (e.g. sport)
- some youths express these subterranean values in the wrong place and at the wrong time and are consequently labelled as delinquents by teachers, the media and the police.

Evaluation of Cohen

👍 Cohen's ideas about status and respect are still very relevant to an understanding of contemporary gang culture.

👎 **Paul Willis** (1977) concludes that working-class youth do not not share the same definition of status as middle-class boys. Willis' lads saw educational failure as 'success' because qualifications were not necessary for the jobs they wanted (see page 31).

👎 Feminists observe that Cohen ignores female delinquency.

👎 **Walter Miller** (1962) argues that working-class juvenile delinquency is not the result of strain. Instead, working-class youth are merely acting out and exaggerating the mainstream values (**focal concerns**) of working-class culture, such as heightened masculinity, smartness, trouble, excitement and anti-authoritarianism.

Now try this

1 Why are feminists critical of Cohen's theory?

2 Outline **two** reasons why Matza claims that the concept of subcultures are not that useful in explaining crimes committed by young people.

Other subcultural theories

Other subcultural theories have further developed Merton's ideas about strain to explain the existence of criminal and deviant subcultures.

Cultural transmission

Shaw and McKay (1942) examined the ecological organisation of cities.

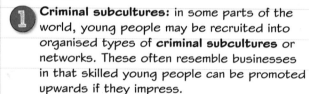

Delinquent subcultures engage in cultural transmission – they transmit criminal behaviour, skills and values from one generation to the next.

Most inner-city zones are characterised by a lack of community spirit and social control and therefore by delinquent subcultures and high crime rates.

Their observations

The constant movement of people in and out of inner-city areas prevents the formation of stable communities and undermines existing social controls.

Differential association

Sutherland's (1939) concept of '**differential association**' suggests that it is very difficult for young people living in urban areas to be law abiding because their frequent association with people who make their living from crime is likely to lead them into trouble with the law.

Illegitimate opportunity structures (IOS)

Cloward and Ohlin (1960) argued that if young working-class people are denied legitimate opportunities, such as jobs, they may turn to an **illegitimate opportunity structure** (IOS). However, their access to these depends on the availability of deviant subcultures in the locality in which they live. They identify three types of IOS, or deviant subcultures.

1. **Criminal subcultures:** in some parts of the world, young people may be recruited into organised types of **criminal subcultures** or networks. These often resemble businesses in that skilled young people can be promoted upwards if they impress.

   The most well-known criminal network in the UK is the Kray gang which dominated crime in South London in the 1960s.

2. **Conflict subcultures:** some inner-city areas may be dominated by **territorial street gangs** (conflict subcultures), which engage in highly masculinised violence.

   Between 2011 and 2014, the police estimated that 6600 crimes and 24 murders were committed by gang members in London alone.

3. **Retreatist subcultures:** those who fail to gain access to either the criminal or conflict subcultures may form **retreatist subcultures**, in which the major activities are drug use.

   Warburton et al. (2005) note the existence of a heroin 'scene' in most major British cities, where addicts probably commit the majority of inner-city crimes (street robbery, burglary, shoplifting) to finance their habit.

Evaluation of Cloward and Ohlin

- They assume that the official picture of crime – which portrays the 'typical' criminal as young, male and working-class – is accurate and fail to acknowledge that such statistics may tell us more about police stereotyping or profiling than about criminal activity.
- They fail to account for white-collar or corporate crimes.
- Their subcultural categories may not be as distinct as they claim.
  Research by **Kintrea** (2008) into London's territorial gangs suggests that they have strong links to organised crime, especially global drug-trafficking networks, and their members frequently use drugs recreationally.
- **Marshall's** (2005) research suggests that Cloward and Ohlin may have exaggerated the criminal opportunities available to young people. His research suggests that most youths never come into contact with subcultures. Instead, they mainly hang out in informal and disorganised groups he called 'crews'. These engage in incidental anti-social behaviour rather than crime, caused by high spirits, boredom and drunkenness, rather than subcultural pressures.
- Postmodernists such as **Katz** (1988) and **Milovanovic and Lyng** (2001) argue that most delinquency is not committed as part of a subculture. They argue that it is often individualistic, opportunistic and spontaneous. Most delinquent actions are fuelled by the excitement and adrenalin that results from the risk of being caught.

Now try this

1 What are the **three** types of illegitimate opportunity structures identified by Cloward and Ohlin?

2 Explain how Marshall is critical of Cloward and Ohlin.

Marxist theories of crime

Marxists argue that crime is caused by the organisation and nature of capitalist society.

Inequalities in income and wealth

According to traditional Marxism, capitalist societies are characterised by class inequalities in the distribution of, for example, wealth and income. Consequently, poverty, unemployment, low-quality housing or homelessness, debt and food banks are 'normal' facts of life for those at the bottom-end of capitalist society. As a result, crime reflects these inequalities, and is therefore an inevitable, realistic and rational response to these circumstances.

Criminogenic capitalism

David Gordon (1976) argues that the very nature and organisation of capitalism is **criminogenic**. This means that the culture or value system that underpins capitalism causes criminal behaviour in all social classes. He argues that the population of capitalist societies is socialised and immersed into a set of capitalist values – competition, individualism, materialism and money as a measure of success. These promote selfishness, greed and, consequently, criminal behaviour among rich and poor alike.

Powerlessness and alienation

Marxists argue that work was traditionally the main source of identity, creativity and satisfaction for working-class men. However, in the drive for greater profits and control, work has been reorganised so that all power, job satisfaction and creativity has been removed from the worker. This has led to alienation – feelings of disaffection or dissatisfaction.

Marxists argue that some working-class men may seek alternative sources of power and consequently commit crime.

For example, sexual and domestic violence may be an attempt to compensate for this alienation.

The law as social control

Marxists believe that the law and agencies of social control such as the police, the courts and prisons function to benefit the interests of the ruling class. **Althusser** (1969) calls the law '**an ideological state apparatus**' because it functions to hide the true extent of class inequality. Although the law claims to protect all sections of society equally, this is untrue because, as **Chambliss** (1975) argues, the law mainly protects capitalist interests, particularly wealth, property and profit.

For example, in the 18th century, British authorities in the British colonies introduced laws which made it illegal to help a slave escape.

The social construction of the law

Steven Box (1983) argues that the law is socially constructed by the ruling class to protect capitalist interests. He claims that the ruling class often engage in activities that result in death, injury, fraud and theft.

For example, according to the HSE (2016), 25 000 workers have died from accidents in the workplace over the past 30 years. It is estimated that 70 per cent of these deaths have occurred because of corporate infringement of health and safety rules (source: HSE). Box argues that employers are rarely charged with criminal offences such as manslaughter or criminal negligence because the ruling class has deliberately prevented laws being passed that might criminalise employers and ensured that violation of health and safety remains a lesser civil offence.

Selective law enforcement

Marxists argue that law enforcement is biased and selective. Statistics give the impression that crimes are mainly committed by working-class people (street crimes) rather than by the wealthy and powerful (white-collar and corporate crime).

Reiman (2001) argues that the more likely a crime is to be committed by higher-class people, the less likely it is to be treated as a criminal offence.

For example, social security fraud is largely committed by the poor and nearly always results in criminal prosecution. In contrast tax evaders rarely face criminal prosecution.

Marxists also argue that laws aimed at protecting powerless groups such as workers, women and ethnic minorities (e.g. health and safety, equal pay and opportunity laws) are weakly enforced and punished.

Now try this

1 Outline **three** reasons why people commit crime according to Marxists.

2 What do Marxists mean when they describe capitalism as criminogenic?

White-collar and corporate crime

Marxists are particularly interested in crimes committed by powerful individuals and institutions, particularly **white-collar and corporate crimes** such as fraud, accounting offences, tax evasion and insider share dealing.

White-collar crime

Chapman (2002) defines white-collar crime as: *'crime committed in the course of legitimate employment by managers, executives, directors etc. that involves the abuse of power and trust to financially benefit themselves.'* Such crimes are therefore committed overwhelmingly by people from middle- or upper-class backgrounds.

Marxists observe that both white-collar and corporate crime are crimes of the powerful because these high-status offenders can use their position and authority to cover up their crimes.

Corporate crime

Chapman defines corporate crime as: *'illegal or morally suspect behaviour carried out by high-ranking company officers (owners, directors, executives and managers) aimed at enhancing the share price or profitability of a company rather than for personal gain.'*

Crimes against employees
Death or injury in the workplace through accident or exposure to toxic materials that cause occupational diseases, such as coal dust which leads to the fatal black lung disease.

Crimes against consumers
The morning sickness drug thalidomide was manufactured in the UK in the 1950s by Distillers without proper testing. This led to around 2000 unborn deaths and around 10 000 serious birth defects.

Corporate crime

Environmental offences
Companies may commit 'green' crimes such as allowing their industrial plants or products to emit illegal amounts of carbon, carcinogenic or radioactive materials, with negative environmental effects.

Financial fraud
Bribery and corruption, and false accounting.

Under-reported and under-policed

- These offences often have low visibility or are hidden from the public gaze – people may not realise they have been a victim of corporate crime.

- White-collar or corporate crime is not feared in the same way as robbery or violence.

- These crimes are very complex and often beyond the understanding of the general public and juries.

- It can be difficult to prove individual responsibility for particular corporate actions.

- **Croall** (2001) notes that there is often a fine line between what are morally acceptable and unacceptable business practices.

  Nobody likes paying tax so the general public might not view tax evasion as a serious problem.

- Corporate offenders are often warned rather than charged with a criminal offence.

- The police are affected by a lack of specialist resources and personnel.

Sociological explanations

1. The neo-functionalist **Robert Reiner** (2008) observes that financial success breeds a desire for more money rather than job satisfaction. Corporate and white-collar crimes are therefore caused by the anomic pressures resulting from societies that value monetary success.

2. Marxists argue that bankers and executives of global corporations subscribe to a corporate subculture underpinned by **criminogenic capitalism**. This emphasises the importance of the pursuit of wealth and profit and the taking of financial risks. For some, breaking the law may be worth the risk if it increases profits.

3. Marxists also argue that the law fails to take the crimes of the powerful as seriously as the crimes committed by the poor and powerless.

4. Left realists argue that the merely-rich may feel relatively deprived when they compare themselves to the mega-rich, and so be tempted to commit white-collar crime.

Now try this

1 How do Marxists explain the difference between white-collar and corporate crime?

2 How does Croall (2001) explain why the general public is generally unconcerned about corporations and wealthy individuals engaging in tax evasion?

Neo-Marxist theories of crime

Neo-Marxists are critical of the notion of criminogenic capitalism because they suggest it is too **deterministic**. This means that it sees the working class as the **passive victims** of capitalism, driven to criminality by factors beyond their control.

The New Criminology

Although now 40 years old, the 'New Criminology' of **Ian Taylor, Paul Walton and Jock Young** (1973) is the most well-known example of **neo-Marxism**. It generally agrees with the traditional Marxist analysis:

- Capitalist society is based on exploitation and class conflict and is characterised by extreme inequalities of wealth and power.
- The state makes and enforces laws in the interests of the capitalist class and criminalises members of the working class.

However, neo-Marxism is critical of traditional Marxism, especially the idea that the working class is driven to crime by factors beyond their control, such as inequality and powerlessness.

Hall et al. (1978)

Stuart Hall et al. suggested that **moral panics** about crime were used to reassert the dominance of ruling-class hegemony (see page 81) during the 1970s, when capitalism was undergoing a crisis. News stories about black muggers were exaggerated by the tabloid press and were used to justify an increase in police powers and to deflect attention away from the mismanagement of capitalism by the powerful.

Interpretivism

Neo-Marxists are interpretivists (see page 7). They see the working class as **active agents** who have free will and voluntarily choose (or choose not to) commit crime as a political response to their negative experience of capitalism. Criminality is therefore a form of **political protest**.

The ruling class is aware of the revolutionary potential of working-class crime and has taken steps to control it – state apparatuses such as the police target working-class areas whilst the State has introduced 'repressive' laws, such as the Criminal Justice Acts, to control the 'problem' population. **Hall et al.** (1978) referred to this as '**policing the crisis**'.

Crime as a form of political protest

Neo-Marxists see criminals as revolutionaries struggling to alter capitalism and to change society for the better. They argue that:

- **economic crimes** such as burglary, mugging and robbery are an attempt to redistribute wealth from the rich to the poor
- **vandalism** is a symbolic attack on capitalism's obsession with property
- **drug use** indicates a rejection or contempt for the material values of capitalism.

Also see **Gilroy's** (1982) theory of crime as a protest against a racist capitalist society, page 191.

The fully social theory of deviance

Taylor et al. (1973) argued that any theory of crime must consider the following six elements, which interact with one another.

1 The wider social origins of the deviant act: E.g. how crime and deviance is linked to the unequal distribution of wealth and power in capitalist society.

2 The immediate origins of the deviant act: the particular social or economic situation that led to the criminal or deviant act. E.g. unemployment.

3 The meaning of the act for the actor: the meaning the perpetrator attached to the criminal act. E.g. a form of rebellion against capitalism.

4 The immediate origins of societal reaction: the reaction of those close to the criminal, such as family and community.

5 The wider origins of societal reaction: how society and especially those with power to label others react. Who decides who or what should be labelled deviant/criminal? E.g. how do police officers police? Why do some crimes result in moral panics?

6 The impact of the reaction on the individual: the relationship between labelling and the deviant. E.g. how does labelling affect the offender? Does it lead to further deviance?

Social theory of deviance

Now try this

1 Outline **two** ways in which the ruling class attempts to control the working class according to Hall (1978).

2 Why are neo-Marxists critical of traditional Marxist theories of crime?

Evaluation of critical criminology

You need to be able to evaluate Marxist and neo-Marxist explanations of crime.

Evaluation of the Marxist theory of crime

👍 It challenges the functionalist idea that law is the product of consensus and recognises that the law and criminal justice system can be manipulated by powerful, wealthy interests.

👍 **Richard Wilkinson and Kate Pickett** (2009) have provided empirical data that demonstrates a clear link between inequality and crime. In societies such as the USA and UK, which demonstrate very wide inequalities between rich and poor, crime rates are high. However, crime rates are relatively low in capitalist societies that demonstrate low levels of inequality, such as Sweden and Japan.

👎 Marxists have highlighted the importance of examining harmful activities committed by the powerful and attempted to explain why these activities are often not defined as illegal, and why they are largely invisible to the public eye.

👎 Marxists over-emphasise social class and fail to explain other patterns of crime relating to age, gender and ethnicity.

👎 Marxists are criticised because they tend to over-focus on property crime and have little to say about violence and sex crimes.

👎 The criminal justice system does sometimes act against the interests of the capitalist class.

Corporate crime is punished on occasion – in 2011, a number of MPs were prosecuted and imprisoned because of the Parliamentary expenses scandal.

Evaluation of the neo-Marxist theory of crime

👍 The theory makes sense with regard to crimes that are overtly political, such as those that may result from confrontation with the police at political demonstrations, breaking into laboratories and rescuing animals, sabotaging the Oxford–Cambridge boat race, terrorism, squatting, assassination of political leaders, the suffragettes, and so on.

Sabotaging hunts is an overtly political crime.

👎 Left realists (see page 183) have criticised New Criminology for over-romanticising working-class criminals as 'Robin Hoods' who fight capitalism by stealing from the rich and giving to the poor. The reality is that most victims of working-class criminals are other working-class people.

For example, burglary, car theft.

👎 Crimes such as domestic violence, rape and child abuse are not committed for political reasons.

👎 Right-realist criminologists argue that most crime is opportunist and committed on the spur of the moment rather than as an attempt to right some perceived injustice.

👎 Left realist **Hopkins Burke** (2005) concludes that the New Criminology is too idealistic and therefore impractical in its attempt to explain and tackle crime.

Now try this

Evaluate the neo-Marxist theory of crime from a left-realist perspective.

Interactionist or labelling theory

Interactionist or **labelling theory** approaches to crime and deviance belong to the interpretivist or social action theory tradition (see page 13). These theorists are interested in how people **interpret** normality and deviance. They believe that crime and deviance are socially constructed.

The relativity of crime and deviance

In his classic study Outsiders, **Howard Becker** (1963) argues that there is no value consensus on normality or deviance – these concepts mean different things to different people and groups.

Interpretivists argue that definitions of 'right' and 'wrong' behaviour differ according to the following:

- **Social context:**
  nudity is fine in private but may be interpreted as criminal if carried out in public.

- **Historical period:**
  homosexuality and suicide were illegal activities until the 1960s.

- **Culture:**
  drinking alcohol is illegal in Saudi Arabia but is regarded as a normal social activity in the UK.

- **Subculture:**
  young people's ideas about what constitutes 'normal' behaviour may differ from those of adults.

The role of agents of social control

Interactionists argue that the powerful often socially construct crime and deviance through **agents of control**.

These agents label and define the behaviour of less powerful groups as a problem. As a result, their behaviour is subjected to greater surveillance and control by these social agencies.

The role of the police

Interactionists argue that the police socially construct official crime statistics by interpreting and labelling the activities of groups such as young working-class and ethnic-minority males as more criminal than other social groups. They then target and over-police these groups.

Holdaway (1998) argues that racial profiling by police officers may be responsible for the criminalisation of black people. This stereotyping may account for their disproportionate appearance in official crime statistics. So, crime statistics may tell sociologists more about police racism than black criminality.

Interpretation

Interactionists believe that deviance is a matter of **interpretation**. For the same act – for example, killing a person – there may be several possible interpretations. Killing enemy soldiers in war time or police officers killing terrorists in a hostage situation are generally considered more acceptable and legitimate forms of killing than murder or manslaughter.

Becker argues that no act is inherently criminal or deviant in itself, in all situations and at all times. Instead, it only becomes officially criminal or deviant when it is interpreted as such by others – he calls this **societal reaction**. Interpreting an act as deviant is usually the province of somebody with more power than the person who committed the act.

For example, parents judge whether their children are behaving or misbehaving whilst teachers do the same for their pupils.

The social construction of deviance

Becker claims that deviance is a **social construction**. It requires two groups – one powerless group acts in a particular way and another with more power interprets the action as wrong and **labels** both the activity and the group as deviant or criminal.

Becker notes that powerful groups create rules or laws in order to define what counts as crime and deviance. They then label those who fail to conform to these social controls as criminals or outlaws (outsiders).

For example, employers define what counts as deviance in the workplace.

Cicourel (1968)

Cicourel concluded that definitions of criminality can be negotiated by some groups. In his study of delinquency, he observed that, when arrested, a middle-class youth was less likely to be charged with a criminal offence than a working-class youth because his social background did not fit the police's stereotypical view of a 'typical' delinquent.

Middle-class parents were also more able than working-class parents to convince agents of social control that they would monitor their child and ensure they stayed out of trouble. As a result, he was 'counselled, warned and released', whilst working-class youths were more often charged with a criminal offence.

Now try this

In what sense are definitions of crime and deviance socially constructed?

Had a look ☐   Nearly there ☐   Nailed it! ☐

The consequences of labelling

Labelling theory was the first sociological theory to draw attention to the consequences of labelling and stereotyping people as 'criminals'.

Primary and secondary deviance

Edwin Lemert (1967) distinguishes between **primary deviance** and **secondary deviance**:

- **Primary deviance:** insignificant deviant acts that have not been publicly labelled. These have little significance for a person's status or identity. Primary deviants do not see themselves as deviant and neither does society.

- **Secondary deviance:** the result of societal reaction (labelling). Being publicly labelled as a criminal involves being stigmatised and excluded from normal society. **Hughes** (1994) observed that the criminal label can become a **master status**. This means that society interprets all the labelled person's actions in the context of their initial criminality.

Self-fulfilling prophecy

According to Lemert, labelling a person as a deviant or criminal can result in prejudice and discrimination. Interactionists argue that this makes it extremely difficult for the 'deviant' to adopt 'normal' modes of behaviour.

As a result, **Becker** (1963) observes that the deviant may be forced to seek the company of those similarly labelled and to become part of a deviant subculture. This increases the potential for a **self-fulfilling prophecy** because membership of the subculture (although offering comfort and normality) may tempt and offer the individual other opportunities to reoffend.

Evaluation

👍 Labelling theory has shown that defining deviance is a complex process.

👍 It has shown that definitions of deviance are relative and therefore not fixed, universal or unchangeable.

👍 It has highlighted the importance of studying the societal reaction to crime and deviance.

👍 It shows that society's attempts to control deviance can sometimes backfire and create more deviance rather than less.

💬 **Akers and Sellers** (2004) argue that the deviant act is always more important than the societal reaction to it. Deviants know that what they are doing is wrong even if their acts go undiscovered.

💬 Labelling theory does not explain why people offend in the first place, before they are labelled.

💬 It is too deterministic because it heavily implies that labelling inevitably leads to a deviant career. It doesn't account for free will, choice or a reduction in deviance due to societal reaction.

💬 Left realists **Lea and Young** (1993) claim that labelling theory neglects victims of crime.

💬 Marxists argue that it fails to explain why some groups have more power to get laws passed that are more beneficial to themselves than others.

Deviancy amplification

This is the process by which the official attempt to control deviance or crime leads to an **increase** in the level of deviance. According to **Wilkins** (1964), when people and certain acts are defined as deviant, the 'deviant' social group are stigmatised and cut off from mainstream society.

For example, negative publicity might be generated by newspapers and subsequently the police and courts may announce a 'crackdown' in order to 'make an example' of the group.

The 'deviant' group may react by going underground and becoming more secretive, which in turn may lead to greater attempts to control the group's activities, and so on.

Labelling theory therefore argues that a great deal of deviance is actually caused by the way agencies of social control react to the initial deviance.

Now try this

Why are Marxists critical of labelling theory?

Right-realist theories of crime

Right realists see crime as a real and growing problem that undermines social cohesion and destroys social communities. They believe that people are inherently selfish, individualistic, greedy and 'naturally' inclined towards criminal behaviour if it can further their interests. There are three types of right-realist theory.

Underclass theory

Charles Murray (1984) and **David Marsland** (1989) argue that most crime is committed by a highly deviant, immoral and work-shy subculture called the **underclass**. This is made up of 'problem families' living on inner-city council estates who socialise the next generation into crime as well as encouraging them to be dependent on state benefits.

According to **Murray**, a key New Right theorist, these problem families are often headed by single mothers. Children lack a stable father figure in their lives and are often influenced by negative role models – older boys involved in gangs, drug-dealing and so on.

The New Right argue that the main reason that the underclass has grown in the last 30 years is the welfare state.

Marsland argues that state benefits undermine work and encourage idleness and welfare dependency, especially among the young.

② Rational choice theory

Cornish and Clarke (1986) argue that criminals have free will and choose to commit crime. The choice to commit crime is based on a rational weighing up of the benefits of crime (material success) against the potential costs (the possibility of being caught and punished).

Felson (1998) argues that crime has increased because:

- the quality of policing has deteriorated (criminals know there is little chance of being caught)
- community controls are weak (ordinary people in high crime areas are too afraid to speak out against criminals)
- punishments have become too lenient (prison itself is no longer a deterrent because conditions are allegedly 'too comfortable').

Wilson and Kelling (1982) in their **'broken windows'** theory focus on the decline of community in inner-city areas. They note that if a community allows its physical environment to decline – for example, it does not mend broken windows, clean up graffiti or disperse anti-social groups – criminals will assume that local social or community controls no longer exist and see this as an excuse to commit even more crime.

③ Control theory

Travis Hirschi's (1969) control theory suggests that most people do not commit crime because they can see that the costs of crime will outweigh its benefits. This is because people have four controls in their lives which mean that they have too much to lose if they are caught and punished for committing crimes:

- **Attachment** – most people fear losing the love and respect of their partners and family.
- **Commitment** – most people fear losing their jobs, their homes or their standard of living.
- **Involvement** – most people fear losing their positive reputation and the respect of their friends, colleagues and community.
- **Belief** – most people have been successfully socialised into respecting others and obeying the law.

Hirschi points out that the underclass and the young are less likely to have these four controls in their lives, and consequently, are more likely to commit crime. As people get older, they settle down and get married, set up home, bring home a regular income – in short, they acquire controls in their lives that may prevent them from committing crimes.

Now try this

1. What is the main cause of the appearance of a criminal underclass according to Murray (1984) and Marsland (1989)?
2. What **four** controls in a person's life mean that the costs of crime are likely to outweigh its benefits?

Right realism and social policy

In the UK, right-realist perspectives on crime have influenced the crime policies of British governments since the 1980s. They have also influenced anti-crime policies in the USA.

Zero tolerance policing

Wilson and Kelling (1982) stress that the certainty of capture is a risk that outweighs the benefits of crime. They particularly recommend '**zero tolerance**' policing. The police should keep the streets clear of all deviant elements, especially crimes that threaten the sense of community in neighbourhoods (such as prostitution, begging, drug-dealing and drunkenness). They believe that the streets should be flooded with police in order to deter crime and so that law-abiding citizens can feel safe.

Three strikes rule

Van Den Haag (1994) argues for tougher laws and longer prison sentences in order to deter people (particularly the poor) from committing crimes.

He particularly approved of the **three strikes rule** that has been implemented in over half of the American states since 1994. The federal government has also enacted three strikes laws that make an offender's third felony punishable by life imprisonment or another severe sentence.

Designing out crime

Criminologists based at the Home Office in the UK have devised policies that increase the risk of being caught. These include **target hardening** or **designing out crime** in which householders and car owners are encouraged to invest in alarms, locks, property-marking and so on, and increased surveillance through the use of CCTV and Neighbourhood Watch Schemes. It could be argued that this transfers the responsibility for crime from the offender to the victim, because this view implies that people should take more responsibility for ensuring they are not victims of crime. More CCTV surveillance may also increase the risk of being caught and reduce the benefits of crime.

The Investigatory Powers Act 2016 gives the security services the legal power to hack into and collect personal data from the personal computers, smartphones and social network profiles of British citizens without alerting their owners.

Evaluation

- 🗨 **Rex and Tomlinson** (1979) agree that an underclass exists but disagree that this is a deviant subculture responsible for its own situation and devoted to criminal behaviour. They observe that survey evidence suggests the poor subscribe to the same values as everybody else and that their poverty is often caused by factors beyond their control, such as economic recession, globalisation and government policies.

- 🗨 **Murray** is criticised by labelling theorists for scapegoating the poor and long-term unemployed and encouraging the State to engage in the negative surveillance and treatment of this social group.

- 🗨 **Stanley Cohen** (1979) argued that right-realist policies on crime lead to class inequalities in victimisation, because the rich can afford to live in 'gated communities' guarded by private security. This displaces crime to poorer, less protected areas such as council estates and inner cities.

- 🗨 There is a danger that zero tolerance policing policies may lead to police discrimination against groups such as ethnic-minority youth and the homeless. The use of 'stop and search' and military-style policing can result in hostility and possibly more crime committed as a reaction.

- 🗨 Right realists are criticised by Marxists and left realists (see page 183) for ignoring the wider structural causes of crime, such as poverty or the criminogenic nature of capitalism.

- 🗨 Left realists criticise right realism for over-emphasising the control of disorder, rather than tackling what left realists see as the underlying causes of neighbourhood decline – governments and businesses failing to invest money in inner-city areas.

- 🗨 Right realism may be guilty of over-stating the rationality of criminals. It is doubtful whether much crime is underpinned by rationality. **Jack Katz** (1988) argues that much delinquency is spontaneous and opportunist.

Now try this

1 Outline **two** criticisms of the right-realist idea that criminals rationally weigh up the costs and benefits of crime.

2 Identify a potential drawback of zero tolerance policing policies according to labelling theory.

Left-realist theories of crime

Left realism developed as a response to Marxist and neo-Marxist theories. Left realists such as **Lea and Young** (1984) generally aim to explain the street crime committed by black and white youths in urban areas.

Explaining 'left realist'

- **Left:** like Marxism, left realism argues that capitalism is a deeply unequal system and that this is one of the main causes of crime.
- **Realist:** Lea and Young carried out a victim survey – the Islington Crime Survey – which found that for residents of inner-city London, crime was a very **real**, daily problem that blighted their lives.

Lea and Young were particularly critical of the neo-Marxist New Criminology for romanticising criminals as modern-day 'Robin Hoods' (see page 178). They claimed that Marxists fail to take the treatment of victims of crime seriously and that they do not offer realistic solutions to crime.

Left realists claim that crime is caused by four influences.

Individualism

Lea and Young believed that society has become less community-orientated due to the growing dominance of capitalist values such as consumerism and monetary success. Great inequalities in income and wealth now exist in modern societies like the UK. Lea and Young argue that capitalist culture has become more **individualistic**. People have become greedier and selfish, leading to a decline in community social controls. Parents, extended family and neighbours no longer have the power to deter crime.

Relative deprivation

Those at the very bottom of society may feel **deprived** compared with their middle-class peers. They see these peers enjoying material comforts and a better standard of living and feel that they should have access to the same. They feel frustrated, angry and hostile because they see their route to these material things as blocked by society. It is not deprivation that causes crime, but whether people feel themselves to be deprived relative to others.

Marginalisation

Feelings of relative deprivation are worsened by feelings of **powerlessness**. Those at the bottom of society may feel **marginalised** – this means that they may feel frustrated and hostile towards the police and wider society because they have been unfairly stigmatised for their poverty or ethnicity and they lack the power to change their situation. Lea and Young liken much of the policing of inner-city areas to a military occupation and suggest that policing strategies such as 'stop and search' are often the result of institutional racism. Consequently, there may be pent-up frustration and hostility amongst inner-city populations that may occasionally erupt into riots and looting.

Subcultural response

The combination of relative deprivation and marginalisation may result in a **subcultural response** as people with similar experiences and frustrations come together. **Deviant subcultures** may form as young men attempt to relieve their feelings of deprivation and marginalisation through violence, gangs, drug-dealing, and so on.

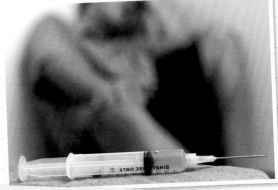

Subcultural responses may also be **retreatist** as people become addicted to hard drugs as a means of coping with the boredom and humiliation of poverty.

Late modernity

Jock Young (2003) describes UK society in the 21st century (a period he calls 'late-modernity') as a 'bulimic society'. This means the media has created a culture in which hunger for consumerism, celebrity and monetary success are worshipped. Those on the margins of society are excluded from this 'get rich' culture but their hunger for and desire to binge on the materialistic world created by the media often results in criminality.

Now try this

What do left realists mean by marginalisation?

Left realism and social policy

In the UK, left realism is associated with New Labour policies such as being 'tough on crime and tough on the causes of crime'. Some examples of these policies are given below.

Left-realist policy solutions to crime

Left realists argue that the only way to cut crime is to understand the relationship between the four elements of crime.

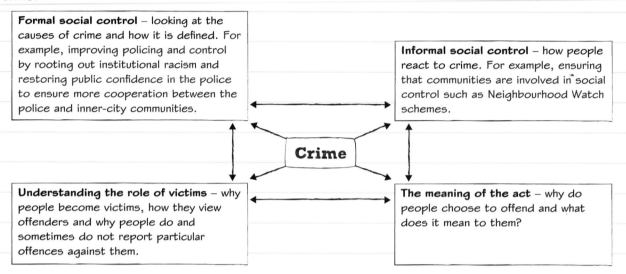

Formal social control – looking at the causes of crime and how it is defined. For example, improving policing and control by rooting out institutional racism and restoring public confidence in the police to ensure more cooperation between the police and inner-city communities.

Informal social control – how people react to crime. For example, ensuring that communities are involved in social control such as Neighbourhood Watch schemes.

Crime

Understanding the role of victims – why people become victims, how they view offenders and why people do and sometimes do not report particular offences against them.

The meaning of the act – why do people choose to offend and what does it mean to them?

Ultimately, there is a need to deal with the deeper structural causes of crime by reducing inequalities in wealth and income, by improving educational and employment opportunities in inner-city areas and by improving inner-city housing and environments.

Evaluation

👍 **Hughes** (1998) notes that left realism should be valued because **Lea and Young** (1984) have drawn our attention to the brutalising reality of street crimes in the inner city. Unlike other theories, especially labelling theory and neo-Marxism, left realists do not over-romanticise young delinquents and criminals.

👍 Left realists have also highlighted the effect of crime on victims. They have clearly shown that most victims of crime are members of deprived groups – most theories of crime have neglected this.

💬 There is no empirical evidence to support the view that young, working-class or black criminals interpret their realities in the way described by Lea and Young, i.e. on the basis of feelings of relative deprivation and marginalisation. Further qualitative research on the motives of young offenders is required.

💬 Lea and Young do not explain why the majority of working-class and ethnic-minority youth do not turn to crime, i.e. why most conform.

💬 The theory only focuses on collective or subcultural criminal responses and does not explain crimes such as burglary, which are often committed by individuals rather than gangs.

Postmodernist critique

Left realists suggest that crime and delinquency is a rational response to particular circumstances. However, postmodernists argue that crime and delinquency is far from rational – they argue that it is an irrational and often spontaneous activity.

Katz (1988) argues that the main motives for delinquency are irrational and the decision to commit a delinquent action is often spontaneous. Little thought is directed towards the consequence of the action either for the participant or victims. Katz rejects the left-realist view that delinquents are reacting to relative deprivation and marginalization. He points out that the main motive behind criminality and delinquency is a search for 'excitement or thrills'.

Now try this

Outline **two** ways left realism has been influenced by structural and social action perspectives.

The official criminal statistics

Most of our information about crime comes from **official criminal statistics (OCS)**, which are published quarterly (every three months) by the government.

Sources of data about crime

The OCS come from three sources.

1 Crimes reported to the police by victims and the general public.

2 Crimes recorded by the police.

3 Data collected by the **Crime Survey of England and Wales (CSEW)**, an annual survey in which a random sample of about 47 000 people are interviewed face to face about their experiences of crime in the previous calendar year.

Problems with the recording of crime

It is difficult for sociologists to compare past trends and patterns in crime with the present because there have been several changes to how the police record crime (PRC).

For example:

- the counting rules for crime used by the police are subject to frequent change by the Home Office
- in 2002, stalking and hate crimes were criminalised
- some offences – for example, white-collar and corporate crimes (such as tax or VAT fraud, or health and safety infringements by employers that result in the death of employees) – are not included in the OCS because they are dealt with by civil agencies such as HM Revenue and Customs and the HSE.

The decision to pursue historical crimes – those committed in the past – can also seriously distort the validity of the OCS.

For example, the crimes committed by Jimmy Savile became part of the 2014 OCS despite the fact that they had been committed over a 40-year period. The 2015 murder statistics jumped 20 per cent compared with 2014 because the official inquest into the deaths of 96 Liverpool football fans in 2015 resulted in a verdict of 'unlawful death'. These were added to the 2015 OCS for murder despite the fact that these deaths had occurred in 1989.

Recent patterns and trends in crime

The OCS are used to establish trends and patterns in criminal activity. For example:

- **The volume of crime** – how much there is and whether it is increasing or decreasing.

  Since 2002, the overall crime rate in the UK has risen only slightly. In 2002, there were 6 million recorded crimes in England and Wales, which rose to 6.5 million in 2015 (a 7 per cent rise).

- **The main types of crime** – those against **people** (such as violence, robbery and sex offences) and those against **property** (such as theft and burglary).

  Property crime in England and Wales has fallen steeply from 9 million in the mid 1990s to 2.9 million in 2015. In contrast, violent crime has risen most years to just over 1 million incidents in 2015 (about 23 per cent of all crime).

- **The 'typical' social characteristics** of the people who are reported, arrested and convicted of crime.

  The OCS suggest that the 'typical' criminal is likely to be young, male, working class, and in some urban areas from Black, Asian and Minority Ethnic (BAME) backgrounds.

Evaluating the usefulness of the OCS

👍 **Positivists** accept the **validity** of the OCS, believing them to be a realistic picture of crime in the UK. Hence, they have constructed sociological theories to explain why particular social groups appear to commit more crime according to these statistics. Functionalist (see pages 171–172) and subcultural theories (see pages 173–174) are good examples of this.

👎 **Interpretivist** sociologists question the reliability and validity of the OCS. They argue that the OCS do not measure actual crime – rather they are a **social construction**. This means that the OCS are the end product of decisions made by several social groups, especially politicians, civil servants, victims and the police.

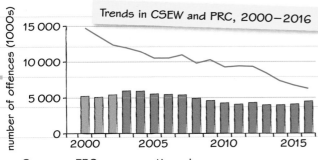

Trends in CSEW and PRC, 2000–2016

(number of offences (1000s): 0, 5 000, 10 000, 15 000; years 2000, 2005, 2010, 2015)

Orange = PRC – new counting rules
Red = PRC – new recording standard   Blue line = CSEW

Now try this

What do interpretivists mean when they say that the OCS are 'socially constructed'?

185

Self-reports

Self-reports are a type of confidential and anonymous **questionnaire** (see page 72). They ask people whether they have committed particular crimes for which they have not been caught or punished.

Nature of self-reports

Self-reports can be official (such as the Home Office *Offending, Crime and Justice Survey*, 2003–2006) or non-official sociological research, for example **Campbell** (1986).

The results of these surveys suggest that the OCS may underestimate crime in general but especially that committed by females and white people.

Self-reports and female crime

Campbell used self-report data to demonstrate that the OCS did not reflect an accurate picture of the number of crimes committed by females. Campbell's research found that the ratio of male crime to female crime is 1.33 to 1 rather than 9 to 1.

Research carried out in Glasgow by **Burman** (2004) found that, increasingly, girls are perpetrators of gang violence but violence committed by girls is still relatively rare compared with that committed by boys. Another self-report study by **Hales et al.** (2009) found that males engage in substantially more serious criminality than females.

Self-reports are, however, useful with regard to gender because:

- they suggest that the difference between male and female crime is not as big as the OCS suggest
- they support the view that young females may be treated more leniently by the police than young males because boys report more police cautions in self-reports than girls.

Self-reports and crime committed by those from BAME backgrounds

Graham and Bowling (1995) carried out a self-report study involving 2500 people and found that white and black offending rates were very similar, whilst Asian people had much lower rates. This challenges the view seen in the OCS that some ethnic minorities are more criminal than white people.

Evaluating self-report studies

👍 They may provide a more accurate picture of crime levels and trends associated with groups such as young males and females.

👍 They may give some insight into the **dark figure** (see page 187) of unreported and unrecorded crime.

👎 The lists of crimes included tend to be dominated by fairly trivial crimes because people are unlikely to admit to serious crimes, especially those that carry strong social stigma such as domestic violence against wives or children, or hate crimes.

👎 They are **unreliable** – some people will never own up to committing certain offences because of fear that the information will be used against them.

👎 Some, especially boys, may exaggerate their delinquent or criminal behaviour to manage the researcher's impression of them as 'tough'.

👎 There may be **ethical** problems with self-reports because they inevitably produce 'guilty knowledge' – knowledge of crimes committed.

👎 The **validity** of the data collected by self-reports may be undermined by selective or false memories.

👎 There is no guarantee that the sample shares the definitions of crime held by the researchers. Some offenders may not see particular offences as 'criminal' and fail to report them to the study.

👎 They may be unrepresentative of criminality because they are mainly aimed at adolescents rather than adult offenders.

👎 **Junger-Tas** (1989) claimed that teenagers with a criminal record were less likely to cooperate with self-reports.

Now try this

1 Outline **two** reasons why self-reports may be more useful than the official crime statistics.

2 Outline **three** weaknesses of self-reports in producing an accurate picture of crime.

Evaluating the OCS

The **official crime statistics (OCS)** have been criticised by a range of sociological theorists, who are not convinced that they provide an accurate picture of crime and criminals.

The role of victims in the social construction of the OCS

Interpretivists observe that the OCS depend on victims reporting crimes against them to the police. However, interpretivists point out that this may not occur for several reasons and as a result there may be a **dark figure** of unreported crime:

- Some institutional victims of crime – for example, banks – choose not to report employees who defraud them so as not to lose the confidence of their customers.

- Working-class people and BAME people living in inner-city areas may not report crimes against them because their relationship with the police is poor.

- Some victims may not be aware that a crime has been committed against them.

  For example, children may not understand that they are victims of abuse.

- Some victims, especially rape victims, may fear being blamed. They may wish to avoid humiliation at the hands of the police, defence barristers and the media, and so might be reluctant to report rape.

- Some crimes are victimless because they involve buying and selling an illegal service (for example, sex) or goods (for example, drugs). Neither party has a vested interest in reporting the crime.

The labelling theory critique of the OCS

Labelling theory argues that the official criminal statistics are a **social construction** in that they originate in the interaction between police officers and suspects. However, the OCS probably tell us more about the institutional prejudices of the police and their stereotyping of particular communities than they tell us about criminality.

For example, there is evidence that the police engage in racial profiling and this may partly account for the disproportionate number of BAME people found in the OCS.

The Marxist critique of the OCS

Marxists argue that the OCS are deliberately constructed by the capitalist state in order to perform two ideological functions:

- They give society the impression that the working class and BAME groups are a 'social problem' in need of social control, thereby justifying repressive laws and greater policing of these communities.

- They serve to distract society from the true extent and cost of white-collar and corporate crimes committed by the powerful.

The OCS and left realism

Left realism is sympathetic to both the interpretivist and Marxist critiques of the official criminal statistics. It agrees that the media and police pay disproportionate attention to powerless social groups and that ruling-class crime is not paid enough attention by law enforcement agencies. However, **Lea and Young** (1984) argue that these explanations are insufficient in explaining why working-class and black youth are more likely to turn up in the criminal statistics.

Using data from their own Islington Crime Survey, **Jones, McLean and Young** (1986) suggest that working-class and black youth really are the main perpetrators of crime in the inner cities. Moreover, the types of crime committed by these groups, such as violence, mugging and burglary, are the types of crime that ordinary people fear and these fears are especially justified in many inner-city areas. However, Left Realists seek to explain these crimes in the context of inequality, deprivation and marginalisation.

Left realism is critical of both interpretivist and Marxist approaches for suggesting the OCS are a social construction, i.e. the product of police and ruling-class practices. They argue that it is irresponsible of these theories not to recognise the devastating effect that everyday crime and fear of crime is having on inner-city communities.

Now try this

Why do left realists argue the OCS are an accurate picture of crime in inner-city areas?

Gender and criminal behaviour

Official criminal statistics tend to show that women commit less crime than men. Approximately 80 per cent of those convicted of serious crimes, especially violent crime such as murder, are men. At least one-third of men are likely to be convicted for a criminal offence during their lifetime, compared to only 8 per cent of women.

Types of crime by gender

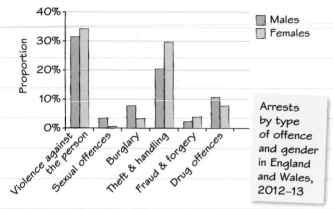

Arrests by type of offence and gender in England and Wales, 2012–13

Men and women tend to be convicted for different types of offences. Males dominate violent offences. In 2011–12 89 per cent of those convicted of murder in the UK were male. Only 11 per cent were female (source: ONS, 2013). The majority of female convictions are for property offences. In 2013, shoplifting accounted for 45 per cent of all female indictable convictions, up from 39 per cent in 2009 compared with only 22 per cent of males convicted for the same offence (source: Ministry of Justice, 2014).

Debates about female criminality

These statistics can be interpreted in two ways.

1. **Pollak** (1950) argues that the statistics are incorrect – women are more deceitful and commit more crime than is officially acknowledged in the statistics but are often treated more leniently by the police and the courts. Consequently, their crimes are less likely to be recorded, reported and prosecuted.

2. Feminist sociologists argue that the statistics are largely correct: women do commit less crime because they are simply less criminal than men.

The chivalry thesis

Pollak suggested that women commit just as much crime as men, but that their crime is more hidden because they are supposedly more deceitful. He argued that the **criminal justice system** (which is male-dominated) is 'paternalistic' and takes a more 'benevolent' view of female crime. Females do not fit police stereotypes about 'suspicious' or 'criminal' behaviour and so are less likely to be stopped, arrested or charged. If women are caught committing an offence, Pollak argues they are subjected to 'softer' treatment than men and are often released with a warning. This lenient treatment of women by male police officers is known as the **chivalry thesis**.

Evaluation of the chivalry thesis

The idea of the **chivalry thesis** has been lent support from the following areas:

👍 Statistics on cautions issued by the police – according to Ministry of Justice 2013 statistics, just under a quarter of people issued with a caution were female.

👍 **Graham and Bowling** (1995) and **Flood-Page** (2000) issued self-report surveys that asked young females to admit to crimes. The results are often cited as evidence that females are committing more crime than is officially recorded, although these surveys tend to focus on fairly trivial crimes.

👍 Research by **Steffensmeier and Allan** (1996) found that women are treated more leniently by the courts because judges are reluctant to separate women from their children and regard women as less dangerous than men.

👍 **Hood** (1992) studied over 3000 court cases in which males and females were found guilty of similar crimes and found that women were one-third less likely to be sent to prison.

Evidence against the chivalry thesis also exists:

👎 **Farrington and Morris** (1983) studied the sentencing of 408 convictions for theft and found that women were not sentenced any more leniently than men.

👎 Women may appear to be treated more leniently simply because the offences they commit are less serious than those committed by men.

👎 Women are more likely to be victims of crime rather than offenders.

👎 Feminists such as **Heidensohn** (1985) argue that women are actually treated more harshly than men, especially if they don't fit the judge or jury's stereotypical view of femininity.

For example, women who are not seen as good mothers or are seen as sexually promiscuous are more likely to be given prison terms.

👎 The chivalry thesis does not take account of factors such as social class, ethnicity and age.

For example, certain groups of women are more likely to be treated harshly by the police and judiciary because of police stereotyping and racial profiling.

Now try this

What is the chivalry thesis and how does it affect the criminal statistics?

Theories of gender and crime

Feminist criminologists have attempted to explain why women appear to be less criminal than men. Some suggest that this is the result of **gender role socialisation**, while others regard **social controls** as key. **Pat Carlen** (1988) suggests criminal women have **weaker attachments** to family and jobs than other women and so turn to crime as compensation.

Gender role socialisation

Liberal feminists claim that gender role socialisation may have an impact on the potential criminality of males and females. **Smart** (1976) and **Oakley** (2015) suggest that males are socialised into aggressive, self-seeking and individualistic behaviour that may make them more inclined to take risks and commit criminal acts, whereas **Messerschmidt** (2000) argues that boys in the UK are socialised into a powerful **hegemonic** masculine value system that stresses difference from femininity and the importance of being a 'real man'. The norms that boys have instilled in them such as 'being tough' and the need to exercise power over women may create the potential for criminal behaviour. **Barak et al.** (2001) believe that the reason women do not commit as much crime is because they are socialised into a culture of femininity that stresses communality, cooperation, empathy and compassion for others.

Control theory

McRobbie and Garber's (1976) classic feminist study concluded that teenage girls' lives in the 1970s revolved around a **bedroom culture** (see page 122). This meant they were more likely to socialise with their friends in the home and had less opportunity to engage in delinquent activities. Boys, however, were more likely to spend time with their peers in public spaces, especially at night when opportunities for delinquency are more likely to arise.

Heidensohn (1985) notes that women are more likely to be controlled by their family roles as wives and mothers, so they have less time for illegal activity. Women are less likely to commit white-collar crime because discrimination in the workplace means that the top jobs are often occupied by men. She also argues that young females face greater social stigma and negative labelling if they are involved in deviant activities. The possibility of this may ensure their greater conformity to the rules and deter any potential deviance.

 Key study   **Weak attachment theory**

The radical feminist **Pat Carlen** conducted a study in 1988 of 39 working-class women convicted of a range of crimes. She found that they often had a weak attachment to family because they had been abused, run away from home and/or had spent time in care. Many also had a weak attachment to paid work because they had failed to gain qualifications due to family breakdown or abuse. This meant they found it difficult to find a job and earn a legitimate living, which left them feeling powerless and aggrieved.

Carlen argues that the rational conclusion of many of these women was that crime was the only route to a decent standard of living. However critics of this theory suggest that Carlen fails to explain why many women in poverty choose not to commit crime.

Feminisation of poverty

Some feminist sociologists suggest that poverty has become feminised in the last 20 years, as women are increasingly more likely than men to experience low pay and benefits due to the patriarchal nature of society. Some types of crime dominated by females, notably shoplifting and social security fraud, may be a reaction to poverty. **Walklate** (2001) notes that shoplifting and prostitution are often motivated by economic necessity – to provide children with food, toys and clothes.

Liberation theory

Adler (2001) argues that women's liberation from patriarchy will lead to a new type of female criminal, one with greater opportunity and confidence to commit crime.

For example, female convictions for violence – a typically male criminal activity – have seen a dramatic rise in the last 30 years. The number of women arrested for violence in the UK more than doubled between 1999 and 2008 (source: Katharine Quarmby 2016). However, violence committed by males far exceeds that committed by females.

Now try this

Suggest why Adler claims that female crime rates are likely to increase.

Ethnicity and crime: patterns and trends

Black, Asian and minority-ethnic (**BAME**) people are over-represented in the official criminal statistics and in the prison population. Evidence from victim surveys such as the Crime Survey of England and Wales (**CSEW**) suggest that people from BAME backgrounds are also disproportionately likely to be victims of crime.

Rates of offending by different ethnic groups

- Statistics on police activity reveal that in 2014 police stopped and searched Black Britons 4.3 times more than White Britons (65 compared to 15 per 1000 people), and mixed ethnicities twice as often as White Britons.

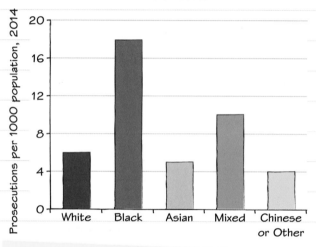

In 2014, black people were three times more likely than white people to be prosecuted for a criminal offence.

- In 2015, 25 per cent of prisoners came from ethnic-minority backgrounds despite the fact that only 12 per cent of the population of England and Wales belong to BAME groups.

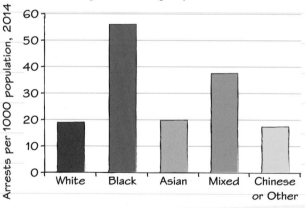

In 2014, the black and mixed-ethnicity groups' arrest rates per 1000 people were almost three- and two-times higher respectively, compared with other ethnic groups.

- Forty per cent of 15 to 18-year-old boys held in youth custody in England and Wales were from BAME backgrounds in 2015.
- In 2009, 29 per cent of the female prison population was made up of BAME women.
- Muslims made up 14.6 per cent of the prison population in 2015.

Victimisation and ethnicity

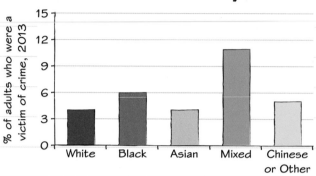

The risk of being a victim of crime is significantly higher for BAME groups compared with the white ethnic group (2014).

- In 2014/15, just under 54 000 racist incidents were recorded by the police; equivalent to around one racist incident per 1000 population.
- CSEW figures show that the risk of being a victim of violent street robbery is significantly higher for adults from the mixed, black or Black British and Chinese or other (C&O) ethnic groups than for adults from the white ethnic group.
- There was a 15 per cent increase in racially or religiously aggravated offences (hate crimes) recorded by the police in 2014/15 compared to 2010/11; 83 per cent of these were committed by white people and BAME people were mainly the victims.
- In 2015, hate crimes against Muslims (Islamophobia) in London rose by 70 per cent. Reported incidents ranged from cyber-bullying and assaults to extreme violence.

Demographic explanations

Morris (1998) observes that BAME groups in the UK contain a disproportionate number of young people compared with the white population. Morris concludes that the disproportionate number of BAME people recorded in the official criminal statistics is a **statistical illusion** caused by the fact that most crime is committed by young people.

Now try this

Why does Morris dismiss the disproportionate level of BAME offending in the official criminal statistics as an 'illusion'?

Ethnicity and crime: explanations

You need to understand the various sociological explanations of the social distribution of crime by ethnicity.

Labelling and institutional racism

Interpretivist or labelling theory suggests that criminal statistics are **socially constructed** (see page 179) and do not tell us much about black or Asian criminality. They simply tell us about their involvement with the **criminal justice system** (CJS). Statistics may simply reflect levels of **discrimination** towards ethnic minorities by the police and other criminal justice agencies.

- **Phillips and Bowling** (2007) argue that oppressive military-style policing has resulted in the over-policing and criminalisation of ethnic minorities.

- **Simon Holdaway** (1983) argues that police canteen culture is still characterised by racist language and jokes and this often underpins the disproportionate 'stop and search' of BAME youth.

- The **MacPherson Report** (1999) into the death of Stephen Lawrence, the black teenager, concluded that the London Metropolitan Police was guilty of 'institutional racism' in its failure to tackle such discrimination.

Paul Gilroy (1982): crime as political protest

Neo-Marxist **Gilroy** argues that young black men feel:

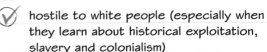 hostile to white people (especially when they learn about historical exploitation, slavery and colonialism)

✓ alienated by their everyday experience of casual racism and what they perceive as a racist police force (racial profiling and disproportionate 'stopping and searching').

As such, crime is a form of **protest** against a racist capitalist society. Street disorders (e.g. London, 2011) are political uprisings rather than riots. Other street crimes such as robbery are revolutionary acts of **resistance** aimed at eventually overthrowing white domination. Gilroy also claimed that black youth viewed the police as a predominantly white military force occupying black areas (like an invading power).

However, black people rather than white people are most often the victims of black criminals which undermines Gilroy's argument.

Right realism: control theory

Right realists such as **Hirschi** (1969) argue that young people, whether white or black, commit crime because they lack the social controls of attachment, commitment, involvement and belief in their lives. Asian families, in contrast, exercise stricter controls over young people, which may limit their opportunity for crime. Asian youths are also more likely to be economically involved in their community and are therefore less likely to be marginalised or frustrated by racism. Asian culture may also provide a safety net if members 'fail' in mainstream society.

Left realism

The disproportionate **relative deprivation** and **marginalisation** of ethnic-minority communities leads to the development of **subcultures** as a means of providing support and status. These can take deviant forms in response to feelings of powerlessness, thereby leading to higher levels of crime (see page 183).

Triple quandary theory

Tony Sewell (2003) identifies three risk factors (or quandaries) responsible for the relatively high levels of crime amongst black boys.

1. **Lack of a father figure:** many black boys are brought up by single mothers. In seeking a father figure, they often look up to powerful male role models in their community such as gang leaders or drug dealers.

2. **Negative experience of white culture:** black boys are disaffected because of their experience of school, policing and employer racism.

3. **Media:** black boys are influenced by media role models such as rap and hip-hop stars and believe that status can be achieved in two ways:

   - via the acquisition of status-symbol designer clothing and jewellery
   - by the construction of a hyper-masculine identity based on violence and sexual conquest.

Consequently, they see street culture as more important than education and jobs.

Now try this

What does Sewell mean by a triple quandary?

Class and crime

The government does not officially collect statistics on key trends associated with social class and crime. However, **Reiner (2007)** and **Young (2007)** observe from prison data that the majority of those in prison for street crimes – both male and female, white and BAME – come from semi-skilled and unskilled manual backgrounds, whereas those convicted for white-collar and corporate crimes are mainly middle-class.

Crimes committed by different social classes

Higher classes	Working class
White-collar and corporate crimes	**Street crimes**
Functionalism: strain theory **Robert Reiner (2008)** – there is no limit to monetary success (see page 176).	**Functionalism: strain theory** **Robert Merton (1949, 1968)** – working-class individuals cannot attain cultural goals by legitimate means, so turn to crime to achieve them (see page 172).
Functionalism: differential association **Edwin Sutherland (1949)** – differential association (see page 174) into corporate crime could be part and parcel of the culture of some businesses. For example, corporate lawyers may look for ways to pay less company tax, which may be on the cusp of legality/illegality.	**Functionalism: subcultural theories** **Albert Cohen (1955)** – working-class boys may suffer from status frustration and turn to crime as part of an alternative status hierarchy (see page 173). **Walter Miller (1962)** – young, working-class men may be exaggerating aspects of working culture, called **focal concerns** (see page 173).
Marxism: criminogenic capitalism **David Gordon (1991)** – criminogenic capitalist culture encourages those already rich to further enrich themselves through illicit means (see page 175). **Marxism: white-collar crime** **Hazell Croall (2001)** – the powerful have greater opportunities to commit crime and to cover it up (see page 176).	**Marxism: criminogenic capitalism** **David Gordon (1991)** – criminogenic capitalism brings about cultures of envy and hostility; the working class is driven to crime to survive as a consequence of capitalism; they are alienated in a capitalist society and commit non-utilitarian crimes to vent their frustration (see page 175).
Marxism: social construction of the law **Steven Box (1983)** – the social construction of the law and selective policing encourages such crimes because the perpetrators are less likely to be detected, charged and, if caught, to receive severe sentences (see page 175).	**Neo-Marxism: the New Criminology** **Taylor, Walton and Young (1975)** – the working-class deliberately choose to commit crime as a political response to their perceived exploitation (see page 177). Street crime is therefore a political act aimed at redistributing wealth from rich to poor.
Left realism: relative deprivation **Lea and Young (1984)** – left realists believe that even the rich can experience relative deprivation (see page 183).	**Left realists: relative deprivation** **Lea and Young (1984)** – working-class crime is caused by relative deprivation and marginalisation (see page 183).
Hegemonic masculinity **James Messerschmidt (2000)** – middle-class men such as city traders may feel the need to show off their hegemonic masculinity (see page 189).	**Hegemonic masculinity** **James Messerschmidt (2000)** – working-class crime is encouraged by socialisation into hegemonic forms of masculinity (see page 189).
There is evidence that corporate crime is widespread but rarely prosecuted (**Frank Pearce, 2003**).	**Right realism: underclass and control theories** **Charles Murray (1984)** – a criminal underclass is responsible for most street crime (see page 181). **Travis Hirschi (1969)** – working-class criminals are more likely to lack important controls or bonds in their lives (see page 181).
	Interactionist: labelling theory **Becker (1963)** – the working class is unfairly targeted by the CJS. They are also less likely to negotiate their way out of justice. The police discriminate against them by patrolling working-class areas more intensively, resulting in more working-class crime in the crime statistics (see pages 179–180).

Now try this

Outline **two** ways in which right realists explain working-class crime.

The media and crime

The general public's main source of information about crime is the **mass media** – newspapers, television news, documentaries, crime novels, videogames, films and television dramas.

Mass media and crime

Some sociologists have studied the relationship between crime and the mass media, and a number of key links have been made between media reporting of crime and actual crime.

Why is crime so newsworthy?

Does the media create the conditions for crime with its emphasis on celebrity culture and materialism?

Mass media and crime

Does the violent and anti-social content of films, television programmes and rap music result in imitative criminal behaviour?

Does the media sensationalise crime and cause moral panics?

Does media coverage of crime create a fear of crime?

The newsworthiness of crime

News is a **socially manufactured product**. This means that it is the end result of a complex process involving journalists and editors applying a set of criteria known as **news values** in order to judge whether a story is newsworthy and will therefore attract a large audience and/or sell newspapers.

Jewkes (2011) observes that crime is newsworthy for several reasons:

- It is bad news. Negative news sells more papers and attracts larger television audiences than good news.

- It has a human interest element – it can happen to anybody. We are all at risk of being victims of crime.

- Crime is dramatic in terms of its effects on the victim.

- Particular crimes – violent crimes committed by women or those in which children are victims – attract more media attention as they are relatively rare.

Is news coverage realistic?

Many sociologists argue that news coverage of crime is often exaggerated and creates problems, including:

- **moral panics** (see page 195) about crime, which often result in some groups being unfairly discriminated against by society and the criminal justice system

- unfounded **fear** of crime, especially among women and the elderly.

Ditton and Duffy (1983) found that nearly half of media reports about crime focused on murder or rape, despite the fact that these types of crimes only make up about 3 per cent of crimes recorded by the police.

The fallacies of crime

Felson (2002) claims media reporting about crime reinforces myths or fallacies about crime.

For example, that women and middle-class people are the main victims of crime and that most crime is planned, when in reality most victims are male and working class and most crime is opportunist and spontaneous.

Sociological theory and media effects

- Functionalists such as **Reiner** (2007) claim that media and advertising representations of material success are partly responsible for crime because they have created anomie or moral uncertainty among poorer sections of society. Reiner believes that the media falsely raises people's expectations and hopes with regard to monetary success and access to consumer goods. The gap between media representation and reality may result in the weakening of the moral certainty that crime is always wrong.

- Left realists argue that these media representations serve to highlight and reinforce the sense of relative deprivation and social exclusion felt by poorer groups who cannot afford the 'good life' shown in media reports of celebrity lifestyles.

- Marxists believe that mass media reporting of crime is shaped by ruling-class ideology in order to give the impression that working-class crime is more costly to society than white-collar or corporate crime.

Now try this

Why is the media partly responsible for crime according to Reiner?

The media as a cause of crime

There has long been concern that media content has a negative effect on the **behaviour** of impressionable young people, especially children. Television, films, comics, music lyrics, the internet and computer games have all been accused of causing young people to engage in **violence** and **anti-social behaviour**.

The media as a secondary agent of socialisation

Elizabeth Newsome (1994) claimed that impressionable audiences such as children or teenagers may be negatively influenced by violent, immoral or anti-social media content. Newsome saw the media as a powerful **secondary agent of socialisation**, shaping the behaviour of young people. Her media-effects approach is commonly known as the '**hypodermic syringe**' model because media content is compared to a drug in the way that it affects individuals. Newsome claimed that mass media content, especially violent content, results in copycat behaviour as children imitate deviant media role models.

The hypodermic syringe model also accuses the media of teaching criminal behaviour, of de-sensitising viewers to the distress caused to victims of violent crime, of the glamorisation of crime and criminals and of encouraging the idea that crime is an acceptable means of solving problems.

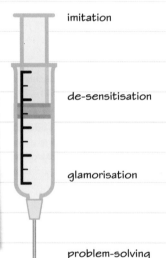

imitation

de-sensitisation

glamorisation

problem-solving

Evaluating the link between media content and crime

Many sociological research studies have investigated the possible link between media content and crime. However, most sociologists observe that this link is too simplistic for the following reasons:

- It fails to recognise that audiences differ in terms of factors such as age, social class, intelligence and level of education and consequently do not react in the same way to media content.

- Most experts on violence argue that it is caused by a complex range of factors: poor socialisation, bad parenting, peer-group influences, mental illness, drugs or alcohol.

- **Richard Sparks** (1992) notes that many media effects studies ignore the meanings that viewers give to media violence. There is evidence that audiences interpret violence in cartoons, horror films and news quite differently, whereas the hypodermic syringe model implies that the effect of these very different media portrayals of violence is much the same.

- **David Buckingham's** (1993) research into how children use the media suggests that even very young children are **media literate** and interpret and use the media in a very responsible way.

- **Gauntlett** (1998) argues that the hypodermic syringe model is often based on flawed methodology, and dubious experimentation.

 Key study ## The social context of violence

David Morrison (1999) showed a range of violent film clips to groups of women, young men and war veterans. All of the groups thought that a very violent scene from *Pulp Fiction* was humorous because there was light-hearted dialogue. However, a scene from *Ladybird, Ladybird*, showing domestic violence, caused distress for all three groups because of the realism of the setting, the perceived unfairness and because child actors were part of the scene. Morrison therefore criticises the hypodermic syringe model because it fails to consider that the context in which onscreen violence takes place affects its impact on the audience.

Guy Cumberbatch (2011)

Cumberbatch reviewed over 3500 studies on the relationship between the media and violence and failed to find one that proved a clear link. However, he also points out that no study disproved such a link either. Overall, he concludes that the actual evidence supporting a link between media violence and real violence is very weak.

Now try this

1 Outline **one** study that is critical of the media effects model.

2 Identify **two** alleged effects of media content on impressionable young people.

Moral panics

Interactionists or **labelling theorists** believe that the media contributes to the social construction of crime by labelling powerless groups as criminal or deviant through the creation of 'moral panics'. A **moral panic** refers to intense public anxiety about a social problem or group that has been brought to public attention by the mass media, especially the tabloid newspapers. The moral panic usually amplifies the threat of the problem or group out of all proportion to its real threat or seriousness.

 Key study **Folk Devils and Moral Panics**

Stan Cohen's (1972) classic study focuses on the media's representation of two opposing social groups – Mods and Rockers in the 1960s. He argues that the media generated a moral panic about the behaviour of these groups in 1964 through exaggerated reports of minor vandalism and low-level violence. This led to widespread public fear and a police crackdown. The distorted reporting encouraged youths to identify with one of the two groups, which had not previously seen each other as rivals.

Examples of moral panic

- **Jock Young** (1971) argued that a moral panic in the late 1960s, which focused on hippy cannabis users, went through the same set of stages that Cohen identifies.

- **Redhead** (1993) notes that a moral panic regarding acid house raves in the late 1980s led to the police setting up roadblocks on motorways, turning up at raves in full riot gear and eventually led to the passing of the Criminal Justice Act (1990), which banned illegal parties.

> The media identifies a problem group and generates interest in the group through negative, sensationalised reporting.
>
> ⬇
>
> **Symbolisation:** articles focus on the symbols of the group (dress, behaviour) so that they are identifiable and visible to the public.
>
> ⬇
>
> **Demonisation:** the group are **labelled** as '**folk devils**' (a group to be feared) and stereotyping occurs.
>
> ⬇
>
> **Condemnation:** those with influence (politicians, experts) condemn the group and the media **predicts** further trouble with the group.
>
> ⬇
>
> **Stamping down:** there is pressure from the media to curb the problem; the group resists attempts to control it, leading to more arrests and more negative reporting (self-fulfilling prophecy).
>
> ⬇
>
> **Deviancy amplification:** the group feels hostile and resentful, creating further deviance.

Evaluating moral panics

👍 **Muncie** (1987) notes that moral panic theory has drawn our attention to the role and power of the media in defining and labelling behaviour as normal or deviant.

👎 **McRobbie and Thornton** (1995) argue that the concept of moral panic is outdated because of the existence of social media platforms such as Facebook and Twitter. Audiences are now exposed to more interpretations about potential social problems and so are less likely to respond with panic or anxiety. Moral panics are less likely to occur today because of the sheer diversity of media outlets.

👍 **Awan** (2014) criticises McRobbie and Thornton and observes that sometimes moral panics that begin via social networking are uncritically reproduced/recycled by conventional news outlets.

👎 **Critcher** (2003) believes that the concept of moral panic is too abstract and vague to be testable.

Causes of moral panic

- Interactionists such as Cohen believe that moral panics occur when societies are undergoing social change. This change is seen as undermining the traditional social order. The moral panic is an attempt to reassert authority over the group perceived to be threatening that order.

- Neo-Marxists (see page 177) such as **Stuart Hall** (1978) see moral panics as deliberately engineered by the ruling class to divide and rule the working class and to distract people from a 'crisis of capitalism'.

- **Ulrich Beck** (1992) sees moral panics as a symptom of the risk consciousness that characterises late modernity (see page 198).

- Left realists argue that moral panics are often based in reality or fact – the groups identified are often a very real threat to those living in inner-city areas.

Now try this

1 What is a 'folk devil'?

2 Why is Critcher critical of moral panic theory?

3 Explain how Cohen's study demonstrated the concept of deviancy amplification.

Globalisation and crime

Glenny (2009) refers to global organised crime as the '**global shadow economy**' and estimates that it accounts for about 15 per cent of the world's gross national product (GNP).

Defining globalisation

Waters (2001) defines globalisation as a social process in which the constraints of geography on economic, political, social and cultural arrangements have declined. It refers to the increasing interconnectedness of societies and is caused by factors such as the development of digital technologies, cheap air travel, mass migration, the removal of trade barriers and the increase in the number of transnational corporations.

For more on globalisation, see page 86.

Why sociologists study global crime

Despite the difficulty of measuring the extent of its influence on local crime rates, it is a fact that those addicted to global-crime products such as heroin and crack cocaine are responsible for a great deal of domestic crime.

Globalisation has led to new crimes such as people-trafficking. Gangs of traffickers have profited from the plight of migrants desperate to escape from poverty- and war-stricken parts of Africa and refugees from Syria, resulting in hundreds of deaths in the Mediterranean. This suggests that more knowledge is required about the causes of this problem in order for politicians to tackle it.

The difficulties of investigating global crime

There is no accurate way in which the value or cost of global crime can be estimated.

It is difficult to measure the precise extent of global crime.

Sociologists are over-reliant on secondary sources such as Interpol and Europol which may exaggerate the problem in order to justify extra funding.

Global crime

There is disagreement as to how global crime should be defined.

The impact of global crime on local crime rates is difficult to operationalise and therefore observe and measure.

Primary sociological research into global crime is likely to be dangerous.

New types of crime

The spread of **global capitalism** has produced new opportunities to commit pre-existing crimes, such as theft, as well as new types of global crime.

Containerisation

This is the transport of goods across the world in container ships, which can be inter-changed between ships, trains and trucks. Drugs, people, weapons and counterfeit goods can easily be trafficked via these containers. Due to the quantities involved it is difficult for law-enforcement and customs officials to check their contents. Global gangs may try to bribe port officials to ensure the smooth passage of their criminal merchandise.

Darknet

The 'darknet' is a part of the world wide web that is intentionally hidden in which users can anonymously gain access to encrypted websites offering a range of illegal products and services, such as illegal forms of pornography, drugs, weapons, stolen identities, and so on.

Cybercrime

The growth in new communication and media technologies have led to an increase in **cybercrime**. The UK government estimates that the annual cost of cyber-attacks for British companies is £27 billion per annum. Organised criminal global networks often focus on the following types of cyber-fraud or theft because they offer attractive rewards for minimal investment and low risk:

- **Identity theft** – acquiring personal data in order to steal from victims' bank accounts and credit cards.

- **Hacking** – illegally gaining access to online banks or businesses for financial gain, or to gain information to further political goals.
  In 2015, the Islamic State claimed to have hacked into the US military and government databases.

- **Online scams** – extorting money.
  For example, 'phishing' (sending bogus money-transfer requests).

- **Viruses** – infecting computers with viruses that criminals will only remove when the owner pays a fee.

Now try this

In which ways can cybercrime be described as traditional crime?

The effect of globalisation on crime

Globalisation has affected crime in a number of ways.

The influence of global crime on local crime

Hobbs and Dunningham (1998) observe that global criminal networks often serve and feed off established criminal networks in Western countries. They argue that crime is increasingly '**glocal**' in character. This means that it is still locally based but is now more likely to have global connections.

For example:

- **The illegal drugs trade** – local prices for drugs and the profits made by British drug dealers depend on their availability, which in turn depends on how efficiently global drug trade gangs can move drugs around the world while avoiding detection.
- **Prostitution** – according to a National Crime Agency and UK Human Trafficking Centre report (2014), it is estimated that 3000–4000 women are trafficked every year into the UK by organised Eastern European gangs in order to work against their will as constrained prostitutes.
- **Smuggling** – **Glenny (2009)** estimates that the UK loses about £6 billion a year in taxes from cigarettes smuggled into Britain from Eastern Europe.

The effects of globalisation on local crime rates

1 In the UK and other Western countries, globalisation resulted in the devastation of many manufacturing industries (coal-mining, shipbuilding, iron and steel) and communities – it was more profitable to import materials such as coal and steel from the developing world.

2 The removal of trade barriers also means that industries such as shipbuilding have been badly affected by competition from nations such as Japan and Korea.

3 Global trade agreements meant that it became more profitable for companies to manufacture their products in factories and sweatshops in the developing world because of cheaper labour costs.

4 The decline of traditional industries in the UK and USA has resulted in mass unemployment.

5 Job loss has a damaging effect on self-esteem and psychological stability and may heighten the possibility of addiction as a means of coping with the loss of both income and status.

6 **Drugwise (2016)** estimate that there are 306 000 heroin users in the UK who are responsible for over 50 per cent of property crime, the proceeds of which are used to buy drugs produced and distributed by global criminal networks.

The impact of globalisation on crime

Inequality

Globalisation has resulted in mass unemployment and poverty in the USA and UK, which Marxists and left realists argue is a major cause of crime because the poor feel envy/hostility or relative deprivation (see pages 175 and 183).

Consumerism

Globalisation has spread mass consumerism throughout the world. **Reiner (2007)** argues that the inability to achieve the status and goals marketed by capitalism leads to rising crime levels in Western societies (see page 193). Marxists argue that capitalism, whether local or global, is criminogenic (see page 175).

Opportunity

New opportunities for carrying out crime have emerged due to the ease of container transportation (smuggling, trafficking) and advances in digital technology.

For example, international money laundering, hacking.

Crimes of the powerful

Companies now operate globally and many move their manufacturing and services to countries with lower costs and often with less stringent health and safety regulations. This can lead to exploitation and negative environmental effects. **Taylor (1997)** points out that the wealthy have also been able to take advantage of the 24-hour digital global banking system and the existence of offshore global tax havens to avoid paying tax.

Now try this

1 Outline **two** ways in which globalisation may lead to people committing more crime in the UK.

2 Identify **two** opportunities for crime that globalisation offers the powerful.

Global capitalism and transnational crime

Over the past two decades, as the world economy has globalised, so has its illicit counterpart. Consequently, the global impact of **transnational crime** has risen to unprecedented levels.

Features of the global criminal economy

Glenny (2009) uses the term 'McMafia' to describe the way that organised global crime networks operate in the same way as legitimate global businesses.

For example:

- The global drug economy has distinct **zones of production**, mainly situated in developing countries (just like garment factories, for example). The raw materials involved in the manufacture of heroin are grown and processed in the developing countries of Afghanistan and Pakistan.

- The organised drug economy, like the legitimate capitalist economy, operates using **zones of distribution**. Heroin is trafficked to the UK via Turkey and Holland whilst Mexican cartels control the flow of cocaine into the USA.

- The **zones of consumption** or biggest markets for global criminal goods such as drugs (or services such as prostitution) are in the developed world – the USA, Europe and the UK.

These organised crime networks might take the form of Mafia-style organisations or newer groups such as drug cartels (**Farr**, 2005).

The overlap between legitimate and illegitimate global economies

- Glenny notes that 24-hour digital banking and off-shore banking/tax havens have mutually advantaged both global banks and global criminal networks. They have made it easier for gangs to launder cash from their illegal activities through mainstream banks and tax havens. Consequently, it has become more difficult for police forces to track this illegal money.

- Global gangs often seek to intimidate or corrupt law enforcement officers or public officials in the developing world to ensure that they turn a 'blind eye' to illegal activities.

- Transnationals, legal or illegal, may take advantage of weak or lax laws in developing societies to exploit the local labour force and take risks with health and safety in order to enhance profits.

- Legal transnational companies can also commit green crimes (see page 199), which are damaging to both the local and global environment.

- Transnational organised crime can have an impact on political stability in the developing world. There is evidence that they have funded military coups that have overthrown democratically elected governments such as that of President Allende in Chile in 1973.

Theoretical perspectives on the relationship between globalisation and crime

- The Marxist economist **Castells** (2010) observes that there is a '**perverse connection**' between global capitalism and crime. This was apparent in post-communist Russia in the 1990s when it switched from being a centralised command economy to a free market capitalist economy. Castells argues that corruption, speculation, privatisation, money laundering and investment merged as criminals were able to take advantage of the political and economic chaos in Russia as the old communist system collapsed and to take control of the Russian economy and most of its big businesses.

- Similarly, Castells refers to money laundering as the '**matrix of global crime**' and shows that it is under the control of the main global drug traffickers but being performed by specialised agents in respectable banks and financial institutions.

- The late-modernity thinker, **Beck** (2000) argues that the risks associated with global crime are the result of new technologies developed by industrial capitalism. He argues that the development of cyber and digital technology such as the internet has produced a set of risks unique to our age and the main role of governments in late modernity is the management of such risks.

  For example, to prevent terrorists using such technology to bring harm to Western populations by using the internet to recruit jihadists or to promote their cause.

Now try this

According to Beck, why are capitalist societies more at risk of global crime such as terrorism?

Green crime

Green criminology, as an area of sociological study, is fairly new. Those who study green crime, such as **South (2008)**, argue that the **physical environment** in which humans and wildlife live is under threat from unlawful and harmful behaviour committed by corporations and governments, and that this behavior is threatening the future existence of humanity and the planet.

Green crime as a global crime

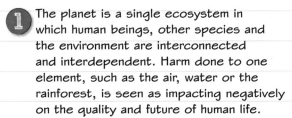 The planet is a single ecosystem in which human beings, other species and the environment are interconnected and interdependent. Harm done to one element, such as the air, water or the rainforest, is seen as impacting negatively on the quality and future of human life.

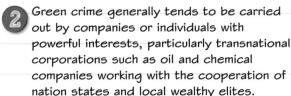 Green crime generally tends to be carried out by companies or individuals with powerful interests, particularly transnational corporations such as oil and chemical companies working with the cooperation of nation states and local wealthy elites.

Types of green crime

South classifies green crime as either a primary or secondary crime:

- **Primary green crimes** are the direct result of the destruction and degradation of the planet's resources.
  For example, air pollution from industrial carbon and greenhouse gas emissions, **deforestation** such as illegal logging, and fresh water and marine pollution such as oil spillages.

- **Secondary green crimes** involve breaking existing laws and regulations.
  For example, dumping toxic waste (which is strictly regulated) and breaches of health and safety rules, which result in avoidable disasters such as Chernobyl (1986) and Bhopal (1984).

Green crime and radical criminology

Radical criminologists such as **Rob White (2008)** observe that:

- countries cannot agree on what should constitute green crime
- international law is inadequate and is weakly enforced
- there is no global agency that has the power to police global green laws
- laws differ globally and are too influenced by the economic power of transnational companies
- governments, especially in the developing world, are generally reluctant to rein in the harms done by global corporations because they are too dependent on the income generated from them in the form of taxation
- environmental disasters have global effects.

Evaluation of green criminology

👍 It recognises the growing importance of environmental issues and manufactured global risks.

👍 It recognises the interdependence of humans, other species and the environment.

👎 What counts as 'harm' is implicitly a moral judgement and consequently subjective and potentially loaded with bias.

👎 Green criminology is often accused of being both anti-progress and anti-capitalist.

Explaining green crimes

White argues that green crime should be defined as any deliberate harm to the natural environment and the creatures (including humans) that live within it, even if no law has technically been broken. His approach is sometimes referred to as **zemiological** (it focuses on harm rather than crime) and '**transgressive**' (it oversteps the boundaries of traditional criminology which is usually concerned with breaking laws).

White claims that nation states, such as China, and transnational corporations take an '**anthropocentric**' view of environmental harms (they see them as a necessary part of human progress and essential in order to maintain materialist lifestyles). He argues that sociologists instead need to take an '**ecocentric**' view (to stress the inter-dependent relationship between humans and their environment). From this perspective, environmental harm will lead to major harm to humankind if it is not addressed.

Globalisation and green crimes

Ulrich Beck (2000) points out that many of the threats to our ecosystems are **manufactured risks** and are the result of the massive demand for consumer goods and the technology that underpins it. Human demand for manufactured goods potentially has grave effects for both humanity and the environment.

Manufacturing across the world is responsible for greenhouse gas emissions, which it is alleged are contributing to global warming and climate change.

Now try this

Why is White's view of green crime described as zemiological and transgressive?

State crime

State crime is defined as illegal activity carried out by agents of the state (armed services, secret services, police and prison services) on behalf of governments and political leaders in order to further state interests. Such activities are illegal in that they break both domestic and international laws.

Examples of state crimes

McLaughlin (2001) identifies four major types of state crime.

1 Crimes committed by **state security and police forces** – war-crimes such as illegal invasions, genocide (e.g. the Holocaust) and ethnic cleansing (e.g. in Rwanda 1994), torture, executions of prisoners of war, the massacre of civilians (e.g. Syria 2016) and the use of illegal chemical or biological weapons.

2 **Political crimes** – imprisonment and execution of political opponents without trial, censorship of the media, unauthorised surveillance of citizens.

4 **Social and cultural crimes** – failing to protect human rights (freedom of speech and religious expression) or tackle institutional racism and sexism.

Types of state crime

3 **Economic crimes** – theft of public funds by political elites, corruption and bribery of state officials by global corporations.

Difficulties in defining state crime

It is difficult to define state crime because what is defined as crime or violence is an **ideological construct**. Governments have the power to define killing as a problem when carried out by an enemy, but as justified if carried out by a soldier.

Herman Schwendinger (1975) takes a transgressive approach (see page 199). He argues that definitions of state crimes should include any **violation of human rights**, including suppression of free speech, institutional forms of sexism, racism, homophobia, economic exploitation and enforced poverty.

Stan Cohen (2001) argues that there is not enough agreement about what constitutes 'human rights'. For example, most people accept that freedom should be a human right but not everyone would agree that freedom from poverty is a right.

States of denial

Cohen argues that it is difficult to find out the true extent of state crime.

For example, if civilians are wrongly killed during a bombing mission, a government might:
- deny responsibility for the action
- claim that civilian casualties were unfortunate collateral damage in the fight against a greater threat to national security.

Measuring state crimes

R J Rummell (1997) claimed that governments have murdered six times more people than have died in combat in all 20th century wars.

- Over 11.5 million (est.) Jews, Soviet prisoners of war, Poles, Serbs, Gypsies and institutionalised disabled people were systematically exterminated by the Nazis during the Holocaust.
- In 1995, 8373 Muslim Bosniak men and boys were executed by Serb paramilitaries in the Bosnian town of Sbrenica.

Criticisms of 'state crime'

Critics of the concept of 'state crime' argue that it is sometimes necessary to go beyond the limits of the law for the greater good.

For example, it could be deemed a 'necessary evil' to torture or assassinate a terrorist.

Explaining state crimes

Techniques of neutralisation

Cohen notes that perpetrators of state crimes often do not see themselves as criminal. This is because they employ techniques of neutralisation to justify their actions, such as 'I was just following orders'.

Crimes of obedience

Kelman and Hamilton (1989) argue that those who commit state crimes are conforming to the norms of a higher authority. There are three processes for this.

1 **Authorisation** – the morality of the act becomes less important than the need to follow orders.

2 **Dehumanisation** – the offender is socialised by propaganda into viewing victims as creatures to whom the normal rules of morality do not apply.

For example, the Jews in Nazi Germany.

3 **Routinisation** – execution teams/torturers are encouraged to see their activities as routine jobs, necessary in order to protect their country or loved ones.

Now try this

Suggest why it is difficult for sociologists to research crimes committed by the state.

Control and prevention: left solutions

Most theories of crime have suggested ways in which crime might be **controlled** and **prevented**. Left-wing theories such as Marxism and left realism suggest that the way to reduce crime is to make **structural adjustments** to capitalist societies with the aim of reducing inequality and deprivation.

Marxist ideas to control crime

Cause of crime: inequality, poverty, criminogenic culture.

Solution: politicians need to make **structural adjustments** to the organisation of capitalist society aimed at:

- reducing poverty, unemployment and homelessness as well as inequalities in income and wealth
- improving the quality of life in inner-city areas via greater investment in housing, education and jobs
- transforming capitalism as an economic system into a more compassionate and community-minded economic system in order to reduce its criminogenic potential.
- Like Right realists, Left realists also promote the idea of building communities, providing facilities and strengthening social bonds.

Left-realist ideas to control crime

Cause of crime: relative deprivation and marginalisation.

Solution:

- The eradication of the institutional racism that exists in the **criminal justice system** (CJS – i.e. the police and courts) and particularly the police's use of racial profiling in 'stop and search'.
- Government investment in inner-city schools to increase the number of school leavers with qualifications.
- Implementation of legislation to raise minimum pay to a 'living wage' in order to avoid dependency on benefits and to reduce inequalities in wealth and income.
- Businesses should be encouraged to invest in poorer urban communities and to create jobs.

Labelling theory

Labelling theory argues that the CJS needs to stop the process of negatively labelling and alienating powerless groups. The CJS tends to be based on **retributive justice** (punishing or penalising the offender, for example, by publicly humiliating or labelling them and perhaps removing them from society altogether). However, **Braithwaite** (2002) argues that societies can have lower crime rates if they communicate shame about crime effectively.

Cause of crime: the labelling of people as criminals, which makes it more difficult for them to integrate back into society and increases the potential for reoffending.

Solution:

- Train those who work in the CJS to treat everyone equally and to root out discriminatory labelling processes such as racial profiling in police 'stop and search' activities.
- Monitor sentencing to ensure that gender, class and ethnic bias is minimised.
- Reform the CJS and introduce **restorative** forms of justice.

Restorative justice

Restorative justice brings victims and offenders together in mediation meetings to help repair harm done and to show offenders how their crimes have affected the victim, allowing them to explain their actions and apologise. The intention is that offenders will realise that they need to be accountable for their actions.

Punishments also need to be applied in a respectful, forgiving way in order to maintain an offender's 'normal' status within the group. Society must avoid negatively stigmatising or shaming offenders, which prevents their reintegration into society and increases their chances of reoffending.

Evaluating left solutions to crime

👎 Structural changes, if put into action, would be extremely costly and may need decades to take effect.

👎 It is not clear how a caring, compassionate capitalism can be brought about.

👍 Left Realists agree with Right Realists that communities and the police need to work together more effectively to combat crime.

👍 A review of restorative justice schemes currently operating in the UK by **Shapland et al.** (2008) found that offenders who had been through the process were less likely to reoffend.

Now try this

Which theory argues in favour of restorative justice?

Control and prevention: right solutions

Right realists have had a significant influence on state policies towards crime control, both in the UK and USA. British crime policies in the 1980s and 90s were underpinned by the idea of **situational crime policies** as these transferred the responsibility for preventing crime from the police to potential victims.

Right-realist ideas to control crime

Charles Murray (1996)

Cause of crime: an immoral and idle underclass which is unwilling to work and is too dependent on an over-generous welfare state.

Solution: members of the underclass need to be weaned off benefits. Murray advocates reducing benefits and introducing penalties which force people to look for jobs.

Cornish and Clarke (1986)

Cause of crime: the benefits of crime outweigh the costs of crime (the possibility of being caught and punished). **Felson** (1998) cites the decline of community controls as one reason why the benefits of crime now outweigh its costs.

Solution: situational crime prevention (SCP) – opportunities for committing crime need to be reduced and the risk of being caught needs to be increased. **Clarke** (1983) identified three SCP measures.

1. **Target hardening** – potential victims need to 'design out' crime from their lives by investing in more personal security, such as locks and alarms (see page 182). The aim of this type of SCP is to increase the effort of crime.

2. **Greater surveillance** – CCTV and Neighbourhood Watch increase the possibility of criminals being caught.

3. **Environmental management** – public space needs to be made more 'defensible' to make criminality more difficult.

   For example, car parks should be made more secure, shops should have visible security such as security guards, streets should have more lighting and cameras.

Environmental crime prevention (ECP)

This is a **social and community** approach advocated by **Wilson and Kelling** (1982). They argue that crime is caused by 'incivilities' or anti-social behaviour such as vandalism, drug use, littering and physical harassment. If these behaviours are allowed to continue, areas deteriorate and a sense of 'anything goes' develops (see page 181). This sends a clear signal to criminals and deviants that the community does not care or lacks the power to confront them, thus encouraging more of the same behaviour.

Advocats of ECP recommend that:

- any sign of environmental decline such as broken windows must be tackled immediately
- public housing should not exceed three floors and residents should be strongly encouraged to take collective responsibility for communal space
- the police need to be more visible in their support of communities and should react with **zero tolerance** and aggressively tackle all types of crime and disorder (see page 182)
- curfews should be imposed on particular age groups
- parents should be punished if their children truant or offend
- communities need to be more proactive in 'chasing out' those who commit criminal and delinquent behaviour in their neighbourhoods.

Environmental crime prevention has been particularly influential in the USA in cities such as Chicago and New York.

Evaluating right solutions to crime

👎 Marxists and left realists argue that SCP schemes ignore the root causes of crime, such as poverty and inequality.

👎 Not all sections of society can afford to design crime out of their lives. **Shover** (1991) argues that SCP is expensive and creates a new type of social inequality because poorer sections of society cannot afford to make themselves harder targets.

👎 SCP strategies displace rather than reduce crime. Criminals simply move to where targets are softer (often in poorer areas).

Research by **Chaiken et al.** (1974) found zero tolerance of crime on the New York subway merely displaced the problem to the streets.

👎 SCP schemes ignore white-collar, corporate and state crimes, which Marxists argue are more costly to society.

👎 Crime may not be due to criminals rationally weighing up costs and benefits. The evidence suggests that a lot of crime committed by the young is actually opportunistic and may be an attempt to find excitement. **Lyng** (1990) argues that some young offenders may be seeking thrills by gambling with the risk of being caught.

Now try this

Why are Marxists and left realists critical of right-realist solutions to crime?

Surveillance and punishment

Systematic surveillance has become a routine part of everyday life in the UK. Right realists argue that **punishments**, particularly prison, need to be tougher so that the costs of crime clearly outweigh its benefits.

Surveillance

Post-structuralist **Foucault** (1975) argued that surveillance indicated a new form of state power, which had replaced more brutal forms.

He saw surveillance as a form of '**disciplinary power**', which was more effective than brute force as citizens were more likely to conform if they felt they were being watched. However, he argued that surveillance goes beyond CCTV: experts such as doctors, psychiatrists, social workers and teachers all practice disciplinary power. They are engaged in surveillance and control and, most importantly, the prevention and correction of deviant behaviour.

Imprisonment

In 2015, there were nearly 85 000 prisoners in British prisons. Right realists argue that there are two ways in which prisons deter and reduce crime.

1 Prison works as a deterrent if it is seen to be tough. Right-realist critics of British prisons argue that prison life is too 'cushy' and does not deter criminals. They argue that **retributive justice** should be applied – proportionate punishment for the crime.

2 Prison incapacitates criminals by taking them off the street.

Panopticon

Foucault illustrates the notion of surveillance and disciplinary power with the **panopticon**.

In Bentham's (1791) prison design, all inmates can be observed by one guard. The observer is not visible to the inmates who generally conform to the rules because they do not know when they are under surveillance.

Prison as rehabilitation

Prison can also reform and rehabilitate criminals through educational programmes and training. Supporters argue that inmates should be given more responsibility and freedom in prison to give them the confidence and social skills needed to change and not reoffend.

Retributive justice in practice

Societies that practise retributive justice often have prison systems in which the human rights of prisoners are routinely violated. These societies often employ other severe deterrents such as capital punishment, amputations for theft and stoning.

Evaluation of surveillance and Foucault

- 👍 **Beck** (1992): surveillance is an essential component of a risk society, used to sift out those who put the rest of society at risk (e.g. terrorists).
- 👎 **Mathieson** (1997): Foucault neglects the surveillance of the powerful by the masses. For example, social media can quickly mobilise public opinion against powerful groups.
- 👎 Foucault may underestimate people's ability to resist surveillance. For example, vandalising traffic speed cameras.
- 👎 Labelling theorists: surveillance may disproportionately focus on those who have been negatively labelled as a problem. This may lead to hostility and deviancy amplification (see pages 179–180).

Evaluation of punishment

- 👍 Labelling theory favours rehabilitation because it avoids stigmatising prisoners as non-people.
- 👎 **Mathews** (1997) describes prisons as '**universities of crime**'. He suggests they make bad people 'worse'.
- 👎 **Solomon** (2006) claims that many people in prison require treatment rather than punishment because they are mentally ill or drug addicts.
- 👎 Statistics suggest prison does not deter. Two-thirds of ex-prisoners reoffend within two years of their release.
- 👎 Right realists believe that rehabilitation is a soft option and that it does not convey to criminals the seriousness of their offence.

Now try this

Outline **two** reasons why surveillance could be described as a form of disciplinary power.

Victims of crime

Watts, Bessant and Hill (2008) argue that, historically, criminologists paid more attention to criminals and offenders than the victims of crime. However, they suggest that this ended in the 1970s because the Left realists **Lea** and **Young** drew attention to the very real fear and hurt caused by crime to victims.

Perspectives on victimology

Victimologists explore **patterns of victimisation**. They are interested in why some groups are more likely to be victims of crime than others. There are three distinct perspectives on victimology.

1. **Miers** (1989) – **positivist** victimology focuses on identifying those factors that make certain individuals or groups more prone to being victims of crime.

2. **Realist** victim surveys focus on victims of crime who live in the inner city (see page 205).

3. **Critical** victimologists argue that definitions of victimhood depend on power relations (see page 205).

Positivism and victimology

This is the most influential contemporary approach to victimology. It is concerned with identifying **patterns of victimisation** and **trends** in the distribution of victims across social groups such as social class, age, gender and ethnicity.

For example, **Von Hentig** (1948) claimed that most victims of violence belong to 'vulnerable' status groups such as females and the elderly. He also implied that their lack of status invited the crime against them. **Wolfgang** (1958) researched over 500 murders in one city in the USA and concluded that some victims, especially women, precipitated their killing by initiating the violence.

Victims of crime

A good example of a modern positivist victim study is the **Crime Survey of England and Wales** (CSEW) which is carried out annually by the **Office for National Statistics** (ONS) and the **Home Office**. The CSEW regularly concludes that:

The poor and the homeless are most prone to repeat victimisation.

The older a person gets, the less likely they are to be a victim of crime.

Young males are two times more likely to be victims of violence compared with females.

The average person's chance of being a victim of crime is fairly low.

Patterns of victimisation

BAME groups are least likely to report crimes as they do not trust the police to take crimes against them seriously.

Most victims of murder are male (70 per cent).

Poorer households are more likely to be burgled than higher-income households.

Women are more likely to be victims of domestic violence, rape and stalking.

People from ethnic-minority backgrounds are more likely to be victims of crime compared with white people.

Victimisation has many **effects** such as physical harm, financial loss, anxiety, fear, anger, depression and post-traumatic stress disorder.

Evaluation of positivist victimology

- It tends to blame the victim.

- Marxist victimologists would argue that the victims identified by the CSEW are the victims that the state chooses to 'see'. They claim the state ignores those not readily identified as 'victims'.

  For example, people shot by the police are often not recognised as victims.

- Critical victimologists such as **Tombs and Whyte** (2007) argue that the victims of corporate, white-collar, state or green crimes are unlikely to appear in positivist victim surveys because questions are not included which cover these types of offences.

- **Mawby and Walklate** (1994) criticise positivist victimology because it does not criticise the role of the CJS in creating secondary victimisation.

  In rape trials, for example, the victim's reputation and actions may also be questioned and 'put on trial'. This may put off other victims of rape from coming forward and reporting the crime.

Now try this

Suggest **two** ways in which critical victimologists are critical of positivist criminology.

Critical victimology

Critical victimologists argue that positivist victimology tends to conceal the extent of victimisation and its true causes. They point out that whether a person is regarded as a 'victim' depends on their position in the power structures that underpin society. In this sense, victimhood is **socially constructed**.

The social construction of victimisation

Media

Some victims of crime may be put off reporting crimes against them by the way that the **media** or the police treat victims. **Sue Lees** (1994) estimates that about 66 per cent of female rape victims never go to the police – and therefore are never officially recognised as victims – because they fear that the police and courts will blame them for precipitating the offence against them.

Christie (1986) argues that some victims of crime are considered more newsworthy by journalists.

For example, child victims such as Madeleine McCann and Ben Needham fit the media's profile of the 'ideal' victim, whereas other victims from either poorer or BAME backgrounds may not.

Police

The police play a key role in the social construction of victims.

For example, some police officers may not treat domestic violence cases seriously. They may prefer to give the offender a warning and so deny the wife victim status.

The state

Walklate (2000) argues that victimologists need to pay attention to the role of the state. The state has the power to define who is regarded as a victim through law-making. It is the breaking of the law that defines a victim's status. The state therefore has the power to label and deny particular individuals and groups as victims.

For example, in 2016 the people killed in the Hillsborough football disaster of 1989 were officially recogised as victims of unlawful killing.

Mawby and Walklate (1994) relate this to crimes against women. They argue that state definitions of what constitutes rape or domestic violence are too narrow and consequently many women who are victims of abuses committed by men are not officially recognised as victims.

For example, the law does not recognise emotional and psychological abuse and bullying as crimes and therefore victims of this type of male behaviour are not officially recognised as victims.

Marxist victimology

Marxist victimologists point out that the poorer sections of society are often the victims of crimes or harms committed by the powerful, such as price-fixing, green crimes, and negligent practices caused by state cuts in spending. These victims are often not visible because in many cases they are unaware that they are victims.

Left-realist victimology

Lea and Young (1986) surveyed victims of crime in inner-city areas and discovered that both the poor and women stood an above-average chance of being repeat or regular victims of crime, and that women's fear of sexual assault was well-justified. Lea and Young criticise the sample (householders) used by the CSEW because it misses groups such as the homeless. According to **Newburn and Rock** (2004), the homeless are 13 times more at risk of being victims of crime than homeowners (source: Crisis, 2004).

The Merseyside Crime Survey carried out by **Kinsey** in 1984 found that the poor, especially those from BAME backgrounds, suffer more than the wealthy from the effects of crime. This is because they do not have the resources to protect themselves from repeat victimisation. They often cannot afford insurance and may not report crime because of poor relationships with the police or the police may not take their victim status seriously.

Evaluation of critical victimology

👍 Critical victimology has highlighted the role of power, especially the power of the state, the police and the mass media, in how the status of the victim is constructed.

👎 New Right criminologists argue that some victims may be responsible for the crimes being committed against them because they have not sufficiently invested in the technology required to make themselves 'harder targets' for criminals. However, this criticism does imply some unpleasant sexist ideas – for example, that some women are 'asking for it' because of the way they are dressed.

Now try this

1 Which groups were more likely to be victims of crime according to realist victimology?

2 What is the role of the mass media in the social construction of victims?

Exam skills 1

These exam-style questions use knowledge and skills you have already revised and will help you to prepare for Paper 3. Have a look at pages 176, 185–187 for a reminder about white-collar and corporate crime, and the official crime statistics.

> Spend a maximum of around 5 or 6 minutes on this question.

Worked example

1 Outline **two** reasons why white-collar and corporate crimes go under-reported. **(4 marks)**

- These crimes often involve the manipulation of complex technical rules and information. Consequently, some victims of these sophisticated crimes may not realise they are victims.

- The main victims of white-collar crime are institutions such as banks who may fear the bad publicity if they report the crime.

2 Outline **three** trends relating to the social distribution of crime. **(6 marks)**

- The official crime statistics suggest that males commit five times more crime than females and far more violent crime: they are 15 times more likely to be convicted of violent crime whereas women are more likely to be convicted of property crimes.

- Secondly, the official crime statistics show that young people commit the most crime. A general trend is that as people get older they commit less crime.

- Thirdly, the statistics show that most crime is property related, although this type of crime has halved since 2004. Violent crime makes up about a quarter of total crime but it has slowly risen since 2004.

Outline

Both of these questions will ask you to outline two or three ways (or patterns, trends, reasons etc.). The command word 'outline' means that you should set out the main characteristics of what is being asked for. You should:

 write (a) an identifier – outline the reason or trend – and (b) a qualifier – an explanation

 write your answer in continuous prose

 use brief examples to illustrate your points if appropriate

 use sociological terms, concepts and studies whenever possible.

You could also bullet-point your answer as this will help you to focus on the need for two or three reasons.

> To work out how long to spend on each question, multiply the number of marks by ½. For example, a 4-mark question would be 6 minutes (4 + 2) and a 6-mark question would be 9 minutes (6 + 3), or 15 minutes for both of these questions.

> We get our information on the social distribution of crime from the official crime statistics, so this answer should focus on trends in these statistics.

> Here the answer gives an example to support the point being made.

Exam skills 2

Have a look at pages 181 and 182 for a reminder about right-realist theories of crime, right realism and social policy. Aim to spend a maximum of 15 minutes on this question.

Worked example

3 Read **Item A** below and answer the question that follows.

Item A

Postmodern theories of crime oppose those theories of crime which suggest that criminality is either the result of rationally weighing up the costs and benefits of crime or because criminal individuals lack social controls in their lives. In contrast, postmodern theorists of crime such as Jackson Katz argue that crime is a spontaneous affair committed because young offenders are gambling with the excitement of committing what are often opportunist crimes and the possibility of getting caught. Crime from this perspective is adrenaline-fuelled rather than the result of rational thought.

Applying material from **Item A**, analyse two reasons why people commit crime according to right realists. **(10 marks)**

Item A refers to cost-benefit analysis. This right-realist theory of crime, which is associated with Clarke, suggests that criminals assess their chances of successfully committing a crime by weighing up the possible costs (the possibility of being caught and the type of punishment) against the possible benefits (the economic rewards or status they might receive from their peers). Clarke and others argue that in order to prevent crime, the costs need to be increased through situational crime prevention strategies. This means that the situation or context in which the crime takes place needs to be made tougher in order to increase the risk of being caught and so deter the criminal. This should be done by educating potential victims to 'design crime out of their lives' by making themselves 'harder targets' by investing in better security – alarms, lighting, surveillance cameras and so on. Others have called for increasing the costs of crime by ensuring tougher or more punitive punishments. However, target-hardening strategies have been criticised for displacing crime to poorer areas that do not have the economic resources to design out crime...

...In contrast, as Item A observes, postmodernists like Katz reject the idea that the decision to commit crime is rational. Other postmodernists such as Lyng see crime and delinquency as 'edgework' – a spontaneous gamble in reaction to boredom, in which the protagonist is excited by the risk of getting caught. Katz sees most crime as opportunist – it is not planned or weighed up. It is a spur of the moment act with little thought for the consequences for either the victim or offender.

Item A contains information that will lead you to the two reasons required by the question. Here, two possible reasons are given in the opening sentence: cost-benefit analysis and control theory. Make sure that you refer to the item in your answer. The point of the item is to guide you and to help shape your reasoning. Try to put the bits you use into your own words. Read through the item and highlight things that will help you answer the question.

The question asks you to 'analyse', which means that you need to **identify** and **clearly explain** the general components of two right-realist reasons or explanations mentioned in the item. Analysis should also include some discussion of the strengths and weaknesses of the reason or explanation in order to add evaluation. Your answer needs to be fairly detailed. It must use sociological concepts and ideas, and be written in continuous prose.

Once you have identified a theory, it should be linked to a specific sociologist. Here, sociological concepts such as 'status' and 'peers' are also accurately used.

The candidate develops the reason by showing how it has shaped right-realist strategies for dealing with crime.

The response shows sociological knowledge and understanding with regard to situational crime prevention.

Now you would need to analyse a second right-realist reason/theory as to why *people commit crime*. For example, you could discuss Hirschi's theory of accumulating controls (see page 181).

For these questions, your analysis should include some evaluation of each reason or explanation. If the item makes an evaluative point, you should employ it too (for example, Katz and Lyng).

Exam skills 3

Your answer to this final crime and deviance Paper 3-style question needs to be detailed and to show good evaluation. It must use sociological concepts and ideas, and be written in continuous prose.

Worked example

4 Read **Item B** below and answer the question that follows.

Item B

Some Marxist sociologists argue that crime and deviance are caused by the criminogenic character of the capitalist system. They argue that the dominant values of capitalist societies, such as self-interest, monetary success and conspicuous consumption, encourage criminality among all sections of society. However, neo-Marxists argue that some working-class individuals choose to commit crime to symbolise their objection to inequalities and injustices brought about by capitalism.

Applying material from **Item B** and your knowledge, evaluate the usefulness of Marxist approaches in understanding crime and deviance. **(30 marks)**

Spend around 45 minutes on this question.

This question asks you to **evaluate** the usefulness of Marxist approaches in understanding crime and deviance, which means that you need to **form a judgement** by **discussing** the evidence. Outline the Marxist theory of crime in some detail. Then, illustrate it with evidence from the item and your own knowledge, such as sociological studies or examples of events that support it. Finally you should make a judgement about the validity of Marxist arguments about crime after discussing its strengths and weaknesses **or** after briefly contrasting it with another theory of crime.

The item will contain information that will directly or indirectly help shape your response, so make sure that you refer to the item in your answer.

Possible plan of action

- Begin by referring to the item and **explaining** what Marxists mean when they describe capitalism as criminogenic. Use concepts mentioned in the item (e.g. self-interest, monetary success and conspicuous consumption) as well as the work of David Gordon to illustrate this idea.

- Extend your **analysis**: refer to how Marxists such as Althusser and Box see the law as being constructed by the capitalist class to protect their interests and to control those they define as threatening those interests.

- Include **further analysis**: refer to the selective enforcement of the law, using examples such as contrasting the treatment of benefit fraud with tax fraud.

- **Evaluate** by weighing up the strengths and weaknesses of the Marxist approach.

- Neo-Marxism: make clear the similarities between Gordon's version of Marxism and neo-Marxism.

- Clearly **analyse** the difference between the two Marxist approaches, focusing on the idea that crime is a voluntary act committed to make a political point. Use examples to illustrate your points.

- **Analyse** the strengths and weaknesses of this neo-Marxist approach.

- **Evaluate** the Marxist approach/approaches by outlining any opposing or contrasting approaches of which you are aware. Try to identify any strengths and weaknesses of the view(s) to create a debate. If you are still within the time limit, you could contrast Marxism with another sociological theory of crime such as functionalism. Make clear their similarities and differences (for example, they are both structuralist theories but one argues that crime arises out of consensus and the other that crime arises out of conflict).

- Based on your argument so far, draw an appropriate conclusion and/or **form a judgement** on the usefulness of Marxist approaches in understanding crime and deviance.

Exam-style practice

These exam-style questions will help you to practise for the crime and deviance section of your A Level Paper 3 exam. You will find answers on page 228.

1 Outline **two** reasons why ethnic-minority crime might be over-represented in the official crime statistics. **(4 marks)**

> Questions and 1 and 2 will ask you to outline **two** or **three** reasons (or ways, patterns or trends). 'Outline' means that you must **identify the reason** but you must also **describe** or explain its main characteristics or illustrate it with an example. Spend no more than 15 minutes on these two questions combined.

2 Outline **three** reasons why a dark figure of unreported or unrecorded crime might exist. **(6 marks)**

> Make sure that you use sociological terms, concepts and studies where relevant and also give examples to support your points. The question asks for **three** reasons so make sure you do include three.

3 Read **Item A** below and answer the question that follows.

> Highlight parts of the item that will help you to answer the question and which relate to the two reasons Question 3 requires.

Item A

Left realists such as Lea and Young partly blame capitalism for crime. They believe that the culture of capitalism, with its emphasis on monetary and material success, results in people never being happy with what they have got. These feelings of relative deprivation often lead to marginalisation – feelings of frustration, hostility and envy as the deprived realise they are powerless to change their situation. Crime is the inevitable result.

Applying material from **Item A**, analyse **two** reasons why people commit crime according to left realists. **(10 marks)**

> 'Analyse' questions want you to both **identify** and **critically discuss** the two reasons. Refer to the item in your answer – for example, to expand on the concept of relative deprivation. The item also refers to the effect of the culture of capitalism. Use this and your own knowledge to further explain that this leads people to compare their standard of living with other social groups. Note that the Item also illustrates what is meant by marginalisation – for example, 'feelings of frustration, hostility and envy... they are powerless...'. Use your own knowledge to explain which social groups feel this way.

4 Read **Item B** below and answer the question that follows.

> Try to put the bits of the item you use into your own words, don't just copy out sections.

Item B

Subcultural sociologists such as Cohen suggest that crime is an outcome of status frustration. Cohen claimed children aspired to status but their access to the institutional means of conferring status is blocked. However, not all subculturalists agree with Cohen. Miller, for example, blames working-class subculture for crimes committed by working-class youth, whereas Cloward and Ohlin blamed the availability of illegitimate opportunity structures. However, critics of subcultural theory point out that subculturalists often neglect the power of some groups to negatively label working-class youth as delinquent.

> Plan your answer before you start and make sure that you include sociological concepts, theories and examples to help you to create a debate and to support your points.

Applying material from **Item B** and your knowledge, evaluate the usefulness of subcultural theories in understanding crime and deviance. **(30 marks)**

> The command phrase 'evaluate the usefulness of' means that you must both **describe** and **critically discuss** the strengths and weaknesses of the theory in understanding crime and deviance. The item contains three clues as to what you should be discussing: status frustration (Cohen); alternative subcultural theories and critics of subcultural theory.

Answers

Where an exemplar answer has been provided, it does not necessarily represent the only response. In most cases there are a range of responses.

Core themes

1. Culture

1 The value of privacy is important in the UK. Consequently, it is the norm not to barge into people's homes or rooms without invitation. Reading other people's mail or diaries without their permission is likely to be met with social disapproval.

2 Although the majority of the British population are white and many subscribe to Christian beliefs, there are significant ethnic and religious subcultures that exist alongside that majority – for example, the Chinese community.

2. Socialisation

Some biologists and psychologists believe that behaviour is strongly influenced by nature, especially by the genes we have naturally inherited from our parents. In contrast, sociologists believe that behaviour is learned or acquired from our parents who are significant role models during the parenting or nurturing process.

3. Types of socialisation

It is suggested that television and films may expose children to criminal or deviant behaviour, such as violence and drug-taking, and may present such behaviour as 'normal'. Peer groups such as gangs may be criticised because they may put peer pressure on children to behave in deviant ways.

4. Identity

The self is your subjective awareness (how you see yourself), whereas social identity refers to how others judge your performance in particular social roles. For example, do your teachers or your mum and dad think you are a good student?

5. Social differentiation and status

1 Marriage is an achieved status because in Western societies it is chosen and achieved rather than imposed.

2 Prince Charles occupies an ascribed status because he was born into that role.

6. Stratification

Class systems of stratification are more open than caste systems. People from different social classes can marry. Marriage between people from different castes is generally prohibited. In class societies, people can experience upward social mobility and improve their class position. In contrast, membership of a caste determines the job a person does for life. Social mobility is only possible through death and reincarnation.

7. Sociological perspectives

1 Marxists are critical of functionalists because functionalists believe societies are based on consensus. Marxists argue that consensus is a myth and that societies are actually based on conflict.

2 Giddens argues that social structures and institutions are created and reproduced by the repetition of acts by individuals.

8. Functionalism

1 The specialised division of labour refers to the fact that work, which fuels the economy, is composed of thousands of specialist jobs or tasks. Let's use the example of education: some people specialise in teaching particular subjects like sociology; some specialise in managing educational establishments; and some specialise in maintaining aspects of schools, such as caretakers, secretaries, cleaners and catering assistants.

2 Social integration is best defined as the social process whereby individual members of a society feel united as members of a larger common community or society. They feel a strong sense of belonging or loyalty to the society in which they live.

9. New Right

1 Neo-liberalism is a set of economic ideas that believes free market competition without any state regulation is the best way to efficiently and cheaply produce greater choice for consumers of goods and services.

2 Murray believes that state provision of welfare services, especially benefits, creates welfare dependency. Recipients of benefits are not motivated to search for work because welfare benefits guarantee them a regular income.

10. Marxism

The infrastructure refers to the economic base of the capitalist system which, according to Marx, is the most important part of the capitalist system because this is the site of the bourgeoisie's exploitation of the working class, resulting in huge gaps in income and wealth, and therefore class inequality. In contrast, the superstructure is made up of non-economic institutions such as the education and political systems, religion and culture. The function of the superstructure is to convince the population – especially those being exploited – that the capitalist system is fair and works in the interests of all its members, despite the fact this is simply not true.

11. Feminism

Firestone argues that women experience patriarchal inequality because of their biology, which means they get pregnant and are in need of protection by men who assume that women should be responsible for childrearing because they give birth.

12. Marxist, liberal and difference feminism

Difference feminists point out that women do not exist as one homogeneous group in which all experience similar degrees of inequality and exploitation. Some women – for example, wealthy and well-educated women – have more power than others to resist patriarchal pressure. Others, for example, may face multiple exploitations because they are poor or because they are members of a very patriarchal religion.

13. Social action theory

People socially construct society by choosing to come together in social groups. They also apply meaning to the behaviour of others – for example, some people's behaviour may be interpreted as 'normal' or 'deviant'.

14. Postmodernism

1 Globalisation refers to the fact that the world has become a smaller place because digital technology in the form of the internet and email means that geographical distance and time are no longer important. We now live in a globalised world that consumes much the same brands.

2 People in postmodern societies are distrustful of bodies of knowledge such as science and religion. Knowledge in postmodern societies is seen to have relative value.

Education

15. Educational policies, 1870–1978

1 Both cultural and deprivation theories inspired Educational Priority Areas (EPAs). EPAs were areas identified by the government as 'deprived'. Extra money was allocated to schools in these areas in the 1960s in order to compensate children for their parents' poverty. For example, money was spent on encouraging parents to get more involved in their children's education. This stemmed from Douglas' (1964) view that working-class or poorer parents were less likely than middle-class parents to take an interest in the education of their children.

2 Marxists would see the tripartite system as serving the interests of capitalism by reproducing class inequalities. For example, they might argue that grammar schools ensured that middle-class students would end up in professional and managerial work and that secondary moderns churned out manual workers and the factory workforce.

16. Comprehensive schools

Selection by mortgage means that affluent middle-class parents can afford to buy homes in the catchment areas of high-performing schools. A good school can considerably raise house prices in catchment areas and therefore price working-class parents out of the housing market. Consequently, working-class students are more likely to be found in schools in catchment areas in which housing is cheap or socially provided by councils or housing associations. Unfortunately, many of these inner-city schools academically under-perform compared with schools in middle-class areas.

17. Educational policies, 1979–1988: marketisation and parentocracy

1 A parentocracy is an educational system in which parental choice is the most important characteristic. Power lies in the hands of parents rather than local authorities or schools as to which school children should attend.

2 The main aim of encouraging competition between schools was to drive up the standard and quality of education. Good schools would supposedly benefit by attracting high-ability children and the best teachers. Moderately performing schools would be forced to improve or face closure because of lack of demand.

18. Educational policies, 1979–1988: The ERA

The national curriculum was viewed as meritocratic because it ensured that all students were taught the same knowledge, and consequently all students experienced the same SATs and exams such as the GCSE.

19. Evaluating marketisation policies

1 According to Gewirtz (1995), middle-class parents are able to use their economic, cultural and social capital to enhance their choice of school for their children. Working-class parents, on the other hand, lack these advantages and often have no choice but to send their children to failing or average schools because the best schools are full.

2 Most parents of high-ability children (who are likely to be middle-class) will attempt (probably successfully) to get their children into the schools at the upper end of the league table. These schools fill up quickly. Parents with children of middling or low ability will probably have to be satisfied with whatever school places are left in schools lower down or towards the bottom of the table. The schools at the top are likely to remain there because they have creamed off the best students. Other schools are unlikely to be able to compete equally with them because their intake is less able.

20. Labour educational policies, 1997–2010

For example:

- Labour expanded the number of specialist schools that could decide their own admission procedures and consequently select part of their intake.

- Labour introduced the Private Funding Initiative (PFI) – local authorities were encouraged to enter into financial partnerships with private contractors to build new schools.

21. Labour's social democratic policies

On the one hand, the Educational Maintenance Allowance (EMA) and the Aimhigher programme were positive policies aimed at encouraging poorer students to aspire to higher education. However, Labour introduced tuition fees and replaced student maintenance grants, which were means-tested, with loans that had to be repaid with interest.

22. Educational policies, 2010 onwards

The 'pupil premium', which was inspired by the Liberal Democrat wing of the Coalition government, aimed to give extra resources to those schools, mainly found in inner-city deprived areas, that had disproportionate numbers of students eligible for free school meals. The pupil premium aimed to improve the educational opportunities of these poorer students.

23. The Conservatives and privatisation

In January 2016, the Conservative government scrapped higher education grants for poorer students and replaced them with loans.

24. The impact of educational policies

Any two from:
- EMA
- Aimhigher
- Gifted and Talented.

25. Globalisation and educational policy

Increased global migration means there will be more ethnic-minority students in schools. This may encourage multicultural forms of education.

26. Functionalism and education

1 British state schooling is based on equality of opportunity – all students are treated in the same way. Furthermore, all students are objectively evaluated and judged in the same way through the use of examinations and qualifications.

2 Subjects such as history and language link the individual to society, past and present, and encourage students to take pride in the historical and cultural achievements of their nation. In Wales, for example, the Welsh language is compulsory in schools in order to remind children of their Welsh heritage.

27. Functionalism, education and the economy

1 Role allocation should produce a more efficient economy if people's abilities and skills are matched effectively with their jobs. For example, medical students spend years training in order to gain the appropriate skills to become doctors. Many drop out in the process. Those who qualify, therefore, ought to be very good at medicine and are paid accordingly.

2 Role allocation depends on equality of opportunity. People should be rewarded with qualifications on the basis of merit – that is, because they have talent and skills, and have worked hard.

3 An over-qualified workforce is a problem because it means employers are not effectively matching jobs to ability.

28. Neo-liberal or New Right perspective

Neo-liberals believe that the role of the state in providing education needs to be lessened and that education should be marketed as a commodity. Schools need to compete with one another in a free market to drive down costs and drive up standards.

29. Neo-liberal or New Right influence

For example:
- Private building companies have entered into Private Finance Initiative (PFI) agreements with local authorities to build schools.
- Private companies are running local educational authorities such as Islington.

30. Marxist theory of education

1 Marxists claim the hidden curriculum is negative because it subtly encourages working-class students to passively accept aspects of inequality such as hierarchy, blind obedience, differential rewards and so on. The hidden curriculum aims to produce students who will grow up into conformist citizens and compliant workers who do not question inequality and authority.

2 Education encourages competition and the notion of different rewards or status for different abilities. Similarly, work encourages workers to compete for promotion and is often organised into a hierarchy where workers are on different pay scales. For example, skilled manual workers tend to earn more than semi-skilled and unskilled workers, while managers have more power than office workers or workers on the factory floor.

3 Social class.

31. Evaluating Marxist approaches

1 Giroux (1984) notes that working-class children often resist schools and education by truanting, forming anti-school cultures and getting themselves excluded. Willis (1977) points out that his working-class 'lads' did not share the same goals as their teachers or more academic students. They went to school for a laugh rather than for an education.

2 In postmodern societies, people are more individualistic and less likely to take notice or be influenced by traditional structures such as class. Students have greater choice and their identities are more likely to be shaped by the diversity of fashionable ideas that exist with regard to gender, sexuality, ethnicity and religion than social class.

32. External factors: social class and education

1 Belief that they provide a higher standard of education compared with state schools; smaller class sizes; more one-to-one interaction with teachers; better facilities; better discipline.

2 Easier access to Oxbridge; social connections; access to better paid and high status jobs.

33. External factors: cultural deprivation theory

1 Working-class children lack the language skills for success in education.

2 Middle-class parents supposedly (a) teach their children how to speak and think in abstract ways, (b) encourage their children to be ambitious and to aim for higher education, (c) are more interested in the educational progress of their children and, consequently, are more likely to regularly communicate with schools and teachers, and (d) are keen to give their children cultural and educational experiences, for example, by taking them to museums.

34. External factors: material deprivation

Fear of debt and lack of funds because of their parents' inability to offer financial help support the view that poverty reduces the numbers of working-class students applying to university.

35. External factors: cultural capital

Poverty means that working-class children are likely to lack educational capital in that parents are unable to buy them extra educational supports. They are likely to live in a deprived area in which there are few highly achieving schools. Their parents are unlikely to have the social capital or contacts that might assist their education.

36. Internal factors: school-based factors

1 The researchers lied to the teachers. Their actions may have led to the remaining 80 per cent of students underachieving.

2 The 'ideal student' is likely to be middle-class and female because these students are more likely to fit the teacher's perception of what a hard-working, motivated and well-behaved student should look like.

3 A teacher may judge a student on the basis of social class, gender, ethnicity, family background, the area in which the student lives, their appearance or the teacher's experience of other siblings. The judgement becomes a label that shapes the attitude of the teacher towards the student on a daily basis. If the label is positive, the teacher may pay the student more attention and stretch and challenge them. If the label is negative, the teacher may treat the student negatively by, for example, constantly criticising their behaviour or by simply having low expectations of them. Students internalise these labels and become what is expected of them.

37. Streaming, identity and subcultures

Triage is based on teachers using labels (which are often based on social class prejudice rather than intelligence or ability) to place middle-class and working-class students into streams.

38. Gendered inequality

Girls at mixed schools may be reluctant to choose subjects dominated by boys. They may be influenced by peer and parental pressure to choose stereotypical feminine subjects. Girls at single-sex schools do not experience boys dominating particular subjects. They are also likely to see more female adult role models in the form of female physics teachers.

39. Girls succeeding: external influences

Beck suggests that people have become more self-orientated or individualistic and are now less influenced by family or peer pressures to get married and start a family. Today, as Sharpe's (1976) surveys show, it is acceptable for a female to look out for herself first and foremost. Consequently, the pressures to become a wife and mother have been abandoned in favour of education and the possibility of a career.

40. Girls succeeding: internal influences

White working-class girls are more likely to underachieve compared with white middle-class girls. This implies that social class and/or access to economic, cultural and social capital may help overcome gender barriers in education. Evidence suggests that African-Caribbean girls do better than white working-class girls. This suggests that, despite sharing a similar social class background and therefore economic circumstances, there must be cultural or ethnic factors that account for these differences.

41. Failing boys

1 Girls are encouraged from an early age by their parents to conform to adult expectations and consequently they know how to behave in classrooms. They are also taught the value of reading and listening from a very early age.

2 If boys are overconfident, they are less likely to work hard or revise for exams because they over-rely on their 'natural' ability. They are also more likely to put exam failure down to bad luck rather than lack of ability or effort.

42. Ethnicity and external factors: 1

Girls seem to achieve better qualifications than boys regardless of ethnic group.

43. Ethnicity and external factors: 2

Black boys from African-Caribbean backgrounds.

44. Ethnicity and internal factors

They may turn to other similarly labelled students and form anti-academic subcultures and award each other status for creating further disruption in the classroom. These students are likely to either fail their exams or be excluded from school.

45. Institutional racism

1 Any two from: some ethnic-minority students may be entered for lower-tier exams at GCSE; the curriculum may be ethnocentric; very few teachers or head teachers are from ethnic-minority backgrounds; cleaning staff may be disproportionately from ethnic minorities.

2 Schools publicise their exam success when competing with other schools. They may be less willing to admit some ethnic-minority groups – for example, African-Caribbean boys – if they see these as a threat to future exam results. They may even exclude them prior to exams in order to meet their targets.

49. Exam-style practice

1 • Studies of parents, especially those from African and Asian cultures have found that these cultures place a high value on education and consequently parents constantly encourage their children to achieve because they see education as a way out of poverty.

   • Sewell observes that African-Caribbean cultural norms favour matrifocal families in which boys are raised by single mothers. He claims that such boys are educationally disadvantaged by the lack of positive male role models in their lives. In particular, they lack the discipline that might be provided by a father figure.

2 Answer may focus on areas such as:

   • They may truant to avoid the system.

   • They may re-define the goals of education. For example, the lads in Willis' study went to school to 'have a laff' rather than to work hard for qualifications.

   • They may seek out other alienated members of their peer group and, as part of an anti-school subculture, bully more academically minded students and cause disruption in class in order to gain status from their peers.

3 • As Item A observes, some sociologists believe that the British educational system is institutionally racist. They argue that this means that organisations such as schools are failing to provide the same quality of service and opportunity to all ethnic groups. Coard, for example, argues that an ethnocentric curriculum is taught in most British schools, which means that it focuses almost entirely on white culture, history and literature and language and only pays lip service to ethnic-minority culture, for example, through Black History Month. This may cause ethnic-minority students to lose interest in education because they cannot see the relevance in what they are being taught. Some sociologists argue that learning about slavery and colonial conquest may transmit the hidden message that white people are superior to ethnic minorities, which may create hostility between ethnic minority pupils and white teachers. Tickly found that African-Caribbean students were aware of their lack of visibility in the curriculum, resulting in frustration due to the focus on white and European people.

   • Another aspect of institutional racism might be found in the marketing and selection policies of schools, which some sociologists suggest may be biased towards white pupils. As discussed in Item A, this discrimination may result in an unequal distribution of quality and opportunity, where ethnic minorities are not offered the same level of quality. Gilborn suggests that this produces a form of deep-rooted discrimination and inequality, which is self-perpetuating. He argues that the reports prepared for secondary schools by primary schools and interviews for school places may racially stereotype both parents and pupils as culturally deficient, especially in terms of their language ability, which may mean they are more likely to end up in unpopular and failing inner city schools. Similarly, according to Gilborn and Youdell the marketisation of education (where schools are encouraged to compete for 'customers') creates a rationing of education. Teachers neglect students labeled as 'no-hopers' and 'high-achievers' to focus on the borderline students, to show improvement. Many black students are often unfairly judged as belonging to the 'no-hoper' group, meaning that they are not given the same focus of attention. Tickly also found that teacher decisions to enter students for either Higher or Foundation GCSE exams resulted in ethnic inequalities in achievement, again showing an unequal distribution of opportunity along class lines.

- **4** • Your introduction should explain and give examples of working-class underachievement, for example, in terms of GCSE results or numbers of working-class students at university or not at Oxbridge.

  • The item deals with cultural differences first, so move on to this next. Outline the theory of cultural deprivation and the sociological studies associated with it – for example, Douglas, Bernstein and Sugarman – and clearly show how this type of deprivation allegedly leads to educational underachievement. Don't forget to use those sentences in the item that support the notion of cultural deprivation to illustrate aspects of the theory.

  • Once you have outlined and described the cultural deprivation theory, you need to evaluate it. The second part of the item deals with alternative theories that purport to explain working-class underachievement – for example, Bourdieu, as well as critics of cultural deprivation who argue that material and in-school factors are more important than cultural factors. The item also identifies material factors that might be responsible for working-class underachievement. You therefore need to outline material deprivation theory as well as Bourdieu's cultural capital theory and use this as a criticism of the cultural deprivation theory.

  • You might then finish the essay with a paragraph or two exploring the possibility that in-school factors such as teacher labelling of working-class students might be to blame. Attempt to draw a reasoned conclusion based on the evidence you have presented throughout the essay. For example, you could conclude that there is no one single factor responsible for working-class underachievement and that a variety of cultural, material and in-school factors are probably to blame.

Methods in context: Education

50. Research context and characteristics

Schools produce a large amount of secondary data in the form of official statistics – for example, relating to the educational performance of their students at various exam levels.

51. Researching parents and teachers

1 If students are aware they are being observed their behaviour may become unnatural. They may be anxious that the observer is working on behalf of the school management and that their 'normal' behaviour will get them into trouble. Some children may be excited or curious by the presence of a stranger-observer and may exaggerate their normal behaviour. These aspects of observer or Hawthorne effect will render data gleaned from observation invalid.

2 The local education authority, governors and head teachers are extremely unlikely to agree to a sociologist taking on covert roles such as teaching assistants or supply teachers because the covert role involves direct contact with students. Such research would be regarded as extremely unethical because all adults who come into contact with children in schools must undergo a police check. Moreover, children and their parents have not given their consent to be subjected to such research.

52. Researching students

1 The presence of their friends or peers may give them confidence in responding to adult researchers.

2 They may be anxious that the researcher might report these views back to their teacher or head teacher and they might get into trouble. This is why it is important that the researcher should stress to the children that everything they say will be kept confidential and that the research even when published will guarantee their anonymity.

3 The more formal the environment, the more likely the child will perceive a power difference between him/herself and the researcher, which will impede the validity of the responses. If the formal structure is removed and the child is interviewed in a more informal context, for example alongside other children, the greater the likelihood of valid responses.

53. Questionnaires and education

1 It would only be effective if those parents who did not frequently attend parents' evenings were questioned as well. This might uncover reasons other than lack of interest – for example, lack of transport, working hours unsuited to attending evening sessions at the school and so on.

2 The imposition problem occurs because the researcher has not only decided on what experiences are important in terms of the questions asked but also the list of possible responses offered for those filling in the question to tick. However, the respondent's experience may not be listed. The sociological researcher ends up imposing their version of reality on the group being researched because they have failed to speak to members of the group beforehand to ascertain the extent of their possible experiences to turn into a valid closed question with fixed responses to tick.

54. Interviewing teachers and parents

Aggressive interviewing is similar to an interrogation. Statements made by interviewees are aggressively challenged so that people reveal their true feelings. Becker believed that such an interviewing style could reveal behaviour or opinions that would normally remain hidden.

55. Issues with interviewing teachers and parents

Bhatti used female interviewers who could interview Asian parents in Asian languages such as Urdu and Punjabi.

56. Interviewing students

Frosh recruited young male interviewers because he believed that boys would not feel threatened by them and were more likely to trust them.

57. Observation and education

Staffrooms; meetings between staff and parents about confidential matters such as factors that make students 'at risk'; and meetings between teachers that discuss student progress or problems.

58. Observation in education

1 (a) Corrigan observed students and talked to them in their own social spaces –for example, the playground.
  (b) He pretended to be a novelist doing background research for a book he claimed he was writing about a group of students in a comprehensive school.
  (c) He deliberately made a point of not talking to teachers or even acknowledging their presence because he did not want students to associate him with adult authority.

2 Because Lacey immerses himself in the life of the school. He runs the school's cricket team and teaches lessons.

59. Official statistics and education

1 The DfE produces statistics that have been collected in a scientific and reliable fashion about a range of educational topics including achievement across ethnic groups and gender at different levels (SATs, GCSE, A-level and higher education) as well as school exclusions. It also produces league tables showing how schools in specific areas are performing. In addition, schools themselves produce statistics on, for example, attendance, for marketing purposes. All of these statistics are extremely cheap to obtain and are current. A great deal of effort, money and time is therefore saved by using this type of secondary data.

2 First, interpretivists argue that many statistics are socially constructed, which means they are biased because they are the end result of people choosing to record or ignore a particular activity. For example, schools can manipulate exam results so that they look favourable by not entering low-ability students for particular exams by excluding them or by constructing an admissions policy that favours the selection of high-ability students. Second, statistics give little insight into why people behave the way they do. For example, statistics tell us little about why teachers positively or negatively label groups of students and the effect of these labels on student self-esteem and achievement, or why some students choose to mess around at school or are truant.

60. Documents and education

- The content of official documents may be biased because it often seeks to justify the political ideas that a particular government believes in.
- The brochures and prospectuses of schools may lack objectivity because they aim to attract parents as customers and often present an over-idealised version of the school rather than a more genuine warts-and-all picture, which might put off prospective parents wanting to send their children there.

61. Experiments and education

Asking for informed consent means that participants in the research know they are being experimented on. It may be this knowledge that is responsible for their actions during the experiment rather than the variables introduced by the researcher. This is known as the experimental, or Hawthorne, effect.

63. Exam-style practice

- The introduction to this essay should include a brief definition or description of self-completion questionnaires and how they might be distributed to parents – for example, by hand, by post, online to parents via school website or by letter home to parents via pupil delivery.
- Outline and describe the practical strengths of using questionnaires to investigate parental involvement in education – for example, low-cost, time-efficient, the possibility of distribution to large-scale samples of parents, existence of ready-made sampling frame in the form of school registers and records, can ask closed questions about jobs, income, housing and so on to ascertain the socio-economic status or class of parents, can use questionnaire as a comparative tool to compare working-class and middle-class parental input into children's education.
- Outline and describe the ethical strengths – for example, can explain research aims to parents via letter and ask for informed consent.
- Outline and describe the theoretical strengths of questionnaires. Explain why positivists see this method as scientific, reliable, objective and so on.

- Evaluate the practical problems in using questionnaires to research parents – for example, the possibility of non-response, students failing to pass on the questionnaire to their parents, the possibility that some parents might not have the literacy skills to understand the questions and so on.
- Evaluate the potential ethical problems. Some parents may be embarrassed by their economic situation and be reluctant to pass on information, some might feel 'threatened' by the research because they feel that the questionnaire is implicitly critical of their parenting skills. Some researchers get around these problems by stressing anonymity and confidentiality.
- Evaluate the theoretical problems associated with questionnaires. Some interpretivist sociologists might reject their use because of, for example, the possibility of parents engaging in impression management, the artificiality of questionnaires, why data collected by questionnaires may lack validity. Briefly mention why interpretivists might use other methods to collect information about parental involvement in education.
- On the basis of the information you have presented during the course of your essay, draw some reasoned conclusions about the effectiveness of using self-completion questionnaires to investigate the role of parents in educational achievement.

Theory and methods
64. Types of data

1 Secondary data is collected by non-sociological sources. One such source is the government, which collects a range of official statistics relating to most areas of social life – for example, crime statistics as well as GCSE and A-level results. The government also commissions reports by experts into social problems and these are published as official documents. Another source of secondary data is the mass media. For example, sociologists might use newspaper reports about exam results to work out whether society believes exams are getting easier or whether society is concerned about boys' achievement levels relative to girls.

2 A transcript is a written or typed record of an interview. Most researchers ask permission to record an interview because this allows the sociologist to accurately quote word-for-word what the interviewee said. In this way the data 'speaks for itself'.

65. Research design

1 Validity refers to whether the results of research are true or authentic, and whether they reflect the reality of what the sociologist is investigating.

2 A reliable research design makes it easier for another sociologist to repeat the research so that its findings can be checked and verified.

3 Bias refers to prejudice that might creep into a particular piece of social research. This might be a result of poor question design or flawed sampling. Most sociologists aim for objectivity in their research design in order to minimise the possibility of bias.

66. Practical and ethical factors

1 Sociologists, like other professionals, want promotion and pay rises, and have ambitions to rise high in the academic world. Consequently, they might carry out research in order to be noticed. They may deliberately choose a research topic because it is controversial and in the news or because it is a social problem that the government and/or the general public is very anxious about. They will also be aware of what is currently fashionable in the academic world. In recent years, for example, themes such as student identity and parental choice have been very popular as arenas of sociological research, while issues such as private education have attracted very little research.

2 Survey-based research, especially involving the use of questionnaires, can be turned around very quickly. Structured interviews can also be carried out fairly quickly.

67. Theoretical factors

1 Verstehen, or empathetic understanding, means that the interpretivist sociologist employs methods that attempt to understand the experience of the research subject – to experience life in their shoes, to get inside their heads, and to see and understand whatever is being studied first-hand through the subject's eyes. For interpretivists, validity underpins the research process and is best achieved by establishing trust and goodwill between researchers and their subjects. Verstehen enables this to happen.

2 Positivists believe that research methods should be scientific. This means that the research design should be standardised, highly reliable and objective in order to produce quantitative data that can be observed for correlations.

68. Stages in the research design

First, most research begins with a hypothesis that the researcher sets out to prove right or wrong. Second, a research method needs to be chosen and, third, the research population – who is to be studied – needs to be decided on. Fourth, the hypothesis needs to be broken down into parts that can be measured by a questionnaire or interview or observed. Fifth, a cross-section of the research population needs to be sampled. Sixth, a pilot study needs to be carried out to iron out potential problems. The research is then carried out and, finally, the findings are summarised in a quantitative and/or qualitative form in the final report.

69. Sampling techniques

1 Quota sampling depends on the judgement of the researcher who is looking for a certain type of person – for example, women aged between 40 and 60 years – to stop in the street and ask questions. However, evidence suggests that researchers are more likely to stop people who they think look 'respectable', 'cooperative' and 'intelligent' and that they are less likely to stop people who do not fit these stereotypical characteristics. Their sample, therefore, is unlikely to be representative of the general population of women aged between 40 and 60. Opportunity sampling is fine if a particular target audience is required, but there is no guarantee that people who attend a particular institution used by a sociologist are typical of the wider population the sociologist is interested in. Finally, snowball sampling is useful for accessing deviant groups such as drug addicts or criminals, but there is no guarantee that people who agree to take part are representative of addicts and criminals as these groups are generally reluctant to share their experiences with sociologists.

2 Other examples of sampling frames include the electoral roll (a list of those eligible to vote), the Postcode Address File® (a list of every address in the UK), the membership lists of political parties, and lists of subscribers to magazines, newspapers or websites.

70. Laboratory experiments

1 Laboratory experiments have all of the scientific characteristics preferred by positivists. A well-designed experiment will be standardised, controlled, logical, reliable and objective, and will produce quantitative/statistical data that can be compared for correlations.

2 Informed consent means that people have agreed to take part in research. However, this knowledge can undermine the validity of the results because the scientist can never be sure that the participants' behaviour is the result of the variables introduced into the experiment or whether it is the result of people knowing they are taking part in an experiment.

3 Interpretivists dislike laboratory experiments because they generally do not take account of free will – people's ability to choose how they behave or interpret something. For example, interpretivists argue it is impossible to construct human control and experimental groups that are exactly alike because, although they may share the same social characteristics, they may not share the same interpretation of what is going on. Moreover, people who are subjected to experimental research may be reacting to the experiment rather than what the experimenter is interested in.

71. Social experiments

1 Statistics are socially constructed, which means that they are the end result of decisions taken by people as to what statistics should or should not be collected. For example, it might not be possible to compare educational statistics because some schools may use different criteria to collect statistics on absences and truancy, so the sociologist may not realise they are not comparing like with like.

2 First, their experiment may have resulted in harm in the form of underachievement for the other 80 per cent of students. Second, they deceived the teachers by lying to them about the ability of the other 20 per cent of students. Third, they failed to ask for the informed consent of the management of the school, teachers or parents because it was a covert piece of research.

72. Survey questionnaires

Poor response rates produce unrepresentative samples, which make it impossible to generalise from the results.

73. Structured interviews

1 Young people and children may associate adult researchers with authority and be reluctant to open up to them. Members of ethnic-minority groups may interpret white interviewers as threatening, especially if the research subject is racism. Female interviewees being interviewed by male researchers may be disinclined to answer questions about being victims of sexual harassment or crime.

2 Giving to charity, obeying the law, being good parents and contributing to the community.

74. Unstructured and group interviews

1 Unstructured interviews involve interviewers who are especially trained in building up trust and rapport between themselves and their interviewees. They can do this because they are trained in listening and empathy skills, so interviewees may feel less inclined to manage the researcher's impression of them.

2 Positivists regard unstructured interviews as unscientific because they are not based on a standardised interview schedule or questionnaire. They are regarded as less reliable because they are based on a unique relationship between the interviewer and interviewee, which is difficult for another researcher to repeat and verify. Positivists also argue that they lack objectivity because the interviewer emotionally engages with the interviewee. The qualitative data generated by such interviews is difficult to analyse for correlations.

75. Observation

1 Participant observation lacks scientific characteristics. For example, it is not carried out in a standardised or controlled fashion; nor can it be repeated because it involves very personal relationships that cannot be easily replicated.

2 Covert observation involves the sociologist hiding his or her true identity as a researcher and going undercover, perhaps taking an occupational role that allows them to observe up close a particular group of people whose behaviour ought to be very natural because they are unaware they are being observed.

76. Official statistics

1 GCSE and A-level exam results are hard statistics because they are the product of objective examinations. Statistics relating to the number of racist incidents in school are soft because schools may define a 'racist incident' in different ways.

2 The UK Census is a 10-yearly survey questionnaire carried out by the government and aimed at every household in the UK. It produces masses of statistical data on most aspects of British social life.

77. Personal documents

1 Respondent validation is the process by which the sociologist's interpretation of a particular event can be checked with that of those who took part in the event – for example, by checking their diary entry for their experience and understanding of an event observed by the sociologist.

2 Reflexivity refers to researchers reflecting on the research process – especially the interaction between themselves and the research subjects, and how he or she might have influenced that interaction. A research diary may sensitise the researcher to his or her prejudices and any other possible bias.

78. Public and historical documents

1 Content analysis is a quantitative technique that involves the researcher counting particular categories that are present in a document, especially those produced by the mass media, for example, a newspaper or magazine. These categories might be specific topics, words, headlines, photographs, etc.

2 There are problems of reliability. For example, we often do not know the source of many online documents or how scientific they are in terms of the way the information was gathered. There are also problems of validity – for example, it can be difficult to ascertain whether the information is fact, fiction or opinion.

79. Functionalism: consensus theory

Goal attainment; adaptation; integration and latency in the form of pattern maintenance and tension management.

80. Functionalism and social change

In order for pattern variables to change, particularism (judging people on their particular characteristics, for example, as a relative) must be replaced by universalism (judging everybody using the same criteria, for example, on the basis of exam results). Secondly, collectivism (putting the group or society first) needs to be replaced by self-orientation (where individuals mainly act on a basis of self-interest).

81. Neo-Marxism: conflict theory

The ruling class has achieved hegemony because social institutions like the media have successfully persuaded the working class to consent to the rule of the bourgeoisie. The media's focus on trivial entertainment – for example, television soap operas and football – distracts working-class attention away from inequality and injustice. Workers are also distracted by consumerism and the acquisition of false needs.

82. Structuralist Marxism and evaluation

Both Marxism and neo-Marxism are accused of being determinist. Marx is an economic determinist because he sees actions as determined by the economic infrastructure. Althusser sees the superstructure as shaping people's thoughts and behaviour. However what goes on in the superstructure is determined by the infrastructure.

83. Triple systems theory and postmodern feminism

Postmodern feminism rejects the idea that there is one universal female experience of patriarchy. Female experience can differ according to class, age, ethnicity, sexuality and so on. Post-structuralist feminism argues that both verbal and body language is central to how people view and judge both gender and sexuality.

84. Social action theory: phenomenology

Phenomena are things that are held to have characteristics in common according to our senses, which we then put into social categories. For example, we interpret and class certain combinations and shapes of plastic, wood and metal as furniture and treat them accordingly.

85. Ethnomethodology and structuration

1 Reflexivity refers to the way that two individuals in a social interaction will mirror each other's behaviour and talk, so that the interaction makes sense to them.

2 Ethnomethodologists prefer conversational analysis and informal social experiments aimed at disrupting everyday routine and order.

86. Postmodernism: globalisation

Marxists do not agree that societies have evolved into a postmodern society. In contrast, Marxists argue that societies have merely entered a stage of capitalism in which greater profits are sought in the global arena. Secondly, postmodernism states that people have greater consumer choices to assist their construction of personal identity. In contrast, Marxism believes that people's consumption and identity choices are manipulated by capitalism in order to create greater demand for consumer products.

87. Late modernity

1 According to Beck (1992), social class has become a zombie concept.

2 According to Beck (1992), technology is the main cause of risk.

88. Is sociology a science?

1 The hypothetico-deductive model looks for evidence to prove a hypothesis right whilst Popper's (1963) conjecture and refutation model sets out to collect evidence that the hypothesis is wrong.

2 Reliability refers to the ability of other sociologists to repeat the research and verify the original findings.

89. Defining sociology as a science

1 According to Kuhn (1962), in order to achieve scientific status, a set of beliefs requires paradigmatic unity.

2 The following theories deny sociology scientific status:
   - Popper (1963), because sociology does not engage in enough refutation
   - Kuhn (1962), because sociology has never achieved paradigmatic unity
   - interpretivism, because humans have free will and do not behave in predictable or standardised ways
   - postmodernists, who argue that all knowledge is relative and sociologists and scientists have no more claim to the truth than any other belief system.

90. Subjectivity and value freedom

Marx (1888) believed it was important to change society for the better. He valued communism over capitalism.

91. Debates about value freedom

1 It is almost impossible to prevent values impinging on social research because some research subjects will attempt to work out the value position of the researcher and give them particular answers in order to gain their approval. Some researchers may also over-identify with the values of the group they are studying.

2 Domain assumptions make up the world view into which members of a culture are socialised and which people take for granted. These values may unconsciously seep into the researcher's research focus and findings. For example, a functionalist sociologist who believes in consensus and equality of opportunity may ignore findings which uncover conflict or inequality.

92. Sociology and social policy

Marxists argue that social policy always works to support the interests of the capitalist class and helps to hide or disguise and justify exploitation and inequality. Radical feminists argue that social policy has generally been patriarchal and aimed at reinforcing women's traditional family role as mother–housewife.

95. Exam-style practice

1 • Positivist sociologists believe that sociology is a science. They believe that just as the natural world is underpinned by natural laws, so the social world is underpinned by social laws or facts. For example, Durkheim believed that even highly individualised behaviour such as suicide is shaped by social forces beyond the individual's control, such as social integration. Positivists therefore believe that sociological research can be scientific so long as it adopts the logic and deductive methods of the natural sciences: observation–hypothesis and deduction from quantitative evidence that is collected in a controlled, standardised, objective and reliable fashion. Consequently, positivists argue that sociological research should use scientific methods such as variations on the laboratory experiment (for example, the comparative method, social surveys and official statistics). Sociological data must be quantifiable and produce statistical data that can be compared for correlations.

   • Scientific realists like Andrew Sayer (2000) reject the view that science needs to focus on observable phenomena. He suggests that many sciences are 'open sciences' – they often hypothesise about events or things that are difficult or impossible to observe, detect and measure (for example, the 'Big Bang' cannot be directly observed by scientists). Sayer defines science as an attempt to explain the effects of underlying and often unobservable structures and processes. It can therefore be argued that sociology is an open science because sociologists observe the effects of invisible social forces such as consensus and integration.

2 • One advantage of structured interviews, according to positivists, is that they can be used to collect large amounts of quantitative data from large geographically scattered research populations. These types of interviews usually use a standardised questionnaire or schedule. The interviewer merely reads out the question to the interviewee and records the response. For example, the Crime Survey of England and Wales (CSEW) is focused on a representative sample of over 40 000 people drawn from every part of the country who are randomly selected from the Postcode Address File. As the structured interviews used by the CSEW interviewers take, on average, 20 minutes, this sample can be large and therefore more representative of the population of England and Wales.

   • Positivists would also argue that an advantage of structured interviews is that they have a high degree of scientific reliability because they are standardised. Every interviewee is exposed to the same set of questions and it does not matter who is reading them out. Interviewers can be trained to conduct each interview in precisely the same way. They do not depend on the interviewer's personal characteristics and, as such, are less prone to interviewer bias. Anyone wishing to repeat the research using the same interview schedules should obtain very similar results. The CSEW is a great example of a standardised measuring instrument because it is essentially a list of closed questions and fixed-choice responses.

3 Possible essay plan:
   - Begin by defining and outlining what is meant by patriarchy.
   - Using both Item C and your own knowledge about the lack of women in positions of political power, include an analysis of patriarchy by illustrating how it is related to political power.
   - Extend this analysis further by discussing how patriarchy might be found in the workplace. Use Item C and your knowledge to discuss what is meant by the 'glass ceiling' as well as pay inequalities and other forms of gender discrimination in the workplace.
   - Introduce the notion that different feminist theories have developed to explain the nature of patriarchal inequalities. Explain the reference in Item C that feminists are 'not united in their explanations of the source of patriarchy'.
   - The ability to identify the differences between feminist theories will demonstrate your evaluative skills.
   - Describe and weigh up the strengths and weaknesses of the liberal-feminist theory of patriarchy.
   - Describe and weigh up the strengths and weaknesses of the Marxist-feminist theory of patriarchy; for example, the ideas of Benston or the concept of 'the reserve army of labour'.
   - Describe and weigh up the strengths and weaknesses of the radical-feminist theory of patriarchy; for example, Delphy's ideas about 'sex-classes'.
   - Briefly consider how well feminist theories hold up compared with other theories of society such as Marxism and functionalism.
   - Sum up and come to a considered judgement or conclusion about the usefulness of feminism in explaining how society works.

Families and households

96. Different family types

There are three main causes of the beanpole family:
   - Lifespan has increased and consequently grandparents and great-grandparents are living longer.

- Women are marrying later and having fewer children.
- The number of extended kin in the form of aunts, uncles and cousins has also declined because of the fall in birth rates.

97. Defining more family types

A family is a household because it normally shares common residence – that is, family members often live under the same roof. Family members are usually related by blood, marriage or adoption ties. However, a household is not necessarily related. People who share a flat, students who share a house and elderly people who share a care home are all examples of unrelated people who can be classed as households because they share common residence.

98. Functionalist theory of the family

For Murdock the 'educational function' of the family is (through) socialisation – i.e. handing down a culture of how to fit in to society and teaching children to be good citizens.

99. Evaluation of Murdock

1 Ethnocentrism is a type of bias because people see their own cultural experience as superior to other cultural experiences. Murdock sees the American norm of the nuclear family as superior to other family types because this was the cultural norm in the USA when he wrote his theory.

2 The Nayar family does not contain a heterosexual couple tied together by conventional marriage. The father of the children does not live with the mother of the children. The mother is assisted in childcare by another female relative.

100. Talcott Parsons

Structural differentiation was brought about by industrialisation, which saw the development of specialised agencies that took over many of the functions of the family leaving it with only two basic and irreducible functions: primary socialisation and stabilisation of adult personality.

101. Evaluation of Parsons

Parsons claimed that the pre-industrial family was mainly extended, but Laslett's (1965) research contradicts this. Parsons also claimed that the nuclear family was functionally best suited to industrial societies, but Anderson (1973) found that the extended family was actually better suited to the characteristics of early industrial society, such as the poverty caused by low wages and high rents.

102. New Right theory of the family

New Right sociologists see social policies as threatening and weakening the nuclear family which they view as the ideal type of family to live in.

103. Evaluation of the New Right theory of the family

Familial ideology is a dominant set of ideas that suggests people should aspire to a nuclear family ideal. It is particularly disseminated by advertisers via the cereal packet norm – a nuclear family closely resembling that outlined by both functionalist and New Right theories (a father, mother and two children, with the father being the breadwinner and the mother staying at home).

104. Marxist theory of the family

Engels believed that the nuclear family had evolved in order to protect male ownership of property and acquisition of wealth. Monogamous marriage made it easier for men to identify their male heirs and to arrange for inheritance of property and wealth to travel down the male line.

105. Marxist-feminist theory of the family

- First, it produces and raises the future labour force free of charge.
- Second, it maintains the health-fitness and efficiency of the present male workforce free of charge.
- Third, wives soak up male frustrations with the capitalist system in the form of domestic violence.
- Fourth, mothers and housewives make up a reserve army of labour that can be hired cheaply in times of economic boom and let go in a recession.

106. Feminist theory of the family

The main source of patriarchal ideology according to radical feminists is gender role socialisation in the family.

107. Social policy

1 Feminists would approve of social policies that support individualistic gender regimes because this type of social policy sees men and women as equals both in the family and workplace. Consequently, social policy aims to provide state-subsidised nurseries and crèches to get women back into the workplace and policies that help men play a positive role in raising their children.

2 Donzelot (1979) believes that social policy aims to police families and help ensure adults within so-called 'problem' families conform to social expectations about how parents and children should behave.

108. Changing pattern of marriage

The New Right believe marriage is essential to the maintenance of traditional conservative values due to its emphasis on commitment and morality. However, the New Right are concerned by the decline in marriage and the rise in different family structures, which, in their opinion, are inadequate structures to socialise children effectively.

109. Changing pattern of cohabitation

1 Cohabitation refers to a couple who live together but are not married.

2 By 'testing the water', Smart and Stevens believe that cohabiting couples are just as committed to each other as married couples but are testing the compatibility of their relationship before getting married. Consequently, couples use cohabitation as a trial period that can be ended if the relationship doesn't work.

110. Changing pattern of divorce

One reason for the rise in divorce could be the development of serial monogamy within British society. It is now deemed to be normal behaviour for an individual to experience more than one serious relationship in their life – which, in turn, has led to a rise in divorce.

A second reason for the rise in divorce could be due to legal changes. Before 1969, divorce was difficult to achieve due to the process of divorce being very expensive, difficult and potentially embarrassing. As a result of the Divorce Reform Act of 1969, couples were granted a divorce if they could prove their marriage had experienced an 'irretrievable breakdown' that consequently led to a rapid increase in marital breakdown.

111. Theoretical views of divorce

1   An increase in individualism and choice could lead to a rise in divorce if individuals prioritise their own personal interests over their relationship, which could cause tension. Also, if individuals are aware of the choice of alternative lifestyles that are available, they may be more willing to leave their unhappy relationship to try something new.

2   Charles Murray claimed that the underclass is a social group that relies on state benefits for survival and suffers from cultural deprivation due to their immoral family structures. Murray suggested that divorce is one of the main causes of the emergence of this group.

112. Consequences of divorce

1   A reconstituted family is another name for a step-family in which a new family is created from the members of at least one previously broken family. The main cause of this family structure is divorce.

2   Perverse incentives, according to the New Right, are the benefits provided by the government that encourage young girls to have children in order to gain access to the welfare state.

113. Personal life perspective

Theorists from the personal life perspective, such as Smart, tend to believe that biological connections are not essential within a family unit. In cases where parents have adopted a child, they may not be biologically connected, but a bond can develop that can be just as strong as a traditional family unit, according to Nordqvist and Smart (2014).

114. Family diversity: the debate

1   The neo-conventional nuclear family refers to an evolved version of the traditional nuclear family in which the expressive leader can now participate in employment alongside performing their traditional roles. This is usually part time or low paid compared to the instrumental leader.

2   Examples of diversity according to the Rapoports (1982) include: cultural, life-stage, organisational, generational and social class diversity.

115. Examples of family diversity

By LATs, Duncan and Phillips are referring to couples who choose to 'live apart together'. This means that, although they are in a relationship, the couple choose to live separately in order to maintain their independence and personal space. This is usually a temporary phase before cohabitation or a break-up.

116. Domestic labour

If a couple experience segregated conjugal roles, they have very distinct male and female roles within the family. In contrast, joint conjugal roles suggest more sharing of housework and childcare, and more equality between the sexes in terms of the distribution of domestic labour.

117. Critique of the symmetrical family

Chore wars refer to the conflict between couples that results from inequalities in the distribution of domestic labour.

118. Criticisms of equality in domestic labour

Heterosexual couples tend to have unequal domestic labour set-ups because men see domestic labour as mainly a female responsibility. There is evidence provided by Dunne (1999) that lesbian couples are more likely to share domestic labour.

119. Social construction of childhood

1   As families needed their children to work in order to help the family survive, they were seen as economic assets as they produced vital resources or generated extra income. Parents therefore saw children differently compared to today's society, as children are restricted from full-time employment until the age of 18.

2   A social construct is something that is created by the society that it exists within. In this case, childhood is seen to be a social construct as it was not a natural occurrence, which explains why different societies have different understandings of the concept.

120. Development of childhood

1   The five different forms of abuse are: physical abuse; emotional abuse; sexual abuse; neglect; and bullying.

2   When referring to the 'golden age of innocence', Pilcher (1995) was discussing how, in her view, childhood is a protected stage of life that is clearly different from the adult world. She claims that because the actions of children are restricted, children are protected by their parents and the state so that they can enjoy this distinctive life stage.

121. The erosion of childhood

1   By 'social blurring', Postman (1994) was referring to how the distinction between adulthood and childhood has become less clear due to the influence of the media. As a consequence, he believes that childhood is disappearing, as children are no longer protected from the adult world.

2   Jenks' (2005) view contrasts with that of Palmer's (2007), as he claims that the bond between parents and their children is still significant. Instead of neglecting their children, Jenks believes that children are the only source of stability for their parents in an ever-increasing uncertain world.

122. Conflict view of childhood

Experiences of childhood can differ in many ways, for example:

- A child's gender can influence their experiences of childhood, as it is argued that parents tend to give more freedom to boys while restricting the movements of their daughters in order to protect them.

- If a child is raised in a low-income family, their life experiences can be different to a child from a wealthy family, as they may not have the same resources needed for a healthy lifestyle.

123. An action approach to childhood

One insight from the personal life perspective that differs from other theoretical views of childhood is their view of how children are active agents of their own upbringing rather than being completely shaped by external factors. Mason and Tipper (2008) suggest that it is children who determine who their family members are and therefore biological ties are not essential.

124. Demographic trends: birth rate

The fertility rate refers to the number of live births per 1000 women aged between 15 and 44 over a year. The total fertility rate is the average number of children that a woman is expected to have.

125. Decline in the birth rate since 1900

1 One reason for the general decline of the birth rate since 1900 is the availability of contraception. This has given women more power over their childbearing. They can now choose to have children later in life, should it fit with their lifestyles. A second reason for the decline in the birth rate is the cost of raising children in today's society. Due to pressure from advertising and peers, children desire the latest trends and fashions, which increase the costs of their upbringing along with increasing living costs and tuition fees. As a consequence, adults may choose to have fewer children, as they cannot afford to raise a large family.

2 Some couples could choose to remain childless if they prefer to focus on their careers instead of raising a family. Due to the decline in traditional pressures, it is more acceptable for couples to choose this option. Another reason for a couple choosing to remain childless could be because they may not be able to biologically reproduce due, perhaps, to being in a same-sex relationship. Although adoption routes are available, it could be difficult to have children due to the emotional stress and potential financial costs that could occur if the couples pursue this option.

126. Decline in birth rate: implications

- Family sizes have declined as people have fewer children.
- Family diversity – different types of family have emerged – such as the 'dual-career' family – to handle the expense of raising a family today.
- Concern with the dependency ratio – there may not be enough young people to replace the ageing population when they retire.

127. Demographic trends: death rate and life expectancy

1 The death rate has decreased and the life expectancy of an individual has increased from 1900 to the present day.

2 One reason for the decline in the death rate could be the improvement in health care in the UK. Before the Second World War, health care was not accessible for everyone and therefore people died of what we now refer to as preventable diseases. As health care has developed, new medicines and treatments are prolonging people's lives and therefore decrease the death rate.

128. Implications of the ageing population

In some ways, family sizes could decrease because of the ageing population, as there has been an increase in one-person households due to one partner passing away before the other. However, family sizes could increase if elderly relatives move back in with their children and their families, creating an extended family.

129. Migration

1 Net migration is the difference between the level of immigration and emigration that occurs over a period of time. As it stands, more people are currently entering the UK compared to those who are leaving.

2 Globalisation has encouraged the increase in migration in many ways. One of the most obvious ways is through the development of transport, as it is now possible for an individual to travel to any other part of the world if they choose to. Additionally, large political organisations such as the European Union endorse and encourage migration through the freedom of movement policy that is central to its ideology.

130. Implications of increased net migration

1 A hybrid identity usually applies to young Asian people who have been raised in the UK, have a commitment to British culture, but still make an active attempt to stay true to the heritage.

2 The African-Caribbean community are the most likely group to marry someone from a different ethnicity – particularly white people.

134. Exam-style practice

1 For example:

- One way in which marriage could be described as more egalitarian or equal is that conjugal roles such as caring for a child are more likely to be jointly shared between parents rather than segregated, which means that 50 years ago women were mainly responsible for this task and men played a very limited role in the bringing up of their children. Evidence now suggests that men are more likely than 50 years ago to attend the birth of their child and play a more active role in their children's lives. Beck, for example, argues that fatherhood is an important source of identity for men today. In contrast, feminists argue that men only involve themselves in the more enjoyable aspects of childcare such as play, but women are still overwhelmingly responsible for the maintenance of children – for example, the cleaning and feeding of children.

- Second, some sociologists such as Young and Wilmott claimed in the 1970s that housework tasks were more fairly shared between spouses. The evidence, however, suggests that, although men are doing far more housework than they were doing 50 years ago, it is still less than half of that done by females. In fact, the evidence suggests that many working women work a double shift. They spend their day working and then return home and are responsible for much of the housework such as washing, shopping and cooking meals. A BBC survey in 2014 claimed that modern marriage is characterised by chore wars. The main cause of arguments between husbands and wives is a wife's dissatisfaction with the amount of housework her husband does or the quality of the housework that he does.

2 - As Item A observes, functionalists believe that family life in the UK is dominated by the nuclear family. Parsons, for example, argued that the isolated nuclear family is functional and beneficial for both the individual and for industrial modern society. However postmodernists point out that functionalist theory is a conservative ideology, which attempts to define what is a 'right' and 'wrong' way of organising family life. This fails to acknowledge recent social changes such as divorce, the feminisation of the workforce, changing female attitudes towards motherhood and changes in the birth and fertility rates, which have brought about greater choice and diversity in family life. Unlike functionalists, postmodernists argue that all types of family have equal value.

- As indicated in Item A, postmodernists believe that social change has altered people's interpretation of who they think belong to their family. Some postmodernists, especially Smart, argue that sociologists should now research 'personal life'. This involves talking to people about who or what they regard as members of their family at particular moments in time. For example, Chamberlain found that African-Caribbean mothers were often assisted by 'fictive kin' (close friends who were known as 'auntie' or 'uncle' to the children), whilst Tipper's research found that children often regarded pets as important members of their families.

3 Begin this essay by briefly identifying and outlining the main view in the title – i.e. Parsons' functionalist theory of how the nuclear family evolved.

- Use the item to organise your answer. It deals with the functionalist theory first, so you should too. Outline Parsons' theory of the family in as much detail as possible and use concepts such as multi-functional, structural differentiation, basic and irreducible functions, structural-isolation, and geographical and social mobility in your description to demonstrate knowledge and understanding.
- Explain why the wider extended kinship network was no longer required according to Young and Wilmott. Use examples from the item or your own sociological knowledge, such as to illustrate why there was no longer a need for a family mutual support system.
- The second half of the essay should mirror the item and focus on an evaluation of Parsons' theory. The item stresses Young and Wilmott's study of families in Bethnal Green, but other key critiques of Parsons that you could mention include Laslett, Anderson and Fletcher. Chester could be used to support Parsons' view that nuclear families are the norm today.
- Make sure you draw a balanced conclusion based on the evidence you have cited. For example, you might conclude that, although most families today are nuclear, family members still see extended ties as important and/or the extended family did not disappear as quickly as Parsons argued.

Beliefs in society
135. Definitions and types of religion

1 An inclusive definition of religion suggests that anything could be a religion. An example of such a definition would be a functional view of religion, which states that anything could be a religion as long as it performs certain roles that benefit society. Alternatively, an exclusive definition of religion, such as a substantive definition, focuses on what features religions are made up of and therefore only certain movements can officially be classed as a religion. The most common feature that is emphasised is generally a belief in a supernatural being.

2 A New Age movement focuses more on the individual development and growth of a believer rather than the worship of a god. Postmodernists believe that these movements are becoming increasingly popular within contemporary society.

136. Religion as an ideology

1 A closed belief system is an ideology that does not allow its beliefs to change as a result of the challenges it may be faced with. Catholicism may be seen as an example of a closed belief system because of its traditional views on contraception and homosexuality.

2 A 'monopoly on the truth' refers to the belief that one ideology has the only answers to life's questions. It suggests that all of its rivals are wrong and all challenges must be deflected or ridiculed.

137. Science as an ideology

1 The CUDOS norms are: communism, universalism, disinterestedness and organised scepticism. They all promote the core beliefs of science whereby criticism is encouraged in order for knowledge to grow.

2 A paradigm is a way of thinking that governs how something works and how it is defined, along with many other things. If a fixed paradigm is in place, it can be difficult for change to occur as its followers are discouraged from deviating from agreed norms that may have been in place for generations.

138. Theoretical views of ideologies

1 A 'free-floating intelligentsia', according to Mannheim (1929), refers to a group of thinkers who are objective and able to relate to society as a whole, rather than committed to a particular worldview such as a religion.

2 Science is seen as a meta-narrative by postmodernists because it attempts to portray knowledge as a universal truth. However, postmodernists believe that there is no absolute truth in the fragmented postmodern world as knowledge is now relative to the individual. Consequently, any ideology that claims to hold a monopoly on the truth is inaccurate.

139. The functionalist view of religion

A collective conscience is where a community shares a set of beliefs that make them feel a sense of belonging to a society. By worshipping together, a community becomes stronger as the beliefs that they share are reinforced.

140. Understanding the functionalist view of religion

According to Malinowski (1951), the rites of passage performed by religious leaders assist their followers in overcoming stressful life events that could disrupt social order.

141. The Marxist view of religion

Marx (1844) suggested that religion maintains a false class consciousness by acting as 'the opium of the masses'. It promises them salvation in the afterlife should they accept their lack of power in this life.

142. Evaluation of the Marxist view of religion

Norris and Inglehart's (2004) study supports the Marxist claim that religion is generally targeted at the poor in order to appease their frustration with society. As the poor are more likely to question their existential security, they require religion more than the wealthy who feel secure about their future survival because of the advantages they have. The poor turn to religion, which in turn allows the religious institutions to have a strong influence over them.

143. The neo-Marxist view of religion

By stating that religion has a 'dual character', neo-Marxists are claiming that whilst in many ways religion promotes stability, it can, under certain circumstances, influence radical change through conflict. This can be evidenced through the liberation theology movement that emerged in the 1960s and 1970s in South America.

144. Max Weber

According to Max Weber (1905), the three different forms of leadership are charismatic leadership, traditional leadership and legal-rational leadership. Weber claimed that charismatic leaders were the most likely to influence change as they could challenge the status quo rather than relying on it for authority.

145. The Protestant work ethic

For Calvinists, 'the elect' referred to a group of individuals that God had decided would be going to heaven. This decision was made before birth and could not be influenced by any individual action. The anxiety this caused within Calvinism drove believers to devote themselves to their work in order to acquire vast amounts of wealth, thus proving to others and themselves that they were the chosen ones who benefitted from God's favour.

146. Steve Bruce: religion and social change

According to Steve Bruce (2003), the key to achieving social change is to use religion to unite and integrate the majority of the population through shared cultural values and therefore to gain public support. By reaching out to all communities and finding common ground, religions can often engage because they act on a moral high ground.

147. The feminist view of religion

El Saadawi's (1980) view differs from that of other feminists because she states that it is not religion that is patriarchal. Instead she claims that it is men who control religion and wider society, using religion to help maintain gender inequality by twisting the messages of the sacred text to justify their dominance.

148. The postmodernist view of religion

1 Postmodernists claim that an individual within the postmodern world no longer has a fixed identity and therefore constructs new, constantly changing identities throughout their life. As a consequence, an individual is less likely to subscribe to one particular religion for life as there are so many competing views available through the media that are equally attractive.

2 New age movements do not focus on the religious elements of spirituality. Instead, they promote self-spirituality. This means that individuals can customise their own experience rather than be dictated to by an established hierarchy. This would appeal to modern views, according to postmodernists, because identities are fluid and knowledge is now relative to the individual so there is an absence of absolute truth. New Age Movements therefore offer the individual the ability to tailor spirituality to their own beliefs and find a spiritual experience relevant to their identity. They can become 'spiritual shoppers'.

149. Religious organisations

1 Secularisation refers to a decline in religious influence on society. Many sociologists claim that this has happened in the UK as rival ideologies, such as science, may provide a more relevant explanation of the big questions asked by the majority of individuals.

2 Loss of community and a more individualistic society. Individuals are therefore more focused on their individual well-being rather than those of the greater community.

150. Classifying religions

Three characteristics of a sect could be that they have short lifespans, they usually have a charismatic leader who claims some connection to a supernatural power and they tend not to have a professional hierarchy.

151. New religious movements

1 A millenarian movement is a world-rejecting group who predict some form of divine intervention that could lead to a judgement day. As a consequence, they seek radical social change to avoid such events or distance themselves from the mainstream in order to achieve salvation in the afterlife. At times, this has led to groups committing suicide in order to escape from the world that they reject.

2 World-rejecting movements are completely intolerant of mainstream society and therefore cut themselves off from society, whereas world-accommodating movements may not be satisfied with wider society but still seek to live within pre-existing communities. They wish to improve those communities by influencing change to return to conservative values that have been diluted due to liberal world views within society.

152. The lifespan of sects

The five stages of Stark and Bainbridge's (1986) sectarian cycle are:

- schism – the initial break away from the church
- initial fervour – the leader creates an intense value-base that conflicts with society
- denominationalism – the movement loses momentum over time
- establishment – the movement begins to compromise with the outside world
- further schism – disillusioned members break away to create a new sect.

153. Growth of new religious movements

'De-traditionalisation' is defined by Hervieu-Leger (2000), who claims that traditional customs and values are not being successfully transmitted through the generations in the same way as they were in the past. Consequently, this provides younger generations with more freedom to choose their own beliefs.

154. New Age movements

1 The 'congregational domain' referred to those who attended traditional church services within the local area. The 'holistic milieu' was a collection of New Age movements that Heelas et al. (2005) claimed would become dominant if current trends continue.

2 Today's society is a more individualistic society and NAMs have a focus on the 'self' rather than community as seen in more traditional religions such as the Church of England.

155. Social class and religiosity

'Lifelong theists' tend to come from working-class communities and have always believed in God, while 'lifelong atheists' are those who have never believed in God. According to Lawes (2009), lifelong atheists are more likely to come from middle-class backgrounds.

156. Ethnicity and religiosity

Modood et al. (1997) acknowledge that religious belief remains higher amongst ethnic-minority groups when compared to the White British majority. However, the research suggests that as an ethnic-minority group become established within the UK, religious belief declines with each generation. This may support Steve Bruce's (2002) view that some ethnic-minority groups use religion as a form of 'cultural transition'.

157. Age and religiosity

One reason why the elderly may be more religious than the young could be the 'ageing effect'. This process describes the trend whereby people become increasingly interested in religion as they get closer to death. This may be because they are becoming more concerned with the afterlife or may be seeking some sort of forgiveness for sins they have committed in the past.

Another reason the elderly may be more interested in religion could be due to the 'generational effect', which refers to the experiences they have had throughout their lives. As they are more likely to have suffered from poverty than the current young generation, they are also more likely to have engaged with religion, as statistics suggest that the poorest are the most likely to have religious belief.

158. Gender and religiosity

According to Woodhead (2004), a 'juggler' is a woman who balances all areas of contemporary life whilst also engaging in a form of spirituality. As she may not have the time to dedicate to a traditional religion or new religious movement, Woodhead believes that the 'juggler' is more likely to engage with a New Age movement that is more aligned to her needs.

159. Defining and measuring secularisation

Sanderson (1999) claims that the church's 'core business' is those people who only attend specific services that the church has traditionally hosted, such as weddings, funerals and christenings. As there are now many secular alternatives, individuals are choosing alternative venues to host their 'rites of passage', which leads to the church losing its role in society.

160. Explanations for secularisation in the UK

Due to religious pluralism, Berger (1969) stated that all religions are in direct competition with rival religions. If each religion claims to provide the absolute truth about how the world works, and, by implication, that other religions are incorrect, followers begin to doubt the teachings they have always believed in. Overall, Berger argued that this could cause people to distrust the ideology and so to lose interest in religion. He has since distanced himself from this view and now suggests that religious pluralism stimulates interest in supernatural debates, which may lead to growth in religious participation.

161. Arguments against secularisation in the UK

The term 'vicarious religion' refers to the process whereby religious worship is practised by an 'active minority' on behalf of the majority who do not attend places of worship. Grace Davie (1994) argues that the majority do not attend church regularly but still believe in religious principles in an individualistic way. Therefore, measuring religious belief is problematic as people do not have to go to church to practise their religion.

162. Religious belief in the USA

1   By referring to American religious participation as 'superficial', Wilson (1962) is suggesting that Americans who state religious affiliation are not always believers and tend to over-exaggerate their participation in order to fit into American culture, rather than being genuinely religious.

2   Robert Bellah (1991) noted that America has its own civil religion known as 'Americanism' that instils a sense of nationalism in its citizens in order to unite a diverse population under a common banner and therefore promote social solidarity. The worship of the American culture can unite its citizens better than any other religion.

163. Religious market theory

Lyon's (2000) 'sphere of consumption' refers to the way in which religious believers are now seen as customers within the religious market in America. Denominations are aware that they need people to buy into their 'business' if they wish to survive and must therefore ensure that their services are as attractive as possible. This contrasts with Bruce's (2011) view that instead of leading to secularisation, the adaptation of religious beliefs to meet the needs of individual followers is enhancing engagement in religion rather than devaluing it.

164. Religious fundamentalism

- One potential reason for the rise in religious fundamentalism is that fundamentalist groups emerge as a response to globalisation and the acceptance of a cosmopolitan lifestyle (Giddens, 1999).

- Another reason for the growth in fundamentalist movements could be their targeting of the marginalised in society who crave social inclusion. Max Weber (1922) believed that by providing a definitive theodicy, new religious movements could be highly attractive to the marginalised.

165. Types of religious fundamentalism

1   Bruce (2008) claims that Christian fundamentalist groups in the West are fighting against secularisation within their own society, whereas Islamic fundamentalist groups are resisting changes from external influences, such as Western values that are being imposed upon them.

2   Among others, examples might include: abortion, gender equality, immigration, homosexuality, gay marriage.

166. Religion and economic development

Weber's (1905) study of Calvinism can be applied to the impact of Pentecostalism in South America because both movements attempt to inspire their followers to value wealth rather than seeing it as a sin. By encouraging their followers to devote themselves to their work, both Calvinism and Pentecostal movements have been credited as influential in stimulating economic development in regions where poverty used to be prevalent.

170. Exam-style practice

1   One reason that explains why ethnic-minority groups tend to be more religious than the White British is provided by Max Weber (1905) who claimed that it is often the most disadvantaged who are attracted to religion. Weber believed that new religious movements will preach 'theodicies of disprivilege' to help their followers understand their marginalisation from the mainstream. As ethnic minorities are more likely to suffer from poverty and have opportunities blocked by racism, they are more likely to be attracted to the supportive message of a new religious movement that attempts to assist its followers towards future prosperity. To support Weber's claim, Bird (1999) discusses how Pentecostalism increased in popularity in the UK after many members of the African-Caribbean community felt rejected by the Anglican Church. Therefore, one potential reason for ethnic minorities being more religious than the white majority is due to the disadvantages they face in society.

Another reason that explains why ethnic minorities are more likely to be religious than the White British is provided by functionalists. Durkheim (1915) believed that ethnic minorities would use religion as a way of integrating into a new society by adopting the values of that culture, and therefore becoming part of the 'collective conscience'. This can be evidenced through Abby Day's (2007) study of 'believing in belonging', in which she claims the existence of 'ethnic Christians' who affiliate themselves to Christianity in order to fit into the British culture. Day claims that they do not hold religious belief but believe that assimilation to British society is important to their opportunities. Steve Bruce (2002) refers to this as using religion as a form of 'cultural transition' but believes that once assimilation is achieved, the need for religion decreases. In summary, the need to integrate into a new society is a reason why ethnic minorities are more religious than the White British.

2 Item A suggests that one explanation for science replacing religion as the dominant belief system is due to 'rationalisation' within the Western world. Max Weber (1905) refers to this process as the 'disenchantment of the World' as the pursuit of evidence to explain supposedly 'supernatural' and 'sacred' experiences has meant that religion has lost its validity. Instead of believing the irrational tales of religion, Steve Bruce (2011) claims that the majority within Western countries hold a 'technological' world view as they attempt to explain global events such as natural disasters and plane crashes using scientific evidence rather than linking the event to a form of divine intervention. This claim is criticised by Lyon (2000) who claims that the emergence of new religious movements within the 'religious marketplace' has led to the 're-enchantment of the world' and therefore believes that religion has not been defeated as a belief system. To conclude, Weber believes that one reason behind science becoming the dominant belief system is due to rationalisation within the Western world.

A second explanation suggested in Item A for the argument that science has replaced religion as the dominant belief system is due to its 'open' nature. Sir Karl Popper (1959) claims that science has become the dominant belief system as it is open for challenge and discussion. One of the core principles of science is to encourage criticism of research (known as 'falsification') so that the understanding of the discipline can grow over time. This view is supported by Robert Merton (1942) who claims that the CUDOS norms of Communism, Universalism, Disinterestedness and Organised Scepticism ensure that science continues to grow due to its open nature as a belief system. This is opposed to religion which is traditionally described a 'closed belief system' (Item A) as challenges to authority are often seen as blasphemy and therefore discouraged. This claim is criticised by Herberg (1960) who states that religion's reputation of being a 'closed' belief system is changing due to 'internal secularisation'. In order to remain relevant to an increasingly cosmopolitan culture, traditional religions are having to dilute some of their conservative values. Herberg claims, therefore, that religion is now increasingly becoming an 'open' belief system which contradicts traditional assumptions. In summary, the 'open' nature of science is often seen as a reason for its dominance over religion as a belief system.

3 Possible essay plan:

1 Introduction – define fundamentalism and globalisation. Link to the item and set out the debate.

2 Giddens (1999) – rapid growth in cosmopolitanism (define this term and provide examples) and then apply Herberg (1960) to how traditional religions are diluting their beliefs, which is alienating their more conservative followers. Remember to link to the item.

3 Postmodernism – support the previous point using Bauman (1992) and Castells (2010). Use specific terms like 'project identities' and 'resistant identities'.

4 Evaluation – use Beckford (2011) to criticise Giddens and postmodernists by suggesting that globalisation has led to an increase in other forms of religious movement. This would be a good place to use an example like the rise of Pentecostalism and how it is helping disadvantaged groups to transform their lives (use Lehmann, 2002, or Bird, 1999).

5 Steve Bruce (2008) – link back to the question and item. Agree with Giddens/postmodernists but then discuss the different forms of religious fundamentalism and how they have been influenced by globalisation. Use specific terms like 'cultural defence' and 'monotheistic religions'.

6 Evaluation (in support) – use Grace Davie (2013) and state how globalisation has also triggered 'secular fundamentalism'. Link to recent political events such as Donald Trump's election and the Brexit vote as evidence.

7 Evaluation (in criticism/contrast) – use Huntington (2002) and state how globalisation has led to the 'clash of civilisations'; it is not necessarily about cosmopolitanism. Use this to criticise Giddens and postmodernists.

8 Evaluation (in criticism/contrast) – use Max Weber (1922) and state how rise of fundamentalism is caused by marginalisation rather than just cosmopolitanism.

9 Evaluation (in criticism/contrast) – use Eileen Barker (1984) and state how rise in fundamentalism is due to relative deprivation rather than cosmopolitanism.

10 Conclusion – make a judgement: to what extent does the evidence suggest that the growth in fundamentalism has been caused by globalisation?

Crime and deviance

171. Functionalist perspective on crime

Durkheim (1893) blames the rise in crime on increasing egoism and anomie. He suggests that in modern societies like the UK, crime has risen because of a weakening of social controls. This has undermined consensus and led to 'anomie' (instability resulting from moral uncertainty about rules/values). Some societies no longer have the power to deter or socially control individuals from committing crime or deviance. Agencies such as the family are less influential and members of society are exposed to ideas that challenge tradition and authority.

As a result there is no longer clear agreement about what constitutes right and wrong behaviour. Social mores change so that previously deviant acts are no longer deviant and, at the same time, punishments have grown weaker and offer less of a deterrence.

172. Strain theory

Merton fails to explain white-collar and corporate crime, as well as crimes that do not involve economic gain.

173. Cohen's subcultural theory

1 Feminists point out that Cohen only focused on working-class boys and ignored delinquent girls.

2 Matza suggests that young people subscribe to the same subterranean values as other members of society but express these at the wrong time and in the wrong place. He suggests they also drift between delinquent and conformist behaviour and grow out of the former as they get older.

174. Other subcultural theories

1 Cloward and Ohlin identified criminal, conflict and retreatist subcultures.

2 Marshall's (2005) research found little evidence of organised subcultures. Instead he found that most young people were in disorganised 'crews' which committed anti-social acts rather than crime.

175. Marxist theories of crime

1 According to Marxists, people commit crime because of inequalities in income and wealth, powerlessness and alienation, or the influence of criminogenic capitalist culture.

2 Marxists argue that the values that underpin capitalist culture, such as competition or the focus on money, cause criminal behaviour in all social classes.

176. White-collar and corporate crime

1 White-collar crime tends to be committed for self-gratification or enrichment whilst corporate crime is committed to gain some advantage for a company.

2 Croall (2001) suggests that tax evasion is regarded by a lot of people as morally ambiguous because no one likes paying tax.

177. Neo-Marxist theories of crime

1 Hall (1978) suggested the ruling class controlled the working class by generating moral panics about 'problem' groups and introducing repressive laws to control those groups.

2 Traditional Marxist theories suggest that the poor are driven to commit crime by factors beyond their control, whereas neo-Marxists argue that criminals interpret the world around them and choose to commit crime as a political response.

178. Evaluation of critical criminology

Left realists suggest that neo-Marxists romanticise most criminal behaviour and see criminals as 'Robin Hoods' stealing from the rich. Left realists argue that neo-Marxists fail to explain why most victims of crime are other working-class people.

179. Interactionist or labelling theory

According to Becker (1963), definitions of crime and deviance require a powerless group to behave in a way that a more powerful group defines as deviant. The powerful group then constructs a law that renders the activity of the less powerful group as unlawful or criminal.

180. The consequences of labelling

Marxists argue that labelling theory fails to explain where the power to label originates. Marxists claim that it originates in the infrastructure of capitalist societies in which the bourgeoisie or capitalist class acquires wealth and power by exploiting the labour of the proletariat.

181. Right-realist theories of crime

1 According to Murray and Marsland, the welfare state and, in particular, the payment of welfare benefits, is the main reason for the appearance of a criminal underclass.

2 The four controls in a person's life are: attachment to family; commitment to a career or education; involvement in the community; and strong belief in rules.

182. Right realism and social policy

1 Katz (1988) argues that crime committed by the young is spontaneous rather than the result of a rational weighing up of costs and benefits. Secondly, crime may also be the reaction to heavy-handed policing.

2 According to labelling theory, zero tolerance policing may be discriminatory because the evidence suggests that police officers stereotype some communities as potentially criminal and over-police them.

183. Left-realist theories of crime

Marginalisation refers to the feeling held by many poor or young people that they lack the power to change their situation or that nobody is listening to their concerns. This produces frustration which can sometimes spill over into inner-city riots.

184. Left realism and social policy

Left realists suggest that problems caused by the structural organisation of capitalism – such as inequalities in wealth and income, poverty, and a culture that stresses individualism, materialism and greed – are responsible for crime. However, the notion that criminals are experiencing and reacting to feelings of relative deprivation and marginalisation suggests left realism is also influenced by social action theory.

185. The official criminal statistics

'Socially constructed' means that statistics are the end result of decisions made by people like politicians, victims and the police. For example, politicians make decisions to make or change laws, which may result in the creation of new crimes. An example of this is stalking, which became a criminal offence in 2002. Victims were encouraged to report their stalkers whilst the police were encouraged to record this offence for the first time.

186. Self-reports

1 Young people may commit crime but not come to the attention of the police. Data from self-reports confirm that males are more criminal than females but suggest the gap between male and female crime may not be as wide as the OCS suggest.

2 Validity of data collected by self-reports may be inaccurate because of exaggeration, selective and partial memory, or under-reporting because offenders are anxious that the data might be used against them.

187. Evaluating the OCS

Left realist Jones, McLean and Young's victim survey of inner-city London – the Islington Crime Survey (1986) – clearly shows that the main offenders as identified by victims mirror the OCS picture of criminality. Islington victims reported that the individuals who committed crime against them were mainly young, working-class white or BAME males.

188. Gender and criminal behaviour

The chivalry thesis suggests that police officers treat females more leniently than males. The police are less likely to suspect them of criminal behaviour and are more likely to let them off with a warning rather than arrest or charge them. Pollak (1950) argues that, as a result, a great deal of female crime goes unrecorded.

189. Theories of gender and crime

Adler argues that female crime rates are likely to increase as women acquire equal rights and, therefore, enjoy the same opportunities as males to commit crime.

190. Ethnicity and crime: patterns and trends

Morris (1998) argues that it is youth rather than ethnicity that is responsible for the high level of BAME crime. The BAME population in the UK is disproportionately young and young people are more likely to commit crime than any other age group.

191. Ethnicity and crime: explanations

Sewell (2003) believes that black youth commit crime because of three problems that they face. Firstly, they lack a father figure to keep them on the straight and narrow. Secondly, they may have had a negative experience with white people – teachers, police officers and employers – which makes them hostile towards white culture. Thirdly, due to media influences, they see status as wrapped up with violence, being promiscuous and the conspicuous consumption of 'bling'. The pursuit of this type of status is likely to bring them into conflict with the police.

192. Class and crime

Murray (1984) argues that most street crime is carried out by a criminal underclass whilst Hirschi (1969) suggests that working-class crime is carried out by members of that class who lack the necessary controls or bonds such as attachment and commitment.

193. The media and crime

Reiner (2007) argues that the media creates the condition for anomie, which weakens moral certainties such as respect for the law. It does this by falsely raising people's hopes of material success. When they are disappointed, they may consider crime as a means of achieving the material success that is constantly presented by the media.

194. The media as a cause of crime

1 Morrison (1999) argues that the media effects model fails to take account of the social context in which the violence takes place.

2 Young people may imitate what they see on the screen; they may become de-sensitised to the suffering and distress caused by crime.

195. Moral panics

1 A 'folk devil' is a label which implies that an individual or group is a problem that needs to be controlled.

2 Critcher (2003) argues that moral panic theory deals in concepts that are vague and abstract and consequently difficult to measure and test.

3 By giving a role and an identity to the teenagers which involved fighting and low level violence.

196. Globalisation and crime

Much cybercrime is aimed at committing traditional crimes such as theft or fraud.

197. The effect of globalisation on crime

1 Firstly, globalisation has led to mass unemployment, poverty and deprivation which, according to Marxists and left realists, fuels crime. Secondly, some sections of the poor may turn to drugs as a way of compensating for their low self-esteem, shame, etc. However, they may turn to crime to finance their addiction.

2 Many companies that operate globally move their manufacturing and services to countries in the developing world, where health and safety regulations are less stringent. This can lead to exploitation as working practices (such as minimum age and wage) are less well-regulated.

   The powerful may also use the 24-hour global banking system and the availability of offshore tax havens to avoid paying tax.

198. Global capitalism and transnational crime

Beck (2000) claims that capitalist societies have entered a period called late- or second modernity. This has led to the development of new but riskier technologies such as the internet which can be used by global criminals and terrorists.

199. Green crime

White's (2008) ideas are described as zemiological because he prefers to study harms done to the environment (which may not be technically illegal and criminal). His theory is described as transgressive because his analysis is not focused on the breaking of environmental laws which, on the whole, do not yet exist.

200. State crime

States have the power to conceal their crimes. Using the Official Secrets Act they can prevent journalists from reporting on state activities. They may also deny involvement. Equally, perpetrators often employ techniques of neutralisation to justify their actions, so may not believe they have committed a crime.

201. Control and prevention: left solutions

Labelling theory is keen on restorative justice because it avoids the stigmatisation, prejudice and discrimination associated with retributive justice.

202. Control and prevention: right solutions

Marxists and left realists feel that right realists do not pay enough attention to the poverty and inequality brought about by the organisation or structure of capitalist societies.

203. Surveillance and punishment

Surveillance could be described as a form of disciplinary power, firstly, because the fear that actions that break the rules might be observed by those in power disciplines people to conform. Secondly, if surveillance uncovers deviant actions, it results in punishment.

204. Victims of crime

Critical victimologists criticise positivist criminology because it neglects victims of corporate, state and green crimes and the role of the CJS in creating secondary victimisation.

205. Critical victimology

1 Realist victimology identifies the poor and especially those from a BAME background living in the inner cities as the most likely victims of crime.

2 The mass media's coverage of some crimes and their victims, especially rape, may be sufficiently negative to put some victims off reporting crimes committed against them. Some victims of crime (for example, white middle-class professionals) may be afforded more attention than other victims (for example, black teenage victims of gang crime) because they are regarded by journalists as more newsworthy.

209. Exam-style practice

1 In areas with high numbers of ethnic-minority people, BAME young people may commit more crime because they are experiencing blocked opportunities or status frustration. They may feel bitter or resentful because racism is denying them access to the same opportunities or means to achieve status, qualifications and jobs as their white peers.
   They may be over-represented in the official crime statistics because police racism, in the form of racial profiling or stereotyping, means that they are more likely than other groups to be stopped, searched and charged with crime. Hood discovered that people from BAME backgrounds are more likely to be sent to prison than white people, even if the latter are found guilty of the same offence.

2 Some victims of crime may fail to report crimes against them to the police because they are unaware they are victims. For example, children may be unaware that they are being abused whilst elderly people may be unaware they have been defrauded.

Institutional victims of employee fraud, such as banks, may be unwilling to report those who commit white-collar or corporate crimes because they fear the poor publicity and do not want to lose the trust of their customers and clients.

Victims of sexual assault may fail to report crimes against them because they fear they will be blamed for 'encouraging' the attack by dressing or behaving in a particular way. They may not wish to put themselves through a distressing cross-examination in court.

3 Item A refers to 'feelings of relative deprivation'. Lea and Young regard such feelings as one of the two main causes of crime, both for young people and those from BAME backgrounds. They argue that modern capitalist societies are dominated by values such as individualism, materialism and consumerism. As a result, people are now motivated by selfish desires and often compare what they have and particularly what they do not have with other social groups. As Item A suggests, 'people [are never] happy with what they have got' and may turn to crime to make up the difference they perceive between themselves and other social groups.

Secondly, Item A refers to marginalisation – feelings of frustration, hostility, envy and powerlessness. Groups that experience marginalisation are likely to be on the economic, educational and political margins of society. This means that if they are in employment, they are likely to be in low-paid, insecure jobs. They are also more likely to be on benefits. They may have performed poorly at school and consequently lack qualifications. They also feel powerless to change their situation and perceive that politicians write them off as 'wasters' and 'scroungers'. Consequently, as Item A observes, they may feel motivated to commit crime because they feel 'frustrated, hostile and envious' of groups who are better off than themselves.

4 • Begin your essay by describing what is meant by subcultures and how membership of these might be connected to crimes committed by young people.

• Follow the item, which begins with a reference to Albert Cohen's theory of status frustration. You must describe this theory in detail. You should also use your knowledge to evaluate Cohen's theory. Item B focuses next on Miller's version of subcultural theory. You will need to focus on Miller's concept of 'focal concerns'. Give examples of these and explore how these might lead to subcultural forms of crimes.

• The third reference in Item B is to Cloward and Ohlin's theory of illegitimate opportunity structures. Describe and explain this in as much detail as you can in relation to how useful subcultural theories are in understanding crime and deviance.

• Finally, Item B ends with a critique of subcultural theory (labelling theory). Use your own knowledge to construct an evaluation of subcultural theory, including theories that aim to explain why young people commit crime in groups. For example, left realism, underclass theory and postmodernist explanations of youth crime.

Notes

Published by Pearson Education Limited, 80 Strand, London, WC2R 0RL.

www.pearsonschoolsandfecolleges.co.uk

Copies of official specifications for all AQA qualifications may be found on the website:
www.aqa.org.uk

Text and illustrations © Pearson Education Limited 2017
Typeset, produced and illustrated by Tech-Set Ltd, Gateshead
Cover illustration by Miriam Sturdee

The rights of Steve Chapman and Harrison White to be identified as authors of this work have been asserted by them in accordance with the Copyright, Designs and Patents Act 1988.

First published 2017

20
10 9 8 7 6 5 4 3

British Library Cataloguing in Publication Data
A catalogue record for this book is available from the British Library.

ISBN 978 1 292 11125 4

Copyright notice
All rights reserved. No part of this publication may be reproduced in any form or by any means (including photocopying or storing it in any medium by electronic means and whether or not transiently or incidentally to some other use of this publication) without the written permission of the copyright owner, except in accordance with the provisions of the Copyright, Designs and Patents Act 1988 or under the terms of a licence issued by the Copyright Licensing Agency, Barnards Inn, 86 Fetter Ln, London EC4A 1EN (www.cla.co.uk). Applications for the copyright owner's written permission should be addressed to the publisher.

Printed in Slovakia by Neografia

Author dedication
I would like to dedicate my section of this book to the NHS, particularly the wonderful nurses, care assistants and physiotherapists of ward F3, St. Luke's Hospital Bradford who gave me such fantastic care after my stroke in March 2016. You all deserve so much more appreciation for your work in increasingly challenging circumstances.

I would also like to thank my partner Fiona for her selfless dedication to my recovery. I am a very lucky man.

Thanks also to my editors, Sam and Carolyn, for their infinite patience and sensitivity in dealing with the cerebral interruption to the schedule.

Steven Chapman

Acknowledgements
We are grateful to the following for permission to reproduce copyright material:

Graph on page 110, source: Office for National Statistics. Graph on page 124, source: Office for National Statistics. Graph on page 129, source: Data from Office for National Statistics and graph by Migration Watch UK https://www.migrationwatchuk.org/statistics-net-migration-statistics. Pie chart on page 159, source: The National Archives, http://www.ons.gov.uk/ons/resources/sctrfigure1_tcm77-290493.png. Graph on page 185, source: Office for National Statistics https://www.google.co.in/url?sa=t&rct=j&q=&esrc=s&source=web&cd=2&ved=0ahUKEwj89vG7nfPRAhVFv48KHbw6 DWkQFgggMAE&url=https%3A%2F%2Fwww.ons.gov.uk%2Ffile%3Furi%3D%2Fpeoplepopulationandcommunity%2Fcrimeandjustice%2 Fmethodologies%2Fcrimeandjusticemethodology%2Fuserguidecrimestatistics.pdf&usg=AFQjCNH8a4IY1kWVBV_VX4WexdQow-dWiA&sig2= f6A8msULY08DD25Uq-sJxg&cad=rja. Graph on page 188, source: Ministry of Justice https://www.gov.uk/government/uploads/system/uploads/ attachment_data/file/380090/women-cjs-2013.pdf. All three graphs on page 190, source: Ministry of Justice https://www.gov.uk/government/uploads/ system/uploads/attachment_data/file/479990/infographic.pdf.

The publisher would like to thank the following for their kind permission to reproduce their photographs:

(Key: b-bottom; c-centre; l-left; r-right; t-top)

Alamy Stock Photo: 57, Angela Hampton Picture Library 1t, ark 2013 136, Roger Bacon 21, britstock images ltd 111t, David Colbran 162, Douglas Peebles Photography 140t, Ros Drinkwater 178bl, Enigma 140b, Andrew Fox 32, Grant Rooney Premium 135, Graphic79 76, Image Source 122l, Janine Wiedel Photolibrary 31, 33, 130, Janine Wiedel Photolibrary 31, 33, 130, Juice Images 41, Bjanka Kadic 139, Justin Kase zsixz 173, Frans Lemmens 120, Richard Levine 146r, LHB Photo 151tl, Jenny Matthews 149, NetPhotos 161, Picture Partners 114r, Reuters 147, Grant Rooney 186, Adrian Sherratt 29, Ed Simons 178r, The Print Collector 142, Mark Thomas 165, Trinity Mirror / Mirrorpix 17, 103l, villorejo 114l, Alan Wilson 148, World History Archive 99, ZUMA Press, Inc. 121l; **Fotolia.com:** Azaliya (Elya Vatel) 84l, corepics 121r, IRStone 128tc, Leo Lintang 196c, Monkey Business 97; **Getty Images:** Robert Abbott Sengstacke 144, Bettman 143, Bettmann 2, John Chillingworth 101, Christian Science Monitor 149b, Timothy Fadek 163, David Howells 151r, Image Source 126, Jason LaVeris 112, Gideon Mendel 1r, RapidEye 176, The LIFE Picture Collection 146l, Topical Press Agency 124, Underwood Archives 203; **OMBEA, AB:** 70; **Pearson Education Ltd:** Lord and Leverett 123; **Rex Shutterstock:** 151c, Albin Lohr-Jones / Pacific Press 7; **Shutterstock.com:** 1bl, bikeriderlondon 81, Nina Buday 125, Creatista 108, DNF Style 113tl, Eviled 73, Firma V 122r, hxdbzxy 34, Image Source Trading Ltd 137, Eric Isselee 84r, Snehal Jeevan Pailkar 166, Michael Jung 40, Robert Kneschke 128b, Alex Luengo 79, mangostock 109, Monkey Business Images 36, 113br, 127, Nomad Soul 181, Alexander Raths 128t, 128bc, Joshua Resnick 111b, Umberto Shtanzman 129, Gladskikh Tatiana 103r, wavebreakmedia 96, Francis Wong Chee Yen 183

All other images © Pearson Education

Websites
Pearson Education Limited is not responsible for the content of any external internet sites. It is essential for tutors to preview each website before using it in class so as to ensure that the URL is still accurate, relevant and appropriate. We suggest that tutors bookmark useful websites and consider enabling students to access them through the school/college intranet.

REVISE AQA A LEVEL
Sociology
Education with Theory & Methods, Families & Households, Beliefs in Society, Crime & Deviance with Theory & Methods

REVISION
GUIDE AND WORKBOOK

Includes FREE online edition

Our revision resources are the smart choice for those studying AQA A Level Sociology. This book will help you to:

- **Organise** your study with the one-topic-per-page format

- **Speed up** your revision with summary notes in short, memorable chunks

- **Track** your revision progress with at-a-glance check boxes

- **Check** your understanding and exam skills with worked examples

- **Develop** your exam technique with exam-style practice questions and full answers.

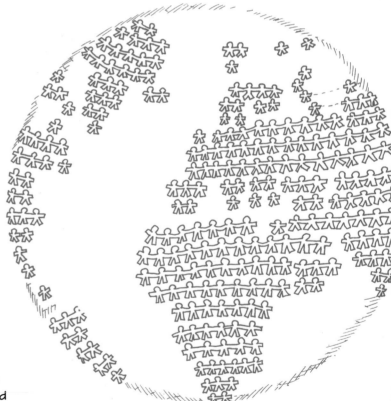

THE REVISE SERIES
For the full range of Pearson revision titles across KS2, KS3, GCSE, Functional Skills, AS/A Level and BTEC visit: www.pearsonschools.co.uk/revise

www.pearsonschools.co.uk
myorders@pearson.com

ISBN 978-1-292-11125-4